SCIENCE AS AUTOBIOGRAPHY

Niels Jerne, by his first wife, Tjek. 1940. (Courtesy Alexandra Jerne)

SCIENCE AS AUTOBIOGRAPHY

The Troubled Life of Niels Jerne

Thomas Söderqvist

Translated by *David Mel Paul*

YALE UNIVERSITY PRESS / NEW HAVEN AND LONDON

Designed by Mary Valencia.
Set in Minion type by The Composing Room of Michigan, Inc.
Printed in the United States of America.

Library of Congress Cataloging-in-Publication Data

Söderqvist, Thomas.
  [Hvilken kamp for at undslippe. English]
  Science as autobiography : the troubled life of Niels Jerne / Thomas Söderqvist ; translated by David Mel Paul.
      p.   cm.
"A revised and abridged version of the Danish edition."
  ISBN 0-300-09441-8 (cloth: alk. paper)
  1. Jerne, Niels Kaj.   2. Immunologists—Denmark—Biography.   I. Jerne, Niels Kaj.
II. Title.
  QR180.72.J47 S6313 2003
  616.07′9′092—dc21

2002012385

A catalogue record for this book is available from the British Library.

The paper in this book meets the guidelines for permanence and durability of the Committee on Production Guidelines for Book Longevity of the Council on Library Resources.

10 9 8 7 6 5 4 3 2 1

The very thing which makes scholarly work difficult is completely overlooked. It is assumed that everyone, and thus also the scientist and the scholar, knows what he ought (ethically) to do in the world—and now he sacrifices himself for his science and scholarship. But the ethical reflection itself should be the first concern—and then perhaps all scholarship would run aground. The scientist and scholar has his personal life in categories quite different from those of his professional life, but it is precisely the first which are the most important.

—Kierkegaard

CONTENTS

ACKNOWLEDGMENTS

A number of people have contributed to this book. My greatest debt is to Niels Kaj Jerne, who placed his large collection of scientific and private papers at my disposal, involved himself in conversations over many hours, and commented on a few draft chapters. Even if he sometimes expressed a little uneasiness over the result, he never formulated this as censorship. Without his generous cooperation this project could never have been realized. His wife, Alexandra, too, showed great helpfulness and hospitality throughout the entire process. For several years I competed with her for her husband's attention, yet she supported the project all the way.

Many others have been invaluable. More than a decade ago, one of my students, Lotte Juul Nielsen, opened the door of Jerne's home and undertook the first series of interviews for her Master's thesis; I am grateful to her for letting me use the transcripts of their talks. Erik Paul Madsen with unusual precision and style made young Jerne's Dutch hand intelligible. Gunther Stent, Perla Avegno, Ivan Lefkovits, and Aase Maaløe generously placed letters from Jerne at my disposal, and Ivan Lefkovits also kindly helped collect those parts of Jerne's archive that were kept in Basel for deposition in the Royal Library, Copenhagen. Other individuals—including Finn Aaserud, Troels Andersen, Carl Erik Bay, Michael Weis Bentzon, Nanna Damsholt, Andrzej Dabrowski, Erik Fischer,

Edward S. Golub, Anders Hald, Timothy P. Jackson, Gustaw Kerszman, Niels-Erik Larsen, John T. Lauridsen, Henk van der Liet, Ole Olsen, Nick Rasmussen, Stig Rosenkilde, Arthur M. Silverstein, Harly Sonne, Willy Thrysøe, and Hanne Westergaard—assisted me in solving a number of factual and interpretive problems. George Moraitis, in a short but useful talk in Palo Alto, helped me over an emotional block in my relation to Jerne. I am very grateful to Birgitte Possing and the staff at the Manuscript Department of the Royal Library, Copenhagen, for excellent working conditions and for giving me extraordinary privileges in the years 1992–96. I am also indebted to my former colleagues at the Department of Biology and Chemistry, Roskilde University, for housing a historian of science and accepting my strange obsessions; my former colleagues at the Department of Philosophy and Science Studies, Roskilde University for their goodwill; and my graduate students at the Department of History of Medicine, Copenhagen University, for their patience.

A large number of Jerne's friends and former colleagues and other contemporary witnesses agreed to being interviewed. A few have asked to remain anonymous; the rest include (in chronological order as I met them): Ole Maaløe, Giuseppe Bertani, Ray Owen, Manny Delbrück, Ivan Lefkovits, Charles M. Steinberg, Lena Skarvall, Anita Söderberg, Ingrid Schnurr, Louis Du Pasquier, Fritz Melchers, Inga Scheibel, Anne Edel Adolph, Johannes Ipsen, Ole Rostock, Viggo Faber, Mikael Weis Bentzon, Karen Guldbrandsen, Ellen Byström, Tove Olafsson, Elsa Falkner, Gunther Stent, Thomas C. Jerne, Piet Swart, L. W. Sluyterman van Loo, Adda Jerne, Kurt Dym, Egill Jacobsen, Helge Kettelsen, Inge Fussing, Hanne Westergaard, Ane Brügger, Tonny Bundesen, Emma Mon Bach, Edith Permin, Gudrun Madsen, Simon Krause, Anders Hald, Marcel Baluda, Lilian Bertani, Melvin Cohn, Renato Dulbecco, Harry Rubin, Hans Noll, Claudia Henry, Karl Gordon Lark, Julius Youngner, Aurelia Koros, Albert Nordin, Gordon Sato, W. Chas Cockburn, Rosemary Newby, Martin Kaplan, Paul Blanc, Valentin Bonifas, Edouard Kellenberger, Horisho Fuji, Arthur Park, Charles Brinton, Aubrey Outschoorn, Vagn Møller, Lis Skovsted, Perla Avegno, Gertrude van der Schalk, Mies van Beurden, Zdenek Trnka, Luciana Forni, Morten Simonsen, Göran Möller, Edward Golub, Arthur M. Silverstein, Herman Eisen, Fred Karush, Baruj Benacerraf, Byron Waksman, Darcy Wilson, Joseph Ingraham, Howard Goodman, Tommaso Meo, Henry Isliker, Alain Bussard, Jeanine de Haas, Ivar Jerne, Antonio Coutinho, Peter Helms, Sara Helms, Margrethe Gade, Jørgen Kieler, Niels Ole Kjeldgaard, Elisabeth Tassing, Bettyann Kevles, Marianne de Loes, and Jørgen V. Spärck. I thank each of them—though only some are quoted in the text.

This book was first published in 1998 in Danish under the title *Hvilken kamp for at undslippe* (*What Struggle to Escape*). Elisabeth Mansén, Tinne Vammen, and Frank Allan Rasmussen read selected draft chapters, and Aant Elzinga, Thorkild Kjærgaard, Gerd Malling, Inger Ravn, and Anna Söderqvist generously gave of their time to read and comment on the manuscript as a whole. In the public debate that followed the Danish edition, and particularly in a review symposium on it as a contribution to the genre of existential biography, Gunnar Broberg, Søren Kjørup, Carl Henrik Koch, Johnny Kondrup, and Birgitte Possing offered useful comments (see "Debat," 1999). The many other reviews in Scandinavian journals and newspapers were helpful, too, and I have also enjoyed a series of postpublication remarks from a number of engaged readers, including Signe Lindskov Hansen.

The present volume is a revised and abridged version of the Danish edition. Readers who wish to see the original Danish, Dutch, French, German, or Swedish quotations, or to consult more extensive footnotes and references, should therefore refer to the previous edition. It has been a pleasure to work with my meticulous translator, David Mel Paul, to produce the English manuscript. Ib Ravn generously helped me cut the text to a size that satisfied my publisher, and versions of it were then read by a wider circle of competent critics: Larry Holmes and Michael Neve commented on selected chapters; Janet Browne, Kenneth Caneva, Louis Du Pasquier, Scott Podolsky, Betty Smocovitis, Craig Stillwell, Matthias Wabl, and two anonymous readers for Yale University Press read the entire manuscript. All these knowledgeable and critical readers improved the text considerably, though the final result is of course my sole responsibility. Great thanks are due my student assistants, Charlotte Ellesøe Hansen and Trine Fastrup, who checked footnotes, original quotations, and the bibliography. My editor at Yale University Press, Jean Thomson Black, has been very helpful and encouraging, and Karen Gangel has been a wonderful manuscript editor.

Presenting topics in this book in the form of seminar and conference papers has been part of my biographical networking. I am grateful for having had the opportunity to discuss Jerne's life and work in seminars at the Department of Theory of Science, University of Gothenburg; the Department of History of Ideas, University of Lund; the Department of Communication, University of Linköping; the Department of History of Sciences, Aarhus University; the Program in the History of Science, Stanford University; the Center for Advanced Study in the Behavioral Sciences, Palo Alto; and the Center for Biographical Studies, University of Hawaii. Aspects of the book have also been presented at a number of meetings: the workshop From Immunity to Cellular and Molecular Immunology, directed by Gustav Nossal on Ischia (Naples) in 1992; a meeting on Interviews in Writing the History of Recent Science, arranged by Horace F. Judson at Stanford University in 1994; a seminar on The Good Life in Science, arranged by Timothy Lenoir at Stanford University in 1996; a conference on Immunology: Historical Issues and Contemporary Debates, organized by Anne Marie Moulin and Alberto Cambrosio at the Musée Claude Bernard, Saint-Julien en Beaujolais, in 1998; and at various meetings in professional societies, including the History of Science Society and the British Society for the History of Science. After publication of the Danish edition I also had the privilege to discuss some of the themes of the book with professionals and lay readers in my adopted home country. These readers-meet-the-author sessions have convinced me that the biographical territory visited in this book—existential biography—deeply resonates with the experiences of both scientists and the general educated public.

The Swedish Research Council for the Humanities and Social Sciences supported my work in Jerne's archive and financed the translation of the manuscript into English, and the Mellon Foundation provided a postdoctoral fellowship for the academic year 1991–92 in the Department of History, Stanford University; at the same time the Center for Advanced Studies in the Behavioral Sciences in Palo Alto offered me an exceptionally fruitful working environment. Horace F. Judson and Timothy Lenoir were a great help to me during this year and later. Finally, a substantial grant from the Danish Research Councils made it possible for me to spend a year completing the Danish edition, and another to revise it, in addition to providing a publication subsidy.

If I were allowed to express my gratitude and admiration for one person only, I would not hesitate to single out Ivar Jerne, Niels Jerne's elder son. I started this journey in admiration for a man who hated mediocrity and made it to the stars—and I came back with a friend who knows what it means to live a humble life. This book is dedicated to Ivar.

A NOTE ON THE TRANSLATION

*T*his book is a translation by David Mel Paul of the Swedish manuscript to the Danish edition, *Hvilken kamp for at undslippe* (Copenhagen: Borgen, 1998). The translation was later revised and abridged.

Niels Jerne's collection in the Royal Library, Copenhagen, contains documents in Danish, Dutch, English, French, German, and Swedish. Most of the material written before 1956 was in Danish and Dutch, some in German. After 1956 most of his professional writings were in English, and occasionally German or French. With a few exceptions, all original quotations have been translated into English. The originals can be found in an appendix to the Danish edition. Interviews with Jerne and others were conducted in English or Danish, and are reproduced here in English with a few minor alterations, such as the removal of repetitions. Jerne's comments to me, in interviews and writings, between 1986 and 1994 are given in *italics* (see the Introduction).

Jerne often used his full name, Niels Kaj Jerne (or Niels K. Jerne in publications). Nowadays he is most well known as Niels Jerne, and I have in the main referred to him as such.

INTRODUCTION:
A SCIENTIST IN HIS LIFE'S PROJECT

*I*n December 1984, a few days after Niels Kaj Jerne received the Nobel Prize in Stockholm for his contributions to the understanding of the human immune system, I attended his address to the public. A large crowd, including many medical doctors and students, had come to get an overview of what was going on in immunology, a field that had just been placed on the social and political agenda by the growing AIDS epidemic.

Jerne, however, had no intention of satisfying his audience's need for clinical or experimental news bulletins. AIDS is of no interest to immunologists, he had told the press a few days earlier. He wanted to talk about language instead, and particularly about grammar, "a science that is more than 2000 years old, whereas immunology has become a respectable part of biology only during the past hundred years." There is an analogy between the immune system and the deep structure of language, he said: the immune system has a basic dictionary, a semantic structure, and a generative grammar; it is a closed cognitive and semiotic system, an autonomous recognition network, an immunological hall of mirrors.[1]

Jerne's Nobel lecture positioned him in the public eye as "the great theoretician in modern immunology," a scientist who strode beyond the prevailing image of biomedical science as a mindless fiddling with experimental and technical detail. This position is not reflected in a comprehensive written output;

his collected oeuvre amounts to only around eighty-five papers (and no books), a substantial portion of which were published in journals without peer review and few of which were experimental. Nonetheless several of his publications had a remarkable impact on immunological research in the 1960s, 1970s, and 1980s, and some are modern classics in the biomedical literature. More significantly, Jerne hovered as a critical spirit over the new discipline. Many saw him as its leading intellectual light, the one who raised discussions above the level of everyday work. He has been called "one of the most intelligent biologists of this century" and "a Leeuwenhoek in theoretical biology," a "living legend" whose theories functioned as "a microscope of speculations." Even his sharpest critic saw him as the "dominant figure" in late twentieth-century immunology.[2]

The foundation of Jerne's fame was laid when, in 1955, he published a radical alternative to the theories of antibody production proposed by chemists like Karl Landsteiner and Linus Pauling in the 1920s and 1930s. It was then universally thought that an intruding antigen (bacterium, virus, etc.) acted as a template that in some way instructed nonspecific globulin molecules in the blood to turn into specific defense antibodies against the antigen. Jerne asserted instead that all kinds of specific antibodies already exist in the organism, preformed, and that the antigen's only function is to select the best-fitting kind. This natural-selection theory advocated a more biologically oriented approach in immunology with, as Jerne himself expressed it, "Darwinian overtones."[3]

The selection theory was largely neglected at first, and Jerne embarked on an administrative career at the World Health Organization (WHO) in Geneva. In 1957, however, his theory was modified by the Australian virologist-turned-immunologist Macfarlane Burnet into the so-called clonal selection theory, and as the selective principle began to be accepted as the central dogma of immunology, Jerne's reputation as the new discipline's leading theoretician grew accordingly. In the early 1960s he was asked to organize WHO's training program for immunology, and in 1962 he was called to the University of Pittsburgh as a professor of microbiology, where he worked out a method for demonstrating individual antibody-producing cells. The so-called plaque technique soon became one of the most used methods in burgeoning cellular immunology. A few years later, Jerne returned to Europe as director of the Paul Ehrlich Institute in Frankfurt.

At the 1967 Cold Spring Harbor Symposium on antibodies—a conference that marked immunology's full acceptance as a life science—Burnet declared that the selection theory was the central dogma of immunology and that Jerne was its "onlie begetter." A year later Jerne confirmed his standing as its leading theoretician when Hoffman-La Roche, the multinational pharmaceutical company, asked him to create, in Basel, Switzerland, what would become the world's largest international immunological research institution. The Basel Institute for Immunology came to occupy a central position in the next phase of post–World War II immunology—the fusion of cellular immunology with molecular biology—marked by two more medical Nobel Prizes, awarded to Georges Köhler (with Jerne and César Milstein) in 1984 and to Susumu Tonegawa in 1987. The institute also became an international scientific mecca, a "cathedral of thinking" that fostered several waves of immunologists before it closed three decades later, in 2001.[4]

Jerne's last major theoretical contribution, the idiotypic network theory, constituted still another radical break with the traditional understanding of the immune system. Against the current understanding of antibody formation as a response to external influence, Jerne drew a picture of the immune system as a self-regulating, cybernetic network. Studies of the immunological network came to preoccupy a whole generation of immunologists, divided into skeptics against and advocates for Jerne's theory. Today, few immunologists believe in it, but it is even now considered one of the boldest biological theories proposed in the twentieth century, and among biomedical scientists outside the inner immunological circle it still has a ring of Grand Theory.[5]

Scientific cultures invariably spin webs of myth and legend around their chieftains, and Jerne is no exception. Many anecdotes have circulated about his power of imagination, his working capacity, and his analytical keenness, but also about the aura of aloofness, elitism, and *Bildung* that surrounded him. Jerne was keen to present himself as an urbane European intellectual who would rather read Shakespeare and Proust than the *Journal of Immunology* and who preferred to sit in a wine bar and talk about politics and life in general than work in the laboratory; conversation was his life's breath. He also declared that he had learned to think creatively while moving in artistic circles in Copenhagen in the 1940s and that he had often been inspired by Søren Kierkegaard—statements which contradict the popular assumption that successful scientists "lose their sense of proportion," as Virginia Woolf once put it.[6]

Jerne certainly did not give the impression of being culturally crippled. But the popular image is more complex than that. His growing reputation also included stories of his problematic private life—rumors that his first wife had committed suicide, that a second wife had been written out of his official life story, that he had an illegitimate son in California, and that he drank too much and too freely—stories that make one think of Yeats:

The intellect of man is forced to choose
Perfection of the life, or of the work.[7]

Archive, Conversations, and Voices

A couple of years after the Nobel lecture I visited Niels Jerne, then seventy-five years old, in his home in Castillon-du-Gard, Languedoc. He had saved quite a bit of paper, he said at lunch. Up in the attic, where the mistral howled in the window frames, the dream of every biographer came true: a room packed with tens of thousands of letters, notes, and manuscripts charmingly stored in hundreds of paper bags from the local supermarket. This was, I realized, an exceptionally rich collection of the papers of a late twentieth-century scientist. Since his adolescent years, Jerne had saved almost everything that had passed through his hands: drafts for scientific papers, lecture manuscripts, notes from scientific meetings, and a wealth of laboratory records, as well as many thousands of private letters, diaries, scraps of paper with passing thoughts, library-loan receipts, movie and theater stubs, chess records, domestic bills, medical prescriptions, ledgers, and so forth. Nothing, except the correspondence with one particular person, seemed to have been destroyed. He was his own archivist, keeping drafts or copies of almost all his outgoing correspondence and reclaiming his letters to parents and wives. He had, in other words, lived a "biographical life," a life lived in apparent expectation of one's biographers. For this reason his letters and other documents must be read with caution—Jerne was constantly engaged in creating and refashioning his persona.[8]

He had already thought of writing an autobiography, and I encouraged him to continue, but he hesitated: *"It's a big job."*[9] So on the basis of our first talks and the scanty secondary literature, I drafted a sketch of his life. He then accepted our collaboration and gave me access to all his papers. By the summer of 1992 I had surveyed most of the collection, worrying the whole time that despite his collector's mania he might make good his occasional thoughts of burning it all. He, in turn, was worried that I would not be able to carry the project through and occasionally doubted whether I was capable of writing his life and works: I knew nothing about immunology, he said, rightly, and, besides, how would I be able to understand his inner thoughts? Eventually, caution gave way to mutual trust, and in August 1992, Jerne donated almost all his papers to the Royal Library in Copenhagen, where I could study them more systematically. A few months before his death, in 1994, he gave me unlimited rights to quote from the material.

During my visits to Castillon-du-Gard, Jerne talked about various aspects of his life and scientific work at length, in all about one hundred and sixty hours of interviews.[10] Even if he felt that he was telling the truth, his memory may well have deceived him, a possibility of which he was aware. He may also have found it in his interest to push me in one direction or another ("the myth-making of the rememberer"), and I often found it hard to decide whether his thoughts and attitudes represented factual experiences, exaggerations, or affectations; in fact he sometimes amused himself with this uncertainty.[11] I have therefore used our discussions (some of which were taped, others scribbled down during the talk) as source material only for events that could not otherwise be substantiated in the archival record. The main use of the interviews is to give Niels Jerne his own narrative presence in this book: the reader hears not only Jerne's voice of the past as it issues from letters, notes, diaries, and his earlier autobiographical commentaries but also Jerne as a present-day interlocutor. In these conversations and in occasional letters to me, he interprets and corrects, clears up and rearranges his life story as he himself wishes to see it and as he wishes for us to read and understand it; an autobiographical narrative (indicated in the text by *italics*) that now complements, now contradicts my own.

The narrative also contains the voices of friends, family, and colleagues, some from the archive, others as interviewees. Helpful as they were, many of the interviewees could deliver only some small additional fact, illustrative anecdote, or brief and sometimes stereotypical assessment of Jerne's persona; only a handful of people knew him well enough to be able to discuss his character, life practices, and work in depth—and always from different perspectives. Their voices required the same caution as Jerne's statements: all my interviews were conducted after the myth-creating Nobel Prize and concern events that took place up to sixty years earlier.

And then my own voice. The extent to which the voice of the writer should be heard in a biography has always been a matter of dispute. For example, Werner Heisenberg's biographer, David Cassidy, maintains that "the less the biographer intrudes, the better." Paradoxically, however, just because Cassidy tries to remain discreetly in the background, he is unceasingly plucking at the reader's attention throughout all the 550 pages of Heisenberg's life. In contrast, J. D. Salinger's biographer, Ian Hamilton, from the very first writes so much about himself, his intentions, and his relationship with the author of *Catcher in the Rye* that the reader's curiosity about the biographer is satisfied after only a chapter or two; thus Hamilton's explicit presence makes Salinger the central figure. I therefore hope that an occasional authorial "I" in the narrative will enhance rather than diminish Jerne's place at the center of this polyphonic narrative.[12]

This polyphony, together with the fact that he had lived a self-conscious "biographical life," made it tempting to reject the idea of a conventional biographical referent. Influenced by various poststructuralist approaches, I played with the thought of picturing Jerne as a subject who was given shape by the multitude of epistolary and conversational interactions.[13] On one occasion, I let his longtime friend Gunther Stent in on my plans; a couple of months later, Jerne called me up and said that he had just spoken with Stent in Berkeley, who told him: "*'You don't exist at all [laughter]; the only thing that exists, is what others have said or say about you and also what you say about yourself, but that is on the same level as what others say about you. But . . . that you yourself have a privileged position in that you actually exist, that's something one disregards in this postmodern biographical philosophy.' . . . It's a construction, yes.*"[14] This incident—although it conveyed a fairly distorted version of the poststructuralist view of the subject—contributed to my giving up the thought of writing about Jerne as a decentered and evasive subject.[15] His evident delight with the idea corresponded all too easily with his own nihilistic self-image and worldview. The idea of a cultural construction of the individual as a subject makes sense as a commentary on a naive realism; but if reality comprehends itself in terms of the linguistic turn, then the constructivist approach becomes "madness in the most literal and terrible sense."[16] Thus my position throughout this book is that the hermeneutics of suspicion must at some point be suspended, that every individual can occasion a number of narratives, each of which refers to a different social role or persona, but that the individual nevertheless remains a coherent biographical subject.[17]

Scientists, like many artists and writers, are rarely pleased by interest in their private lives. In his younger days, Jerne sometimes expressed an attitude toward biography akin to the New Criticism, the view that the life is not the basis for interpretation of the work. When the editors of the Danish biographical dictionary of art asked his first wife, Tjek, for biographical information about herself, Jerne answered on her behalf that her paintings alone were the important thing. But toward the end of his life, he revised this attitude: "Dear reader, please, before discussing my life in immunology, let me dispose of the dominating questions: sex, war, and . . . God, solitude," he wrote in preparation for his planned autobiography. During our conversations, he never resisted my going into the private and, in some cases, intimate sides of his life, and after reading a draft of my analysis of the relation between his personality and his selection theory of antibody formation, he declared that he was *"fully in favor"* of the idea that his scientific theories had *"'autobiographical' traits."*[18]

Despite Jerne's openness about his private life, I occasionally found it difficult to draw the line between what can be published and what should be left silent. How many of the painful circumstances surrounding Tjek's suicide are merely "the chattering nature of life's content," as Kierkegaard called it, and how many have significance for understanding her husband's later life?[19] Jerne allowed me to read diaries and other documents from the days leading up to her death and did not ask me to avoid the subject. I have attempted a balance between regard for the family and the fact that some of the circumstances that led to her last act do in fact clarify his passions, thoughts, and life choices. A similar argument can be given for treating such private themes as his erotic preferences and alcohol abuse. For a reader who considers biographies of scientists only as tools for the history of science, some of this may seem superfluous. Yet if one wishes to understand how science for Jerne often functioned as a way of evading the claims of daily life such as presence, responsibility, and emotional support, then the insights into his intimate life become meaningful; furthermore the short glimpses into his sexual desires, together with his view of himself in relation to the world, do indeed give a clue to the personal and emotional background of his scientific theories. I have nevertheless refrained from including a great deal of material I came across and, to the greatest extent possible, have avoided writing more than absolutely necessary about members of the family now living.

Finally, whether or not one wishes it, the work of writing a biography of a living person leads to a personal closeness between two human beings—something of which historians and biographers have rightly warned.[20] The longer the association, the stronger the emotional reactions such as admiration, sympathy, irritation, or repugnance. My dominant feelings during the first years were admiration for Jerne's intellectual powers combined with a certain uneasiness about how to handle the less virtuous parts of his character, side-by-side with increasing anxiety that he might break off our contact and thereby demolish the project. A short session in April 1994 with the Chicago psychoanalyst George Moraitis, who specializes in working with biographers, led to the release of some of these emotional ties—in short, I allowed myself not to like Jerne.[21] Only after his death six months later did I begin to look on him with greater detachment. My conclusion is that one can hardly set out to write a biography without being emotionally involved with its central figure, but on the other hand, that one has to work hard on establishing distance in the process of writing. The final result should emerge as a happy divorce, a certification that the writer has freed himself from the central figure.

A Choice of Genre

The rich archive and the many conversations I had with Jerne could be used for a number of different narratives.[22] Jerne's scientific career coincided with immunology's development from a scattered field dominated by chemical thinking at the close of the 1940s to a coherent biomedical discipline in the 1970s and 1980s; and since he corresponded with almost every person of importance in the field, the archive might easily have been used for a contextual history of postwar immunology.[23] And vice versa, the history of recent immunology and its wider social and cultural context might be used as a setting for a social portrait of Jerne and to demonstrate how his immunological achievements made sense against the broader background.[24] The abundance of laboratory notes, theoretical scribblings, and successive drafts of manuscripts and lectures could equally serve for a reconstruction of the cognitive and investigative pathways that led up to Jerne's central theories, thereby contributing to our understanding of how scientific theories are constructed.[25] Finally, the rich personal material from Jerne's early years might be searched for documentation for a psychobiographical narrative, in which his scientific theories could perhaps be explained with reference to his childhood experiences.[26]

Aspects of all these narratives can be found in the chapters that follow, but only as subordinate threads. Because as my work in the archive and the interviews proceeded, a further possibility presented itself. The shopping bags in the attic turned out to contain a wealth of documents that testify to Jerne's character and personality. The diaries revealed a Niels Jerne who felt himself an alien in the culture in which he lived and who longed for the sublime. Out of the letters from the Copenhagen years emerged a picture of a man who hesitated over choosing science as his life's work. In the conversations, too, we repeatedly returned to his view of himself and his evaluations and choices of life inside and outside science. I therefore began to put questions to myself such as: What choices did Jerne make during his life, and what consequences did they have for himself, his work, and for others? Which life situations attracted him and which did he try to suppress or flee from? What brought him to pursue science instead of a career in business, a life as a doctor, writer, or philosopher, or the bonds of family and children? How did he bring together, or separate, his life inside and his life outside science? How did he orchestrate his personal potentialities to create a scientific career? What intellectual and moral virtues and vices did he develop? How did he live his life in such a way as to gain a sense of worth, meaning, and connectedness? Finally, even if I do not believe in biography as a "realization" story, I nevertheless wondered whether there was a narrative unity in Jerne's life, in the sense of a recurrent pattern in the transactions between his emotional experiences, his character, his scientific work, and the multitudinous settings of his life.[27]

In asking these questions, I assume that Jerne's scientific work—in the laboratory, in his armchair, or at the desk—was an inseparable part of his life as a whole, that his scientific work was not an investigative pathway insulated from the rest of his life but an integrated part of his life's pathway. In contrast to most biographies of scientists, which inevitably focus on scientific work and public achievements and leave the rest of life (if treated at all) at the periphery, I have chosen to place Jerne's life in the center, well aware of Robert Skidelsky's point that "with the life, rather than the deeds, the achievement," we have entered "a new biographical territory, still largely unexplored."[28] I call this territory existential biography, not to be confused with psychobiography, which is an attempt to explain a person's work from a psychological perspective.[29] Kierkegaard reminds us that "the scientist and scholar has his personal life in categories quite different from those of his professional life," and that "it is precisely the first which are the most important."[30] Jerne's major achievement was his life, his most important deed, as it were, which incorporated his public scientific achievements as a special, albeit important, part.

Consequently this is a biography of Niels Jerne, not a contribution to the history of immunology disguised as biography. If one wants to learn about Themistocles, one should read Plutarch's biography; if one wants to learn about the battle of Salamis, one should rather read Herodotus of Halicarnassus. If this was a biography in the service of the history of immunology, I would have concentrated on Jerne's scientific training, his early research experiences, and particularly his mature scientific contributions, which had such influence on the discipline. But because my purpose is biographical, and because most of the recurrent themes in his life are best documented in the notes and letters of his early years, I emphasize the making of his character and his persona more than is usual in biographies of scientists. Therefore, the thrust of Part 1, "The Making of a Romantic Character," is to give a comprehensive account of young Niels's self-understanding and emotionally laden experiences—his bearing as *puer aeternus* (eternal boy), his romantic feeling of being a stranger, his elitism, his belief in intuition and the power of imagination, his longing for the sublime, his wish to make an impression on the world, and his chameleonic un-derstanding of self—all traits that later came to be resources for the construc-tion of the selection theory of antibody formation.[31] This focusing on the indi-vidual life does not mean that I deny the importance of the social or cultural context. But the cultural and social history of science has a tendency to over-look the *personal context* for scientific work, the accumulation of an individu-ally unique array of cultural interpretations and experiences. By focusing on the possibilities of going beyond the cultural context, normative structure, and moral economy, I wish to give my subject a privileged role in the narrative as an ethically responsible (but not necessarily ethically successful) individual who carves his way out of the cultural wood.

Furthermore, to focus on the man, his feelings and thoughts, and his life's project does not entail any devaluation of his scientific work, because we need to know something about the game of immunology and about Jerne's relations to it to understand what manner of man he was. Therefore a significant portion of the narrative deals with his experimental and theoretical work, and this work is analyzed (as far as possible, given my lack of training in immunology) in the context of the contemporary immunological scene. Part 2, "The Making of the Selection Theory," focuses on the seven years of experimental work between 1947 and 1954 that eventually led to the formulation of the natural selection theory of antibody formation—the theory that would inform all of Jerne's later work. I specifically highlight his researches into the chemical equilibrium be-tween diphtheria toxin and antidiphtheria serum, which placed the study of the early immune response on his personal scientific agenda, as well as his dealings with the early molecular biologists, which gave him the methodological tools that led him to the selection theory. In Part 3, "A Man, His Theory, and His Network," I recount Jerne's success story, culminating in the Nobel Prize in 1984—his growing fame in the wake of the clonal selection theory, his work at the WHO, his development of the hemolytic plaque assay and his later attempt to understand the early immune response in terms of the somatic mutation theory, and finally his creation of the Basel Institute as an international center of excellence, and his construction of the idiotypic network theory. The ac-count of Jerne's contributions to immunology, however, is not an end in itself. It would have been nice to anchor Jerne's scientific ideas and practice in that swarm of hypotheses, experiments, discoveries, clinical advances, and medical policy measures that marked the rise of immunology as a major biomedical discipline after World War II. But the historiography of immunology has only recently been initiated, and the background picture so far is patchy at best.[32]

To write a biography of Charles Darwin or Thomas Henry Huxley in the context of well-researched Victorian science, culture, and society is one thing; to paint both a portrait of Jerne and the larger picture of contemporary immunology on one canvas is quite another, Sisyphean task.

Finally, I do not intend to devalue the power of a biographical explanation of his science. As a matter of fact, it gradually turned out that the rich archival resources made it possible to demonstrate a close connection between Jerne's personal life and his scientific work. In the Parabasis, "The Selection Theory as a Personal Confession," I argue that the source of Jerne's scientific ideas rests primarily in his personal story, as if he were an artist or writer drawing on his or her own life to create a work.[33] Drawing on his diaries and correspondence, I suggest that the selection theory can be seen as a metaphorical projection of his emotional self-understanding. The theory that launched the postwar immunobiological era was, to use Nietzsche's words, "the confession of its originator, and a species of involuntary and unconscious auto-biography."[34] Jerne's view of himself was a major source of inspiration for his science. His life is therefore not only interesting in itself but also provides the key to understanding the unifying thread in his scientific oeuvre. Thus the title of the book.

The personal equation is not limited to the gestation of the selection theory in 1954. That Jerne, in spite of Burnet's modification of the theory into the central dogma of immunology, stubbornly held onto it for the rest of his life, and that it inspired both his experimental work in the 1960s and his network theory of the early 1970s, indicates that the notion of preformed antibodies continued to have a deep personal and emotional meaning for him. In my interpretation, the network theory of the immune system—the climax, as it were, of Jerne's scientific life—grew out of his wish to resuscitate the basic theme of selection theory, namely, to endow the immune system with independence and primacy in relation to the world of antigens, and to reinstate freely circulating, preformed antibodies as the central agents in the immune response. Thus, the network theory, too, can be seen as a metaphorical projection of Jerne's understanding of himself in relation to the world, thereby sustaining the connecting theme of this book—that Jerne's scientific work was an integrated part of his life's project.

An implication of the choice of genre made here is that biographies of scientists can fulfill purposes other than elucidating scientific practices or contributing to a cultural history of science. Biography can also answer the perennial ethical question asked by philosophers from Socrates to Plutarch and beyond: What does it mean to live a good life? This was a major aim of biographical writing from the dawn of the genre in the early seventeenth century to the early twentieth, but it disappeared in the same cultural process that substituted the "hermeneutics of suspicion" for moral discourse as the hegemonic ideology (a movement that Alasdair MacIntyre has problematized in his seminal *After Virtue*, 1981). I suggest, however, that the hermeneutics of suspicion can be replaced by a "second naivete" (Paul Ricoeur), namely, that biographical narratives can even today furnish us with examples with whom, for better or worse, we can compare ourselves and "enlarge [our] possibilities of living," and that Richard Rorty's argument for literature in general is true also for biographies, that is, they are able to "take us out of our old selves by the power of strangeness, to aid us in becoming new beings."[35]

To give today's biographies of scientists this Plutarchian role does not necessarily mean that one has to resurrect the uncritical hero tale. Moral examples need not be uniformly positive, like Samuel Smiles's edifying biographies, but can portray more complex human fates, portraits that present the reader with ethical dilemmas, like John Heilbron's biography of Max Planck as a study in "heroic tragedy." Even Plutarch can be interpreted in a late modern fashion. In Tim Duff's recent reading, the *Parallel Lives* were "designed to make the reader ask new and rather challenging moral questions"; the ethical ingredient of Plutarch is therefore not a simple exposition of advice or injunctions to be put into effect but food for reflection and a "gentle exploration of the realities of human life and the moral dilemmas it raises."[36] In a similar fashion, today's biographies of scientists may provide food for ethical reflection for readers in the centers of technoscience who are asking the perennial questions: What is good, what is bad, and what constitutes a flourishing life?

In spite of all his scientific success, in the end Jerne apparently felt unfulfilled. His story epitomizes MacIntyre's claim that biography is truly "neither hagiography nor saga, but tragedy."[37] Jerne was recognized as "one of the most intelligent biologists of this century" and a "living legend" in his science, and consequently he satisfied all reasonable requirements for the "perfection of the work"—though he felt himself to be "a misfit." A romantic and Faustian theme runs through this narrative: Jerne wanted terribly to be unusual, but he paid for his efforts by becoming a wanderer who continually tried to evade responsibility for his own life and the care of others' lives. All his life was a "struggle to escape." He wanted to be unique. To be number two would signal failure. I am convinced that this kind of tragedy is more widespread in today's scientific culture than we ordinarily wish to acknowledge.

SCIENCE AS AUTOBIOGRAPHY

I

The Making of a
Romantic Character (1911–1947)

1

"I Have Never in My Life Felt
I Belonged in the Place Where I Lived"

On several occasions during his life, Niels Jerne considered writing an autobiography, and in 1985, six months after receiving the Nobel Prize, he came close to doing so. The Alfred P. Sloan Foundation wanted to include him in a series of current outstanding scientists, a project for which he would be well paid. Nevertheless, Jerne hesitated. He was not sure, he wrote, whether it made sense to write an autobiography at a time when there were so many scientists.

In particular he wondered where to begin—with his ancestors or his birth? Or a little more unconventionally, at the end, say, or even midway in life? "The point of my story," he wrote, "is that, quadrilingual by ... education and steeped in fantasies about randomness and diversity, I came face to face with immunology when I was forty years old and found that she needed a new look." But when was it, really, that he first encountered immunology? When he came to the State Serum Institute in Copenhagen, in the early 1940s? Or six years later, when he finished his doctoral dissertation? And was it the encounter with immunology that had been the turning point in his life?[1]

Jerne finally concluded that a conventional approach—going back to his ancestors—suited him best. His Danish roots had always played a major role in his self-image and his reminiscences; ever since childhood, he had been interested in his family's history and "how to preserve some scraps of memories from being extinguished by forgetfulness." He drafted a couple of outlines for his autobiography—in one of them the first thirteen chapters were to cover the forty-five years preceding his breakthrough as an immunologist, while his subsequent international career got only four:

Prelude: The North Sea
An exile from his island
Growing up in Holland
Being both precocious and Spätzünder
I join the United Fruit Company, and study calculus
Philosophy = Science (Hoping to emulate Francis Bacon)
I pretend to study physics, and learn Greek and Latin
Being a polyglot
Going back home (to study medicine). Lectures vs. books
Waiting for the war, Shakespeare and the painters
I enter immunology through a study of probability
I meet scientific super intelligences. Thesis 1950
With Delbrück to US
Geneva
Am I a microbiologist? Pittsburgh
Harvard, Copenhagen, Frankfurt, Basel
Three occasions of "knowing" the truth 1954, 1970, 1973

Only scattered autobiographical notes came out of it, however, and the uncashed check from the Sloan Foundation is still in the archive. But the structure for his spontaneous life story was fixed for him—the early years appeared much more important than the later career in science.[2]

In conversations, Jerne told often and eagerly of being able to trace his father's family through generations of fishermen and shipmasters on Fanø, a small island off the west coast of Denmark, where his father, Hans Jessen Jerne, was born in 1877. After receiving his grammar school diploma in 1894 Hans Jessen became "an exile from his island"; he spent nearly three years as a bookkeeper for an English shipbroker, had various jobs in Germany, and at last returned to Denmark to manage a slaughterhouse. His father's wandering years always remained a source of fantasy for Niels; a few personal dedications written in Hans Jessen's books suggest that, for a time, he may have moved in Copenhagen's artistic and literary circles, a story that bears a striking likeness to the son's bohemian inclinations forty years later.[3]

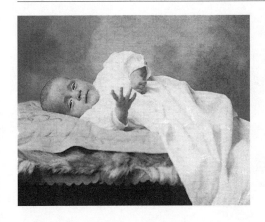

Niels Jerne, a few months old, at home on Dorset Road, Merton Park, London, early 1912. (Medical History Museum, University of Copenhagen)

Before his exile Hans Jessen Jerne had become engaged to Else Marie Jensen Lindberg, a miller's daughter from a little village north of Esbjerg. They were eventually married in 1904. The next year a son, Thomas, was born, and the following year a daughter, Karen. Their growing family did not mean an end to traveling. Hans Jessen experimented with celluloid, the plastic of that day, and discovered a way of making signboards by laying a thin celluloid film on colored cardboard. In 1908 he started a factory to produce a charity badge in the shape of a flower, which quickly became a success and made him well known to generations of Danes as "the first maker of the Autumn Blossom." After their second daughter, Elsa, was born in 1910, the family moved to London, where Hans Jessen established yet another company. There, on the day before Christmas Eve 1911, the family's fourth child, a boy, was born and christened Niels Kaj.[4]

Business went well for Hans Jessen Jerne, and the family soon moved to pastoral surroundings near Wimbledon. In the spring of 1914, however, Hans Jessen became ill and for a time could not support the family. The children were left with their grandparents in Esbjerg. The assassination in Sarajevo and the European war that ensued changed the situation for the better. Hans Jessen is said to have met the owner of a large export slaughterhouse in Rotterdam, who was *"looking for a man who could run a bacon factory for him"* and who *"had the idea that he could make money by supplying the German army, I suppose, with meat."* Hans Jessen was employed to establish a factory in the village of Terwolde in the eastern Netherlands.[5]

At the beginning of 1915 the family, including the last-born daughter, Emily, was reunited. But only the three oldest children, who were Danish citizens, were allowed to pass through Germany to the neutral Netherlands. Niels Kaj, who had a British passport, was stopped at the border. The incident is among his favorite anecdotes: *"So my father . . . he travels to Denmark . . . and picked up his children to bring them to Holland. . . . But he didn't bring me, be-*

Niels Jerne with an older cousin at his grandparents' home in Esbjerg, Denmark, in August 1915, right before returning to the Netherlands after an eight-month separation from his parents. (Medical History Museum, University of Copenhagen)

cause the Germans . . . didn't let me through, so I stayed in Esbjerg, with my grandparents, for about a year." Young Niels Kaj was not able to go home until August 1915, apparently thanks to Hans Jessen's connections with the German army. Unfortunately, the archive reveals little concerning the child's long stay in Esbjerg. The stamps in his passport and the official records confirm his absence, but he has no memory of it: "*No, nothing that I can clearly distinguish from [later episodes]. . . . After all . . . I was only two years old, so it is difficult.*"[6]

"Give sorrow words," says Malcolm in *Macbeth*. But a small child who loses his nearest relations cannot describe his sufferings; his loss cannot be made comprehensible. Psychiatric literature gives no unequivocal answer to the question of how might an early separation affect one's later life? On the plus side is a greater probability of creativeness; on the minus is the increased probability of alcohol dependency, of psychic depressions and of difficulty, later in life, in dealing with the loss of close relatives. All these consequences did in fact from time to time mark Niels Jerne's later life. It is reasonable to suppose that the separation of this three-year-old boy from his parents sheds some light on the feeling of cultural alienation and existential insecurity, of personal detachment, and of desire to live within his own world, which began to be expressed during his adolescent years.[7]

Niels Kaj's first vague reminiscences are of his arrival in Terwolde: "A whetstone? Butchers—blood, on the back of Tom's bicycle?" But beyond that, neither their house nor the flat and lush landscape beside the Ijssel River evoked any memories. His first clear recollections came from Assen, a rapidly expanding city in the northeastern province of Drenthe, where the family moved two years later, when Hans Jessen Jerne became director of a new and even larger export slaughterhouse. The family settled down in the city's prosperous southern environs, in a big house on Wilhelminastraat, *"a very beautiful street . . . and we had a large house, and, we were sort of, we belonged to the best families. We had a house with a large garden and our neighbors were the doctor's family."* Foreigners were rare in this part of the country, far away from the more cosmopolitan western provinces. The five Jerne children seem to have been accepted at once, however, and a neighboring girl recalls that they were "very interesting children" since they spoke a foreign language at home.[8]

Niels Kaj began in the local Fröbel school but was later transferred to the regular community school. His memories of the three years in Assen occur "in a non-ordered, episodic way": he remembers drawing pictures and braiding rugs and busying himself with puzzles: *"Oh, I loved these puzzles, they were of celluloid, and I also had one of wood, in the shape of an elephant."* He also has several strong memories of the grassy meadow behind their home. Many years later, he remembered how he and a schoolmate once had taken off their pants, kneeled with their buttocks in the air, and even though they were afraid to be caught, stuck twigs into each other's rectums "quite deeply, back and forth"; six months later, both boys had appendectomies and he also remembered connecting the illness with this forbidden experience. But the meadow also framed his clearest memory of happiness: "The grass is tall and yellow, taller than me. I am a child. My friend Wim will have difficulty in finding me here in the field. I am perfectly happy."[9]

Hans Jessen Jerne must have managed the bacon factory well, for in 1920 he was hired as director of a cold-storage warehouse and freezing plant in Rotterdam, newly erected as a midpoint for the import of South American meat and its distribution in Germany. Once again it was time to move. Whereas countless Europeans had lost their illusions during the war, the Jernes had let it provide the groundwork for their continuing financial security. They could afford a big house with servants in Rotterdam's new and fashionable Kralingen district, a costly automobile (a Belgian Minerva), and summer holidays in rented houses at the coast.

The earliest direct archival traces of Niels Kaj's life originate in these holidays in the form of picture postcards and letters to family members who stayed

The four elder Jerne children. *From left to right:* Karen (whom Jerne described as "sweet" but "without ambitions"); Thomas ("conventional" but with "technical enthusiasm"); Niels Kaj; and Elsa ("power-hungry" and having "no sense of humor"). Emily, the youngest, is not in the picture. (Medical History Museum, University of Copenhagen)

home. Both these greetings and the later interviews bear witness to a seemingly harmonious childhood home. Niels Kaj's favorite among the siblings was Emily (or Baby, as she was usually called); he also got along well with the two oldest children, Thomas and Karen. With Elsa, the middle girl, it was otherwise. He *"always hated [her], all the way back."* She had "no sense of humor," he felt, and she was "power-hungry" and much too quick to judge other people, not least himself. "You are so small, you can't understand such things," Elsa is said to have remarked scornfully to her little brother. She measured up to Niels Kaj intellectually and remained the only one in the family who, her whole life through, would offer any opposition. Their intellectual equality and their rivalry remained a source of irritation and mutual sarcasm. Late in life Jerne told a scientific colleague that "the reason I would like to be a Nobel laureate is to show my sister, whom I never liked, that I was somebody."[10]

Else Marie Jerne (born Lindberg), in her thirties. Her son once remarked that "she didn't play a crucial role." (Medical History Museum, University of Copenhagen)

It was the positive memories of his early years in Rotterdam that predominated, however. He always remembered his parents' marriage as harmonious and loving; even their long engagement was included in his reminiscences. He relates, for example, how he sat and listened when his mother played the piano and sang an old Danish folk song (he sings from memory):

> 'Twas on a Saturday evening I sat awaiting thee
> 'Twas on a Saturday evening I sat awaiting thee;
> I love you so sincerely, but you didn't come to me
> I loved you so sincerely, but you didn't come to me.

He remembers how, even as a child, he was moved to tears when she played that melody, "*because I think she waited for him six years or so, before he came back.*" Otherwise, Mama does not come up so often in his recollections; she emerges as more of an appendage to the father than an independent person: "*She didn't play a crucial role, I think . . . she didn't really participate.*"[11]

It was Papa, as he continued to call his father throughout his life, who played the leading role in his memories. Jerne's spontaneous life story is replete with anecdotes about a loving and caring father, a father he looked up to and wanted to please. When asked whether he had ever been punished, he answered emphatically: "*No, never, no. Yeah, I beat my own son, but he [Papa] never beat me, no, no.*" The family photos of Papa show a slightly chubby man with round cheeks, a large nose, and a jolly smile; he was a man with great technical talent and imagination, but also a man with both feet on the ground, "a solid West Jutlander, without pretensions but with a sharp sense of realities," as a Danish newspaper wrote on his fiftieth birthday. Jerne described his father as a person with social ambitions, a self-made man who achieved financial and social

Hans Jessen Jerne, around forty years old. Niels wrote of him that "he sort of dominated." (Medical History Museum, University of Copenhagen)

success on the strength of his inherent qualities. In our conversations he brought out the contrast between himself and his father. Papa was a leader; he *"sort of dominated"*: *"I am much more timid. . . . There are some Danes who, in an advanced age, become typical leaders, and wise and gentle and so. I don't belong to them [but] my father belonged to those, who have a charisma of authority. People believed him when he said something,"* he says, adding, *"and that is not true with me."*[12]

Papa had a quality Jerne would admire to the end of his life, namely, that of being a grand old man: *"The man who everybody respects, the pater familias. . . . He never criticized anybody. . . . They were all welcome, everybody, no matter whether they were intelligent or stupid or so, that played no role at all. He just was generally liked as a wonderful person to come to."* Nor did Jerne feel he had lived up to his father's example in this respect: *"I did not inherit that [quality]."* So, while his mother was more or less invisible in his autobiographical writings, Papa became a personality whom Niels Kaj looked up to but felt he did not resemble.[13]

The Jerne family was not actually atheistic—like the other siblings, Niels Kaj was confirmed—but their home hardly evidenced any religious influence; his mother once told him that she did not know "whether or not God exists." Being Danish was more important. Papa was a central figure in the Danish community in the Netherlands, and as time went by the family's ethnic origin would gain in importance for Jerne's autobiographical image. His feelings about his origins were strengthened during the family's annual summer vacations with his paternal and maternal grandparents in Jutland. As he matured, his consciousness and passions revolved around urbane culture, great cities, opera houses, good restaurants, the tokens of modernity; aesthetically, urbanity was the air he breathed. But when he talked about his origins, his thoughts went not to England or the Netherlands— *"it's too confusing to accept as your roots"*—but to the fishermen on Fanø and the millers in Jutland, just as if he needed this secure, traditional platform for his own excursions to the centers of modernity. "Just because I have led such an unsettled life," he said in an interview, "I yearn back to my origins. I have to know where I come from."[14]

From an early age Niels Kaj was regarded as the family's most gifted child. His sister Karen remembers that he was "rather a serious kind of person" who "went around thinking a lot, you could ask him something and he would be completely abstracted" and claims that they all (except Elsa, perhaps) "admired him tremendously . . . always, when there was anything we couldn't figure out, then we said: 'Ask Niels, ask Niels Kaj.'" Karen's description fits well with the general picture of a creative researcher's childhood, namely, that it is not the content in the child's occupations that predisposes him or her to theoretical thinking but rather that the child seeks resources within, finds solitude agreeable, and is accepted on this basis. Jerne's reminiscences add to the conventional picture. He remembers how at an early age he had the experience of finding himself intellectually superior even to his father: *"[Papa] thought he knew certain things, I say 'no, no, that's not true.'"* One episode installed itself firmly in his mind: *"I was ten years old, I'm sure it was the first time I had been in Monte Carlo. Father was playing roulette. He had a system of playing black when the ball had landed on red four times or something of that kind. Then I got an idea: 'Papa, the roulette has no memory. . . . What you're counting up is wrong.'"* This episode was promoted to one of his most important childhood experiences. Yet the suspicion persists that both Karen's and his reminiscences are rationalizations after the fact, that is, that a Nobel Prize winner ought to have had such a childhood.[15]

For the time being the smart one was limited to helping his siblings with their homework and getting himself through school with as little effort as possible. In 1923, after another two years in primary school, his father chose to place him not in the traditional six-year gymnasium but in the five-year Hoogere Burgerschool, which emphasized science and business education. His memories of the high school years vary. "Fear of reading aloud before the class or of telling stories or such" he wrote ten years later, adding that he had been afraid of some of his schoolmates, afraid of the classes in technical drawing, afraid of blushing, and afraid that Elsa would tease him over his poor marks in athletics. Over time, however, mainly a positive recollection lingered

Niels Jerne, editor of the high school literary journal, at the age of fifteen. (Medical History Museum, University of Copenhagen)

in his spontaneous reminiscence; he was *"perfectly adjusted to the situation. . . . I felt that the teaching was easy to follow, and the grades were easy to make."* He remembers especially that he respected the teacher of Dutch language and literature because he *"was teaching poetry or reading poetry for us and trying to make us understand the value of poetry."* The archive confirms: Papa's bookshelves were full of literature about business and technical subjects, but Niels Kaj preferred to sit in his room with Goethe and Schiller; "by then his interest in literary things had awakened," remembers Karen. During his final year at Hoogere Burgerschool, he became editor of the school newspaper, *Libanon,* and one of his last school essays, "The Book-Lover," tells of a young man who goes into his library and surveys the rows of books in the bookshelf; he finally "goes over to a little row of twelve volumes on whose yellow linen bindings letters of gold appear, 'Goethes sämtliche Werke.'"[16]

This dawning literary interest does not mean that Niels Kaj was a stay-at-home bookworm; he joined the local skating club and played tennis with his friends during the summers. But his choice of the world of books meant the beginning of a detachment from the practical world. In contrast to his father, Niels Kaj had no special technical or scientific interests. Many scientists in his generation had such interests when they were young. *"But I don't,"* says Jerne: *"my brother . . . built radios and had sort of engines where electric sparks would fly from one pile to another and so, and all the things he did, I didn't want to do."* Instead: *"I read,"* he says. *"'All the things you do there with your hands, I can read in this book.' . . . 'All that you can do . . . it's already written down here, so why should we bother,' and so. I was, from the beginning, I think, more theoretically interested than manipulator."* The contrast between the theoretical and practical worlds corresponds to an opposition between detachment and involvement. In a little handwritten family newspaper from the summer of 1927, the youngest son appears as a detached social critic who commented in detail and with a tinge of sarcasm on the day's events and topics of conversation. It was not just an adolescent thing. A couple of decades later, when mulling over plans to write a family history, Jerne wrote that he wanted to draw portraits of the family members by studying their behavior, whereby the family atmosphere, usually so boring, would become more interesting, for—referring to Proust's *Remembrance of Things Past*—"my goal is not to enjoy our being together so much as to analyze it and to enjoy the analysis."[17]

It would have been natural to let the family's designated genius continue studying after high school. In connection with the economic depression Hans Jessen Jerne had taken over the warehouse and freezing plant, the enterprise blossomed and the family continued to enjoy a sound financial condition. Papa and Mama do not, however, seem to have had any special academic ambitions for their children. *"So I came home with my little booklet to my father, and he says, 'oh, I see geography you get six, it's not very much.' I said: 'No, it's not so much, maybe it will be better next time.' . . . They never cared . . . they never understood what all this was about."* And since Thomas had failed at the polytechnical university in Delft a couple of years earlier and continued in business school instead, *"my father thought there was nothing gained by study."* So in spring 1928, a few months before Niels Kaj's final examinations, Papa arranged for him to take a trainee position in Elders & Fyffes banana importing company.[18]

Jerne has no recollection of any argument over this decision. *"I was too young to know what I wanted. . . . After the gymnasium I wasn't especially mature. I was a child."* As a sixteen-year-old he was well developed intellectually, but not emotionally and personally. In his autobiographical sketch from 1985 he characterized himself as "being both precocious and Spätzünder [a slow starter]," and on several occasions he felt that his life had been characterized by a combination of childishness and maturity. In a draft of a theater piece from the 1930s he had one of the characters describe the play's "I" as "half man, half child": "You get a kick out of foolishness and children's games, and yet your intellect is developed in many ways. This dividedness makes you want to change Nature's most solemn things into license and derision." Also in another respect he found himself betwixt and between. He was a foreigner, he stood with each foot in a different world. *"We were never part of the Dutch community,"* he says: *"My brother and sisters and I spoke Dutch, and yet we were not Dutch. We were welcome everywhere, people thought this nice Danish family was fun. But, on the other hand, we didn't really fit in anywhere."* His Dutch would always remain better than his Danish, but he had some problems with the written language and could not always distinguish between German and Dutch grammar and spelling. Neither did he have a natural native language. Niels Kaj was the family's polyglot: he wrote in Dutch, Danish, English, and German and combined words and grammatical constructions from the different languages, an ability that he would develop in diaries and notes, and that also cropped up in his later scientific thinking, for example, when playing with "sentences" in the analogy between language and the immune system.[19]

The lack of complete mastery of one language may have contributed to the outsider feeling that came to be a core of his emotional vocabulary. Jerne often emphasized that he never felt truly rooted anywhere: *"I think I have never in my life felt I belonged in the place where I lived."* He did not experience this condition as especially negative, however, but instead asserted its advantages: *"One gets used to being where you don't really belong; it was really not difficult to get to Switzerland, to Frankfurt, to America."* In one of his autobiographical notes he describes himself accurately as a citizen of the North Sea: "Four of its languages, Danish, English, Dutch & German, are my mother tongues that I speak with equal ease & delight." Both he and his friends and colleagues of later years usually characterized him as a European or a cosmopolitan rather than as a Dane or a Dutchman.[20]

Toward the end of his life Jerne felt very strongly that he had lived his life *"in a borderland"* between belonging and not belonging. The romantic sensation of being a stranger, a wanderer, a Byronic hero, alienated from culture and society, followed him his life long. When on one occasion I showed him a quotation from one of his letters to Elsa about alienation, he answered me: *"Yes, that's a feeling I am well acquainted with."* He described himself as *"a kind of misfit,"* one who never quite knew how to comport himself: *"What do you do when you get an apartment in a house? Do you go around and present yourself? . . . You don't know. . . . This is what I mean by misfit."* Much of this experience of marginality and alienation, corresponding to what Wallace Stevens calls "an absence in reality," was subjective. Seen from outside, Jerne was hard to identify as a socially and culturally marginalized person. He never took the next step out into the margin of society—a step later taken by his eldest son, Ivar—but the feeling was presumably real and continued throughout his life. He was a sort of Flying Dutchman.[21]

He did not feel alienation as a handicap, however. It had *"certain advantages,"* for *"it keeps you away from the workings of society. . . . They couldn't place*

you in any category. So therefore you were always welcome in any level of society."
He mixed socially with *"Jews and foreigners"* and had *"a feeling of solidarity with the other minorities."* When he fell in love for the first time, it was with a young woman who, like himself, stood at the perimeter of the national circle of fellowship.[22]

2

"Stylistically, I'm
Best at Irony"

"Right now I am, I think, madly in love with J[e]anine Reyss, a French girl here from Kralingen," wrote sixteen-year-old Niels Kaj Jerne in his first "Dagboek" in the spring of 1928. The tall, slender, dark-haired daughter of a pastor of the Walloon reformed congregation of Rotterdam stimulated his poetic talents and awakened his lukewarm interest in the French language:

> Je t'aime Jeanine, je t'aime toujours
> C'est tout que je veux vous dire
> Je t'aime d'une grande et divine amour
> Je t'aime de tout mon coeur.[1]

The infatuation was mutual, though she was unsure of his sincerity. Maybe he would rather flirt with some of the other girls on the tennis court, she thought, maybe one of those who called him the "Charme of Charmes"? Jeanine's doubts wounded him, and he threatened to turn ironical, for, as he said, "stylistically, I'm best at irony." His tendency to become a detached observer always haunted him: one moment he imagined sitting next to her with his hands around her waist, kissing her without uttering a word; in the next, the feeling vanished and he became "sober as a judge." For the time being, though, he preferred to be in the situation rather than to stand aside and observe his crush on

"Dagboek van Niels Kaj Jerne" (Diary of Niels Kaj Jerne), from 1928, which starts with the words: "It is in fact a little peculiar to start a new diary on 23 April. All proper diaries start, e.g., on 1 January or 1 July." (Jerne Collection, The Royal Library, Copenhagen)

her. "Jeanine and I are two souls with a single thought," he wrote, and despite her earnest pleas not to, he read her diary, because it made him "so tremendously sentimental." The decisive obstacle to young love, however, was not Niels's (he was now called Niels, not Niels Kaj) soberness but Pastor Reyss, who discovered that the young man had kissed his daughter in public and therefore declared that they had to suspend their relationship for a year until it became clear whether they cared sufficiently for each other. "It is just like what happens in a French story," commented Niels. Yet he did not seem overly disturbed by the prohibition and spent most of his time target shooting instead of preparing for his final examination.[2]

At the end of June 1928, Niels received his high school graduation certificate. *"[I] admire myself a little bit,"* he says, since he was *"the youngest student who got his Abitur in Rotterdam"* and *"on top of what was needed."* On the Dutch ten-point scale he received a nine in chemistry and an eight in mathematics; he also did well in the Dutch language exam, but physics did not go well—he scored only seven points. After graduation he left on a month-long tour of Scandinavia. Jeanine followed him in his thoughts, and he now began to imagine her as two personas: "I'm calling you Sonja now. I love that name; that's one of the reasons wherefore I'm calling you so," he wrote her from amidst the summer foliage in Jutland. For him, Sonja was both intellectual and sensual, a completely different person from the dutiful, well-brought-up, and slightly superficial daughter-of-the-family Jeanine with whom he would carry on "silly" telephone conversations. From that time on, he wrote by turns to Jeanine and to Sonja.[3]

Back in Rotterdam in August, Niels started work as the youngest junior clerk in Elders & Fyffes's mail department for a modest salary of ten Dutch guilders a week. He soon felt at home in the routines of the company, developed a fairly relaxed attitude toward his work, and after a while learned to arrange his desk so that it looked as though he were busy.

By the beginning of September nearly three months had passed since he had seen Jeanine; now and then he had spoken with her on the telephone but otherwise had had only glimpses of her. Although both then and later on he seems to have been attracted more by her absence than her presence, the long wait spawned doubts. He alternated between doubt, tender reflections, and ironic commentaries on the situation. All this waiting and longing was "to no purpose, I fear"; he did not know whether he should take his emotions toward her seriously: "Am I infatuated with you—or do I love you?" he wondered. After all, he had never been in love before. Pastor Reyss had promised that if, after yet another year's separation, they still cared for each other, he would allow them to have their way. "He wants this, he wants that—and I am just supposed to submit," raged Niels. Yet he did not want to marry for convention's sake; he wanted to love for love's sake, without interference from other people's "petty wills," and he did not want to commit himself until he could support her. There was no other solution than to "end it, a definitive *end*." She would always remain his "dear Sonja," but in the future he would regard her as a friend. "It is better this way. So long," he wrote in January 1929.[4]

Niels had scarcely ended the relationship with Jeanine before he once again allowed himself to be courted. The insecurity of his school years was less troubling now: he was considered attractive: "He was an awfully good-looking young man," recalls his sister Karen. The lucky one this time was a jolly and more accessible girl, Gertrude Wansinck, whom he saw regularly for the next six months. They went shopping, saw "a sentimental" film, and attended parties together. He liked the rhythms of "jazz-foxtrots and draggy tangos." She remembers the relationship as "puppy love," their erotic relations being limited to kisses and caresses. But young Niels asserted that he was not in love—at least not in accordance with the expectations he had of what love ought to be. He saw her more as a toy than an equal (having described her on one occasion as a doll) and regarded their relationship as a detached observer. In his letters to her, he reused the best phrases and imagery from his correspondence with Jeanine, for example, that of a mosquito flying over the sea, landing on her ear, and softly whispering little words so as not to disturb her dreams.[5]

Gertrude—or Truus, as he called her in the Dutch way—was unaware of this textual recycling; she admired his poetic talents and asked him to teach her how to write letters. "Listen closely," Niels answered, giving her the following recipe: play "five sentimental records of [the tenor] Richard Tauber and five of [the jazz musician] Jack Smith." When the music had sunk in and she had become "deeply moved," she should take down Heinrich Heine's *Buch der Lieder* and read twenty-five pages. Then she would be able to write a good letter. Here, as on so many later occasions, he revealed himself as a creature of moods. The advice had its effect: "It is just as if you hypnotize me, such power you have over me," Truus told him. The word "hypnotize" was not an accidental choice: Niels had developed an interest in hypnosis and suggestion and had borrowed a German textbook on the subject.[6]

Niels was not only a marked romantic who wanted to exert influence over a young woman's mind. He was also, Truus remembers, "a very intensive living young man"; he was "possessed, very driven." She remembers clearly his intellectual and sometimes superior and self-assured bearing: "He always knew better, he really knew everything, and he knew he knew better, he was aware of stupidity in other people." She also remembers that Niels kept "more to himself" and only had "a few very good friends," among them a German Jew, Kurt Dym (in his own words, his "best friend"), in the senior class of the Hoogere Burgerschool. The two young men shared a youthful cynical attitude to their surroundings; during their school years they met almost daily, drank beer and partied together, and lived *"a rather intensive adolescent life."*[7]

Tennis was the favorite sport of well-to-do adolescents. Elders & Fyffes had its own tennis court, and Niels soon qualified for the company's annual international tournament in London, which had the potential to fulfill his dreams of being admired: in one of his nightly images he stood as a tennis champion before an "applauding crowd." In fact, the real tournaments did not go so well (*"I usually lost in the very first round"*), but fifty years later tennis was still the only sport he liked to watch on television; he kept up with ranked players and liked to comment on their skills.[8]

Niels's favorite sport, however, was more mental: chess. He regularly cut out newspaper clippings reporting on the big tournaments, took part as a player in the British Luncheon Club's competition, and after work often went to some of Rotterdam's many chess clubs. He usually placed well and once won his game in a simultaneous exhibition against the visiting Austrian grand master.

"The Charme of Charmes," Niels Jerne (*standing third from the right*), together with members of the Elders & Fyffes's Sports Club, 1930. (Medical History Museum, University of Copenhagen)

Papa asked on one occasion whether his son *"should seriously pursue chess playing,"* to which a chess expert and friend to the family allegedly answered: *"Bananas are better."*[9]

The well-mannered and well-adjusted youngest son continued to live at home and was on the way to making a career in business. In fall 1929, he was promoted to the accounting department. But he also began to realize that he did not wish to remain in the middle-class environment in which he had grown up. The tone of his letters and notes from his first years at the banana company manifest either a youthful elevation, solemnity, and longing, or a detached and cynical stance. Values such as consideration and sympathy were apparently not in young Niels's repertoire. It was as if he had no choice other than irony or convention.

More and more, Niels regarded himself as unique, although he was some-times overcome by "a feeling of being ordinary," for example, when he thought about working in an office "just like millions of other people" and realized that he "had not yet accomplished anything." Despite living during a time that has been called the "age of the masses," he did not want to be one of the multitude. He wanted to reach beyond the everyday and the banal. To an increasing extent, he began to regard himself as intellectually superior and separate from the con-ventional crowd and combined this attitude with a kind of criticism of moder-nity. Reflecting on thoughts that had wide currency in Europe between the wars, he scorned the so-called "machine civilization." "What are we really living for?" he once wrote: "Not to go to the office and be a cog in the great machine that keeps the human race going. Not to fool around and be responsible for hu-manity's continued existence. The main thing must lie in other things, in our feelings, in thinking, in love, in all that which is incomprehensible around us. And that is why I have such a glorious feeling, I am nothing, I know nothing, I believe nothing. Ahead of me lies a life. For me and a world. Everything in my thoughts is chaos. I can become everything, I can learn everything; out of thoughts I can do what I want, 'myself.' "[10]

Chaos is neighbor with God. Niels later quoted Willem Kloos, one of the romantic Dutch poets: "I am a God in the depths of my thoughts." This was a statement, he wrote to Truus, that "pierced him through and through." In his revolt from his father's commonsensical, practical, and socially oriented way of life and his individually oriented view of the world, young Niels recapitulated the revolt of Romanticism against the Enlightenment. If Hans Jessen Jerne was the model of a nineteenth-century progressive industrialist, his youngest son fashioned himself the model of a romantic.[11]

Niels had broken off his relationship with Jeanine but could not forget her. One night late in the fall of 1929 he wrote her a passionate love letter while the rain streamed down the windowpane "sadly and endlessly, endlessly." A "rushing tide" of feelings forced itself from his heart. He was, he said, "raving mad" over having rebuffed the only one he had ever loved. Very likely he realized he was being adolescently theatrical, for the next day he wrote her a more detached postscript. Jeanine, for her part, proposed that they continue to be friends, "only friends," and asked him to pick out some little poems for her. Completely guided by his "own feelings," he spent the following weeks selecting an anthol-ogy of poems and writing them down in his most elegant hand.[12]

The little collection testifies to young Jerne's literary tastes during his intellectually formative years. He concentrated on *de tachtigers* (the Eightyists), a group of Dutch lyric poets who modeled their art-for-art's-sake attitude on the Romantic, Impressionist, and Symbolist movements that had sprung up earlier in the century (his later letters and notes often contain more or less verbatim borrowings from de tachtigers and the German Sturm und Drang poets). The motto of Willem Kloos, their ideologue and leading figure—that lyric poetry should be the most individual expression of the most individual feeling— could have been Niels's own. Another of his favorites, Jacques Perk, introduced the collection with a poem about two lovers who never have each other. For Niels, love was not so much about "love for someone or something, but instead about love for love itself, for the glorious emotional experiences, the lovely dream that men call 'love,'" a view entirely congruent with his later statement that he gained more enjoyment from analyzing sociability than from the sociability itself. Referring Jeanine to Edmond Rostand's play *La princesse lointaine* (1895), he emphasized, too, "how glorious it is to live for an unachievable ideal; to live and dream in a rapture of love for the impersonal."[13]

Yet another favorite writer was Multatuli, the stylistic renewer of the Dutch novel, who touched the nerve of Dutch colonialism. Notes and letters from the early 1930s evidence Niels's strong reaction to reading *Minnebrieven* (1861), a fictional exchange of letters with two young women; just as Multatuli wrote to Fancy and Tine, Niels wrote to Jeanine and Sonja. He was wildly enthusiastic over Multatuli's use of language, for example, in *Max Havelaar* (1860), where the author "sort of plucks out letters and forms them into words which he then hurls upon the page, from which the sentences are whipped up to me in a mighty rhythm." Niels placed at least as much emphasis on the choice of words and on the mood or tone as on the thought content of literature, and he liked to experiment with the stylistic novelties of de tachtigers—writing words together that normally do not belong together, experimenting with irregular spellings and unexpected word orders—thereby affiliating himself with literary Modernism and its restoration of Romanticism's relationship with language. Language became more and more the medium through which Niels could develop Schiller's "third drive . . . the drive to play and to create semblance in place of reality."[14]

During spring and summer of 1930, in letters to Jeanine, Niels's tone became increasingly sentimental, sensual, and melancholy. During a train trip he described how he watched the things gliding by outside but soon shook them off to make room for new things. "This resembles my life," he wrote: "All the events have also glided by me, they have been picked up and then once more forgotten." Now here he was, eighteen years old and expecting new unimportant events to go gliding by him—as if real life was unimportant and could stimulate only detached observations. Young Niels thus made one of the most important romantic discoveries, namely, that the culturally alienated individual, an individual who is doomed to be a wanderer, longs to stabilize his life in isolation and apartness. His best moments, he declared, were those when he was alone with his chosen authors and his thoughts, for example, wandering along the shore and coming to "a place where I'm all alone. I like that." Or when he sat up in his chamber at night and saw the smoke from a Gold Flake cigarette rising toward the ceiling while the gramophone filled the room with "a pleasant sentimentality." He could also be overcome by a heroic longing for the sublime. Although he never used the word, his notes and choice of literature reveal that he knew the feeling well.[15]

Some time during the early fall of 1930, he recorded his ideas about the relationship between sensual love and intellectuality in the form of a dialogue between Cupid and his alter ego, the little, insignificant, and egoistical, but also intellectual, Pietje Kleverjong (an acronym for *kleine verwaande jongen*, "little conceited boy"). Niels, alias Pietje, wished that Cupid not dominate his life any longer. True, he had spent many delightful hours dancing and kissing and being happy in the presence of young women; he had dated "a pretty black girl" with "big soft breasts" that he gladly and often caressed and kissed. But dancing and petting did not satisfy him, and he grew irritated, he told Truus, that he could not "read or work or anything else because of his amorous feelings." What was the point of making an exhibition of yourself in the middle of "a partying herd of people," going to the movies time after time, seeing the same stories, over and over? "Perhaps I am blasé," he wrote in a note, but it seemed a shame to occupy oneself thus when one could instead share "the works and thoughts of the world's greatest thinkers."[16]

When Niels sat in his chamber surrounded by books the little god's arrows were powerless. His tastes reflected a hodgepodge of authors: Homer, Shelley, Keats, Lord Byron, Dickens, Heine, Hugo, Lamartine, Rostand, Zola, and Joost van den Vondel. R. C. Sherriff's new play *Journey's End*, Henryk Sienkiewicz's *Quo Vadis*, Thomas Mann's *Buddenbrooks*, and one of the most popular Dutch novels of the day, Margot Scharten-Antink's *Het leven van Francesco Campana*—they all seemed "irresistibly" attractive. And it was not only with poetry and belles lettres that Pietje confronted Cupid. Here, too, were books on his favorite sport, such as Richard Réti's *Modern Ideas in Chess*, containing the latest about openings and position play; books about mathematics and science; and

Cupid sending his arrows toward the heart of Pietje Kleverjong, alias Niels Jerne, with a greeting to Jeanine, 1930. (Jerne Collection, The Royal Library, Copenhagen)

books on philosophy. "All this and even more I want to plow through," he told his diary, "and, for this, I have no use for you, Cupid."[17]

The dialogue between Cupid and Pietje Kleverjong expresses not only a young man's thoughts about the relationship between sensual love and intellectuality. Retrospectively, it can also be read as a manifesto for his lifelong problem of balancing the banalities of daily living and striving for the unique, abstract, transcendent, and sublime. Not surprisingly, he began to read Nietzsche. "Nietzsche is splendid," he proclaimed to Jeanine after having discussed *Also sprach Zarathustra* with Kurt. A year later he acquired the collected works. "Before me stands a magnificent thought: Nietzsche's," he wrote. The goal of life was, he told a Christian friend, to overcome one's ego and bring forth human beings who stood above the rest of humanity, models whom the others could follow. This superman ideal—to which, in various elitist variations, he would hold fast throughout his life—merged in his mind with the humanistic motto: "I say: How shall I think in order to become myself, to become a human being," a phrase he borrowed from *Minnebrieven*: "The goal of a person is to be a human being." Nietzsche was no temporary adolescent aberration; on the occasion of our very first meeting, the conversation moved to his philosophical sources of inspiration in life, Kierkegaard, of course, and then Nietzsche. *"I don't understand Nietzsche, but it is so inspiring to read . . . and I understand fragments, like Dostoyevsky. . . . Nietzsche he is a poet first of all, and he is passionate, and he expresses some thoughts he has, which are fascinating and extraordinary."*[18]

Niels's reading of Multatuli, de tachtigers, and Nietzsche also elicited thoughts and moods that shaped his relationship with Jeanine, whom he had begun to meet again, secretly, during the fall of 1930. The reunion was not wholly positive for dreamy Niels, for the illusion of Sonja had died and the reality of Jeanine had been reborn. It was as if all the tension that existed between them suddenly disappeared, as if "the distant became close-at-hand and all the dreams glided into reality." Both were now nineteen years old, and Jeanine wanted them to become engaged. This time it was not primarily resistance from her parents that prevented the marriage, nor was it finances. Niels was advanced to the banana company's groceries department, earning around fifteen hundred guilders a year, which would enable him to support a family. The obstacle was rather his ideas about free and ecstatic love versus conventional marriage. Like Kierkegaard's aesthete he was afraid of losing his freedom and was not prepared to tie himself down in marriage. He told Jeanine that he felt like a satellite in her energy field; he began to find "something commanding" in her letters, a voice that expected to be obeyed. He got the feeling that she placed her mind at the midpoint of everything and that "her thoughts and feelings and her surroundings (Niels) rotate around her like the earth around the sun." He did not want to accept this, he did not want to be "subject and object [at the same time]."[19]

Instead he developed a vision of how, together, they would free themselves from convention and daily banalities. If he married he risked "sinking down again into the usual concepts." At New Year 1931, he implored her to tear herself loose from everything that prevented her living wholly and fully, to deliver herself into the glorious ecstasy of love, to "fall up into the depths of her love," where they would drift together, "totally freed from everything." The Neoplatonic imagery was pervasive: the customary picture would be of Niels the seducer pulling the innocent girl down into the abyss. But Niels turned gravity upside down: he evoked decency and convention as the monsters pulling Jeanine down, away from ecstasy. Hand in hand they would fall up into the unknown, up to the essence of things, up to the "divine oneness." He wanted to abandon himself to "an ecstasy beyond restraint and beyond all reason."[20]

In addition he renamed her yet again. In *Jij en ik* (1930), by now the mostly forgotten Dutch novelist Edith Werkendam, he had stumbled over the name Ilja. She became his new dream figure, a woman who could abandon herself to ecstasy beyond restraint, in contrast to Jeanine, the slightly shy family type, and the dead image of Sonja, who had symbolized the thoughtfully passionate. It is hard to understand fully what this dream of ecstasy consisted in. Maybe one can read his letters and nightly notes as an expression of the overexcitement of late puberty, of a more and more sexually excited young man who could not find an outlet for his erotic energy. A decade later, he stated that he had not begun to masturbate until the university years in Leiden, and in an interview, he asserted that he then knew nothing about the sexual act and never had a sexual relationship with Jeanine: *"The active sexual connection was not there. It was simple, I didn't know what it was. I must have missed some conversation with friends. I started reading Jacques Perk instead."*[21]

Although Jeanine did not want or could not play his game, she nevertheless left one door open. In a postscript to her letter of farewell, she wrote that Ilja would be struggling and dreaming on, in secret. With those words she kept hope alive in Niels. During the spring and summer of 1931 he continued to write to Jeanine, alias Ilja; he wrote lengthy, passionate monologues, filled with images of nature in sorrow and longing, teeming with romantic invocations. Words such as "endless," "incessant," "murmuring," "whirling," "floating," "black," "singing," "gloomy," and "longing" recur with even greater frequency than in the letters and notes from the preceding years. Instead of hanging on to a banal and laughable reality, he now wanted to construct adventures even lovelier and more fantastic than the hope that was disappearing between his fingers.

Then in July 1931, Jeanine suddenly let him know that she had become engaged; a young medical student had asked for her hand. Niels, however, refused to admit defeat. He explained that her engagement was an expression of despair, or possibly a way of reaching out to him. "When we are together we must not force ourselves into the normal human pattern," he wrote. Without dreams and shared thoughts, they were nothing else but an ordinary, merely incidental woman and man. "We must live out our dreams," dare to express them, he continued. The goal for both of them, he explained, must be to create something out of life's chaos, to create something which was in keeping with themselves, something of the highest and most beautiful.[22]

Jeanine did not understand Niels's longing for the grand and eternal. She probably wanted closeness, a husband, a family, and an everyday life together. Despite her attempt to follow him in words, his dream of making something other than the "normal human pattern" remained foreign to her. During late fall they exchanged a few more letters; she accused him, among other things, of being detached and indifferent and wished that just once he could rave with real "passion, anger or love." But then, definitely, it was the end. At New Year 1932, Jeanine wrote that she realized that Niels liked her, but that their relationship would not last. As a souvenir, she sent him a lock of her dark brown hair in a little envelope, which he kept among his papers forever.[23]

His feelings for her remained. Jeanine was "the only being I have ever loved, who has ever appealed to me and whom, nevertheless, I have pushed away," he wrote in his diary six months later. For many years, he sent her a bouquet of white roses on the anniversary of their last dance. The meeting with her had been the most important event during the three and a half years from his school graduation in 1928 until he entered the university in 1931. Through his relationship with her, he had made contact with his innermost dreams, his longing for the sublime and his passions; through her reactions he had become more self-aware. "In her, I have learned for the first time to know myself," he concluded. Later in his life, love—or rather the longing for love—would have to compete with other interests, and in the end it would be transformed into a rivulet in the flood of his scientific career. It would never be totally eliminated, however. At irregular intervals it broke through his social mask of the urbane, scientific world citizen.[24]

Perhaps it was specifically to try and forget Jeanine that, during the summer of 1931, Niels fulfilled his interest in mathematics: "*I said to my father, . . . 'What I really would like is . . . to study some calculus.' . . . So I studied calculus, with some private retired professors.*" This interest lasted the rest of his life. Right into his old age he could sit for hours of an evening, calculating prime numbers. "*I wouldn't conclude I'm a great mathematician, but I would be very happy if I could solve a mathematical problem,*" he remarked. Just as many physicists are said to use physics as a means of escape, as a kind of "soma" (in Aldous Huxley's sense), Jerne asserted that all his life he had used mathematical games and puzzles to escape from the problems of everyday life: "*I usually do mathematics when I'm bored . . . when I'm afraid of answering to a letter or something and then I do this instead. . . . I always did that. . . . When I'm sorry or angry I can find a mathematical game and I don't think about anything else.*" This kind of escapism fascinated him. He had a talent for calculation, and even the bookkeeping at Elders & Fyffes matched his temperament. Thomas remembers that his little brother was interested in "everything with numbers" and that in the banana company they were surprised "everything was correct." One of the colleagues of his later years emphasizes his preference for thinking in "algebraic relationships" and his "unusual proclivity for that kind of thinking." Even though these autodidactic studies of mathematics were neither profound nor comprehensive, they are one of the central events in Jerne's understanding of his life's course. In the autobiographical sketch from 1985 he summed up his three years in the banana company laconically with the words "I join the United Fruit Company and study calculus."[25]

Niels also read Henri Bergson, probably in the spring of 1931, when the French philosopher was at the height of his popularity; in 1933 the Dutch translation of *L'évolution créatrice* had its second printing. Several of Bergson's ideas coincide with Niels's later interest in stream of consciousness and the subjective experience of the world. With the help of Bergson he began to develop the views on intuition that would accompany him through the rest of his life. Although the positive sciences translate the unknown into the known with the help of analysis and symbols, Bergson explains that intuition is a kind of intellectual sympathy through which a person becomes one with an object's innermost nature. So the task of metaphysics is to exclude all linguistic expression, translations, and symbolic representations. There is at least one reality that everyone understands through intuition, namely, one's own personality in its flow through time. Consequently, intuition and language, with its logic, are two essentially separate forms of understanding. It is possible, Bergson says in *Introduction à la métaphysique,* that a person has no intellectual sympathy for anything in the world; but for his or her own ego a person assuredly has sympathetic understanding. Certainly the thought of having intellectual sympathy with his ego was an immediate hit with the self-absorbed Niels.[26]

Two of the modernistic authors whom Niels enthusiastically read during these years—Marcel Proust and André Gide—were also influenced decisively by Bergson. At this time Niels was especially preoccupied with Gide. What is a human life about? he asked rhetorically in his diary—and then paraphrased Gide's answer: well, to be born, and with a lot of hubbub circle around your own ego and at last to die; that's all. In his early works Gide had been much occupied with the fundamental conflict between the inner angel and the inner beast. Tityrus, the central character in *Paludes,* is confronted with life's emptiness, a life in which it is impossible to think creative thoughts and blaze new trails. He cannot write nor can he live, and therefore he attempts spasmodically to make changes and find spontaneity in his life. As a writer, Gide could break through his paralysis, but only at the price of an ironic and satiric perspective on existence. In Gide's irony Niels recognized a kindred spirit. "Read 'Paludes,'" he wrote, but "do not only read it, spell it out, involve yourself deeply in it."[27]

3   *"I Wanted to Study Something That Couldn't Be Used"*

*B*y the fall of 1931, Niels had been working at Elders & Fyffes for more than three years. He got along well with his colleagues and had received a promotion. Looking back, he *"felt very happy there"*; it was *"full of charm."* But at nineteen he was far from thinking the work had any future. He had ended up "in bananas" because Papa had been skeptical of the value of academic studies and would rather have his youngest son make a career of business, like his elder brother, Thomas. Now Niels saw before him a life in which one directorship followed another until he ended up as "continental manager" or something else "very, very high up." Looking back some fifteen years later he remembered feeling as though his whole life had been laid out before him, a life as "a series of flattering promotions." So, during the spring of 1931, he decided to invest no more effort in a business career: "[I] suddenly tired of it and wanted out, devoted myself to study—at last, something that had no practical purpose—I wanted to study something that couldn't be *used,* something only existing for its own sake, not in order to accomplish anything." He knew what he did *not* want, he told Papa, "namely, not to get the most money and medals I could in the shortest time possible." Young Niels wanted to drop out of his father's commonsensical, practical, and community-oriented lifestyle and worldview: *"The drive was more to be an intellectual, which my father was not."*[1]

Niels Jerne in January 1931, on his way to becoming a "continental manager" or something "very, very high up" in the Elders & Fyffes banana company. (Medical History Museum, University of Copenhagen)

But what should he study? To continue with mathematics—one of the few subjects that, in his view, could not be put to any use whatsoever—was a possibility. Literature also interested him, as did history. But, above all, he wanted to study philosophy: *"Because I felt that everything was exciting [and] since I was interested in everything, I thought that meant I should study philosophy."* There was just one catch to philosophy. His diploma from the five-year Hoogere Burgerschool would admit him only to scientific, technical, or medical studies. And even if he had been able to complement his certificate with additional gymnasium qualifications in Latin and Greek, Papa, who was going to pay for his studies, did not see much point in letting his son have his way. To resolve the problem, Hans Jessen Jerne is said to have called together some friends from the Danish community, among them the Leiden astronomer Ejnar Hertzsprung and Hendrik Kramers, a professor of physics at Utrecht, who had married a Dane during one of his stays with Niels Bohr in Copenhagen. One of Jerne's favorite anecdotes, the story of the meeting of this advisory council is extant in several versions. In one of them, the advisers explained that anyone who wanted to study philosophy would be best served by getting himself an education in the sciences: *"And there is me, a little rascal boy who doesn't know what he wants. And my father was a little desperate, what we should do with this child, and they had a meeting. . . . And you can understand, a boy of eighteen . . . he just laughs at these big shots there trying to tell me what I should do. . . . These clever guys had then decided that there's no distinction any more. In our time science is philosophy, and the principal science is physics. Okay, so I said to my father: 'Okay, I'll study physics in Leiden.' And that was beautiful."*[2]

At the end of October 1931 Niels left Elders & Fyffes and signed in as the year's 103d and last new student in the mathematics and physics faculty at Leiden, just an hour's train ride from Rotterdam. With the passage of centuries, Rijksuniversiteit te Leiden had become one of the leading intellectual centers in Europe, counting some twenty-five hundred students in the early 1930s. The university had at the time an especially good reputation in science, with names like Heike Kamerlingh Onnes, who had founded experimental low-temperature physics around the turn of the century, Hendrik A. Lorentz, who had been active as professor of mathematical physics for half a century, and Lorentz's successor, Paul Ehrenfest, who had made significant contributions to thermodynamics. The crowning glory of the place was that Albert Einstein had been attached to the faculty for some years as special professor of theoretical physics. The existence of this illustrious assembly of physicists is probably one reason why Jerne later referred to his Leiden years as studies in "theoretical physics and mathematics." But, as a matter of fact, he was registered as a student not of physics but of chemistry; this was probably more in accordance with Papa's interests.[3]

There are not many documents to show how Niels's studies went. He had arrived too late to take part in the applied laboratory courses of the term, but he could choose among a dozen or so lectures every week: *"And that was beautiful."* Adding to the mythical picture of himself as a physics student, he noted: *"I listened to lectures, and I found it quite easy, you know, thermodynamics or whatever they were teaching there."* In another conversation, he specifies going only to the lectures that were given by *"Lorentz's daughter* [G. L. Lorentz, later Haas-Lorentz]." Did he remember other lectures? *"No, because I didn't go to them."* (Is that really so? Or is his memory playing tricks on him? Or maybe his declaring that he did not go to the lectures, a statement that recurs in his account of his studies in Copenhagen ten years later, is part of his self-image as the intelligent young man who developed a certain superior and detached relationship with the academic world.)[4]

In October 1932, Niels rented a room in nearby Leiden while the homebound remainder of the Jerne family moved to the small town of Wassenaar, between The Hague and Leiden. For the next two years, he spent most of his time around Rapenburg, the most beautiful of Leiden's canals, while student life took over completely. *"Now I entered an entirely different world,"* he remembers. Looking back he tells spontaneously and animatedly about Het Leidsche Studenten Corps, the tradition-laden student union at Leiden, as one of the great events of his life: *"I cannot really describe this tremendous experience of being a part of this Studentencorps. . . . It was absolutely remarkable,"* he says, and continues: *"Here, one discussed art, death and eternity, and we drank beer till the*

Niels Jerne, in the crowd, after being elected a member of the Leiden Student Union in September 1932. They have all had their heads shaved. (Medical History Museum, University of Copenhagen)

crack of dawn. . . . It was all compounded by alcohol . . . and you were not admitted to take part in the dinner until you had vomited." The student union also made an appearance in his dreams: "Popular member of the Corps, admired," he described himself in one of his nightly scenes. For Papa, who paid for it all, this occasionally quite wild student life was new and incomprehensible: *"My father, he didn't understand a word of it."*[5]

Het Leidsche Studenten Corps was part and parcel of the Dutch power structure. The members constituted a selection of young men from the political and economical elite who got a brief period of freedom from responsibility between the constrained discipline of adolescence and their subsequent proper, respectable lives as physicians, lawyers, or civil servants: *"And those who were not members of that corps were ignored, you couldn't even speak to them, they were unspeakable proletarians."* The members of the Corps were *"a group of people who knew that they were invulnerable, I mean, in their imaginations."* There are no notes about politics preserved from Niels's Leiden years. But there is every reason to suppose that emerging National Socialism was among the subjects of lively discussion. Within the conservative and elitist student milieu of Leiden thrived many small fascist and Nazi-oriented organizations. Many lasted only a

Dinner with some of the "invulnerable" members of the Leiden Student Union in November 1932. Niels Jerne is seated second from the left. (Medical History Museum, University of Copenhagen)

short time: they were merging and splitting; the debate was lively. It is difficult to say whether Niels sympathized with these organizations; he did in fact express a certain interest in Hitler, but it seems primarily to have been Der Führer's rhetorical skills that stirred his imagination. After Hitler's rise to chancellor in January 1933, Niels made a bet with Elsa over how long he would last in power; hardly a year, she thought, but Niels was less certain and later gave her a copy of *Mein Kampf.* [6]

The Leiden years also brought a further heightening of Niels's literary interests. In fall 1932, he became a member of the student literary society, Utile Dulci, *"a serious literary company of young people who wanted to discuss whether the sweetness, the dulci, also had some utility in life."* If Niels read everything he bought on credit at the bookstores, his time in Leiden must have given him a solid literary ballast. He continued reading Gide and consumed the new generation of modernist writers who had begun to gain fame toward the close of the 1920s, especially Ernest Hemingway and James Joyce. Two fellow students remember distinctly that Niels had unusually big bookshelves in his rented room, that he "bought many books and discussed them," and that he introduced them to *Ulysses.* They valued his intellectual sharpness and sense of humor ("he was surely a pleasant guy"), but they also recall that he was distant, a person who went his own way and did not bother being in touch with others: "You thought you got contact with him, but you didn't." Niels was a little older than the others, "so he found us a bit childish" and was "a little bit superior." They especially remember how, once, they had discussed erotic literature and Niels commented "if you have enough fantasy you don't need it."[7]

This arrogant comment did not, however, keep Niels from interesting himself quite a bit in the erotic genre. On the list of his library books were, among others, Pisanus Fraxi's (Henry Spencer Ashbee) large annotated bibliography of forbidden erotic literature, *Index librorum prohibitorum* (1877), and the Marquis de Sade's *Histoire de Juliette* and *La philosophie dans le boudoir.* De Sade would become a lifelong companion. Some years later, Niels formulated another of his dream pictures: "Abuse and torture of defenseless women, naked." So, a kind of Cupid sneaked into Pietje Kleverjong's chamber, after all.[8]

Parties at the student union, evenings at the chess table, and long hours of reading filled Niels's time during his second year in Leiden. Studies of chemistry occupied a smaller and smaller space in his life. In spring 1933 he does not seem to have attended the class sessions at all. "Instead of learning a lot of chemistry," he later wrote of his year in a letter to Papa, "I learned very little; instead of learning a little mathematics, it interested me so much that I learned too much. And instead of studying by the program and for the examination, I occupied myself for weeks on end with a book or a philosopher." But first and foremost his energies went into the social life of the student union: *"I spent the first year being drunk most of the time."* During the summer vacation—and, by his own account, inspired by Bacon's *The Advancement of Learning*—Niels came to the conclusion that, from a cultural point of view, one was only "half-civilized" if one did not know the classics. At the beginning of the 1933–34 academic year, he did not even register at the university but decided instead to take private lessons in classics, with the goal of passing the *Staatsexamen* the following summer: *"I felt that I was terribly deficient, by not knowing Latin and Greek. . . . I felt that it was an essential accomplishment which I should make."* He also maintains that he wanted to get some distance on the wild student life: *"I said [to the teacher], 'You know I can't stand this life anymore. . . . I just would like you to teach me Latin and Greek.'"* It was, he adds, *"maybe a little bit of an escape from the circumstances I had created for myself in Leiden."* He left the student union and set to work with great determination and energy.[9]

But then, once, he gave in to the temptation to take part in student life and canceled his lesson twice in a row. That was one too many times, and his teacher quit. The situation was unpleasant. He had lapsed from his chemistry studies, and now he was without a teacher of Greek and Latin—and all of this without his parents' knowledge. "At the moment, I am outside of everything," Niels concluded in a carefully written letter (of several drafts) to his father at the end of October 1933. "Maybe it is a sign of a weak will, not completing what you've started," he wrote, implicitly referring to the standing discussion of strength of will in the Netherlands just then, "but I believe that a person first feels the will to achieve something when he is completely and deeply convinced of the goal toward which he is striving." He expressed uncertainty about what he wanted to do with his life. "I truly don't know any longer what it is I'm striving for, and I can see very well that this is not the normal way to go about it, if one wants to attain any outwardly position in this world." He did not know what to do any longer, he told his father. He did not want to follow in Papa's mercantile footsteps, and he did not want to be like everybody else: "I am not especially interested in becoming a banana director or in this job or that in the laboratory of some company or other. There are hundreds of such people, but what have they to do with me? I have my own interests and I go my own way." He realized that he had to earn money and have a job, but that was truly not his ultimate goal. He was so upset, he concluded, "so many thoughts and feelings are raging inside me. And I am trying not to be weary of everything, not to become indifferent."[10]

His phraseology was like a youthful echo of Søren Kierkegaard: "You receive a title, and this brings in its train every sin and evil." Probably it was no coincidence that it was Kierkegaard's words and diction that suffused Niels's letter to his father, just as some years before Jacques Perk and Willem Kloos had been part of his love letters to Jeanine. He later declared in an interview that Kierkegaard was one of his first reading experiences: "I found him in my father's library, and I could read him in Danish." It was certainly not the religious Kierkegaard, hardly even the ethical Kierkegaard, who made an impression on him, but rather the ironical and aesthetic Kierkegaard, a person who "is like me." Even in our very first conversation, Jerne emphasized that he read Kierkegaard as one among the modernistic writers who emphasizes man's isolation and existential insecurity: *"Kafka, he is with me, and André Gide too . . . and Proust were part of the fascination, an existentialist brand, not realist, a close link between them and Kierkegaard. The man cast out in the world without security, he doesn't really know where he's going."* Young Niels did not know, either, where he was headed, and in this mood he apparently found not only Kierkegaard's ideas but also his language an ally. Perhaps his feeling of affinity was strengthened by the fact that the Danish philosopher came from a village in Jutland not far from his mother's birthplace. The family name Kierkegaard occurred on his mother's side, and so Niels imagined that they were even distant relatives.[11]

When looking back on the events he emphasizes that his father became *"terribly disappointed,"* of course: *"So he had ambitions, he thought that . . . after all, now [Niels is] going to become a physicist. But nix, I was drunk most of the time. . . . I think he gave up, said, 'Well, [my] first son . . . he sort of failed, in the university, in Delft . . . and now Niels is also getting crazy.'"* Nevertheless Papa was, as before, forgiving. Niels got his way, found a new private tutor, and spent the remainder of the academic year 1933–34 preparing for the Staatsexamen. His classical studies were "very interesting"; every day it was "as though scales fell from my eyes." He recalls that *"the two years in Leiden produced no real outcome except that I learned Latin and Greek, most of which I've forgotten, but it was very exciting."* If nothing else, he felt that he found a use for his knowledge later, in his immunological work: *"A great many of the words we write derive from Greek, like epitope."*[12]

"So, now I live fairly isolated here, as a nihilist," Niels wrote to a good friend, "looking in books and roundabout, and enjoying myself." He resolved to improve his life, promising himself that he would stop drinking, consider moving back home to his parents, look for permanent work, and try to "improve my handwriting." The last promise grew out of the negative judgment of his personality he had just received from a graphologist. He had been told that he was gifted but lacked backbone, that he was "very vain" and "naturally selfish." For a contemporary observer, the characterization must have seemed amazingly on target, so it is no wonder Niels became unusually angry. He remarked sarcastically on the graphologist's poor Dutch and rejected what he took to be an irresponsible way of categorically expressing opinions on other people's personalities. In the course of a few weeks he began to alter his handwriting and soon developed a controlled and easily readable script that remained almost unchanged up to his death, sixty years later. Thus his handwriting, too, became one of the means through which he protected himself from the outer world's attempts to read his inner thoughts and feelings—one of the personality traits that would later crop up in his construction of the selection theory of antibody formation.[13]

The graphology incident is one of several expressions of Niels's interest in his identity. His autobiographical ruminations, too, testify to his continually circling around his self. In 1932, at the age of twenty, he wrote his first, condensed life story. In another autobiographical note from the same period, he summed up the emotional experiences in his life to date, listing a series of situations in which he had felt anxiety and fear. He remembered, for example, how as a child he had been afraid of being teased by his playmates, of taking the ferry across the Maas River ("bridges, instead"), and of "criticism from my fellow men." He declared that the real reason for his leaving the student union was to avoid delivering speeches. He was also afraid of committing suicide in his sleep, of falling into a canal, of being impotent, and of not having anything to say when he was with a group or with people he did not know. The list of fears is long and confirms not only how he identified himself with an emotional and anxiety-burdened self but also how the unbearable capriciousness of chance was always lurking in the background.[14]

During the entire spring and the early summer of 1934 Niels was fully occupied with his Latin and Greek studies. But what was to become of him after that? The three years in Leiden had not led him anywhere. He had failed in his chemistry studies, turned his back on the student social scene, and disappointed his father. The intensive reading of the classics had given him some intellectual self-confidence, but in any formal sense he was back at square one: he had not earned a degree or a social position. He declared contempt for those who sought such external proofs of success but at the same time understood that he must soon earn a living.

He still had no desire to continue in business, least of all to take over the cold-storage warehouse and freezing plant from Papa. In his correspondence with friends he sometimes expressed despair at the meaninglessness of life, a combination of doubt and indifference, seeking and longing. He described how he sat listening to the radio, drinking whisky, and thinking that everything was hopeless. By playing bridge, going to a bar, and talking with people, he felt he could escape the abyss. He also expressed a wish to travel: "Most of all I would like to go abroad, away from everything here in Holland," he told Papa. Maybe he could go to Denmark, to study at the university in Copenhagen. That would be a way of starting over, of seeing and experiencing something new. After all, he had Danish ancestry. So in the spring of 1934 he applied for a Danish passport.[15]

Again the problem was what to study. The law, teaching, and engineering did not interest him. To specialize as a chemist, an astronomer, an architect, or something similar was a possibility, but he doubted his ability to maintain his concentration and interest in a one-sided course of study. What remained, then, was medicine, though he did not feel a call to the profession—in his opinion people who felt themselves called were boring; it had overtones of the petty bourgeoisie and cheap novels, he confided to his diary. But medical studies had the obvious advantage of being broad in scope: one was able to learn science as well as to deliberate on philosophical, psychological, and social aspects of existence. Medical studies would also allow him to defer his choice of a future even further: *"When you study medicine, you can become a country doctor, you can become a hospital doctor, you can become a ship's doctor and sail around the world, you can work with basic medical research. . . . So it was a course of study where you didn't need to decide in advance what you really wanted to become in the end."*[16]

Nothing has been preserved of the family discussions that followed during the spring and summer of 1934. But Papa did not seem to raise any serious opposition. At the end of August 1934—after having passed the Latin and Greek exams—Niels embarked on the steamer to Copenhagen to begin a new, independent life as a medical student.

4   *"I Have the Feeling That Everything Around Me Is Enveloped in a Mist"*

*A*s August turned into September 1934, twenty-two-year-old Niels Jerne arrived in Copenhagen with the most indispensable part of his baggage—four chests filled with books. He quickly found a rented room with a view over the Lakes and only a ten-minute walk from the City Hall Square and the Central Station.

During the following weeks he observed the life of his new hometown with curiosity. Copenhagen looked like a real metropolis. Things seemed "to roll along" better here than back home in the Netherlands, and he was amazed at how well the Danes fared. He approved of the Danish tolerance and coolness ("Nobody is impressed with anything") and was fascinated by the Danes' democratic temperament; it was not easy to tell a worker by his or her clothes, and restaurant employees were not as deferential as they were at home. Nevertheless, he could not help but notice a certain provinciality—the Danes were "very naive," he reported back to his friend Kurt.[1]

It may seem surprising that Niels did not notice how Denmark, and the capital in particular, was marked by political and social unrest; unemployment had reached a record high. But from the first, Niels moved in the city's wealthier circles, and compared with the rest of Europe, Denmark was a peaceful country that had kept out of the world war and had been spared the more or less dramatic revolutionary upheavals following in its wake. The temporary electoral victory by the Social Democrats in 1924 had signified a breakthrough for political mass democracy, and after the 1929 victory the party pushed through the enactment of a comprehensive social security law, including social welfare and unemployment compensation. Thus from the viewpoint of his class position and as seen from a larger European perspective, Niels's assessment of Copenhagen as "good pastries and good fun" was not unfounded.[2]

However, Niels had gone to Denmark not to celebrate the relative well-being of the Danes but to study medicine. His new alma mater, the University of Copenhagen, founded in 1479, was still the only university in the small kingdom. Between the wars it was thought of as one of the best European universities, known for its solid undergraduate education and, on the research side, a roster of powerful names, such as August Krogh, who had made pioneering contributions in the physiology of muscles and respiration, and the atomic physicist Niels Bohr, who led the Institute of Theoretical Physics on Blegdamsvej; both had received Nobel Prizes, in 1920 and 1922, respectively.[3]

Students in Denmark had to document their competence in the Danish language and culture, so Niels contacted a private teacher who helped widen his literary horizons by introducing him to works by the nation's most important authors: Ludvig Holberg, Adam Oehlenschläger, Steen Steensen Blicher, among others. He was also to practice composition in Danish and commented, jokingly, that he would probably end up "a couple of years from now, in a Fröbel school." Even so, his transition to a new language was not without its problems. Many years later he still felt inhibited in Danish social intercourse and believed his vocabulary was insufficient to express nuances of feeling and thought.[4]

While polishing his Danish, Niels attended Jørgen Jørgensen's lectures for the required preparatory philosophical examination *(Filosofikum)*. Under the influence of Bertrand Russell, Jørgensen had developed formal logic and its relation to mathematics and was close to the Vienna circle of logical positivists. At the time Niels's view of science was in general agreement with Jørgensen's: science acts exclusively to establish measurable connections between entities and to express these mathematically, but it says nothing about the essence of things. "'Value' and 'the true content'" were the tasks of art and religion. This fairly conventional view of the limitations of science Niels would continue to hold for the rest of his life: "I only point out that there are questions that do not allow of scientific answers," he said in an interview fifty years later, and "therefore science must be modest."[5]

He also attended one of Niels Bohr's public lectures, on "Fundamental

Principles of Scientific Research," and was fascinated with the famous physicist's appearance. Bohr was "a very nervous man," he wrote, "who has a very hard time expressing himself, yes, could hardly read what he had written on the paper. He was playing with his fingers all the time, he lisped, and he had ugly teeth," but he also had real "mathematical hands . . . with fingers that handle a bit of chalk like a surgeon handles his scalpel." Young Niels limited his reporting to aesthetic impressions, however; his parents were not told anything about Bohr's views on the principles of scientific research. They did not hear much about their son's premedical studies, either. Probably for good reason: he bought the expensive textbooks in anatomy, histology, and organic and inorganic chemistry, but he does not seem to have touched them. He went to lectures in chemistry for physicians and attended (and later passed) the required laboratory course in medical physics given in the fall. But just as, three years before, he had arrived too late in Leiden, now he was too late for the laboratory course in medical chemistry. And again, he spent more time on philosophy and literature than on science.[6]

Papa paid not only for his lodging, tutoring, and textbooks but also for recreation, so Niels got along quite well financially. The Jerne family had friends and acquaintances in Copenhagen who regularly invited him to dinner. It was not easy to fall in with the Danish lifestyle, however, and as the autumn advanced, the more isolated Niels felt. He joined a chess club and went now and then to Studenterforeningen—Copenhagen's democratic counterpart to Het Leidsche Studenten Corps—where he noticed that female students had achieved greater equality with the males than was the case in the Netherlands. But he made no Danish friends, either male or female.

He felt himself alone, yet romanticized his isolation. A year earlier he had quoted in his diary a long passage from Beatrice Harraden's late nineteenth-century bestseller *Ships That Pass in the Night,* concerning unconditional solitude and our inability to reach one another; most of us discover sooner or later that very few people are interested in others and that "we are, after all, nothing to them." During our conversations, Jerne returned several times to the theme that solitude and isolation are also a means of avoiding taking a position, of evading responsibility for one's own and for others' lives: *"I often went to Copenhagen main rail station, had some coffee and sat for three hours. There was something going on, this ambience, all these people, and I didn't have to be responsible."* The railway station was, as he once wrote, "the only first-rate place in town," a place "without foolishness and cliquishness" where people came and sat absorbed in their own thoughts, bringing something "unreal" with them—

an atmosphere "that for me, who usually am not where I am, is just right." Kierkegaard would have said that Niels took a "human bath." Consequently, the petit bourgeois social life he attended also felt false and unreal. In his letters to his Dutch friends Niels philosophized over how conventional social life could be a way of avoiding existential isolation. Play acting and comedy were required, he explained: "Isn't everyone basically alone? Yet only the cleverer notice this. And notice also that 'company,' 'socializing,' and fitting-in are all just noise, whereby one hears the loneliness less. But this 'relaxation' in company is only relaxation if one leaves at home one's annoyance and contempt for the 'small talk' and 'prattle' of others (and yourself). And that demands comedy, it's hard on one's nerves; sometimes they can't stand it and then the isolation in the midst of 'company' suddenly becomes enormous."[7]

He liked to have people around him, but he was no friend to the age of the masses. Neither did he want to be a "rider upon the masses" like his friend Kurt; he preferred to stand and watch people from a distance and think that "we, the superior ones, don't know how we should live—and yet are proud of it! No, not even proud any more. Nothing." His alienated elitism found constant sustenance in literature. He read with especial pleasure the "major cynics": Stendhal, the shrewd critic Abbé Galliani, and the author of the Dadaist manifesto, Walter Serner, along with the "great ones": Dostoyevsky, D. H. Lawrence, and more of Nietzsche. He emphasized authors who gave expression to passionate love and compassion "which they themselves do not wish to admit." He found this self-contained emotional expression to a pronounced degree in Ernest Hemingway (*"one of the heroes of our early youth"*), because he was conscious of the emotions but limited their expression; he had the ability to capture "a mood through *distancing himself from it.*" Hemingway's glamorous nihilism had come to a poignant expression in *The Sun Also Rises* (1926), a book that won adherents from a whole generation of young nihilists during the period between the wars. "I feel akin to him," Niels wrote to a Dutch friend, thereby confirming Jeanine's and Truus's earlier complaints that he demonstrated no outward sign of his passions. He said that he "possessed the emotional person's disgust at the baring, the publicizing of emotion." When, many years later, his eldest son, Ivar, pointed out that his father was a creature of moods, Jerne corrected him: he was "a creature of controlled moods, a creature of disciplined moods."[8]

After visiting his parents in Wassenaar over the Christmas holiday and New Year, Niels stayed in Germany a couple of days in order to hear Hitler speak in connection with the Saar plebiscite in mid-January 1935. He was still rather naive with respect to the Nazi threat; a year later he gave vent to the idea that "it may be only a matter of time before the Soviets or the Nazis come to Denmark"; "hopefully . . . the Nazis," because then Europe would not risk becoming "the communist or (worse) social-democratic pancake that Denmark seems to be trying to become."[9]

On the train from Berlin to Copenhagen, he met a young woman, an event that not only changed his life but also gave rise to another favorite anecdote: *"A young lady came up, who asked—I was sitting by the window—whether the seat opposite me, also beside the window, was taken. So I said 'No, that seat isn't taken.' . . . And so I was rewarded by being asked to carry her fur and her suitcases up onto the ferry and off the ferry again. . . . The next evening we went to the Royal Theater, and that was that."* Ilse Wahl was born in Frankfurt in 1910 to the Sudeten-German engineer Robert Wahl and his wife, Emilie. The family moved to the small city of Preetz, in Holstein, and Ilse attended high school in Kiel. At the end of 1931, after a European tour, she arrived in Copenhagen, where she began to take art lessons; a year later she was accepted into Kunstakademiet (the Royal Danish Academy of Fine Arts).[10]

Ilse—or Tjek, as she was called by her academy friends—came into Niels's life like a whirlwind. In contrast to Niels, who often flirted with bohemianism and antisnobbery, but, in reality, nourished a well-developed sense of social status, Tjek actually seems to have had little interest in the formalities of social life. She was "very independent," she had "few principles" and a "funny nonchalance," but she was "not especially egotistical," he told his sister Elsa. Besides that, she had "erotic lips"—hence they met almost every day and night in her little apartment. The tone of Niels's correspondence changed abruptly. Once, when Tjek was confined to the hospital, he wrote to her nearly every day; his letters were poetic, written in an engaged style completely different from the detached, nihilistic tone that had permeated his letters and notes since his breakup with Jeanine three years earlier. He remembers that *"Tjek was the first woman I made love to."* A month later he wrote a detailed account in his diary of of how he had spent his first weeks together with Tjek. Of the 864 hours that had passed, they had been together 294 hours and had had "coitus" 18 times; on the other hand, he had spent only 16 hours in the company of other men. He had slept 190 hours and used 40 hours in getting dressed, washing, and shaving; his studies had suffered, at only 98 hours. For several months to come, Niels kept similar minutes of their relationship; later, he referred to "our hours-per-day-together statistics."[11]

Niels Jerne liked to order the world around him in tables. Here he records "hours-per-day-together statistics" with Tjek, 9–22 March 1935. The columns list weekdays; the rows, hour of the day. Circles represent time spent in her company. (Jerne Collection, The Royal Library, Copenhagen)

In Tjek, Niels had finally found a woman who did not want to be burdened by convention; now he saw his chance to realize the vision he had tried to get Jeanine to share. It was probably not coincidental that he sometimes called her "Ilse-Sonja." But with this new Sonja, by contrast, he was more than willing to get married. To break with the convention now meant marrying without obtaining the family's approval in advance. When he looked back on this course of events a decade later, he wrote that "I got married without having any economic foundation of my own because I was weary of all those who postponed their marriages till they had a position, were able to support a family, etc. etc. I objected to creating security first, as everybody else did; I didn't want to let these bourgeois considerations determine my actions, feeling that it was humiliating and banal to let such thoughts decide such instinctive acts as marrying, living with a woman." In the beginning Niels kept the relationship secret, and it was only in the middle of April, after the examination in Danish (which received a mediocre "Passed"), that his parents were informed of the situation. They urged him to postpone the wedding but could not alter his decision: *"There were so many things I would have been able to compromise about, studying medicine for example. But in this case I wanted to impose my own will,"* he remembers. In the beginning of May 1935, Niels and Tjek were married, and after Niels's Filosofikum exam (awarded top grades), the newlyweds visited both parents for introductions. They returned to Denmark at the end of July and moved into an apartment; some weeks later Tjek learned that she was pregnant with a "spinach," as the impending child was dubbed in the couple's domestic code.[12]

The newlywed Niels and Tjek Jerne visiting his parents in Wassenaar. Among the wedding party, Mama (*second from left*), Niels and Tjek (*center*), and Papa (*third from right*). (Medical History Museum, University of Copenhagen)

Papa was eager to support the young family and his son's studies once again, provided they did not take so long. Why not business, insurance, or tourism? Not in the Netherlands, though: Denmark was the country that could give him "the best starting conditions." Niels investigated the possibility of becoming an auditor or an insurance agent or of seeking work in a Dutch company in Copenhagen. He remembers his preference for getting a job over getting a short education: "*I would show him that I could easily get a job, knowing all these languages.*" Unemployment was still high among office workers, but a few days after placing an advertisement in the paper Niels got a bite; a Copenhagen publishing house was planning to set up a Dutch subsidiary to publish a Who's Who of all Dutchmen who had been honored with the Order of Knighthood and wanted Niels to take care of the acquisitions. It seemed just right: his language qualifications seemed tailor-made for the assignment, and he was delighted with the firm's leadership methods and modern, American style. He sounded not wholly disappointed at "undergoing the transformation into an office person again."[13]

After some job training, Niels traveled to Amsterdam and found a small office. The practical work of questionnaires and acquisitions took all his efforts, and he soon complained that when money was the goal of existence there was not much time left over for "contemplative and abstract thinking." When the first acquisitions started coming in, he began to have serious doubts about the whole project, and especially the income level; at the same time, his employer asserted that there were irregularities in the accounts and that little had been accomplished. Niels angrily rejected the accusations and concluded that he did not want to continue. In mid-December, his employer regarded the contract as breached.[14]

Niels was not proud of the situation. He had failed at his first independent job and now had a law suit for breach of contract hanging over him. "The Amsterdam fiasco," as he called it, remained an embarrassment that he preferred to conceal. He did not mention his brief career as a biography hunter in his drafts of an autobiography, and when reminded of it in one of our conversations, he did not remember that he had been fired, but stressed that he himself had decided to leave the job, that he and his father had come to agreement that *"this way of earning money is not my type of life,"* and that the whole thing *"was actually a bit of nonsense."* And when reading a draft of this chapter, he protested; he thought the tone was too negative. Why? Well, he answered, *"it disturbs me that the public will see that I dropped this and I dropped that."*[15]

Hans Jessen Jerne was able to help his son again, however. Papa was approaching sixty, but his fevered inventiveness was unabated. He had always preserved things—eggs in celluloid, meat in cold storage, and colors on celluloid-coated signs—and for several years he had also been interested in what happens during the salt curing of pork into bacon. He had carried out some promising experiments but had little knowledge of chemistry, nor did he write well in Dutch or English. Therefore, just before Christmas 1935, he asked his son to work for him as a kind of assistant for an indefinite period. In return, Niels and Tjek would get four hundred Danish kroner a month to live on (a skilled worker would earn about three hundred kroner a month).

As speechwriter and library assistant to his father, Niels did not need to live in the Netherlands; besides, Tjek was not happy in Amsterdam: the Dutch language tangled her tongue and she wanted to return to the academy. So, they decided to move back to Copenhagen and rapidly found a modern apartment in the suburbs. Life quickly returned to normal, and the Amsterdam fiasco was pushed out of mind. In the middle of February 1936, Niels sent out a swarm of

Tjek Jerne (left) during her first pregnancy in Copenhagen, fall 1935, with a friend. (Medical History Museum, University of Copenhagen)

letters to his family, friends, and acquaintances, to tell them about his new life. In contrast to the melancholy he felt the previous fall, he now felt a certain inward calm. Being together with his pregnant wife, everything was rosy, Niels wrote: "We milk the day of all its joys and sunbeams, and do not grow tired of being together all the time. [Ilse-]Sonja has the instinct of seeing and living life openly, and I try to reach and to understand it with my thoughts." He sometimes went downtown to the library but otherwise spent most of his time in the suburban apartment, studying *Het rijk der Microben* and other books on microbiology, food science, and deep-freeze technology, writing lectures on cold-storage technique and salt-curing methods for his father, as well as meditating on life and the state of the world.[16]

In late February, their first son, Ivar—"a sturdy old fellow," as the midwife called him—was born and an "utterly domestic" life began. It is said that Tjek was not especially interested in household matters or baby tending, that she was nervous and did not seem to have an especially warm relationship with Ivar, who cried every time he was fed; but then, says a friend to the young family, "Niels took over, calm and quiet, and Ivar calmed down and everything went much faster." Niels proudly declared that it was not harder to be a father than to get married, or learn to ride a bicycle, or to start smoking.[17]

But behind the superficial idyll of family life lay uncertainty about the future. Niels soon began to complain about a "chronic cash shortage." Neither he nor Tjek was particularly thrifty: they rented a radio, subscribed to newspapers, spent 10 percent of their monthly allowance on cigarettes, and even found it necessary to hire a girl to mind the child and to have domestic help in the mornings. Above all he felt like a helpless and unemployed observer of his father's bacon adventures. Everything would be a lot easier if only he had work of his own and did not need to "parasitize on Papa's money." He responded to a few Help Wanted advertisements, but nothing happened. The severe unemployment of the early 1930s was beginning to ease, but there were still many looking for the few available jobs.[18]

Niels also felt reproaches hanging in the air. It is true that his parents had assured him that they would always be "the haven you seek, in word and deed." But the two older sisters—now both married, too—were less accepting of their little brother's actions and reproached him over his hastily arranged marriage, and particularly his status as the favored sibling. The relationship with Elsa was especially problematic. Niels referred to the "chilly Gulf Stream" that prevailed between them; he thought she was heartless when she condemned his actions without understanding his underlying motives. She, in turn, thought he was naive and ignorant, that he lived under utterly advantageous conditions, and that he knew nothing of "la condition humaine." Niels felt a "little bitter" about her attack, he told his brother Tom. Why did she not try to understand what was going on in his thoughts and feelings? What really matters, he claimed in a note, is what "penetrates deeper into us." "Thus, *not* witticisms" of the kind he thought Elsa was so good at: "It's amusing but sloshing [plätscherend]. Very seldom, one hears during an extremely, perhaps unimportant, moment, a scream out of someone's innermost secret. That is the *only* important message." Those were the terms he established for human relations. But he did not add whether he himself could live up to these terms or if they were something he desired of others while he himself stood aside and observed the scream, like someone looking at Edvard Munch's painting.[19]

The fact that Niels spent so much time and attention on the conflicts with Elsa indicates that he found it difficult to overlook her denunciations. A few years earlier he had written that the fear of "criticism from my fellow men" was a pervasive feature of his personality. He found it difficult to immunize himself against personal attacks, and any rejections, as in the letters from Elsa, led to a feeling that the world around him was unreal. In a letter to Elsa written in March 1936, but not necessarily sent, he described his dreaming mood:

> People and things around me can thereby arouse in me a moment of unreality that I can dismiss only with difficulty—but I seldom attempt to escape this feeling of irreality; as a rule, I try precisely to continue it: I can walk very carefully through the city with it for hours, being carefully watchful that the tension does not moderate and the mood be broken. For these fantastic dreaming moods in full daylight are "charmante," they give me a kind of sense of power, elevated above the earthly "groveling." For example, I can thereby go into a café, very slowly remove my jacket, very slowly throw an "überlegen" glance around the room and through the guests, and then make my way to an empty table. With provocative slowness I move my cigarette in the direction of the ash tray, a brief flick, the ash drops in, and my hand moves back again. And I have the feeling that everything around me is enveloped in a mist, above which only my feelings protrude into a clearer and higher atmosphere.[20]

This sweetness of alienation was no transient shift of mood. Five years earlier he had expressed similar thoughts in notes and letters to Jeanine. One of Tjek's friends got the impression that "he went around in a kind of dreamworld," and fifty years later his colleagues in Basel recognized the same attitude. ("That was really him," one of them exclaimed after reading the quote above.) The feeling of unreality expressed itself in many ways. "A layer of paving lies between us and the earth," he wrote, in a draft of a letter to his parents, continuing in a style and spirit that is again reminiscent of Kierkegaard: "It is possible, too, that a layer of paving exists between our thoughts and the realities; over that skin of pavement, our thoughts drive away in automobiles, quickly here, quickly there, quickly they are in the papers, quickly on the radio, quickly in the movie theater. One seldom encounters anyone who has left the car to dig down beneath the pavement and find out whether there is any earth underneath, earth that does not smell of metal and paper."[21]

Daily life in the suburbs with Tjek and Ivar, existential deliberations, and reading of microbiology and cold-storage technology did not last long. Papa, though "enormously pleased" and satisfied with the work Niels had presented him with, nevertheless had more elaborate plans than to let his youngest son sit in Copenhagen as a library assistant. He had succeeded in demonstrating that the results of bacon curing do not depend solely on the effects of the salt treatment, but also on the bacterial content and on the natural concentration of lactic acid in the muscle tissues, and that the process could be improved by adding extra lactic acid during the salting. Above all, curing could in principle be kept under control, thereby guaranteeing an even quality and dependable result. Just as the brewing of beer and other biological and chemical processes had been understood and controlled by the end of the nineteenth century, Hans Jessen thought he would be able to standardize bacon preparation through scientific technology.[22]

To obtain the concession of manufacture under license, Hans Jessen wanted his youngest son to take charge of demonstrations of the new method for the agricultural ministries of several European countries. Niels was not overjoyed, but for the moment had no choice but to accept, and soon the letters between father and son exclusively concerned bacon, especially after the Dutch government let it be known that they might consider buying the rights to the new discovery for a sum approaching 250,000 Dutch guilders. The Danish and British agricultural ministries, too, made inquiries. As spring 1936 approached, Papa announced an impending test curing in a slaughterhouse in Ipswich, England. For a time the plans were threatened by a summons Niels had received for Danish military service; but after a visit to a doctor he was "summarily rejected because of a weak heart," a diagnosis that probably reflected his formal status as a medical student rather than the condition of his heart.[23]

Seeing England, and particularly London, once again stirred Niels's spirits. He wrote home, reporting from the tennis courts at Wimbledon during tournament week. There one saw the most modern and elegant people, with "pink-painted lips and eyeglasses with pink rims" as well as "women's legs, naked in transparent short pants on the tennis courts, and perfumed women's legs with fashionable accessories." He insisted on Tjek painting her toenails red when he came home; she was to have a "pretty, well-groomed head on one end, pretty, well-groomed feet on the other, and, midway between, the primeval, everlasting jungle of passion." He dreamed of how, when their finances improved, they would bed down in "coal-black sheets" and pictured their lying there like "two bananas"; not for one second would he let her be: "Like macaroni in a black pan we will wriggle and writhe and wind about each other until the match lights and, like a red dragon, spits fire inside you, and we both rise up, like white phoenixes, out of the flames, and then, afterwards, like quenched cigarettes, lie beside each other in the black ashtray." But, he concluded, "that's enough of vulgar instincts!" and shifted to a more romantic description of their love.[24]

The London trip also gave him the chance to think over how much Tjek meant to him and how strongly he was attached to her. She had helped him leave behind his earlier cynical and nihilistic view of life: "You have given me everything you are and all you own, with spontaneous, absolute devotion— and that may be even more than you suspect, and something that is probably given only to a few men. Sharing life with you has satisfied my thirst for love in the most beautiful way. Your natural, free, pure, unprejudiced and yet innocent thinking has drawn me out of my sophistry and carried me in an honest, positive direction." It was the first time Niels had ever expressed an alternative to the great cynics and to the mastery of emotions. The detached observer had not forgotten his capacity for observation but, for a moment, apparently allowed love and sensuality to break through the facade.[25]

5 "When I Look at Other Scientists . . . None of Them Have Wasted as Many Years as I Have"

As June turned into July 1936, Niels was able to move back to Tjek and Ivar and his books in Copenhagen, at least for a while. The great intellectual happening in the Danish capital at the time was the Second International Congress for the Unity of Science, held for one week in June under Jørgen Jørgensen's supervision. Maybe it was newspaper reports on the radical empiricists' discussion of problems of causality that inspired Niels to throw himself into David Hume's writings when he returned home. He also familiarized himself with Bertrand Russell, probably because of Jørgensen's introductory book on the English philosopher, published the year before.[1]

But he was allowed only a few weeks to delve into *On Education* and *Sceptical Essays*. The English bacon experts had remained unconvinced of the advantages of the new curing method, and so Hans Jessen began a new and larger series of tests in the Netherlands. At the end of July, Niels had to travel again, this time to help out in a slaughterhouse in Utrecht: "Just now, my thoughts are dissolved in distilled water, and, by turns, they become oxidized with potassium permanganate, colored brown by phenyldiamine, and neutralized with $CH_3CHOHCOOH$," he wrote home to Tjek. As the summer went by, he became increasingly pessimistic and defeatist about the world and his situation, gradually slipping into a new phase of melancholy. Everything was "a monotonous expanse of sameness," he had "made a kind of pause in life, like a hibernation," and his ego had "withdrawn into his innermost, since everything outside was so empty." As usual his mood changed quickly, however. A few weeks later, after having received instructions to take charge of a bacon demonstration in Denmark, the depressing thoughts were only a memory; now he proposed to Tjek that they set fire to the whole correspondence, dance around the fire "like Hottentots, and make a hellish racket with pot and pan covers in our hands until we fall down on the bed from fury and exhaustion."[2]

When Niels returned in October, Tjek was wholly absorbed in her majolica work, Ivar was getting his first teeth, and the letter burning was postponed indefinitely. Niels got busy with the planned bacon demonstration, but the experiments did not give clear-cut results. The Danish agribusiness was interested in anything that could improve their export opportunities, so Papa was still enthusiastic, but Niels had not much confidence that the companies wanted to invest in changing their accustomed methods. For a time he considered trying to earn money at journalism, for example by writing about Denmark in Dutch newspapers. He even tried writing a crime novel. To be sure he had talent: certain passages showed his capacity for observation and flair for suspense. With practice, and a larger helping of stylistic courage, he might have made a career in fiction. But *"it really wasn't serious,"* he says, when reminded of it. *"No deeper thought lay behind it; probably it was mostly a way to earn money."*[3]

During the dark fall and winter evenings, Niels also found time to explore further a few of the subjects closest to his heart: philosophy and mathematics— and sadism. Russell's *Principia Mathematica* and *Introduction to Mathematical Philosophy,* as well as the Marquis de Sade's collected works, were on his list of library books that fall, representing the two sides of his attempt to get control of himself and his surroundings. Mathematics would tame the unruly mind, sadism the unruly bodies of others. He was also fascinated with the surrealists, in whom he found support for his ideas about spiritual and sexual freedom. André Breton's first manifesto on automatic writing, which, Niels claimed, could release an individual from the control of common sense, aestheticism, and morals, was a fitting backdrop to his "stream of consciousness" exercises as he sat at his newly rented typewriter. Breton's motto in *Manifeste du surréalisme* (1924)—"Man's imagination should be free, yet everywhere it is in chains"— resonated deeply with Niels yet so far remained only an idea. He was eager to be unconventional, to break with established points of view, as he flirted with bohemian and deviant ideas. In some ways he succeeded, but to a much greater degree than he realized he seldom strayed far from his bourgeois up-bringing.[4]

The future was still uncertain. The inconclusive results of the bacon experi-ments created a sense of despondency as the family celebrated Christmas over roast duck. Their worries increased with the news that Karen's husband had suddenly developed financial difficulties, prompting Papa to send Niels as an envoy to sort out the consequences after the New Year. Both in these family in-vestigations, and later, during spring negotiations with the Danish bacon con-trol commission, Niels displayed engagement and inventiveness when it came to gaining maximum financial advantages—a talent for business he would put to good use thirty years later in Geneva, Pittsburgh, Frankfurt, and Basel. He was also involved in efforts to market the new curing method, though much of his time was spent idly. When his parents sent him a little extra money, he ex-pressed gratitude, since his suit had been worn shiny, but added: "Hopefully this period will soon be over; it has lasted long enough, now, and it truly shouldn't become a habit." As usual he used the waiting time to read: the En-glish Fabian G. D. H. Cole's *The Intelligent Man's Guide Through World Chaos* symbolizes his literary efforts during the winter of 1936–37. Receipts from the annual book sale show that he also went through a Scandinavian period—reading August Strindberg, Georg Brandes, J. P. Jacobsen, Johannes V. Jensen, and J. Anker Larsen.[5]

At the end of May 1937, Niels was again summoned by Papa to carry out experiments at a full factory scale in a small Dutch town where the off-work amusements were "limited to drinking beer and listening to the radio" with the other hotel guests. Tjek stayed with her parents-in-law in Wassenaar and saw Niels only on the weekends. The summer passed slowly. The whole pork-pro-duction line was processed with the new curing method and shipped to En-gland to be sold on the market. Niels took samples to monitor the process, but *"without any enthusiasm."* The closing date was postponed again and again, be-cause the Dutch bacon commission remained skeptical. The eternal waiting and uncertainty continued. Not even his love for Tjek seemed able to counter his sense of meaninglessness: "Should I go on writing that I love you, dear Ilse-line, and that I am happy, so happy that I have you and little Ivar, even though it's a pity we must so often be apart? These truths are almost trivial, but maybe you want them repeated and repeated anyway?" This was the high point of a summer of dispirited weekday letters.[6]

In the beginning of September 1937 Niels received instructions to travel to

London to discuss the method with the English bacon importers. He was freed again from Dutch stagnation; once again he felt he had air beneath his wings. Even the discussions in London suddenly felt encouraging. He reclaimed his poetic gift: "There are so many thoughts inside me, dearest, a whole landscape of thoughts, little thoughts that mean nothing, but press upward between each other like grass in a meadow . . . and in the middle of the meadow you are lying, and you look into my eyes until I smile, and you smile back, and that smile is like a breath of wind through the grass, and all the little thoughts bend toward you, whispering softly I love you." He remembered their lovemaking moments in Copenhagen, how "wonderful it was to weep together in bed." It was also "wonderful to ride tandem together," but it was "more wonderful to weep together."[7]

In October, Niels, Tjek, and Ivar returned to Copenhagen with yet another winter of waiting facing them. Tjek had begun to make a name for herself in the capital's artistic circles and had several works accepted for a major exhibition, including six majolica plates. Meanwhile, Niels sat writing abstracts of American and German bacon patents, drafts of the family's patent application, and the long report of the summer trials in Boxtel. That fall and winter he also placed Shakespeare firmly on his spare-time reading agenda, with a brief digression into Goethe's *Faust*. Six months later, having finished *Antony and Cleopatra*, he informed Tjek that he had "read all 37 plays." No other author, not even Kierkegaard, had ever inspired such intensive reading. Shakespeare remained the leading figure in his personal literary canon. "He always quoted Shakespeare," says one colleague; "he burst out in long Shakespeare quotations," another relates. People who had not read *Macbeth* or *Julius Caesar* were, in his eyes, inferior—on one occasion, he vented his *"disappointment"* even *"dismay"* over his limited familiarity with the Bard. Beyond reading Shakespeare, however, the late fall of 1937 and the winter that followed were spent waiting. *"There were months where I really had nothing to do,"* he recalls.[8]

Despite two years of factory trials and several patent applications, by the winter of 1938 the new curing method had still not made a breakthrough. The English producers opposed the patent application on the grounds that it too closely approached already existing methods, and the Danish bacon industry supported the opposition. Niels did not want to put his trust in the patent plans. Several times during the past three years he had looked for work and had constantly been "hunting for money." For the present there was nothing to do but continue a third year on the bacon project. His only consolation was that four new volumes of André Gide's collected works had just arrived, "and the man is still living. If only I have the time to experience the last volume before I die."[9]

In May 1938, Niels spent a third summer on-site at a factory, leaving Tjek in turmoil as she struggled to find time for her artistic work in between the washing, cooking, and caring for Ivar. Sometimes she was on the verge of collapse: "This afternoon, I wandered around with the boy, aimlessly," she wrote one day. She sometimes left him alone, asleep at home, just to have an evening to herself and to get "completely drunk but feeling fine." Bar hopping, however, was a brief relief, and she finally decided to put the furniture in storage and to move with Ivar to Løkken, a small coastal village on the northwest coast of Jutland, well known as a gathering place for Copenhagen artists. She wanted to rent a small house there until Niels returned, whenever that might be. Immediately after their arrival in Løkken, Ivar got sick and everything came apart for her: "I can't handle this—often it's as though a brutal dentist were drilling and drilling away on the same nerve. I no longer have the least interest in myself. I renounce all responsibility for the boy, there is a question whether he is going to make it through all this, he is skin and bones now, but I have sacrificed myself for him, so we'll see how it goes." From his Dutch exile, Niels recommended that she turn Ivar over to a nursemaid, which apparently helped. She found a local girl in the village and considered "being a little more cold-blooded with Ivar."[10]

Meanwhile Niels immersed himself in the company business. Every Saturday, all summer long, he sent reports of the past week's work to the Dutch bacon-control commission in the Hague. Sometimes commission representatives made visits to evaluate the results: "There was slicing and looking and tasting . . . and everything continues just about like last year." His days, like the year before, alternated between the factory and the hotel, where he sat in the evenings and played chess and talked politics. The European situation had become more and more integrated into Niels's life and way of thinking as the 1930s advanced. Despite the long wait, he remembers the 1930s as one of the most important decades in his life and declares that younger generations *"never will be able to realize [that] the period between the two wars . . . [was] enormously productive. . . . It was a fantastic period."* His earlier fascination with Hitler had been transformed into the opposite; a couple of months earlier, the German army had marched into Austria; war hung in the air, and Niels's political sympathies now lay basically with England and its conservative elite. However, he did not engage in politics primarily to change the situation or to moralize over the state of the world. Political events were, first and foremost, a reason to keep an inter-

One of Niels Jerne's favorite pastimes: chess. The other was discussing politics. Ca. 1938. (Medical History Museum, University of Copenhagen)

esting and critical conversation going. This was no transient youthful attitude. Throughout his life, he would remain a mere observer of the world scene.[11]

He described his tendency to take part in a conversation without really taking any fixed standpoint as the expression of "an unusual (intellectual) flexibility." He also possessed, he said, "a fine sense of other individuals' attitudes toward life, at least once I have known them for a while." The following self-characterization seems to capture well his identity at the time:

> My experience is that nearly all the persons I have come to know have an attitude toward life that is much more deeply rooted in their personality, perhaps more principled, than my own. In my contact with people I may take two approaches: either I position myself on their platform and achieve, to the greatest extent possible, a harmonious contact, or I position myself on an opposing platform and counter them, usually, however, with so much tact that no direct antagonism arises. In me, such an antagonistic feeling arises extremely seldom since I usually only *position* myself on a conditional platform, while most people stand upon a platform to which they

are rooted. If my temporary platform should be shaken, it cannot evoke the same emotion in me as when others' permanent platforms are shaken. And if antagonism should arise in my interlocutor, then I can be content to look at him with a superior smile, as if not really concerned, as if I was looking at a man who was angry because his hat had been blown away by the wind. Yes, sometimes I feel like a wind, one that can be needed to blow through some people's dusty viewpoints, to blow the hats off their narrow brains.

This "intellectual flexibility," he added, "can be confused with, and actually is not so distant from, various qualities that are usually considered unfavorable, namely negativeness, deficient strength of character, dishonesty, superficiality, cold intellectualism, lack of seriousness about life, and cynicism."[12]

While Niels devoted the summer of 1938 to developing his intellectual flexibility in political discussions over a couple of beers in a small Dutch hotel, things at last began to ease for Tjek. As an artist she had specialized in oils and had tried ceramics, with success, but it was as a watercolorist in Løkken that she made her breakthrough. She felt like "a real watercolor machine"; an exhibition at the local gallery was a success, receiving positive reviews in the press and selling well. She learned to drive a hard bargain for her art now—one of her friends described her as "decidedly a business talent."[13]

Tjek's artistic success was accompanied by an active social life. Soon she had so many new acquaintances that she could not "satisfy all of them; they are waiting for me, every evening." She realized that she was erotically appealing: "Men, anyway, are crazy [about me]—and I [am] haughty and enjoy myself." She wanted Niels to come soon to show him off: "Hurry, now," she wrote, "the whole crowd is excited now at the prospect of seeing you—God knows what you may think of all these bohemians—they build up such expectations—Tjek's husband—the husband of sophisticated Tjek." But Niels was not in such a hurry to be shown off. In the beginning of August the test curings and taste samplings for the year were completed and at last the Dutch bacon commission declared that it was satisfied. Strong interests opposed to the new method also existed, however, thereby delaying the date when Niels could decide whether to take the "bacon path" or not.[14]

Tjek was enraged. The other summer guests would be on their way home, and soon she would have no one to show Niels off to. But when his wife became angry, Niels became detached. He thanked her for her letter, which he had read with "his well-known calmness," and tried to explain the situation. He did not want to set out "headlong" but to talk the situation over with Papa first. But nei-

Tjek Jerne at the beach in Løkken. She knew she was attractive and wrote to Niels that "men are crazy [about me]—and I [am] haughty and enjoy myself" (20 June 1938). (Medical History Museum, University of Copenhagen)

ther did he seem especially eager to meet Tjek's summer friends: "Perhaps it's a pity I cannot share in your intellectual, but departing, acquaintances; hopefully, a few of them will remain in Løkken when I arrive; otherwise, in my pocket I carry Shakespeare and Bertrand Russell, who give me at least as great satisfaction." Maybe this was a test of strength between the spouses? "The one who has the least use for the other is the strongest," he wrote two weeks later in his diary. In her reply, Tjek enclosed an open sign of strength and independence: a photo of herself in a provocative pose on the beach together with the Danish writer Jacob Paludan, fifteen years her elder: "He is your type—intellectually." Was Tjek unfaithful? A friend describes her as "very flirty": she was "something of an adventuress, who was out to get herself acquaintances." Another friend thinks she had "absolute sex appeal" and seemed to attract "mature, virile men"; there was always someone who was "wildly interested in her. . . . All the men became fascinated." Nothing in the archive suggests that Tjek was adulterous during this or the following summer in Løkken. That would happen later.[15]

In the end, Niels came to Løkken, stayed there three weeks and got to know the remaining members of the local artists' colony. Apparently he and Tjek succeeded in getting along, for in the middle of September 1938 he traveled to Copenhagen to find new lodgings. After a week's intense search, he found an "incredibly suitable" five-room apartment on Amaliegade, just behind the Royal Palace, in central Copenhagen, precisely what he wanted: "It's not highly polished with steel windows and beechwood parquet, like the modern barracks have, but it has room to breathe," he reported to Tjek. He was exhilarated again, ordering their first telephone, buying his first typewriter, and fencing three times a week, "because I'm getting stiff as a board and smoke too many cigarettes."[16]

And then he read, of course, especially books on the emotional life, in both normal and abnormal forms. Earlier he had read Freud, Adler, and Jung and

Tjek Jerne with the Danish author Jacob Paludan. "He is your type—intellectually," she wrote to her husband on 18 August 1938. (Medical History Museum, University of Copenhagen)

had clipped magazine articles about psychological subjects; now he went to the university library and borrowed scholarly German volumes on sexual psychopathologies, sadism, and masochism. One day he wrote a long entry in his diary about his own sexual development. He saw himself as "quite normally sexually developed," yet "with a strong latent sadistic tendency," and reminisced about some of his sadistic impulses during his life, about "bondage activities" in elder brother Thomas's room some time during the Rotterdam years, in which one of them had lain like a "bow over the chair." He remembered how he had been fascinated by the description of the torture of a poison maker and by youthful conversation about the bloody terror of the Spanish duke of Alba against the Dutch liberation movement. The horrific images were mixed with fragments of his own sexual history. Did Tjek know anything about this? Was she herself at the receiving end of his tendencies? There is nothing to indicate that Tjek ever experienced Niels's attraction to sadism. He was to save that until later, for others.[17]

On 1 October 1938, Tjek arrived like "a schoolgirl in her broad-brimmed green hat," to help put the new apartment in order. The weeks went by in furnishing the place and in socializing with visiting artist friends. There are not many documents concerning what thoughts Niels had about the future, but it is easy to imagine that he questioned once again whether it was reasonable to wait around for a possible career in the bacon or freezing-plant business. He remembers that he had long been haunted by the feeling of being a failure: "*I was about to become desperate, ten years had passed since my baccalaureate.*"[18]

But, as on so many previous occasions, he had a hard time pulling himself together. His only really unequivocal act, as an adult, had been his marriage to Tjek. A close friend of the family characterizes him as a person who did not take initiatives but waited passively so as to allow himself to catch temporary, passing events that he found interesting; only then did he express his opinions or exert his will. She also recalls how Ivar, some years later, when asked what he wanted to be when he grew up, answered "I want to be a passenger, I want to see life pass by." "And that also applied to Niels," she comments. "I see him as an almost perversely onlooking person," says another acquaintance, who got to know him many years later.[19]

The thought of resuming medical studies kept reentering Niels's mind. It seems to have been Tjek who made the decisive step, by writing a letter *("the contents of which I have forgotten")* to her father-in-law, saying that, if Papa did not want *"his son to go to pieces,"* the only sensible thing was to let him take up medicine again. Actually, it seems as though Niels's parents had been hoping for an initiative in this direction, for a few days later Mama referred to the "news that Papa and I are *endlessly* glad to receive." Hans Jessen committed himself to paying four hundred Danish kroner a month through the entire course of studies, as an advance against Niels's inheritance.[20]

Right after New Year 1939, Niels traveled to the Netherlands once more for a two-week inspection tour to conclude the work of the previous years and returned to Copenhagen "loaded with energy!"—just in time for the beginning of the spring term in February. This was his "farewell to the bacon matter." With the outbreak of war and the German occupation of the Netherlands, Hans Jessen Jerne's entire bacon project was thrust into the background and would never be taken up again.[21]

Events in an (auto)biographical account are seldom evenly spaced through chronological time. Likewise all the phases of life are not equally spaced in the memory. In certain periods of life, a single day's experiences can give rise to whole chapters, sometimes whole books, like a day in Stephen Dedalus's life. Other phases in a life story can stretch out across years apparently vacant, as if life was on hold. In his reminiscences, Jerne regarded the fall of 1935 as a publisher's agent and the three following years with his father's bacon experiments as "the dark middle ages of my life."[22]

In several respects, the archive supports the image. For almost four years he had been torn between economic dependency and loyalty to his father and the tie to Tjek and Ivar at home. He had read and thought a great deal, yet without a goal, as if living in an intellectual no-man's-land, lacking any connections with a formal field of study or any specific intellectual circles. Several times he had tried to get a job but had failed. The long trips to the Netherlands on bacon business seemed an exile. His absences of many months from Tjek, his uncertainty about the future, and his feeling that the whole bacon project was meaningless made him, at various times, depressed and apathetic. The years comprising the dark middle ages were not especially fecund in external events, nor—if we may trust the archive—in internal experiences of the kind that Kierkegaard calls the "moment of possession," the moments of instantaneous intensity that characterize the aesthetic life. The lively descriptions from the two brief London trips, in the summers of 1936 and 1937, stand out like lights in darkness. At the same time, Tjek had begun her own career and had achieved a certain standing in the circle of younger artists in Copenhagen. It was still unusual for a woman to gain the outward status traditionally expected of a man, so perhaps this, too, put heavy pressure on the couple's relationship. In particular, Tjek's social and artistic breakthrough in Løkken, in the summer of 1938, put their original closeness to the test.[23]

Looking back, Jerne considers his father's bacon experiments to be largely meaningless, even though *"it gave me something to do,"* and he regards these years of waiting as mostly a waste: *"Why did I waste those three years,"* he asks, *"why didn't I say at once that 'I want to be a doctor'? When I look at other scientists, well-known people, every one of them had an almost identical life story. None of them have wasted as many years as I have."* At the same time, every experience sets the conditions for the rest of one's life. Without lapsing into teleology, one can reasonably assert not only that Niels's bacon standardization experiences prepared him for the later practice of standardizing vaccines and sera but also that the work of writing the reports gave him experiences in comprehending literature and experimental data, skills that later impressed both the staff of the World Health Organization and his colleagues at the Basel Institute for Immunology. One can similarly assert that the long winter evenings in company with Russell, Shakespeare, and Gide helped him to broaden the independence of thought that made him, later in life, go his own way to create his own biological theory, instead of allowing himself to be guided by the prevailing scientific understanding.[24]

A final reflexive note: after having read a first draft of this chapter in the summer of 1992, Jerne seems to have modified his view of himself: *"I no longer think darkly about the middle ages of my life,"* he wrote to me. Hence, at least in this case, the biographical process contributed to the refashioning of his narrative self.[25]

6 "Now I Think Nobody Can Keep Me from Becoming a Doctor"

A t the beginning of February 1939, nearly four years had passed since Niels Jerne had interrupted his premedical studies, during which time he had hardly touched his textbooks. There was nothing to do but start over. He arranged for a place in the medical chemistry laboratory exercises and took the premedical science courses once more. Most of this was repetition, which allowed him plenty of time to play chess and browse in the library and secondhand bookshops. He borrowed or bought literature on the relationship between art and medicine, on the history of medicine, and especially on history in general, for example, the Dutch historian Johan Huizinga's recently published *Homo ludens,* on the play element in human culture.

Most of Niels's leisure reading in history concerned the opposite of playfulness, however. What fascinated him was the world of evil—the witch trials, the German terror in Belgium, the Inquisition—appropriate reading in a time that lived up less and less to Huizinga's cultural analysis. In the middle of March 1939, Hitler took Czechoslovakia, and two weeks later General Franco defeated the republicans and ended three years of civil war in Spain. A few weeks later, general mobilization was begun in England. Like so many others, Niels expected a new European war to break out.

On the home front, peace reigned. The hyperactive Ivar had just started kindergarten, and Tjek had equipped one of the rooms of the apartment as a studio. Watercolors still interested her, but now she also began working in oils. The past autumn she had had several works accepted for the Copenhagen artists' fall exhibition, including a ceramic tile table and an oil painting; her works also began to sell. To earn a little extra money she considered joining the staff of decorators at a department store, but Niels rejected the idea. He idealized her: "You are an *artist*, they must realize that, and you cannot be shut in when the sun is shining."[1]

As spring advanced Niels concentrated increasingly on the upcoming premedical examinations, and when Tjek traveled with Ivar to Løkken at the beginning of June for another summer with the artists' colony, he remained in Copenhagen. During the warm summer evenings he sat among the fragrant lilac bushes down by the harbor front and studied while people strolled all around him. That was how he preferred to read; it was like sitting in a train station, anonymously and with life passing by. The cramming was exhausting, but the lectures in Leiden had not fallen on barren ground. As one of very few, Niels passed all three premedical exams in early June with honors, and for the first time in many years he could write to his parents with pride: "So I passed . . . with the highest marks. . . . Very good, if I may say so myself." He had at last demonstrated his "worthiness as a med. stud," he wrote to Tjek.[2]

Soon the spouses were reunited for another apparently uneventful summer in the rented house in Løkken—Tjek painting, Niels reading; they did not return to the capital until the end of August, just before the news of the Molotov-Ribbentrop pact. Shortly thereafter, the German army entered Poland; the English and French governments presented Hitler with an ultimatum, and on 3 September 1939 war became a fact. A few days later Niels began his real medical studies. Beyond Filosofikum and the premedical exams, the three-year preclinical program included anatomy, physiology, and biochemistry. He was expected to learn thousands of details by heart, most of them through independent study. Although many students sought the help of tutors, almost half failed the anatomy examination. Niels could hardly have deluded himself that he would complete his degree in record time, and when looking back he remembers that his studies were not without problems. He had *"a very strong tendency not to believe"* what was printed in the book or stated in the lectures, and his biggest problem, he claims, was to keep track of the lecture schedules, the meeting times, and places for the laboratory sessions: *"All these things which you can read on the blackboards or on the notice boards, and which, of course, all nice students, they seemed to communicate to each other."* Here, once again, are the ingredients of the autobiographical story of *"a kind of misfit"*—maybe an affectation, because when I pointed out that he seemed highly organized both in the banana company and later, in Pittsburgh and Basel, he became uncertain: *"Yeah [long pause], yeah [long pause], I don't really know, but [long pause] I don't know."*[3]

The aging Jerne also recalls how he had a problem feeling at home in the student milieu: *"I didn't get along with the other students, either. I was a little older than they. . . . I didn't feel comfortable together with the others."* One contributory cause could be that he was contemptuous of many of them: *"I often wondered: 'Is this stupid to become a medical doctor?'"* The only fellow student with whom he felt comfortable was a certain Preben Torp (later Avnstorp), whom he had met at a first-aid course in the fall of 1939, and who soon became a regular breakfast and lunch guest in Amaliegade (*"We were together almost every day"*), and as a result he became *"one of the only friends I had. . . . We were both equally lazy."* In frequent letters Torp expressed his admiration for his more experienced and more brilliant study companion—"Taj," as he called him. Torp was devoted and loyal but sometimes felt injured and disappointed.[4]

Thus continued the fall of 1939 and the winter of 1940. The daily routines were not noticeably disturbed by the war, not even on 9 April 1940, when Niels and Tjek were awakened by "an indecent roar of airplanes." German army units had crossed the border in southern Jutland, and seaborne troops had landed in Copenhagen. The Danish forces were completely unprepared and after a few hours of half-hearted resistance the order went out to surrender. "In the morning, great tumult . . . occupation by the Germans," wrote Tjek in her diary that day. Torp and Niels hurried to the harbor to look at some warships where "sailors on the deck were playing the guitar." In the streets German soldiers were directing traffic as though it was a day like any other. The first fright abated in a few hours. Later in the morning Niels went on to his tutoring in anatomy and thence to hear King Christian X give a speech in the palace square, before he "went back home to listen to the radio and to continue to study the 1200 pages or so of Cunningham's textbook of anatomy." That same evening, windows were to be blacked out. The illuminated advertisements and the street lamps were extinguished. The daily life of war had begun.[5]

During the early years of the war, the Danes were comparatively well treated by the Germans. Apart from the rationing, the scarcity of commodities, and the shortage of fuel, the Occupation brought relatively small changes to everyday life. Of course people lived in the shadow of the war. Sometimes air-

An ex libris (linoleum print) designed by Tjek Jerne for her husband around 1940. The book in front of him may be Cunningham's textbook of anatomy. (Medical History Museum, University of Copenhagen)

raid sirens went off, and sometimes the population was forbidden to go outdoors. But compared, for example, with Rotterdam, where Allied bombs fell only a few hundred yards from elder brother Thomas's apartment, the war was far enough away from Copenhagen to be somewhat unreal. Niels noticed it mostly in indirect ways: a shortage of butter, sugar, flour, cocoa, coffee, and tea and a lack of coke for heating and, eventually, of woolens and leather goods. Worst of all was the shortage of tobacco, he thought.

In summer 1940 Niels and Tjek did not go to Løkken but instead rented a small house on the northwest coast of Zealand. His diary recounts more than two months of company and excursions, but not many studies. "Beyond that, I understand that you two have it like Adam and Eve in Paradise," a couple of friends wrote them. The result was not long in coming: Tjek became pregnant again.[6]

Back in town in the beginning of September, Niels started his required dissection course and studied with Torp in the afternoon: "Torp and Taj palpated each other, here—with shirts off," Tjek noted in her diary. The anatomical assignment was comprehensive, but the examination was still six months ahead. "I am 28 years old and am studying anatomy," he thought back many year later: "It is not my favorite subject. Nerves, vessels, muscles, bones and membranes crossing one another in the most elaborate ways. It is hard to force your memory to keep track. It is also hard to study medicine at the university when your fellow students are eight years younger, when it is twelve years ago since you finished [high school], and when German troops occupy your country."[7]

The winter of 1940–41 continued under the signs of painting, anatomy, literature, and war. With a new baby growing in her womb, Tjek stood most of the time at her easel and later got a few works accepted for the annual counterestablishment exhibition. Niels went to daily dissections and lectures and sat at home reading his anatomy books, some with greater interest than

Ivar, Niels, and Tjek Jerne on summer vacation, a regular family activity in the late 1930s and early 1940s. (Medical History Museum, University of Copenhagen)

others, for example, those that dealt with the nervous system (*"That was my favorite, the nervous system. I read several books"*), but otherwise he was quite willing to be interrupted to go to the library and investigate the hidden aspects of the inner life, through titles such as *La pathologie des émotions* and *Sadismus und Masochismus.* In the evenings he worked, or constructed, crossword puzzles or conversed with the many artists who visited their home day and night. He and Tjek often sat up half the night drinking coffee, chatting, and reading and got up late in the mornings.[8]

In the summer and fall of 1940 Niels also "rediscovered" Søren Kierkegaard. Just as a couple of years earlier, he had studied the Shakespeare literature systematically, now he went through the scholarly writings on the Danish essayist and philosopher. He browsed Copenhagen's secondhand bookshops: "Strolled around downtown this morning and bought some small 1st editions of Kierkegaard," he wrote in his diary one day. Kierkegaard made a deep and lasting impression on him; sometimes Jerne describes him with such intensity that one might suspect the Danish writer of being his first and greatest source of inspiration: "Oh, how he has impressed me," he once told a journalist, "for he writes with a power, an intelligence, a joy, indescribable. . . . It is the whole thing that attracts me. He is so funny, you can laugh, and at the same time, so deep. There is a resonance to him, like when you listen to Mozart." And when he later wrote that he had "always been a troublemaker in this life, always been attracted by the unusual, the opposite moves," the wording, as so many times before, echoes Kierkegaard's.[9]

The hunt for first editions of Kierkegaard was followed by a long winter devoted to making lists and tables of different kinds. Niels went through his correspondence and receipts for the past five years in an effort to outline his life history; incoming and outgoing letters were carefully listed by date, as if he were archiving documents. This was not his first attempt at organizing his experiences; during his first spring with Tjek, he had kept "hours-together-per-day statistics," and now he treated science the same way: Sir James Jeans's *Astronomy and Cosmogony* (1929) contained "good tables!" Arthur Stanley Eddington's *The Expanding Universe* (1933) provided the physical dimensions of the cosmos, which were duly added to the lists. His mind was able to imagine both incomprehensibly large dimensions (10^{79} protons in the universe) and the infinitesimally smallest: the mass of a hydrogen atom is 1.6618×10^{-24} gram. Between these boundaries extended the known world—a bacterium, Niels noted, weighs 10^{-12} gram, and a human hair, 10^{-3} gram, whereas a small galaxy weighs 10^{43} grams. Everything could be calculated and expressed in finite numbers. There were small dimensions, but not infinitely small; many protons, yet not infinitely so. This way of thinking made a lasting impression on him and was later instrumental in the construction of the selection theory of antibody formation.[10]

He also set to work listing world events. He filled a whole notebook with historical personages divided into twenty-five-year periods and, some months later, catalogued the entire Dutch literary history in a corresponding way. He did not try to interpret events; he asked no questions, sought no explanations. His notes were restricted to a simple chronicle of kings and great writers, with names and dates that could be surveyed like a careful listing of household finances. That winter, hour after hour, evening after evening, went into the making of such lists. On one occasion he also summarized the things he would most like to do in his life, for example, to make some chessmen and a terrestrial globe, to "write a poem as beautiful as 'the lips of water,'" to write inventories, to "[divide] history into named generations, and [to edit] a book consisting of pure schemes."[11]

This encyclopedic—almost compulsive—overview of the world and the sciences became an intellectual way of life: "Kaspar Hauser steps up and observes: the World," he dubbed his occupation. Tjek could not help notice this bent for imposing order, for, as she said a year later, when asking him to do an inventory of the house in Løkken, "I know that it amuses you beyond words to root through everything and note it down in the greatest detail." She herself had no tendencies in this direction. Her art was the opposite of an ordered universe; she gave expression to the storms of emotion in her inner self through an expressive language of colors. The two spouses dealt with their emotional lives and their dreams in two diametrically opposed ways.[12]

The making of art was a recurring theme in Niels and Tjek's daily life. The two summers in Løkken had widened their circle of acquaintances, and the Jernes were drawn into an intense life of entertaining and sociability. Tjek liked to sit at one of the fancy cafes "every day and drink a cup of coffee," while Niels preferred a few glasses of beer or wine in shabbier surroundings in what was called Minefeltet (the Minefield district) in downtown Copenhagen. With a bit of imagination, one could find there something resembling the bohemian life in Paris.[13]

Thanks to Papa's generous support, Niels and Tjek had more money at their disposal than most of their poverty-stricken friends, so there was always a little food or beer or wine to spare whenever anyone came by. Two of her female friends remember that "it was Tjek who ruled" and "it was Tjek's friends who filled the house." She had a need for company and adored having people around her, even though it apparently had to be on her own terms: "One day you were welcome, the next day they could almost throw you out," an artist friend relates. Jerne best recalls two of the modernist painters of his own generation; one was Egill Jacobsen, who had begun to make a name for himself as one of the prime movers in burgeoning Danish abstract art (*"came very often, daily almost"*); the other was Asger Jørgensen, who, as one of the initiators of the international Cobra movement some years later, would become better known under the name Asger Jorn. *"So I lived in a sort of happy community, you know, of all these people. They were all painting, they all agreed that all peasants are idiots."*[14]

Niels liked Tjek's friends and acquaintances from the very start. "They are agreeable people, straightforward and without snobbery," he told his parents. Their company became a constant source of inspiration and allegedly made a lasting impression on him. "The average painter is more intelligent than the average scientist," he jotted down many years later. He was especially fascinated by the motivation and the psychological characteristics of artistic work, and remembers asking himself: "What is it, really, that drives a painter to paint?" Niels himself could not paint. Once, and only once, he tried make a picture, but by his own account *"it was terrible, and in addition I had mixed the colors and the turpentine all wrong. It never dried, and I really felt ashamed."* His practical involvement in art was limited to helping Tjek prepare exhibitions, fetching frames and canvases, and shipping the works that had sold.[15]

A continual topic of conversation was the relationship of the pictures to reality. Did they represent something, or not? Abstract painting had made its entrance into Danish art in the middle of the 1930s, when the group of artists calling themselves Linien (The Line) organized a much talked about exhibition.

For a long time, however, the general public remained negative—and so did Niels. He used to admire the Dutch old masters, where one could see "every thread in the lace collar"; that was real art, he thought, the product of hard work. Slowly, though, he came to understand a little more of modern art and began to realize that certain similarities exist between modern art and modernistic literature, even chess. His attitude became more positive when he began to understand that art had "developed from the object and inward to the subject: the artist's mind." This was a perspective he understood and shared.[16]

Asger Jorn, the rising theorist of Danish abstract art, wrote articles in the new avant-garde journal *Helhesten* that set the tone for discussions of the fundamental principles of the new movement. It is difficult to judge the extent to which Jerne and Jorn inspired each other. In Tjek's diary there are brief notes of Jorn's regular visits to Amaliegade but nothing about the subjects of their conversations. The fact that Jerne, in the course of our own conversations, repeatedly brought up Jorn's name may simply be an expression of his need to associate himself with a famous artist—but it may also be true that the young artist actually did make a lasting impression on the young medical student. Jorn's rebellious temperament, his interest in surrealism, and his provocative views on Danish culture ("a Dane cannot understand . . . that it is possible to be disciplined and independent at the same time") may have contributed to making him a welcome guest in Amaliegade.[17]

Jerne believes that his association with the world of Copenhagen's artists helped to sharpen his intellectual powers. He remembers, for example, how he once discussed a painting with one of the artists who had the ability to evaluate good pictures: "It's better if we stand it on its head," the artist is supposed to have said, as if anticipating Georg Baselitz's works, "then I can see it better. It's only confusing if you are able to see what it depicts." From this Jerne believes he learned that in science, too, it might sometimes be better to stand a thing on its head: "Under these conditions, you see more clearly what's not right with the thing." He also believes that this attitude helped him find his way to the natural selection theory of antibody formation fifteen years later: he started with the template theory of antibody formation then generally accepted, but then he thought, "this can't be right, makes no sense, you've got to stand this on its head." He was also struck, he says, by the painters' critical attitudes. Jorn, for example, had a striking and unsentimental attitude toward artistic quality: "Do you know what they cultivate in France?" he once asked. "They cultivate nastiness," he answered; "critical self-assurance is a fancier way to put it. But, no matter which way you turn it, it's the same." Given that Niels already had a reputation for being a critical person, and later developed a widely recognized ability as a scientific critic, it is easy to assume that the two men found much in common in that respect.[18]

To be sure, the association with Jorn, Jacobsen, and other artists strengthened the elitist attitude Niels had adopted in late adolescence and had revealed in his admiration for Nietzsche. Many Copenhagen artists were socialists or communists and thought of themselves as an aesthetic avant-garde. In his notes Niels expressed his conviction that the experience of art is the secret of a small cultural elite. He became irritated with a newspaper columnist who had asserted that the general public is not so bad: "Isn't it so, on the contrary," countered Niels, "that the taste of the 'general public' is the worst conceivable?" It was "a kind of silliness" to talk about "the general public": "For a work of art, no general public exists, and it is true that the finer the art, the fewer the number of devotees. The air is thin up on the mountain tops, and the masses are wallowing down in the valley. Art is aristocratic par excellence; art is the diametrical opposite of the vulgar, the ordinary (translated: the folkish, the usual! The language speaks for itself, if only one makes use of it!). Art is the simple, rare, cultivated, original, etc., that is to say, a concentration of precisely all the qualities lacking in the plebeians."[19]

"Who is reading William Blake? Keats? François Villon? Baudelaire? et cetera," he continued, rhetorically: "The 'general public' has not the faintest idea of this, zero, nix, nihil, they stand before Rembrandt, van Gogh, etc., *as illiterates* stand before Shakespeare, Blake, etc." The same elitist attitude returned time after time in his notes and letters during these years: "The *smart* will always be on top," he once wrote; "you *can't* keep them down." In a letter to Tjek a few years later he expressed his contempt for "that clot of sluggish, weeping, struggling people, each desperately clutching the other, who live in a delusionary outer world which they populate with their stupid narrow-mindedness and with the shadows of their day-dreams, pale with undernourishment and gross with spiritual poverty, while they move, as if blind, toward eternal annihilation."[20]

His distaste for the masses was concrete and palpable. Among the worst things he could imagine, he once wrote to Tjek, was to sit in a train compartment with a group of "fat middle-aged ladies who sweated and chatted and ate greasy sandwiches"; at such times he felt himself becoming "more and more misanthropic," and at last "[he] crept into [his] snail shell." This was not an unusual point of view among European intellectuals between the wars. But the medical student on Amaliegade held it to such a great extent that his Danish friends noticed and reacted to it. He would never give up that attitude, and therefore all his life several of his colleagues would regard him as "haughty." From here on, too, it affected his view of scientific research; he always maintained that science is an elite activity that can be popularized only with difficulty. He consistently followed the principle of fewer but better. "A single good [scientist]," he proclaimed a quarter century later, "is worth more than any number whatsoever of middling ones."[21]

On 10 March 1941, their second son, Donald, was born, "a charming black-haired little fellow." Life seemed to be going so well, he told his parents: Donald thrived, Ivar was "utterly lively," and Tjek was their "caring and beloved little woman." The summer of 1941, again in a rented house in Løkken, turned out to be Niels and Tjek's happiest together. Tjek had a show of the watercolors and oil paintings she had done the preceding spring, in which, once again, she demonstrated what an admirer called the "well-known temperament of her brush." Niels began to mix with the village doctor, who became a partner in chess and politics, and sometimes went along on house calls, where he got to talk with patients and apply bandages—his first clinical experiences.[22]

He tried to read anatomy ("tomorrow I must start studying intensively for the examination. Nothing new from the Eastern Front"), but there was so much to distract him. The war was always in the background. While Ivar played and Tjek stood painting—sometimes on Mecodrin (an amphetamine), her vacation pills—Niels sat in the sand dunes and wrote down his opinions of the world situation and the possible future course of events, all interwoven with brief notes about daily life in Løkken. Was Europe heading toward its downfall and disintegration? Would the communists seize power in the end? All summer long he, like so many others, had "a map of the world war hanging on the wall"; he clipped war maps out of the papers regularly, coloring the front lines and marking the troop movements—a kind of real-war chess game! That he supported the Allied powers there is no doubt. His friends and acquaintances were on the whole pessimistic and afraid of the Germans and believed that England would eventually fall. "I don't believe that," wrote Niels, though he didn't sound overly optimistic. Tjek was an eager anti-Nazi and feared the worst. She felt overwhelmed by the German successes and wondered what the Allies were waiting for: "Why don't they hurry?"[23]

In the last week of August 1941, summer vacation was over. Tjek continued painting at home, and Niels was to review two years of studies in physiology, anatomy, and biochemistry, hoping to be ready for the examinations before

Christmas. Time after time, however, he allowed himself to be distracted. During his busiest study period he devoted himself to writing some twenty pages of observations and meditations on Ivar; maybe they could be used for a children's book, he thought. He also spent time reading the Italian philosopher Benedetto Croce, writing notes about his theory of art as intuition and concluding with a paraphrase of Croce's aesthetic compendium, reminiscent of his earlier fascination with Bergson's ideas of intuition as a kind of intellectual sympathy, through which a person becomes one with the innermost nature of an object: "What gives intuition its unity, what animates the symbol, is emotion. Intuition is intuition precisely *because* it produces an emotion. Not the idea, but the emotion gives art symbolically hovering lightness. Art is an excitation of emotion enclosed within a circle of representation."[24]

Approaching the middle of November, Niels was plagued with doubts about whether he was going to pass the preclinical examination. His earlier feelings of failure seem to have returned; he became despondent and apparently even considered giving up. In December he rented a room farther down Amaliegade so as to read in peace and quiet. The physiology examination "went very well," but in anatomy his "weak points" were exposed. His chances of getting a high grade in biochemistry, thereby passing on his average, were not good, so he decided to make a new try in the summer.[25]

The winter of 1942 was the second severe winter of the war in a row: the water in the kitchen froze by morning and the family (and sometimes their artist guests) had to huddle together in a single small room. But the happy life continued without notable disruption as Niels philosophized about art and Tjek continued to practice it. When spring arrived, Tjek moved with the children to Løkken—where they had now purchased their own little house—to continue her painting and left Niels facing a stern regimen on his own: "I studied until late at night, walking up and down the floor and around the round table in the dining room, in a nightmare with the most horrible thoughts, while the most dreadful byways of my brain pictured the most miserable future, so that it took all I had to tear myself away from that and drive myself back to the endless books. It was good that Torp came by once in a while and brought with him a whiff of healthy perspective (he says I was 'totally stupefied')." In the end, the exams went well, and he passed with flying colors.[26]

The hardest part of his medical studies was over. Tjek's nerves had cracked a little while Niels was preparing for the exam, and she was extremely happy when she heard that everything had gone well. His parents, too, could breathe easy. A year before, his brother Thomas had followed in his father's footsteps and taken over the freezing plant and cold-storage warehouse, and now Niels—fourteen years after finishing high school—had at last lived up to his parents' expectations. It was generally considered that anyone who had passed the pre-clinical subjects would more or less automatically pass the clinical part, too. Now Niels no longer doubted that he would succeed: "So now I have the first part of my studies done, and *now I think nobody can keep me from becoming a doctor!*" he wrote triumphantly to Tjek in Løkken.[27]

7

"To Be Able to Let Nature Reflect in the Depths of My Own Soul"

*I*n June 1942, during the week that Niels stayed home in Amaliegade to rest from his examinations, he began an affair with the physician Erna Mørch. They had met at a midsummer party some years before and had bumped into each other from time to time thereafter. After a particularly lively gathering he had written to her, begging her pardon for having been "very noisy and talkative." He continued with a long disquisition on the difference between artistic, scientific, and religious knowledge, launching out from his newly acquired insights into Croce's theory of art: "The main thing is for one to experience art, and only with that artistic insight as a basis can there be any point in a conceptual definition of art." Scientific knowledge, on the other hand, "speaks alike to everyone" and "applies alike to everyone." "It is objective, makes no claims on personal feelings or on the individual's life. Its highest expression is a formula. It is 'easy,' from an ethical standpoint," he explained to her.[1]

Erna, too, was easy. They had continued to meet, more and more regularly, through the spring of 1942, right up to the week after the examination, when their relationship was transformed into the "stage in which [her soul] loved me." Erna was two years older than Niels, she was divorced, and for a couple of years she had been involved in research at Statens Seruminstitut (the Danish

State Serum Institute). Earlier that spring she had been appointed an associate professor and before long would become one of the few female doctors in Denmark to defend a thesis for a medical Ph.D. She was tall and slender, with an appetite for life. Allegedly she could not "resist men." She had, Niels wrote, "every one of the qualifications I had so long missed: her burning erotic abandon, her intellect, her bourgeois ways, her mildness, her tenderness; she was so well-groomed, Danish, admiring, everything else you can name." Qualities that he had begun to find lacking in Tjek.[2]

Neither could Erna resist Niels. Tjek's friends differed in their opinions of Niels's sex appeal. One found him "shy and withdrawn," but also "an attractive man"; another saw him as "very private" and "mysterious," a man with "a charm invisible to me," although some women were obviously "crazy about him. . . . They almost threw themselves at him"; a third remembers him as "a little bit like Raskolnikov, you know, you could very well imagine him beating such a disgusting old woman to death, yes, I couldn't bear him, and, also, he was a male chauvinist beyond all measure." It might have been the combination of *puer aeternus* and the demonic in his personality that worked its attraction upon Erna, a trait that soon expressed itself in a partly sadomasochistic relationship: "*I remember whipping her breasts with a whip, because I liked that, and she said, 'Why don't you do it.' And she gave me the whip and said, 'Do it now, do it now.' So I did it.*" "*I always had a sadistic tendency,*" he adds. "Have always been terribly heterosexual—inflicting pain," he jotted down in an autobiographical note. A colleague at the Basel Institute in the 1970s and 1980s claims that Jerne told him of a masochistic "variation: whipping himself or being whipped as he was listening to Beethoven's quartets."[3]

After two weeks with Erna in June 1942, Niels journeyed to Løkken for the annual vacation—a summer that is otherwise lost in documentary oblivion. At the end of July he returned to Copenhagen to begin the clinical portion of his medical studies, while Tjek remained in Jutland with the children for another month. On 1 August, Niels, at this point thirty-one years old, reported to Sundby Hospital, the most modern hospital in Copenhagen.

Sundby opened up a whole new world. The daily encounter with clinical reality was overwhelming. For the first time in a decade he had to get up early in the morning, find time to shave and eat, and then throw himself onto his bicycle to arrive in the hospital by eight o'clock: "In the beginning it was completely hopeless," he wrote to Tjek, with his usual mixture of surrealistic dislocation and self-satirizing style:

It looked as though the patients were being carried in and rolled in from every direction, and we moved from one operating table to another, machines and instruments were everywhere, big flasks and little, tables, faucets, buttons, a beehive with swarming nurses, sterile people everywhere who must not be touched, and no matter where I stood I was in the way; nothing could I find of whatever was demanded of me, I could not make sense of light switches, it was completely hopeless, and the patients screamed and the doctors swore at us, and I stood or glided around on the wet marble floor in my rubber shoes and did not know whether I should hold my arms behind my back, across my chest or over my stomach.

After a couple of days, however, he began to adapt to the rhythm: "It won't be so very long before I begin to feel like a doctor," and soon the hospital work became a "routine"—it "was great to be there." To pass time out of the clinic, Niels began to go to dance classes, where he danced the jitterbug with Erna and her sister "as if I had never done anything else, it's terrific." He lived a bachelor's life.[4]

Meanwhile in Løkken Tjek was struggling to combine painting and child rearing. The year before, she had received some recognition in the Copenhagen art world by being appointed judge of the decorative arts section of Den Frie Udstilling (The Free Exhibition), but she was not as lighthearted as she had been ten years before, upon her arrival in Denmark, and complained that she was "extraordinarily receptive to all ugly impressions." Painting never came easily to her: it was difficult to find time and calmness, the children required her presence, and domestic help was not always dependable. On occasion, as the summer came to an end, she broke down in despair when help proved unobtainable: "I am completely beside myself. . . . I am entirely lost. . . . I may well go straight to Hell." A few days later she dispatched Ivar and Donald, along with a new nurse, to their father in Copenhagen in order to get a week's peace and quiet for painting. It helped; soon after her return to Copenhagen in the middle of September she got all seven pieces accepted for the Charlottenborg Fall Exhibition.[5]

While Tjek prepared her big show, Niels continued in the surgical and medical departments at Sundby; afternoons he pedaled downtown to attend the introductory courses in pharmacology and elementary surgery and the required laboratory course in medical bacteriology. He also acquainted himself with a field of science he had never heard of before—immunology. He learned

Niels Jerne (with dark hair and glasses in the middle of the second row from the back) in the anatomical theater, now the Medical History Museum, University of Copenhagen, in the 1940s. "I was always sitting in the back row." (Medical History Museum, University of Copenhagen. Photo: Torkild Henriksen)

the principles of immunity and natural resistance, vaccination, and serum therapy, and that both living and dead bacteria, along with their metabolic products, can function as antigens for the production of protective antibodies. Judging by his notes, though, immunology made no great impression on him: antibodies, he wrote, are a kind of "protein in serum." That was it. Immunology was decidedly not love at first sight.[6]

At home there was not much natural resistance. The whole family took turns going to bed with colds, sinusitis, fevers, nausea, and indigestion. In between Niels found time to immerse himself in literature. During the fall and winter of 1942–43 he spent much time reading literary criticism and poetry, and judging by the newspaper clippings, he followed the progress of Danish literary debate with interest. He also had sufficient "psychic energy" to discuss every possible aspect of politics. One evening Tjek wrote in her diary that they had been at a party where Niels had talked politics with a German lawyer "until we were worn out." He also had enough left over to keep hours-per-day-together statistics again—this time concerning his relations with Erna, "the gentle and womanly one," as his friend Torp called her.[7]

In January, 1943—when the battle for Stalingrad reached its culmination (again war maps hung on the wall)—Niels completed his six-month hospital service with a month-long autopsy course. Simultaneously Tjek was admitted to a private clinic, probably to get an abortion, and on arriving home was so fatigued that Donald, now almost two, was turned over to a children's home and not brought back again until they had hired a new nurse and maid one month later. For the rest of the spring term Niels continued at the medical and pediatric clinic at Rigshospitalet (the National Hospital, also the university hospital), attending daily demonstrations and ongoing lectures.

Household finances were a constant problem. The money that was transferred from Papa's account every month (Hans Jessen Jerne had collaborated with the German Occupation authority from the very beginning, so the warehouse and freezing plant in Rotterdam were thriving) barely covered the expenses of a two-child family with a large circle of acquaintances and dissipated habits. Bills lay unpaid for months, and the bill collector often had to leave empty-handed. Having enough money meant a lot to Niels, and scarcity of liquid assets is a recurrent theme in his autobiographical reminiscences (*"During the war we were terribly short of money. . . . I mean it was disaster"*), and they were sometimes forced to sell to the pawnbroker. The few quarrels he and Tjek had openly were apparently about money.[8]

Several times in past years Niels had opposed Tjek's taking a job. However, he had nothing against a little extra income, and when the chance came, he took it. One of Erna's good friends and colleagues, Johannes Ipsen, headed a small department at the Serum Institute and was "*in need of a secretary*." Right before Easter 1943 Niels went to a job interview and was immediately promised a half-time appointment through the end of the summer—a most welcome supplement to the budget and a good chance to experience something new. "Taj met Dr. Ipsen, got the temporary job for the summer, very happy," wrote Tjek in her diary.[9]

Over Easter Niels familiarized himself with an introduction to the Serum Institute. The history of serum research goes back to the end of the nineteenth century. Two years after Emile Roux's and Alexandre Yersin's isolation, in 1888, of the toxin of the diphtheria bacterium, Emil von Behring and Shibasaburo Kitasato had shown that injection of the toxin produced an antitoxic substance (an antitoxin) in the blood and that this could be used therapeutically. The expectations were high that the same serotherapeutic method could be applied to a long list of diseases; hence serum institutes were established in several countries for the production of antitoxic sera. In Copenhagen, Carl Julius Salomonsen, the first professor of general pathology at the university, started the production of antidiphtherial serum in the early 1890s. In 1902 the operation, now led by Salomonsen's assistant, Thorvald Madsen, was transferred to the newly established State Serum Institute.

Under Madsen's leadership the institute expanded rapidly. Because of its status, the institute was given a large grant from the Rockefeller Foundation in the mid-1920s. The production of diphtheria serum continued to be the institute's main business, but the staff also busied itself producing sera against tetanus, meningococci, streptococci, pneumococci, and gangrene. The preparation of whooping cough and smallpox vaccines eventually played a large role, as did production of the Calmette vaccine against tuberculosis. They prepared typhus, paratyphus, and cholera vaccines for epidemics in foreign countries and developed methods for the serodiagnosis of syphilis, gonorrhea, and tuberculosis as well as means for blood typing. By 1940 the Danish State Serum Institute was one of the largest biomedical institutions in Europe, employing 376 persons in sixteen departments and undertaking everything from the production of sera to basic serological and bacteriological research.[10]

The institute was well known for its deep pockets: "Money was no problem at the Serum Institute, it was something you had," Ipsen recalls. Madsen had great international prestige, and was able to pump the ministry for funds. His successor, Jeppe Ørskov, who took over in 1940, did not have the same international standing, but the institute was still considered an ideal place to work and do research, especially among physicians who wanted to write a routine doctoral thesis in order to qualify for a clinical career. The infrastructure—instrumentation, supply of laboratory animals, assistance—functioned beyond reproach. It is also said that the institute operated as a cover organization for the Resistance movement, which had just begun to accelerate during the spring of 1943. Activists who had gone underground were reportedly vaccinated, weapons were test-fired in the cellar beneath the animal stalls, "sabotage was planned, the transporting of refugees was organized. There was hardly anything the staff of the institute did not get mixed up in," asserted one of the active Resistance members after the war. The new secretary probably knew nothing yet about the institute's purported role in undermining the German Occupation forces. Niels's involvement in the war was limited to following the news on the BBC—in March and April 1943, the Germans' U-boat offensive in the Atlantic peaked—and he hardly considered taking an active part in the Resistance, in contrast to his friend Torp, who dropped his studies because of his engagement in underground activities. *"It was things like going up to Elsinore and laying bombs on the rails; it gave you a short popularity."*[11]

Niels had his attention fixed instead on his new work. Some years earlier he had learned that the bacon market valued standardization of the product; in his current work, he realized that vaccines, toxoids (that is, weakened toxins), and antisera for clinical use required similar standardization to guarantee effect and safety. The spread of various forms of serum therapy during the first decades of the twentieth century had led to what Madsen called an ever more "widespread desire for uniformity in the measurement of healing sera." Just as there were international units of length and weight—the standard meter and the standard kilogram—there ought to be international vaccine, toxin, and antitoxin units. Faced with the problem of poorly defined toxins and antitoxins early on, Madsen had insisted on the importance of international standards in the field, and when he became presiding officer of the Health Committee of the League of Nations in 1921, he set up a commission on biological standardization. In addition it was soon decided to create an international central laboratory for the establishment of international serum standards, and as the State Serum Institute in Copenhagen was considered one of the most outstanding, along with the institutes in Paris, Frankfurt, London, and Washington, Madsen succeeded in having it located in Denmark, with financial support from the League of Nations. In the early 1940s about thirty substances were on the Health Committee's list of international biological standard preparations: among them a number of antitoxins, several vitamins, a number of hormones (insulin, androsterone, gonadotropin), and digitalis. The strength, or activity, of these substances was expressed in international units (IU) and incorporated into the national pharmacopoeias.[12]

While other departments at the institute were oriented toward clinical problems, the task of the Standardization Department was the production and investigation of international standard sera. Twice a year samples of twelve kinds of sera were distributed to institutions all over the world, to be used as local standards for serum production. (Only the British Commonwealth continued to standardize vaccines and sera at the Department of Biological Standards in the National Institute for Medical Research, at Hampstead.) The department's work was also supposed to function as a center of education for visiting physicians and as a research institution—from the very beginning Madsen had stressed that standardization practices should be based on research. The first head of the department, Claus Jensen, had worked on methods of biological measurement for the standardization of diphtheria toxin and diphtheria antitoxin, and Johannes Ipsen, his successor, had published his dissertation, *Contributions to the Theory of Biological Standardization,* on the evaluation of the death rate and the time of death of test animals as biological measures of toxin strength. It was to this department that Niels Jerne reported in April 1943.[13]

Working in the Standardization Department during the late spring and summer of 1943 did not leave Niels much time for his family, who had left for another summer in Løkken. The spouses wrote to each other about everyday matters and not least about Tjek's painting. The watercolors were "blossoming" in her hands, "while the oils continue to be withering and heavy." As usual, Niels answered by idealizing her artist's life: "I know how you fight for your life as an artist, with daily duties and sorrows like heavy blocks tied around your feet." Alone in Copenhagen he had few duties and sorrows and liberated his mind from the "daily chaos of worries and trifles" by diving into some statistical problems Ipsen had set him.[14]

Niels was supposed to do secretarial work; "he sat and wrote all the letters when we sent out the standards," the laboratory technician Jens Ole Rostock recalls. But soon Niels was allowed to try the scientific side as well. He was learning "something about . . . measurement of diphtheria antitoxin," he reported to Tjek in early June. Because all methods of biological measurement are affected by error, the practice of biological standardization also involved statistical treatment of the test results. Biostatistics was something new to Niels: *"Before I came to the Serum Institute I had never done any probability calculation."* Ipsen remembers giving his new secretary a copy of his dissertation, which immediately seemed to stir a sympathetic response in Niels, who suggests, in retrospect, that his mind was prepared for biostatistics and that he had always had a natural talent for probability calculations: *"Things like roulette have always interested me."* The notion of chance played a large role in his self-understanding; it is *"something very essential. . . . I am a very big fan of randomness."* That his being a statistical prodigy is more than a self-constructed myth is confirmed by the archive; his notes contain scattered comments on the play of chance, such as the phrase "chance governs all."[15]

In a series of letters to Tjek in the summer of 1943, Niels described being totally absorbed by his statistical studies. It amused him much more than writing business letters in French and German, and he got so involved that he seldom had time to dive into his "little pet projects of digging through" his papers. He borrowed textbooks on the subject from the library, particularly the latest (1938) edition of R. A. Fisher's *Statistical Methods for Research Workers,* "a book that is 'the bible' in this field." He sat up with these volumes and let calculation problems fill his thoughts "so that the hours and the whole night run away from me without my having finished it."[16]

One of the routine calculation problems that kept him occupied consisted of determining the uncertainty in the strength of an unknown serum preparation. Test animals cost money, so the problem was to achieve a reliable measure of strength on the basis of a small number of tests. "Now, if you give animals two different sera that are to protect the animals against a bacterial toxin," Niels explained, then the purpose is to "decide whether one serum has a stronger effect and how much stronger than the other": "We are now mixing sera with different doses of toxin and injecting this into some groups of animals. A few of the animals die and so we take note of a series of mortality percentages for the different doses and the different sera. With a specific dose, we find, for example, that the one serum gives a mortality of 15% and, with the same dose, the other gives a mortality of 26%." Was it possible to say "with assurance" that the one serum is better than the other? How great was the probability that there is no difference between the two sera? "How large is the percentage of error? All this requires a colossal calculation using a bunch of formulas," he told Tjek.[17]

Most of the biostatistical methods of the time presumed that the observation data were distributed according to a so-called normal distribution, a bell curve. Ipsen had used a so-called probit (probability unit) method for many years, and probit calculation now became one of Niels's daily work assignments, and even a leisure-time enjoyment. One summer Sunday, for example, he wrote to Ipsen about his musings at the beach: "I walked along the water's edge and began counting the people at a place far out to one side where a little dog was lying, and I wrote down the number of people in bathing suits every 50 steps: 13, 20, 29, *36*, 23, 28, 20, 31, 34, 44, 51, 83, 69, 67, 80, 104, *141*, 79, harbor. They were the most concentrated outside the beach hotel (141). . . . I have not had time to carry out a test of Departure from Normality. Unfortunately there was not any normal distribution on the train home, I looked for a place to sit, using the Maximum Likelihood Method, but in vain." The probit method is burdened with a systematic error of uncertainty for small series of observations, however, and Ipsen and Jerne found that they could eliminate this error if they used a somewhat different method, which they called rankit (unit of ranked data). They soon realized that Fisher and Frank Yates had already published a table of rankits but had not determined the uncertainty of the rankit values in their table. So to be able to use the method routinely and to give an expression for uncertainty, Ipsen felt that a new table of rankit values had to be prepared. This required a numerical calculation of an integral to work out the degree of uncertainty. *"Together, Ipsen and I had already calculated five cases,"* Jerne recalls, adding that the calculation of every single value in the new rankit table took two days, with the help of their mechanical calculation machine.[18]

At the end of August, Ipsen took off on vacation, and Niels, along with Rostock, the technician, busied himself with making a toxicity determination on neosalvarsan preparations. In a letter to Ipsen he vividly described his irritation with the statistical apparatus he had to rely on in comparing the results of two tests. Envisioning the statistical work that lay ahead, he continued: "I climbed on board the big calculating machine, more or less as you would do in cutting a little lawn in the garden with a self-propelled hay baler. You know it is a little silly and you hope the neighbors aren't looking while you are doing it, but, on the other hand, you own the machine and it cuts grass very well, and then it's fun, too, driving it around!" Would not someone be able to construct "a machine of somewhat reduced caliber" for simple calculating tasks? Sitting alone at the Serum Institute he figured out that *"when it took two days for every calculation, then it was going to take two hundred days [all together], and Ipsen was going to be coming back in thirty days, so, I thought, there has to be a smarter way to calculate it."* Apparently, his motive was aversion to boring routine work. On several occasions during our conversations, he described himself as *"gifted but lazy."*[19]

Over the next couple of days, Niels developed a calculation method that simplified the work and saved time (it was probably the use of a standard formula for the so-called binomial distribution summation), and when Ipsen returned they wrote it up in a little article that was submitted, with Ipsen as the first author, to the journal of Scandinavian serologists, *Acta Pathologica et Microbiologica Scandinavica*. Not many people referred to it in the subsequent literature, so the rankit article was a rather insignificant contribution to science. The difference between the two methods proved to be negligible for test series with more than twenty-five observations (*"The whole thing is only a slight improvement on the probit tables"*), hence from a historical perspective, it is hardly worth mentioning.[20]

What seems a trivial detail in the large picture, however, can be of great importance for the individual in his life's project. In our conversations, Jerne returned again and again to the rankit calculation episode, describing how he found *"a method that only took two hours for each calculation . . . and when Ipsen came back, he said, 'You are a genius' and then we published my method, that is my first paper."* He says that was the first time he realized he was smarter than Ipsen, *"and that made me a little 'Watsonistic.'"* It was the same kind of experience he had had as a child when he visited Monte Carlo with his father, and the rankit episode was elevated to one of the most important in his life: *"I think that was the essential departure of me into science."* The story about the rankits thus entered Jerne's repertoire of stories about how he gradually discovered that he was brilliant and thereby overcame his feeling of being a failure. Actually, the event made such a great impression on him that, years later, he decided to title one of the chapters in his planned autobiography "In which I am given a half-day job in the Danish State Serum Institute, and finally discover (suddenly) that I am a scientist." The choice of words is significant—the phrasing suggests Jerne's romantic self-image of having a latent scientist within, who, in the right environment, had finally revealed himself.[21]

It was not long before Niels began to speculate on the possibility of pursuing research on his own. Ipsen remembers that Niels often talked about settling down as a general practitioner although it was probably "a little affectation, that thing about being a country doctor." Niels did not seem to have had "any great urge to do something to benefit humanity," and the medical studies were rather a kind of "chess game . . . a kind of hobby he pursued, as a sideline." Jerne, in his later autobiographical musings, agrees—being a practicing physician *"was only a very last refuge, so to say."* The dream of a placid life as a doctor in the country only came in brief glimpses. In his daily habits, he remained an urban intellectual.[22]

Even if "it would be a good move to write a dissertation," he was not sure he wanted to devote his life to research. In a letter to Tjek, he questioned "whether it is sensible, humanly speaking, to invest such great energy and powers of concentration in something so specialized, something that doesn't even slightly impinge on your personal sense of life": "To employ your time in the demanding assignment of familiarizing yourself with a thought-structure that others have already built up to completion; to develop this part of your life as a dilettante in peripheral abstractions, while the pulsing purple-red blood in your veins and the feelings in your heart have to take care of themselves until 'later.'" His ruminations about scientific work are like an echo of Kierkegaard, for whom the subjective view of life was diametrically opposed to the scientific and who did not find the choice a hard one: "It does no good to get involved with the natural sciences. . . . The researcher immediately begins to distract us with his particular projects. . . . Who in the devil can stand that!" Later Erwin Schrödinger would come to the same conclusion when realizing that science as a life project has its price, because it is "ghastly silent" about every single thing that "is really near to our heart," about everything that "really matters to us."[23]

Then what could Niels imagine as an alternative? In "one word," he wrote to Tjek, "if only one was an artist!" It was not the technical aspects of the artist's work that attracted him but the creative side. Niels conceived of an artist as a person who could express what his or her soul contained:

> To be able to impress his personality like a stamp in colors and form; to be able to let nature reflect in the depths of my own soul; to be able to cultivate my inner garden of emotions and express myself in pictures, instead of expressing abstract qualities of distant things in numbers. To be able to listen to life within and without, feeling in touch [with] everything that bubbles, pulses, strives, works, lives. To be able to work with that multitude I myself contain; to be able to train one's hand and one's eye to master the technique of creating just the form that is prepared to receive one's own imprint. To be able to bend one's will toward recreating oneself in harmony with nature.

That he wished to come in contact with what "bubbles, pulses, strives, works, lives" does not mean he dreamed of getting in touch with concrete, everyday reality. In this respect he was still thinking like the young, sublime Niels. No, he wanted to "liberate a part of one's soul from the daily chaos of worries and trivialities, and to be able to fix the happiest moments in a bouquet of colors. To be able to stand up and say: cela, c'est moi! This is my work!" He dreamed of "being a world in oneself and God in that world and creator!" It was like an echo from his letters in the beginning of the 1930s when he had cited Willem Kloos: "I am a God in the depth of my thoughts"—words that had "pierced him through and through." None of the romantic poets he had read in his adolescence had expressed themselves more clearly on the spirit's power over matter.[24]

Niels's dream of an artist's life sounds, at first, like the opposite of living a scientist's life, more like a conflict between thought and emotion. But his choice was not whether the intellect or the emotions would be allowed expression. The big question was whether a life in science would force him to limit his thoughts and feelings to the mediocre, the superficial, and the customary or whether he would get a chance to approach the exceptional. The kind of person he described, one who bends his will toward "recreating himself in harmony with nature," need not necessarily be an artist in the literal meaning of the word. A scientist can also be an artist.

In light of his subsequent trajectory, Niels's remarks about the artist's existence can be seen as a manifesto for precisely the kind of scientist's life he would come to live. Such a scientist does not allow himself to be blocked by inconvenient facts or by the confusing life of the laboratory. Such a scientist can attain the sublime through science by abstracting from concrete details, thereby reaching out to universal connections, and by putting his personal imprint on the world. What fascinated many of his later scientific colleagues was the fact that he was able to unite these two modes of existence—rational cognition and artistic creation—in order to transcend everyday "worries and trivialities" and attain the sublime.

Niels's view of the scientist-cum-artist is reminiscent both of historical Romanticism and of romantic thinking in general. The idea of the constructive power of the mind, a mind where "reality is brought into being by experience," is a central theme in romantic poetry as Northrop Frye has put it. This Romantic self is not imprinted by the world; it is the fundamental creative authority, the source of all values. In act 5 of *A Midsummer Night's Dream,* the mythical Theseus gives pregnant expression to the poet's sovereign and absolute creative power:

> The poet's eye, in a fine frenzy rolling,
> Doth glance from heaven to earth, from earth to heaven;
> And as imagination bodies forth
> The forms of things unknown, the poet's pen
> Turns them to shapes, and gives to airy nothing
> A local habitation and a name.

It is certainly not coincidental that Jerne, again and again, in letters and manuscripts, quoted these words of the Duke of Athens.[25]

"I Am Branded with Infidelity, and See That Open-Eyed"

*A*fter a mere week's vacation with Tjek and the children in Løkken in the summer of 1943, Niels continued his combination of medical studies and statistical musings. The fall term continued in the surgical clinic, with courses in radiology, neurology, epidemic diseases, skin and genital diseases, ophthalmology, otorhinolaryngology, and cowpox inoculation, followed by a month's internship at a psychiatric department.

In Niels's spare hours, Fisher's statistical "bible" was his constant companion. In a sense, his preoccupation with statistics was the essence of what he called "peripheral abstractions." But he did not have to suppress his pulsing blood and the feelings in his heart—Erna Mørch took care of that. They lay sunning together on her balcony, went to the movies, and visited the Tivoli Gardens. "For the 7587th time: I like you so much," Erna wrote once. Much about her had began to irritate him, however. She had no taste in poetry, he thought, and no artistic sense; when she read, she paid attention only to the plot, not to "the composition, the emotion, and the art." But even though their relationship was becoming more like a habit, despite feeling more and more burdened by having to satisfy her need for company, and despite his moods about her "unlovely face, impossible hats and banal taste," she satisfied an ever greater need in his life. The magnet of his passion was "her slim, supple body, her lust

for the erotic, for lying naked together, that she surrenders herself completely. . . . In a word: her erotic arts." She brought out the sadistic artist in him.
He described painting her body; he also described "the whip, the rope, the
naked struggle."[1]

Tjek knew of the relationship, but it is not clear how she reacted to it. The
ideology of sexual freedom was widespread in their Copenhagen circle of acquaintances, and it is said that she described her marriage as "open," that "they
did not want to tie each other down," but that they also "would tell each other
when they were heading for trouble." At first she seems to have taken it relatively
calmly. But as the affair continued she was trapped between her ideology and
her own feelings. "Of course you're enjoying yourself hugely, now," she wrote at
the beginning of June 1943, "free and independent; oh, yes, I understand you so
well, have yourself a really good time, for now."[2]

Niels swore that his relationship with Erna meant nothing in the long run.
He told Tjek that he thought about their marriage with "eternity thoughts"; he
wanted to "do [his] best" and "never leave it." Nevertheless, he later confided to
his diary that from time to time he enticed Erna with "marriage plans" and
several times tried to leave Tjek, but each time "after a few days I found it unbearable." Seen from outside, the whole thing was quite banal—he wanted to
have both wife and mistress—but Niels did not have such a banal self-image.
He defended himself by saying that he could not resist his "need for erotic dis-
charge": "There is a conflict inside me. I am branded with infidelity and see
that open-eyed. But I have never been indifferent to you. I have never been driv-
en by an easy, thoughtless mind. I cannot imagine completely soulless sexual
liaisons."[3]

The relationship with Erna was not only erotic. She was, after all, a medical
doctor and an accomplished scientist and as such also evoked Niels's scientific
talents. When, in November 1943, he was admitted to the hospital for a kidney
ailment, he lay there analyzing data from her pneumococci research. "Theory
explaining all results!" he wrote in a note and showed her how he could, point
by point, account for all her data. This combination of erotic and professional
sharing may have contributed further to the deterioration of the relationship
between Niels and Tjek. During Niels's sickness Tjek wrote that she expected
her "substitute" to take over the duty of caring for him, and a month later an acquaintance referred to the "crises in your marriage that people are talking
about." But Tjek clung to the hope that it would be possible to keep their marriage together. To be sure, they could talk with each other, and she had noted
that he had at least "the will, anyway, to share a nice married life" with her.

"Evening at home with Taj, hardly any cigarettes," she wrote in her diary later that winter. "Taj quiet—we talked together half the night—and wept."[4]

After the rankit paper had been sent for publication, Niels's medical studies continued rolling along, now with tutorials and demonstrations in pathological anatomy. During the winter and spring of 1944 he had clinical work in the morning and lectures in pharmacology in the afternoon, so the Serum Institute became a more intermittent experience. Not that his presence mattered that much: after finishing the rankit article, he felt much surer in the saddle and could be more nonchalant about the amount of time he spent in the department. In one of the few letters that got through the German censorship during the war, Hans Jessen asked his son whether he viewed "scientific research work" as his occupation or merely as "a stepping stone to future practical medical work." That was a question Niels could not answer. There were so many more important matters than standardization and statistics to worry about. The war, for example: *"I was sitting at the radio every night,"* he says, thinking back, adding that he knew some people who worked at the Swiss Embassy and that he *"went there every day to read Neue Zürcher Zeitung."* The longer the war went on, the more involved he became—though always as an observer. Ipsen remembers that Niels often was not "much in the mood" for working.[5]

Niels's casual attitude was not an obstacle to his acquaintance with Ipsen, who was rapturous over his new assistant. Ipsen was only six months older than Niels but had already come a long way in his scientific career; he was a *"Frühzünder"* (one who ignites early), as Niels called him, as distinguished from himself, the late-blooming *"Spätzünder."* Despite the difference in their formal status and scientific experience, Niels soon became the object of Ipsen's wholehearted admiration. "He was poor, but he was rich," says Ipsen; it was Niels's gift of seeing science as part of a more comprehensive cultural enterprise that made the greatest impression on him: "I don't know if I was in love with him. I'm not homosexual, but there was something or other about him. [He was one of] those people who have had the greatest influence on me, other than my father. For he drew me out of one-track science." Ipsen noted that his new assistant was "fantastic as a guide" to world literature as well as "an outstanding chess player [who] knew all the theoretical openings by heart." The two men soon became good friends. Yet Ipsen could not help but notice that his assistant had a slightly arrogant bearing based on "a certain feeling of superiority" that sometimes expressed itself in "very sharp comments" that "could irritate all of them." He remembers when Swedish Television broadcast a discussion with the 1984 Nobel

Prize winners, and "there he was again, with his air of superiority, when he criticized the others." He also saw Niels's fondness for making sarcastic remarks as
related to his sadistic tendency: Ipsen's wife, Daphne, was completely crazy
about Niels, who is said to have rejected her advances yet, at the same time, proposed that he be allowed to whip her.[6]

The year 1944 was the summer of the great invasion. On 6 June, 150,000 Allied
soldiers came ashore on Normandy's beaches. "I am huddling over the radio
most of the time," Niels wrote to Tjek, who as usual was spending her summer
in Løkken with the children. The political situation in Denmark, too, sharpened. The Danes became more and more optimistic, and the German Occupation authorities more and more aggressive. The strife in Niels's personal life,
however, consisted mainly of his relationship with Erna. "My mind is be-
witched," he told his wife: "I have tried to tear myself away, it makes me wander
around through the streets for hours on end, until I find myself weeping on the
sofa. I must get through this thing. If only some happy day I find the strength to
turn back to you dear ones." He apparently had strength enough for a short
summer vacation before the family returned to a Copenhagen where hundreds
of people had just been killed in the confrontation with Werner Best's Occupation command.[7]

At this point Niels's interest in the war seemed to diminish—as if he were
waiting for the inevitable end. Once again, he began to focus on science. One of
the most important research tasks, as Ipsen saw it, was to develop methods for
standardization of diphtheria and tetanus toxoids that could be used for immunization. Inspired by the discovery in the 1930s that treatment with forma-
lin could produce a nontoxic, but still immunogenic, diphtheria toxoid, Ipsen
had already set in motion a series of experiments to study the relationship between the dosage of diphtheria toxoid and the serum response. Even before
Niels arrived in the department in the spring of 1943, Ipsen and Rostock had
carried out several hundred experiments.[8]

The measurement of diphtheria antitoxin in serum was done with the help
of a biological assay that had been introduced at the beginning of the century
and developed further by Claus Jensen at the Serum Institute in the beginning of
the 1930s. An unknown antitoxic serum is mixed with toxin, and after a certain
time a small amount of the reaction mixture is injected into the back skin of a
shaved rabbit. The diameter of the skin irritation is, within a certain interval,
proportional to the concentration of excess toxin in the mixture, hence an in-
verse measure of the strength of the antitoxic serum. If a series of reaction mix-

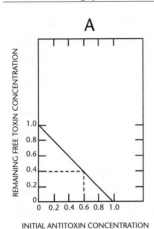
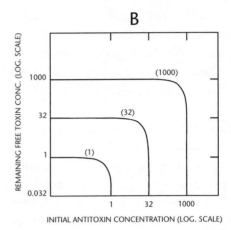

A: INITIAL TOXIN CONCENCTRATION 1
B: INITIAL TOXIN CONCENTRATION 1, 32, AND 1000. LOGARITHMIC SCALE

Theoretical neutralization curves showing the decrease of toxin concentration in a series of mixtures of constant initial toxin concentration and increasing initial antitoxin concentration. *Left:* arithmetic scale; *right:* logarithmic scale. The law of multiple proportions assumes that the curves are parallel. From Jerne's dissertation, 1951. (Jerne Collection, The Royal Library, Copenhagen)

tures with the same initial amount of toxin but with various antitoxin levels is prepared, then the remaining amount of toxin over time can be plotted as a neutralization curve. Standardization supposed that the neutralization curves for standard antitoxin and for unknown antitoxin are parallel on a logarithmic scale, so that the distance between the curves could be used as a measure of the difference in "strength" between the two preparations. This fundamental prerequisite, the "rule of multiple proportions," as Jensen called it, means that if, for example, 1 international antitoxin unit (AU) of serum neutralizes 0.1 ml of toxin, then 0.1 AU of serum neutralizes 0.01 ml of toxin, and so forth.[9]

Jerne later remembered that he began to doubt this assumption, noting that, first and foremost, he was driven "to question the prevailing truths": "For many years, people had set about measuring the antibody content in a serum, there at the institute, in a certain established way. That's how it was done, that's all. But wasn't it possible to improve this established way of doing it?" In the middle of June 1944, he wrote to Tjek that he was "discovering something about diphtheria," and a month later he was again "in a hurry" with experiments. Dur-

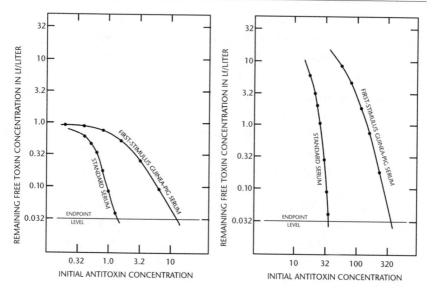

Empirical neutralization curves for standard serum and first-stimulus guinea pig serum.
Left: initial toxin concentration 1 Lf/liter; *right:* initial toxin concentration 32 Lf/liter.
Lower initial toxin concentration makes the neutralization curves less parallel (the dilution
effect). From Jerne's dissertation, 1951. (Jerne Collection, The Royal Library, Copenhagen)

ing the fall, he continued to busy himself with his own experiments in the afternoons, having spent his mornings in the surgical clinic. His occasional laboratory notes show that he carried out a number of experiments with guinea pigs
immunized with diphtheria toxoid and found that the conventional measure of
a serum's strength (the AU value) seemed to be arbitrary, since it varied with the
initial level of toxin concentration chosen for carrying out the measurement. On
an average, he wrote later, "the antitoxin content of the sera was found to be *five
times as high* when measured at the one [initial toxin] concentration level, as
when measured at the other." The guinea pig serum therefore behaved "in total
contradiction" to the law of multiple proportions; the "strength" of an antitoxic
serum evidently depended on the measuring method, in this case on the level of
toxin concentration at which the measuring took place.[10]

Serologists normally worked at high concentration levels. So why did Jerne
try low concentrations? When directly questioned, he answered: *"I worked at
low concentrations because it was much cheaper and much easier."* But he would
also claim that he worked with neutralization at low concentrations in order to

question established methods: *"I was always a bit of a rebel, so I said: 'Why do we do it this way, why don't we do it in a hundredfold dilution.'"* Should his discovery of the "dilution effect," as he called it, then be taken as the result of a kind of rebellion? *"Yes,"* he answered with emphasis. In the same way he discovered the salt effect in the phage-antiphage reaction seven years later? *"Yes, yes,"* he answered even more emphatically. Is that the same attitude? *"Yes, that's right. And I think there are many such attitudes. . . . Why do they do it the way they do it, you could do it quite different."* His responses may be a rationalization after the fact, an attempt to create retroactively a consistent image of himself as a *"rebel."* But whether it is authentic or an element in his retroactive self-fashioning, the image agrees well with his general understanding of his character. It is tempting to compare this story with another, namely, how the painter Egill Jacobsen had taught him to stand things on their heads, a story that, in turn, is also reminiscent of his self-characterization of being an outsider, of being *"a kind of misfit,"* wondering why other people do as they do.[11]

In fact, Jerne's discovery of the dilution effect made so great an impression on him that he long chose to overlook the fact that it was already known in the serological literature. In the beginning of the century, the Austrian bacteriologist Rudolph Kraus had pointed out that the neutralization capacity of an antitoxic serum is determined not only by concentration but also by a quality he termed *Avidität* ("avidity"). Even at the State Serum Institute, the effect was known, at least in principle; already at the end of the 1930s, one of the leading Danish biostatisticians, Georg Rasch—the institute's first real professional statistician, a *"significant"* person and a *"close friend"* who had studied with R. A. Fisher in London in the 1930s and who was *"willing to talk about everything between heaven and earth"*—through a statistical analysis of the neutralization curves, had drawn the conclusion that the difference in strength between two antitoxic sera cannot be given by a single-strength measure; it must be given with two numbers, one corresponding to the "quantity" and one to the "combining velocity." Ipsen, too, had noticed the great difference between guinea pig serum and standard serum with respect to the slope of the neutralization curves, although he had not found it especially significant. (Niels long seems to have repressed the fact that Ipsen already knew about the dilution effect—"for shame!" he wrote in the margin of one of Ipsen's manuscripts on the topic around 1946—and it was only in his doctoral dissertation that he admitted that Ipsen long before had made observations that were "essentially the same" as those he himself had made the summer and fall of 1944.)[12]

The question of priority is of minor interest, however. A more interesting aspect of this episode is the role the discovery played in Niels's self-image. His emphatic interest in the dilution effect was an expression of a personal world-view in which the conflict between normality and deviation had great significance. Objectively, he may only have repeated what others had already found out. But subjectively he experienced it as his own discovery, and this perception had a major and enduring impression on him, perhaps even greater than the "brilliant" statistical solution he had found a year earlier. The dilution effect became the point of departure for his dissertation research a few years later and the key to his independent activity in international standardization work during the decades to come.

While Niels felt he was making yet another personally significant discovery in science, Tjek had an artistic breakthrough at the Charlottenborg Spring Exhibition. Because of the fine reviews she received, she was given an entire hall for the upcoming fall exhibition. She also experienced an economic victory: her works sold for four thousand Danish kroner, almost a year's income, and soon after that she received a large academy stipend. Tjek had become the economic head of the family. She invested her earnings in a second summerhouse, Jægerhuset, some fifteen miles northwest of Copenhagen. The couple spent Christmas of 1944 there together with their children, the "tall, thin Don Quixote" and "short, fat and cheerful Sancho Panza," as Niels called eight-year-old Ivar and three-year-old Donald. But the Christmas and New Year's holiday in the new house did not turn out happily, the relationship with Erna casting a long shadow over domestic harmony. Some months later Niels noted that he "had nearly wrecked [his] marriage." In what way, we can only guess.[13]

9   *"Letters Are a Spiritual Spiderweb in Which You Snare the Dreaming Soul of a Woman"*

*T*he previous two or three years had been a turning point in Niels Jerne's life. At last he had proven himself to his parents; his boss valued him and openly recognized his intellectual capacity; and for several years he had managed to fire Erna Mørch's desires. The nihilistic attitude toward life and the melancholy undertone that had marked so many of the letters and notes of his youth gradually ebbed. And a mood of reckless success began to break through.

Of course one should, like Kierkegaard, speak of "either-or," wrote thirty-three-year-old Niels to Tjek right after New Year 1945; one ought to speak of "the aesthetic and the ethical" if one wanted to keep "nobility of the heart" and "solidity of the character." As usual, it is hard to judge whether he merely flirted with the Kierkegaardian categories or truly felt that he faced a choice between the ethical and the aesthetic life. On the one hand, one ought to adopt the same position as Kierkegaard's ethicist and think in terms of fidelity, faith, spirit, duty, patience, devotion, self-denial, and eternity, he claimed. Maybe such concepts were unusable—indeed morbid—in comparison with the categories of hedonistic philosophy, but for the individual they were nevertheless the most valuable and essential. Hence he ought to work for his children and their future; he ought to fill his life with "work, work, work"; he ought to hurry up and get himself qualified as a physician, he repeated to himself later in the spring.[1]

On the other hand, one should not brood too much, permitting thought and self-examination to take up more room than pleasure and the joys of life. He enjoyed the good in life, he declared; he loved the art of seduction. Tjek's moral strength and personal integrity caused him to adopt an extreme aesthetic position toward life. Even if "in deep contemplation" one could prove the ethical way of life all the way down to "total unselfishness," that would not drive away the "deep satisfaction of body and mind, as nature has framed us, in smiling broadly and lighting a cigarette after having made love." All things considered, he added, "what a boring place this world would be if nobody was brave enough to sin and develop himself."[2]

He still sought certain qualities in Tjek—gentleness, womanliness, absolute devotion—but recently he had begun to find her unfriendly, with a brusqueness in her tone that "totally demolishes any mood whatsoever." He yearned for a "gentle feminine devotion in a slim, attractive body that longs for sex with me." With Erna he had had his erotic yearnings satisfied, and she had become "an obsession" in his soul. But other aspects of their relationship were less satisfying: he was afraid of losing his freedom; he did not want to be forced into a modern apartment with her and her bourgeois taste; and he was frightened by the thought of having to account for his doings and being invited out with her "as the captive of her charms." Tjek, after all, gave him a freedom few other women would grant. She was gifted, and she had "a much sharper eye for human and aesthetic values," he told her.[3]

Erna released him from his dilemma when, at the beginning of March 1945, she ended the relationship. At first he seemed relieved, thanking her "for the thousand days" she had bestowed on him, for always being "so boundlessly loving" toward him. He hoped they could remain good friends, but soon his restless unease returned. Hamlet's words about the "pangs of despised love" became his motto for the spring. Just as, a decade earlier, he had used mathematics to get over his breakup with Jeanine, again mathematical calculations became a distraction. Every time he thought too much about Erna, he sat down and "calculated out the pneumococci." Apparently it helped. More than a month later, when his thoughts were filled with "examinations and other things," the opposite occurred: "Busying myself with your pneumococci kept bringing you into my thoughts and evoked once again some of my previous anguish. I kept away from the pneumococci." Another month after this, he seldom thought about her: "I now busied myself again with the pneumococci, enjoyably, as a convalescent enjoys touching a scar."[4]

The affair with Erna Mørch was "finished forever, you can count on that," he wrote to Tjek, but this did not keep him from launching himself into newer, if still briefer and more soulless, liaisons. During March 1945, while Tjek was feverishly occupied in preparing a new exhibition, Niels moved out to Jæger-huset to study for the penultimate exams in pathology and bacteriology and brought with him a younger female student, "a pretty, cute little . . . piece," as a fellow student described her. Niels conceived of their relationship as comradely but allowed himself a single misstep during the intense weeks of study. He also had a brief but intense affair with an Englishwoman he had met at a party in the Swiss consulate. Wasn't it amazing, he wrote to Erna, that "14 days before" he "had only known 2 women? And now, it is 4." He began to understand Erna's "penchant for renewal": there was "something glorious, fresh, stimulating in a new person you meet and penetrate (fie for shame!)." And "isn't it remarkable," he continued, "the way everything happens without your having really planned it? Well, maybe it's my nature always to expect that my momentary mood will prevail longer than it really does."[5]

These two brief affairs reinforced Niels's boldness and self-confident atti-tude toward life, as though he was rediscovering in himself the power of sensu-ality, of the flesh. But the two episodes also reinforced his feelings of restlessness and anxiety. Like Kierkegaard's aesthete, Niels, too, was easily distracted. Two years earlier, he had complained that his thoughts flitted from one thing to an-other, pulling his will along with them; that he lacked a fixed, purposeful course through life; that his conscience was troubled. As peace in Europe approached, his life became ever more unconcentrated.

In April and May 1945 Niels took leave from the Serum Institute to con-centrate on examinations. Tjek and the children moved out to Jægerhuset to avoid the closing phase of the war and the possibility of gunfire in downtown Copenhagen, while Niels moved into Amaliegade. A few weeks later the Ger-man forces surrendered. On 5 May, Denmark was liberated. His examination in pathological anatomy, at the end of May, proved "a dazzling performance, if you consider how little I knew and how much bad luck I had"; three weeks later he received the highest marks in bacteriology and "saved, thank God, the honor of the Serum Institute."[6]

Niels stayed alone in Copenhagen after the exams, and the correspondence between husband and wife became more heated and bitter in tone as the sum-mer advanced. He missed the erotic contact between them, not only sexual con-tact but everyday bodily contact, he wrote. He thought Tjek was holding herself back from him and that she laid the blame for all their marital problems on him. But it was Tjek who was responsible, he asserted. If she had found it possi-

Tjek Jerne after the opening of an exhibition in spring 1945, approximately six months before her death. (Polfoto, Copenhagen)

ble to live with his erotic "extravagances" during these last years, she should also, he thought, help him find his way back to her heart. He wished she would stop doubting that he really wanted to continue their marriage. Apparently he assumed that Tjek would be able to forgive him and that their life together could just continue as before. One of Tjek's women friends explains that Niels was used to "everybody forgiving him everything"; she sensed that "he was not really grown up."[7]

Tjek was suspicious. Sometimes she regarded him rather indulgently, as though he was a capricious child, thereby adding to the impression of Niels as a *puer aeternus*. "Taj came yesterday," she wrote to one of her friends, "with a lot of meat, and a huge bundle of dirty clothes and all the morning and evening papers, a load of books, glorious French translations, a couple or three flowers from the roadside, dictionaries (typical of him: 3 of them!) and 'The Times' and a lot of news." Most often, however, she was depressed, and at the end of July she raised the possibility of a divorce. She felt like a "miserable scullery maid," like "a house pet who's been dismissed but cannot be driven off." She had nothing left but "a soul completely distressed," filled with "a sense of obliteration."[8]

Niels was shaken by Tjek's frustration. After all, she was his anchor, and the thought of divorce made him feel even more adrift. He respected and admired her, indeed almost worshiped her intellectual and artistic qualities yet felt himself dominated by her: "You are very willing to be escorted by me, but not guided, for you do not believe in my superiority, you only believe in the rightness of your own thoughts. If I were as you wish, and you were the man and I the woman, everything would be perfect," he had written a few months earlier. He struggled against "an inflexibility" in her that compelled him to resistance. Just as, fifteen years earlier, he had felt like the earth orbiting around Jeanine as his sun, Tjek seemed to dominate everything with her "strongly egocentric personality": "Everything organized according to your pattern. When we walk along the street it is you who choose the direction, if I go to the right and you go forward, I must give way. If we are out shopping, it is you who decide on everything, you are always the most sensible." He looked for something in Tjek that he did not find; he wanted a woman who lived wholly and only for him, someone "who, as a woman, is always conscious of my existence as a man . . . a woman who is filled with me in all her thoughts and every cell of her body. A woman who seeks to be close to me, who is pleased when I touch her and tries to make that touching endless. A woman for whom I represent the divine . . . only with me does she really live; who sits at my feet, when I am there, for she has no other thought or wish than to be mine."[9]

Some time during the summer of 1945 Niels had his yearnings fulfilled when he began a passionate affair with Tjek's friend, Adda Sundsig-Hansen, a married hospital worker three years his junior. Tjek and Adda had been in the maternity ward together in 1941; later, Adda had modeled for her a couple of times, and just before the end of the war the two women had lived together briefly in Jægerhuset. Now Adda became Niels's woman, totally his: "I want to own you," he wrote, "[to] feel my power over you, feel that you are filled with me and my soul, that you are nothing else than mine, for I am going to drown everything else in pain and lust until you open yourself and surrender yourself to me." With Adda in the role of submissive slave, Niels once more had the chance to enter the sadomasochistic world that had fascinated him since the Leiden years. Erna Mørch had joined him in his games only partly, but Adda surrendered wholly to his fantasies: "*I remember visiting her at her home . . . and I remember taking my cigarette and extinguishing it on her nipple. Just to see what would happen. And then great orgons, [or]gasms and all that ensued, and so, and that sort of imprisoned me, because she would say: 'Would you like to do that once again, would you like?' and so. That was Adda.*" Years after these events, he recorded his fascination with witnessing female sexuality: "I love a woman's orgasm more than my own."[10]

The sadomasochistic aspect of their relationship was not only physical but also psychic. He played with her as Kierkegaard's Johannes the Seducer played with Cordelia and considered carefully how he could utilize letters in the service of seduction. Letters give a relationship that is otherwise overwhelmingly physical "a *spiritual* luster, too, because the physical passes away and only leaves behind an emotion, perhaps somewhat empty," he wrote in his diary. They "fill out pause and absence, give emotions a spiritual dream, and dream, a content." He conceived of letters as a kind of "spiritual spiderweb in which you snare the dreaming soul of a woman, so that she abandons herself and her body." A letter should be "just so soulful that it is a head taller than the woman's understanding," yet not too advanced: "there has to be material for her, it must aim at her receiving equipment"; and it must be mystical "so that she regards herself as initiated into mysteries" whereby "that other mighty power of love: admiration" is strengthened. "Thou! [Du!] A word cannot be shorter, and no word can be more beautiful than my 'thou' to you, my beloved," he told Adda. These were words that he had not used with Tjek for a long time, words that had their effect. Adda replied that her trust in him was so great that it "has nearly become a religion for me." He continued to weave his web around her, and she continued to let herself be spellbound.[11]

In the beginning of September 1945, and for the first time since the outbreak of the war, Niels saw his chance to travel abroad, officially to sort out certain standardization problems with Alexander Glenny, head of the standardization section of the Wellcome Physiological Research Laboratories in London. In a series of spirited letters to Adda, he resumed the romantic stance on the independence of the soul that on previous occasions he had expressed in letters to Tjek (who this time only got a few noncommittal picture postcards with routine greetings). It is not the world that gives us our distinct form, he wrote—as if anticipating metaphorically both his natural selection theory of antibody production ten years later and his network theory thirty years later—but it is we ourselves who bestow our souls on things: "The things, our surroundings, have no value in themselves, but only gain the value we ourselves are able to confer on them; they are like empty shadows that are colored and animated by what we ourselves contain of thoughts and emotions, and are tinged by our moods. This is how our surroundings can seem inspiring, for our emotions gain new forms to clothe themselves in and become more conscious and multifarious. Nature and things can become gratifying to us because we ourselves have animated them, they are like mirrors reflecting something of ourselves."[12]

The London trip offered a breathing space in the struggle between husband and wife. Tjek had hoped that the trip would give Niels back his old calm and loving self. But on his return their mutual infidelity became the dominating theme. Tjek understood that Niels had begun a new affair but evidently did not know that Adda was the object of his passion. When she at last discovered what was going on, it came as a shock. A friend tells that Tjek had been "sitting on the sofa with Niels and Adda, one on each side, and [discovered that they] held each others' hands [behind her back]." Niels, in turn, was informed by Adda about Tjek's many hitherto secret extramarital affairs, relationships that Adda was supposed to hold in confidence. How he reacted, we can only speculate. Probably the revelations supported his feeling that Tjek organized her life according to her own pattern, even in this area. Having learned in addition that she had had at least three new affairs while he was in London, he began to make inquiries among their circle.[13]

Tjek had earlier threatened divorce. Now Niels did so. Tjek took the threat seriously and pleaded with him to stay with her and the children. But he sensed his power at this moment: "She kneeled down in front of me, after ten years of marriage, and pleaded with me for something. And I said no. . . . I was hard. I knew things about Tjek that she had told her friend in confidence." Faced with the threat of divorce and knowing of her husband's and best friend's betrayal, Tjek broke down. One of her woman artist friends who used to play bridge with her recalls her last words: "She came up with a remark, and such things you remember best afterwards: 'It doesn't matter.' . . . She probably wanted to make sure that it was she who decided the pace, 'I'm going to decide how things go,' that was all [she said]. 'I'll make a decision for all of us,' she said."[14]

Before dawn on 30 October 1945, Tjek took her life. "I have chosen, today—for you, too," she opened her brief farewell letter. Just as, earlier, she had decided which direction Niels would walk across the street, now, too, she decided that he would live the rest of his life in guilt. She wrote a few further words about clothing for the children, and closed: "I love you, in my death." An hour later, Ivar was awakened by the smell of gas, went into the kitchen, and found his mother dead beside the oven.[15]

Some years earlier Niels had described people meeting like ships passing in the night. Now two strong souls had collided on life's dark and stormy sea; the active and outgoing one had sunk.

Early in the morning Niels telephoned one of Tjek's friends who was a sculptor and asked her to go with him to the mortuary to make a death mask. In the days that followed he visited Tjek's closest friends, seeking "all those places where anything of her soul still lived on in another human being." A week after her suicide, Tjek was buried after a brief and simple ceremony, in which one of her lovers, a "young violin virtuoso," provided the music.[16]

For a month, the world stood still. But even amid the sorrow and the pain, practical problems had to be sorted out, and friends of the family came to Niels's aid. The children moved in with relatives outside Copenhagen for a month, and then one of Tjek's closest friends quit her job and moved into the apartment to give a hand with the household, "as a kind of maid, more or less, and nanny." Family and friends could not, however, drive away his sorrow and despair, nor erase the knowledge that he had not done enough to prevent her death. "How humiliating it is for me that I did not succeed in keeping her alive, but let her go alone into death," he wrote to an acquaintance.[17]

Henceforth he would always accuse himself. A year or so later he explained in a letter to his parents that "Tjek's death" was as much due to me as to anything else, and that guilt I am going to have to bear forever." Rostock had "a vague suspicion" that Niels had "a guilt complex about Tjek's committing suicide," that Tjek's paintings became the cross he bore throughout his life; wherever he moved—Pittsburgh, Frankfurt, Castillon-du-Gard—the paintings went along, "and very often most of them never even got unpacked. But he truly had them with him." It was probably because of this guilt that Niels was not able to tell Tjek's parents the truth, instead writing them that she had died of "a heart disease." The reason for his guilt may have been that he had threatened divorce without really meaning it. "Please be so kind as to answer a question for me . . . you must be *completely honest*—did Tjek know that you did not want a divorce? Had you said that to her directly?" one of his female friends asked.[18]

Tjek's death and the related guilt bring to the fore the question of the relationship between life and work. The work of an author, an artist, or a composer can take its theme from, or be colored by, strongly emotional events in the artist's life. No such simple connection applies in the world of science. As will be demonstrated later, the natural selection theory of antibody formation can be interpreted as a metaphorical projection of Jerne's emotionally laden self-understanding. In the case of Tjek's death the logical structure of his later scientific work does not seem to have any direct connection with his emotional life. But the guilt may have impinged on the route taken to the work. Jerne himself makes such a connection: "Maybe my sorrow over having lost Tjek contributed to making me a good scientist," he said in a magazine interview many years later.[19]

How? One possible interpretation is that science diverted him from his thoughts, just as the late nineteenth-century French physiologist Claude Bernard is said to have used science to forget his unhappy personal life. A year earlier Niels had busied himself with Erna Mørch's pneumococci as "a means of distraction." But now the loss was incomparably greater. He may have disappeared into the depths of science for the rest of his life to escape the pain.[20]

Another possibility is that Tjek's death released his scientific creative powers in a more paradoxical way. Perhaps her death was a liberation for him. This does not mean that Niels had not loved Tjek or that her death was not a blow. But a strong emotional tie between two people contains contrary tendencies. We are pressed between the need for closeness to other people and the need to prevent that closeness from turning into surrender. Love gives us the chance to fulfill our yearning for union and belonging; in love, we can escape the anguish of loneliness. But in love we also risk becoming dominated by the other and losing our identity. Niels had, on one hand, sought to share profoundly with Tjek. He considered her one of the most intelligent people he had ever met and attributed to her such traits as strength and will: "She set her stamp upon everything she touched and everyone she met. She had no patience, no resignation, she would not adapt, because she was always herself and only herself, and so was always right. [Tjek] always did what she wanted, what she knew was right, she attained what she wanted. She as it were forced her paintings out, she forced her sensitive mind to express itself. Everything came to life under her firm, sure hand, to life that expressed Tjek. It was not so much that she conserved the life that existed, as that she created life in her own image." He added: "She breathed her own soul into things and into people." It was a quality he admired and wanted to emulate.[21]

But his choice of words also reveals that Tjek's will was stronger than his own—and therefore threatening. During their ten years of marriage, he had been one of those people into whom Tjek "breathed her own soul"; she had created his "life in her own image." As he became aware of his increasing dependence on her, he began to lose some of his identity. For most of those in their circle, he had been "Tjek's husband, the husband of sophisticated Tjek," as she herself had once expressed it. In the summer of 1945 he had accused her of being "the center of your world." Tjek had been stronger and braver in developing herself, and therefore her death may have meant a kind of freedom for him, both from her dominating mind and from the circle of her friends, a freedom that gave him the chance to regain his own identity. When Tjek was gone, Niels, too, could set "his stamp on everything," be the center of his world, and create "life in his own image" instead of conserving "the life that existed."[22]

"Now I have come to rest in my living room," Niels wrote to a friend of the family at the end of November 1945. He was beginning to get back in touch with the rest of the world. He was free now, as free as a man can be who has guilt, the responsibility for two children, and an incomplete medical education hanging over him. At the same time, Adda was becoming more pressing. She no longer wanted to be a little glow in his life—either the glow should be extinguished, or it should burst into flame. She was prepared to leave her husband and child for his sake. He could demand of her whatever he wanted. "Just to live for you and yours can make me happy," she explained. Right after New Year 1946—after again having described her as clothed in the weave of his thoughts—Niels told Adda to come to him. She was welcome to move in, to act as a mother to his children, and to share his bed, but he did not want to make any firm promises about the future. "So if you want to come to us, you must do it of your own free will, in a free relationship, and fate will have to decide the future. . . . Come, and *come soon*." And Adda came.[23]

What did Niels really want with Adda? She does not exist in any of his official autobiographical accounts or in articles about him in biographical dictionaries, and when he spoke about her in interviews she appeared as a shadowy, negative figure, the object of contempt and, occasionally, outright hate. But just then, in the winter of 1946 and for some years thereafter, he needed her, especially as someone to take care of the children. Besides, Adda was the realization of his dream of a completely submissive and devoted woman. He wanted her erotic surrender: "Under my caresses and torments, your body swept against mine like music." As soon as she had moved in, he went to the library to borrow books on suggestion and did experiments on hypnosis with her, the results of which he observed and recorded.[24]

He probably also needed Adda to disperse the thoughts of Tjek's death and to get his neglected studies under way again. He had not touched his books for more than half a year, and four months of work lay ahead before the final examinations. The director of the Serum Institute even gave him permission to reduce his work during the spring to one day a week with no cut in pay. But by March his plans fell apart when he was hospitalized with pneumonia for nearly three weeks. On his return home he realized he was going to have to wait another six months for his final examination. And so he spent most of his time during the rest of the spring and the summer of 1946 in his "cockpit," as he now

Caricature of Niels Jerne published in the Copenhagen medical students' journal, *Bugpressen* (The Abdominal Press), 1946. (Medical Faculty, University of Copenhagen)

called the Standardization Department. Ipsen had just left for a year in the United States, and Niels was alone with Rostock and the secretary.

"About me, there's not so much to tell; I'm trying to study for the examination, and otherwise living in my accustomed way," he wrote laconically to Daphne Ipsen in the middle of October 1946. He had little contact with his old friends and acquaintances. Most of the artist friends had disappeared with Tjek; his old flames tried to keep in touch but he does not seem to have reciprocated their invitations. Instead, he contemplated plans to stabilize his relationship with Adda. "What would you say if I married Adda next year?" he inquired of his parents.[25]

The medical class Niels had joined five years earlier having gone on without him, he became part of a new class. A heavy schedule of examinations lay ahead: childhood diseases, theoretical medicine, internal medicine, and surgery before Christmas, and obstetrics, clinical medicine, forensic medicine, and social medicine after the New Year. In December 1946 and January 1947, he studied nearly day and night, equipped with a yard-high pile of books and a supply of Mecodrin tablets. It was no longer fun to "collect such an enormous material in your mind when one would rather be critical and work through interesting details," he complained. He became so nervous and smoked so much that he developed an irregular heartbeat and diarrhea.[26]

But all went well nonetheless. His final grade was average, which did not really matter. During his more than thirteen-year-long journey, he had encountered many setbacks and one tragedy. He knew by now, he told his parents, that he was "rather gifted." But he also knew that talent and gifts were not everything. He lacked the strength of will and ability to concentrate. Because he had been unable to keep from spreading himself over far too many interesting fields, the consequences had been that he had "not reached . . . depth in any one of them." Besides that, he still saw himself as a late bloomer, and his life was not yet driven by career ambitions: "Comparatively small gusts can blow me off track, since my character has not found its way to fixed principles." He also realized that he probably would never have succeeded in getting started without Tjek's support, that "it was her energy and her persuasion that got me to resume my study plans when she saw that the bacon plans didn't lead to anything and could not make me happy." What did matter was that now, at the age of thirty-five, he had at last accomplished the task he had set himself as a student thirteen years earlier. He was sure of "never again having to submit myself to the risk of being rejected as worthless."[27]

II

The Making of the
Selection Theory (1947–1954)

10

"The Happiness of Feeling Superior to a Lot of People"

*I*n the late 1940s Niels Jerne was a widower, the father of two sons, and a middle-aged man with a medical degree. He had only to go through his internship to be certified as a physician, though the staff at the Serum Institute had already begun calling him Dr. Jerne. On 1 February 1947, a week after his final examination, he started work in the medical department of Rigshospitalet.

Judging from the lack of archival material for that year, the internship took most of his time. The night watches gave him leisure to read; receipts from bookstores indicate that he was devouring books as never before and, as usual, was hungry for everything: history, novels, philosophy. "I'm very happy with my job," he wrote to his parents (who still lived in Wassenaar but were soon to move back to Denmark); "we have a whole lot to do and it is interesting to be plunged suddenly into real life." Retrospectively, he adds that the hospital work also gave him a somewhat cynical view of medicine: *"most of the things doctors do, I don't believe."* After summer he continued his one-year internship, now in surgery. Most of the fall went into rounds, operations, and night watches, and he was able to save no more than two or three afternoons a week for the Serum Institute. The surgical operations he took part in contributed to his repertoire of autobiographical stories; for example, he liked to portray himself as an unpractical conversationalist: *"I did nothing more than hold the forceps and the skin*

to one side. . . . [The surgeon] was happy to have me for his assistant, for such op-
erations often last long, two hours maybe, and then he would be talking with me.
He said 'those others are idiots who don't know anything' . . . and so he was very
fond of me."[1]

Jerne's exchanges with the surgeons and the other interns hardly contributed to the mental concentration he had so long lacked and striven for. The
Standardization Department did not provide the needed environment either—
Ipsen was obviously looking for other opportunities and did not pay much attention to serological problems any more. But in the summer and fall of 1947
everything changed to the better: Ipsen announced that he had been offered a
new job as an epidemiologist at Harvard University, and a doctor from the
Serodiagnostic Department, Ole Maaløe, took over responsibility for the standardization work. It soon turned out that he was precisely the kind of partner
Jerne needed to get it all together. In conversations with Maaløe during that
winter, Jerne began to focus on a scientific problem that gave him the chance to
create some intellectual discipline in his life.

Ole Maaløe had already published his Ph.D. on the identification of the an-
tibacterial serum components alexin (complement) and opsonin and was thoroughly familiar with classical bacteriology and serology, but he did not know
much about standardization. "I was a little hesitant," Maaløe remembers: "Jerne
was a couple of years older than I, but I was a couple of years older in science. . . . I thought, 'How's that going to work, here I come as his junior and
haven't got any experience with standardization.'" Yet it soon became clear that
they "talked unusually well together." They also had a mutual interest in painting and other forms of art, and they talked "a lot about Shakespeare, but on the
other hand, not much about Kierkegaard, with whom Taj was captivated, but
not I." Above all, they discussed scientific problems, for example, Maaløe's new
field of study, namely, how pathogenic *Salmonella* bacteria develop resistance
to complement through mutation. The regular standardization work was "a
routine that did not require too much time or energy" and that did not especially interest either of them. So they *"agreed that we would only standardize on
Mondays,"* turned the daily routines over to the laboratory technician, Jens Ole
Rostock, and devoted the rest of the time to their own research. Jerne confirms
the picture of a continual two-man seminar and emphasizes the open and
searching nature of their discussions, characterized by such questions as, If we
do this, what will happen then? *"We had enormously long, long discussions about
details,"* he remembers. The secretary of the department, too, recalls their "endless discussions."[2]

Friendship is fundamental to close collaboration between scientists ("certainly you have to be personal friends," as Francis Crick says), and Jerne and Maaløe were, and remained, good friends. Even though "no joint achievements resulted" from their almost daily intellectual exchanges, Maaløe describes their collaboration as "fruitful" and compares himself and Jerne with other scientific dynamic duos of the postwar period, such as James D. Watson and Francis Crick, and François Jacob and Jacques Monod. A contemporary observer adds that Maaløe was "a very clear analyzer," a man of action, a skillful experimentalist who wanted to see ideas put into practice in new experiments, whereas Jerne was the intuitive one, a creative thinker who listened closely and then stood everything on its head. Other contemporary observers have similar impressions of the collaboration between the two men. Hans Noll, a Swiss graduate student who visited the department in the late 1940s, asserts that Maaløe was "an excellent discussion partner for Jerne" but also that their relationship was "strange" and "difficult." Maaløe was much more intent on getting "public recognition," whereas "Jerne didn't give a shit."[3]

Jerne, too, did not hesitate to point out the difference between himself as the philosophically oriented thinker and Maaløe as the more practically oriented researcher. He characterized his friend and colleague as a person always willing to discuss the technical aspects of their work, as someone who "is knowledgeable about complement, about phagocytes, about centrifuges—how fast they spin and how large all the different kinds of particles are, and which buttons you should push, and about water baths and substrates . . . and all that hard stuff. . . . It very soon became plain that what I intended, could not, from a technical standpoint, be done at all." Jerne's characterization should be taken with a grain of salt—it was spoken after a good dinner, to amuse the party—but even so it suggests that he chiefly saw his colleague as a source of technical insight. Later he strengthened his opinion: *"Ole was good at all sorts of bodily activity, and also at sound judgment. . . . His expert way of dealing with plates, test tubes, and pipettes was also magnificent."* This in contrast to Jerne himself, who always took pride in having no laboratory-technical insight and who saw himself as the one who carried out the mental work while others handled the methodological and technical details. Jerne's general attitude toward life—as a contemplative and detached observer of existence, a *theōros*—began to make itself more evident in his science, too.[4]

One of the main topics at the blackboard was the classic concern of the Standardization Department: the measurement of the strength of antisera and toxoids. In the fall of 1947 Jerne and Maaløe were discussing how to coordinate the task assigned by the World Health Organization (WHO), that is, to establish international standards for diphtheria and tetanus toxoids. As mentioned earlier, Jerne had taken part in Ipsen's long series of tests with diphtheria toxoid and had done a number of experiments during 1943 and 1944. Now the WHO assignment gave him the chance to play through his entire repertoire of personal doubts about the worthwhileness of standardization in his discussions with Maaløe.[5]

The reliability of measurement methods was, Jerne thought, a crucial but unrecognized problem, not only for the standardization of diphtheria toxoid but for standardization in general. He had personally gained insight into the problem when, in 1944, he had observed the "colossal dilution effect" in guinea pig serum: *"I said: 'It's not just the number of antibody molecules you have to know, but also their quality.' So you cannot say that [the serum] has so-or-so many units. You've also got to know what kind."* As already pointed out, the dilution effect and the corresponding avidity phenomenon (that antisera containing antibodies against the same antigen apparently had differential binding capacity to the antigen) was already known in the serological literature. But it had no practical significance for standardization procedures and was mostly regarded as a disturbing element. In practice, serum 'strength' was measured in relation to standard serum as if avidity did not matter. And there was no satisfactory explanation of the avidity phenomenon. Nobody bothered much about it, and nobody had subjected it to systematic studies.[6]

Here was a good subject for a doctoral thesis for someone like Jerne, who liked questioning what others took for granted. Maaløe, too, rapidly realized that the phenomenon was worth investigating further. In a letter to the director of the Serum Institute in October 1947, he wrote that Jerne had "lately" been "working with an important problem affecting the measurement of small antitoxin quantities in serum" and had thereby "revealed the phenomenon, hitherto disregarded," that the results of measurement depend on the initial concentration of toxin. Shortly after, Jerne received the necessary official sanction—five years after he had first aired the idea of doing research—for using part of his work schedule to write a dissertation on avidity.[7]

But how to tackle it? One explanation of the dilution phenomenon was that the toxin-antitoxin reaction is a reversible equilibrium reaction. On dilution the equilibrium should be shifted toward free toxin and antitoxin. Jerne's mind was prepared to think about this: *"The kinetics of reactions"* had *"always interested"* him, he recalls. Thermodynamics and equilibrium chemistry were the only parts of his chemistry courses in Leiden he had found time for. His thoughts had spontaneously gravitated toward the chemical aspects of the toxin-antitoxin reaction when Ipsen had given him the first serological instruction in the spring of 1943. Yet for the previous four years his spontaneous equilibrium chemical approach had lain fallow. His regular discussions with Ipsen and Georg Rasch had instead led him into statistics, and perhaps matters would have remained as they were had Ipsen stayed and had Maaløe not come on the scene.[8]

The discussions with Maaløe during the fall of 1947 and the spring of 1948 became, in Maaløe's version of the story, "the beginning of Niels's preoccupation with 'avidity.'" A young doctor at the Serum Institute at the time also suggests that the change from Ipsen to Maaløe was of decisive importance for Jerne's new orientation: "I think that Maaløe was central for Jerne. [Maaløe] said 'this is something happening at the molecular and cellular level.' That was a whole different kind of thinking." Jerne confirms that the change of discussion partner meant that he began to redirect himself from statistical investigations to chemistry: "*Ipsen . . . was completely absorbed by statistical considerations. . . . Physical chemistry was—he didn't like that too much, I think. He found it perhaps unnecessary,*" while Maaløe indeed "*took part in discussing avidity. As a matter of fact, it was highly essential and we discussed in detail.*"[9]

These intellectual musings of Jerne and Maaløe about the reaction kinetics of the dilution effect and the avidity phenomenon were mostly preliminary. Maaløe needed time to get himself settled in his new job and develop his recent interest in bacterial genetics, and Jerne had only a few hours left over every week from his internship. Right after the New Year 1948, he at last received word that he would be given a permanent full-time position as a scientific assistant in the Standardization Department. Retrospectively he declares that, by then, he no longer doubted that he wanted to continue with research; working in a hospital didn't appeal to him, and "*the idea of becoming a country doctor, I had soon left behind me.*"[10]

Beginning in February Jerne started working on the dilution effect in earnest. Judging by the quantity of notes that has survived, during the next six months he devoted most of his thought to developing theoretical models of the equilibrium reaction between diphtheria toxin and diphtheria antitoxin. He filled sheet after sheet of the institute's yellow folio-sized stationery with equilibrium reactions, velocity constants, and possible reaction curves. To regard the toxin-antitoxin reaction as a physical-chemical phenomenon was new to him, but not new in the literature. At the turn of the century, Thorvald Madsen and the Swedish chemist Svante Arrhenius had observed that the neutralization curve between diphtheria toxin and antidiphtherial serum resembled a typical equilibrium curve. From the end of the 1930s several theoretical and experimental works on antigen-antibody equilibrium reactions had been published, particularly by John Marrack, and at the beginning of the 1930s, Alexander Glenny and his assistant Mollie Barr at Wellcome Physiological Research Laboratories in London had declared that the differences in avidity among sera varied depending on the "firmness of union" between the toxin and the antitoxin. The literature on chemical reactions between antigen and antiserum was limited, however, in that it explained only the formation of an insoluble toxin-antitoxin complex (a so-called precipitate) in concentrated reaction mixtures.[11]

But Jerne wished to study the dissociation of the antigen-antibody complex in high dilutions. As he saw it, there were two theories of precipitation formation: the univalence theory and the multivalence theory ("framework" theory, lattice theory). More than a decade before, William Boyd, Sanford Hooker, and their colleagues had presented experimental data that made a case for antibodies having one binding site only (univalency), and the Swedish physiologist Torsten Teorell had made their data the starting point of his quantitative theory of precipitation formation. Teorell's 1946 paper was probably the first discussion of this type of equilibrium reaction with which Jerne became familiar.[12]

The multivalence theory, too, entered early into Jerne's thoughts. Some immunochemists, such as Marrack, Linus Pauling, and Alvin Pappenheimer, had given theoretical arguments for antibodies having two or more binding sites, supporting the current ideas of framework and lattice formation. Besides the simple one-to-one reaction between antibodies (Ab) and antigens (Ag), more complex reactions could also occur, they suggested, for example, $AgAb + Ag \rightleftharpoons Ag_2Ab$, and $Ag_2Ab + Ag \rightleftharpoons Ag_3Ab$, and so on, as well as formation of simple chains of the type Ag_2Ab_2, Ag_2Ab_3, and the like. These frameworks could then lead to formation of large lattices and aggregates and, in the end, precipitation. Formation of aggregates was an integral part of the theory, and for this reason Jerne later suggested it was "reasonable to assume that aggregation also takes place at lower concentrations, although invisibly."[13]

His research strategy was to derive theoretical neutralization curves from the univalence and multivalence theories, respectively, and then to match these curves with experimental neutralization data. Jerne simplified his work on the multivalence theory in two ways: first, he limited himself to the two initial steps of the reaction ($Ag + Ab \rightleftharpoons AgAb$ and $AgAb + Ab \rightleftharpoons AgAb_2$), and second, he started with a given (statistically determined) value for the relationship between the equilibrium constants of the two reactions. He was thus able to describe the total reaction with a single equilibrium constant. In the summer of 1948 his thinking about theoretical models got still another push forward from a conversation with the Italian chemist Enzo Boeri, who "drew my attention to the theory of reversible step reactions."[14]

The rabbit-skin assay was the indicator by which Jerne could experimentally follow the course of neutralization between diphtheria toxin and antitoxic serum. The reliability of the method determined the certainty with which he could measure the antitoxin content in a serum. During the next few months he fine-tuned the experimental design so as to minimize systematic sources of error and spent much labor on standardizing the routines of injection and of reading responses. Hunting down sources of error was his great scientific passion in these years. He approached his work with focus and discipline now. Although his personality was still "elastic," as he put it, he no longer seemed to have a bad conscience about it. He was no longer economically dependent on his parents (who had moved to Copenhagen) and could allow himself certain digressions as long as the distraction related to the question of whether one could rely on the measurements and the methods of calculation.[15]

A regularly recurring distraction was, of course, the mandatory standardization work. During June and July 1948, Jerne set to work on the large diphtheria toxoid experiment, while Maaløe wrote up their views in an article that was submitted a couple of months later to the *Bulletin of the World Health Organization*; this was their first attempt to launch the department's rabbit-skin assay internationally. Another legitimate source of distraction was a "tripartite correspondence" with the British statisticians David Finney and Eric Wood, in which "almost every link in the long chain of reasoning and inference from the performance of a biological assay to the statement of its results was critically examined." The three-way correspondence with Finney and Wood sharpened Jerne's attention to the experimental and statistical sources of error in his own work. A year later Jerne and Wood published their views in the newly founded journal *Biometrics*, a paper that contributed further to Jerne's reputation in Copenhagen's scientific circles as, in his own words, an *"expert in mathematical statistics [and] quite well-known mathematical statistician."* In fact, his most frequent contacts outside the cockpit was with Rasch and a young, newly employed insurance mathematician, Michael Weis Bentzon, in the Statistics Department. On several occasions Jerne also helped fellow doctors with statistical problems in their research work and was later invited to write encyclopedia articles on biostatistics and biological standardization. Consequently the first two professional societies he joined were the Biometric Society and the Royal Statistical Society. Even outside Denmark, he soon acquired a reputation as a biostatistician, and in 1950 he was elected to the board of the Biometric Society for a three-year term.[16]

Toward the end of 1948, Jerne set his experimental program going. The first experiment was a paradigm for the whole test series that followed; the laboratory notebook is extant, and the experiments were later described in print. He had already immunized a guinea pig with 50 Lf of diphtheria toxoid (Lf, the limit of flocculation, is a measure of toxin, or toxoid, concentration), and four weeks later he withdrew 5 ml of blood by heart puncture, collected the serum, and kept it frozen. He then prepared 28 serum dilutions in phosphate-buffered saline and mixed these with toxin into three series of dilutions: one with mixtures of 20–64 percent serum with 1000 Lf toxin/l, another with 0.63–5 percent serum with 32 Lf toxin/l, and a third with 0.08–1 percent serum with 1 Lf toxin/l. The reaction mixtures were incubated for two hours in a water bath at 37°C, and then 0.1 ml of each mixture was injected into the skin of five or six rabbits. Forty-four hours later, the skin responses were read.[17]

With this experimental model as the basis, Jerne went on to vary the experimental conditions. Through manipulation of the three equilibrium variables—reaction time, temperature, and initial concentration—"an effort was made to penetrate into the mechanism of the processes responsible for the phenomena observed." The shifting of the reaction curves on the diagram to the right or to the left became his window into the equilibrium reaction. Or, as he later expressed it: *"So we had curves on the blackboard . . . curves when you inject one milligram, and curves when you inject ten milligrams, and so. How do we explain these curves? . . . And there Ole Maaløe and I, we discussed [this for] days and days. Whether there is something in there which is, which leads us to recognize the truth."* For the rest of his life, Jerne would hold on firmly to that experience: that the graphic representation of biological processes as reaction curves was superior to all other ways of understanding what was going on inside the organism.[18]

After the first experiments with four-week serum, a corresponding experiment with standard serum, and some further experiments dealing with methodology (tests of varying the positions of the injections on the rabbit skin, and of the injection time), Jerne became ill and had to stay at home for a couple of weeks. When he resumed work in the laboratory in early January 1947,

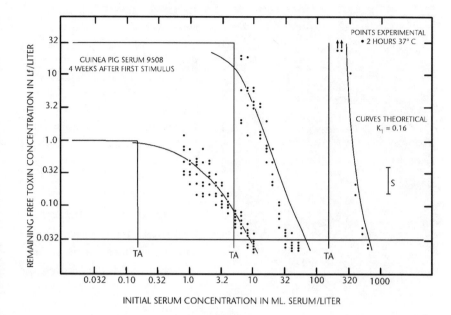

Neutralization curves for mixtures of early guinea pig serum and three initial diphtheria toxin concentrations. (*From left*): 1, 32, and 1000 Lf/liter. The curves are theoretically derived; the dots represent experimental data. From Jerne's dissertation, 1951. (Jerne Collection, The Royal Library, Copenhagen)

Maaløe was on his way to the California Institute of Technology to deepen his insights into the methods of microbiological genetics in Max Delbrück's laboratory and was not expected back in Copenhagen until the beginning of June. So Jerne had to handle the correspondence with WHO and the diplomatically sensitive experiments on the standardization of diphtheria toxoid—as well as his own experiments, when he found the time.

Jerne and Rostock now fused into a team: Jerne planned the experiments and injected the rabbits with the reaction mixtures, while Rostock read the thousands of skin responses. To the question of whether Jerne was technically skilled, Rostock answers: "No, not especially, [he] fumbled a little bit, I must admit. . . . He didn't do so much lab work, really." Hans Noll remembers clearly the "sort of ritual" that took place: Rostock would bring to the lab a shaved rabbit stretched out and strapped to a board, and "then they divided the back of the rabbit into a chessboard-like pattern. . . . Rostock was bringing this thing to him and Jerne put a white coat on and then he himself did the injections."[19]

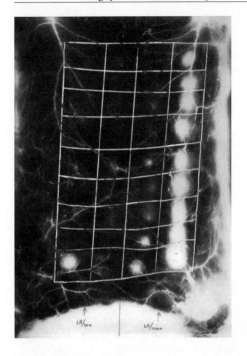

The rabbit skin assay. Close-up photograph of the back skin of a shaved live rabbit. The sizes of the spots (local skin inflammations) are proportional to the amount of surplus toxin after the diphtheria-antidiphtheria reaction is completed. The image is reversed black and white. (Jerne Collection, The Royal Library, Copenhagen)

The course of the experiments can be followed in the laboratory notes and in a series of letters to Maaløe during the spring. The results indicated that the neutralization process can best be understood as an equilibrium chemical process and confirmed the well-known phenomena that the organism begins to form antiserum after a so-called lag phase of about ten days, that sera after a first toxin stimulus are of very low avidity, and that the avidity rises gradually over time. The time at which the dilution was made was also important. When he produced a reaction mixture of toxin and antitoxin by mixing the components in high concentration and thereafter diluting the mixture, the neutralization proceeded more quickly and completely than when he mixed the components in a diluted condition. On the other hand, if the reaction was allowed to continue for a week, the degree of neutralization in each of the two mixtures became similar. In this way, he went on gaining insights into the mysteries of the equilibrium reaction, and when, in late spring, he concluded this new experimental series with individual guinea pig sera under varying experimental conditions, he had obtained more than fifty experimental diagrams.[20]

Thus did Niels Jerne pass the spring of 1949, dividing his time between his own experiments and the obligatory work on standardization of diphtheria toxoid. At the beginning of May he gave a lecture on the department's diphtheria toxoid work at a WHO standardization meeting in London. The discussion after his lecture "proceeded in a somewhat surprising way," he told Maaløe, because he was dubbed the "Savonarola of 'biological standardization.'" To be compared with the fifteenth-century Florentine revolutionary seems to have tickled Jerne's vanity.[21]

Being considered an elitist enticed his vanity, too. During our conversations Jerne referred to *"the happiness of feeling superior to a lot of people"* and declared that he felt himself to be *"superior or more intelligent than the other scientists."* He asserted that many researchers he met, both at the Serum Institute and later in life, were *"so stupid that the lady in the bread-shop is more intelligent than them, she has an awareness and an ability to observe and articulate her observations."* His feeling of superiority was also reflected in some of the contributions he sent to the institute's newsletter, *Mikro.* In the summer of 1949, he wrote a self-satirizing sketch about the activities in the department in which he described, among other things, a fictional hair-counting device, the so-called "Newcombs Pilotrix." The apparatus consisted of a steel mesh wastebasket that was placed over his secretary's head; then, recalls Rostock, "Jerne sat there and pretended he was counting." The whole gag was photographed and furnished with a caption: "Now, you press this button, thank you—oh yes, stings a little. Now look at the counting instrument. You have precisely 253,357 hairs on your head, of course allowing for the margin of error." In another article he satirized statistics as a "conjuring ritual" and "witchcraft" performed with "magical formulas."[22]

This sort of ironical mini-essay was Jerne's favorite genre, for it gave him leave to write about what concerned him while maintaining his distance. His colleagues were not always amused, however: "when I say anything in a discussion, it is often understood as an insult, [so] there must be something wrong with my approach," he once complained to Maaløe. Yet, despite (or perhaps because of) his sharp tongue, several people have testified to being inspired by Jerne's intellectual attitude. Michael Weis Bentzon remembers that he experienced Jerne as "a fantastically bright thinker" and as a person who had a "sense for mathematical curiosities." Hans Noll declares that he always felt "drawn to" Jerne because he was "an extremely provocative discussion partner" who did not let himself be disturbed by peripheral aspects of the problems he studied but selected the data that fitted; he was therefore, in Noll's opinion, among those scientists who have the "right instinct." Noll was also easily impressed by the breadth of his colleague's intellectual interests, for example, that Jerne read Proust at the same time as he was developing the "fairly sophisticated" theoretical models for the equilibrium reaction. Above all, Noll has a clear memory of Jerne being "drawn to Kierkegaard like a magnet . . . because some of his longings and perhaps also some of his experiences, tragic experiences of life, made him understand what Kierkegaard's deepest concerns are."[23]

Noll also maintains that Jerne was underestimated by his colleagues in other departments of the institute. One of those who emphatically did not was a young doctor, Viggo Faber, who became deeply impressed with Jerne's intellectual style, which he says differed greatly from that of the average medical doctor, not only in the Serum Institute but also generally in the Danish scientific community. Jerne was an "intuitive," almost "instinctive" thinker. "He was curious," says Faber; "his starting-point was that whatever is established needn't be what is correct." The young M.D. sketches the figure of a Renaissance man: "I admired enormously [Jerne's] fantastic breadth, from a human point of view. . . . Never mind where or when, he would question people. He wanted to know what they really had inside. He always started from the assumption that there could be something exciting in people. . . . He was generally curious what everyone had in them. . . . I characterize him as a very special man. He had incredible knowledge of every conceivable field: art, literature, language. He could talk about everything. Of course there were a few who were not fond of him, but I think they were part of the envious crowd." But Faber also says that, as open and tolerant as Jerne could be in conversing with others about questions of human and intellectual life in the broadest sense, about scientific matters he could be merciless: "When scientific discussions were concerned, if they could not rise to his level he simply cast them aside."[24]

The technical staff at the Standardization Department also esteemed Jerne. Rostock, another enthusiastic admirer, remembers him as a "nice and likable, gracious and accommodating man" who ("it sounds so banal") was "interested in everything imaginable and who could chat with you about anything." The anecdotes about Jerne's frankness and his childish pleasure in demolishing middle-class prejudices during lunch breaks are legion. "I was divorced, just then," Rostock relates, "and just then we were sitting there. . . . Jerne suddenly asks me: 'Actually, how do you manage, Ole, when you aren't married, do you masturbate?' And then I said, 'Yes, it happens.' And that was the end of that." Other anecdotes reinforce the picture of Jerne's urge to take an opposing position: "He could sit and listen quite a while, seemingly interested in this or that, whether it was something scientific or some perfectly ordinary common knowledge of one kind or another, and sit there with his cigarette, and then interrupt and say, at last: 'No, I really don't believe that, I think so-and-so,' and that would be something to the contrary. But always in an utterly likable, nice way."[25]

Yet there are discordant voices in the panegyric chorus. Finney remembers that he judged Jerne a very skilled researcher but cannot say that he saw in him, at that time, any sign of "a future Nobel winner." More important, one of Jerne's colleagues at the Serum Institute declined to be interviewed, explaining that she did not have "anything pleasant" to say about Jerne: "He wasn't a person one especially admired. That brings us to something called opportunism. . . . I was not any particular admirer of his personal qualities." Such voices, though not common, remind us that an unequivocal picture of a human character is difficult to establish.[26]

"I Think the Work Has Principal Application to Immunology"

By the late summer of 1949, Jerne had sufficient experiments behind him to be able to choose between the univalence theory and the multivalence theory. The theoretical curves derived from the univalence theory did not match the experimental data well, whereas the curves that had been derived from the multivalence theory did; hence the multivalence model permitted a "reasonable explanation of the experimental data." He could show that high values of the reaction constant correspond to the steep neutralization curves obtained on titration of high-avidity sera (for example, standard serum), and low values to the more horizontal neutralization curves obtained from sera produced some weeks after the first toxin injection. In contrast to the prevalent view that phenomena such as "ready dissociation, flatness of neutralization curves, and longer reaction times" were not necessarily related, Jerne could demonstrate that these phenomena would indeed "be expected to go hand in hand." Avidity was therefore just another expression for the reaction constant of the toxin-antitoxin reaction, which he dubbed the "avidity constant."[1]

Jerne began to compose a first penciled version of his thesis in autumn 1949. He was constantly unsure about the results of the lab work, found new excuses to do some additional experiments, and repeatedly interrupted the writing process. Maaløe seemingly played a decisive role in urging him to get it finished: *"Get it printed, so you can [get your Ph.D.] . . . That helped me a lot."* He believes, too, that his father's unexpected death in the middle of January 1950 may have helped him pull himself together to write the final manuscript. He remembers going to the hospital and telling his father that at last he was *"ready to write my doctoral thesis."* A few hours later Papa, who had so long been his recourse and support, died. *"I inherited his fountain pen and then I wrote my dissertation with it."* Judging by the meager files in the archive, for the next four months all other intellectual activity—chess, reading, and the like—was put aside.[2]

He started with a short survey of the state of the art of serology, including the literature about the equilibrium reaction between toxin and antitoxin, and traced the history of the avidity concept. Then, in the first chapter, he went through his experimental material and methods, and in the second, he continued with an account of the early dilution effect studies of 1943–44. In the third chapter he described the experimental work from the late fall of 1948 to the spring of 1950, summarized the results of the reversibility experiments, discussed the univalence theory versus the multivalence theory, derived the theoretical neutralization curves, and demonstrated the agreement between the theoretical curves based on the multivalence theory and the results of the reversibility experiments. In a brief fourth chapter he reported the work done to determine the difference in avidity between a first and a second antigen stimulus.

In the concluding fifth chapter Jerne discussed the consequences of his research for antitoxin measurement and, consequently, for the work of standardization. From the very beginning he had questioned whether the standardization of antitoxins was possible in principle, and the most important result of his investigations was probably the confirmation of his original skepticism. His judgment of the whole tradition was unshakable: "The standardization of antitoxin rests, as has been shown, on a faulty foundation." In Jerne's judgment it was theoretically impossible to standardize antibodies if one stuck with a conventional measurement of serum strength in AU units; it followed that "the basis for standardization of antitoxins must be totally revised." It was necessary to overhaul the terminology and weed out the traditional, arbitrary unit and strength designations for a toxin in favor of purely chemical concepts, preferably a pure molarity value. Henceforth antitoxin values were to be given in chemical terms as a combination of concentration (molarity) and avidity. In a small essay for *Mikro,* Jerne summed up his skeptical attitude toward the current standardization effort: its practical value was perhaps best expressed "in the words of the poet: 'To give to airy nothing a local habitation and a name.'" Now, as so many times later, it was Shakespeare who provided the words for Jerne's description of the state of the art.[3]

For the past three years the agenda for Jerne's work had been set by the discourse of chemically oriented serology, that is, the tradition of studying the chemical reaction between antibodies and antigens. The serological aim was reflected in the early versions of the introductory chapter. The first penciled draft, written some time toward the end of 1949, thus opened with a traditional serological statement: "In highly diluted mixtures of diphtheria toxin with antitoxin serum no visible precipitation occurs."

This serological opening was kept unaltered through the handwritten versions, but it lost its rhetorical status sometime in the summer of 1950, when Jerne added a new short opening sentence: "The diphtheria toxin-antitoxin problem is the classical problem of immunology." It remained unchanged in the printed version. When a few days later he sent the manuscript to the famed Danish protein chemist Kai Linderstrøm-Lang, he wrote in the covering letter: "I think the work has principal application to immunology, since it completely reevaluates the basis of current measurements of antibody formation after antigen stimulus." The new opening signaled a change in Jerne's professional identity. This was the first time he had expressed the idea that his work was a contribution to immunology.[4]

Immunology was a child of late nineteenth-century biomedical thinking, and the field soon became recognized, judging from the Nobel Prizes in medicine that were awarded to some of its pioneers: Emil von Behring in 1901 for his work on serum therapy; Robert Koch in 1905 for his studies of tuberculosis, including the immunodiagnostic tuberculin reaction; Paul Ehrlich and Ilya Metchnikoff, jointly, in 1908; Charles Richet in 1913 for his work on anaphylaxis; and Jules Bordet in 1919 for his discovery of hemolysis and complement fixation. The first stages of its formation as a discipline were reflected in the founding of *Zeitschrift für Immunitätsforschung* in 1908 and the *Journal of Immunology* in 1916 and by the establishment of the American Association of Immunologists in 1913.

One by one, however, the components of this early phase in immunology fell into disfavor during the first decade of the twentieth century. Most important, the early successes with preventive immunization and serum therapy came to a halt. The fact that only one Nobel Prize in the next forty years was awarded for an immunological achievement (Karl Landsteiner's in 1930 for his discovery of human blood groups) indicates that immunology no longer interested the medical research frontier. Furthermore the study of immune phenomena underwent a marked conceptual and methodological shift toward chemical problems. The 1920s, 1930s, and 1940s were dominated by chemists like Landsteiner, Michael Heidelberger, John Marrack, and their students. Studies of the chemical reaction between antigens and antibodies dominated the journals and meetings. The biological aspects were put in the background.[5]

So far Jerne had scarcely trodden outside the conceptual world of chemically oriented serology. So why did he suddenly change the opening of the last manuscript version? The answer is probably to be found in the brief fourth chapter of the dissertation, which deals with the rise in avidity during the immune response in various animal species. During the test series in February 1949, Jerne had established that "after the second stimulus, a guinea pig serum was much more avid, lying somewhere between the avidity of standard serum and that of rabbit serum." After a third stimulus, all sera exhibit an avidity that can be compared with that of standard serum from hyperimmune animals. He found that sera display an improvement in avidity over time, and that this improvement is especially pronounced on repeated immunizations.[6]

The investigation presented in this fourth chapter (of only thirteen pages) was "by no means exhaustive," but, as Jerne pointed out at the end, "the immunological aspects of these facts are interesting." In the final, typewritten version, he even inserted an extra subheading, "Immunological Aspects," for the chapter's concluding discussion. Avidity increase was closely connected to antibody formation, and Jerne knew, of course, the current theories of this central immunological phenomenon well from the standard textbooks: *"Maaløe and I agreed that there were only two books worth reading: Kabat and Meyer['s Experimental Immunochemistry, 1948] and Boyd['s Fundamentals of Immunology, 1943], and I think, really, that Boyd was the best. They were the only textbooks you got anything out of."* According to these theories, specific antibodies were in some way produced out of nonspecific globulin molecules by direct impression of the antigen, like a bit of cast iron in a casting mold. But experiments had shown that the increase in avidity was independent of the strength of the stimulus: in tests on guinea pigs, the final titer of their serum was just as high after two weak stimuli as after two strong stimuli. "How can it be that even a comparatively tiny 2nd stimulus gives such a colossal increase in the yield?" he asked his audience in a lecture at Polymorfien (the Polymorphic), the Serum Institute's seminar series. The occurrence of a lag phase, too, required explanation. According to established theories, the production of antitoxic antibodies should start immediately after an antigen stimulus, so "why should almost 14 days go by before you can show antitoxin?"[7]

To interpret the increase in the antitoxin response after a second immunization as just an increase in the number of antitoxin molecules seemed to him "very dramatic." His experiments made possible another explanation of the immune response: "the 1,000-fold increase [of antitoxic power] after application of a second small stimulus may partly or mainly be due to a sudden increase in avidity." He imagined that specific cells produced unspecific globulin molecules and that the production of antitoxin began immediately after the antigen molecules had penetrated the cells. First, "an antitoxin of almost infinitely low avidity" was produced, which could not neutralize any toxin and "thus would be indistinguishable from unspecific globulin." Gradually the avidity in the antitoxin molecules would rise. What was traditionally understood as a rising concentration of antitoxin could therefore be interpreted equally as the "increasing antitoxic power of a constant concentration of antitoxin of increasing avidity." He asserted that one could reason by analogy in considering the swift increase in antitoxic strength after a second stimulus. "There can be no doubt," he wrote, "that an important part of this apparent rise in antitoxin content is due to the increase in avidity." He advanced no account of the mechanism responsible for this avidity increase, but referred in passing to a largely neglected paper by an English colleague, L. B. Holt, who had advanced the hypothesis that "the second response phenomenon . . . is due to a release in stored preformed antibody."[8]

Jerne's thoughts about the rise in avidity signal a shift from a purely serological and chemical approach to the antibody problem to consideration of the immune response as a biological process. This is interesting in two ways. First, historically, because his thoughts fit into the picture of a growing number of independent observations and discoveries that could not be accounted for within the chemically oriented serological tradition and that were about to add up to the "immunobiological revolution" of the late 1950s and 1960s. Second, biographically, because these thoughts were taken up by Jerne again four years later in his natural selection theory of antibody formation—a theory that in turn was a decisive contribution to the general shift in the 1950s toward thinking about immunity as a basically biological phenomenon. His reference to Holt's idea of "a release in stored preformed antibody" points toward the central concept of the selection theory, namely, that the antigen does not induce the production of antibodies but only participates in the choice of already produced natural antibody molecules. It is true that to Holt it was only the secondary response that consisted of the release of stored, ready-made antibodies from the primary stimulus. But the more radical idea—that is, that the primary response, too, consists of the release of ready-made antibody molecules—lay close at hand.[9]

Another idea in the fourth chapter that turned up again in the selection theory four years later is that early antibody production consists of antitoxin "of almost infinitely low avidity" which is unable to neutralize any toxin and so "would be indistinguishable from unspecific globulin." In the summer of 1954, Jerne would follow the argument to its conclusion when postulating that there is no fundamental difference between antibodies and unspecific globulin. Yet another idea that later emerged in the selection theory lies in the wording of a "possible, but unlikely, explanation" of why the avidity of the antitoxins first produced is so low, namely, that "the producing cells may always turn out a spectrum of antitoxin of widely differing avidity" and that the reason why the early sera are of low avidity is that the antigen still present in the tissues combines with the more avid part of the antitoxin, leaving only antitoxin of very low avidity to circulate in the blood. But this was only speculation, he explained, so long as he had no opportunity to investigate the issue experimentally. The first part of the argument—that the antibody-producing cells produce a spectrum of antibody molecules of different avidities all the time—lies very close to what would become the fundamental idea of Jerne's seminal selection theory, that is, that the organism spontaneously produces a repertoire of specific antibodies.[10]

In June of 1950 all of this flew in the face of the prevailing conception of antibody formation, according to which specific antibodies are formed from unspecific serum globulin through the antigen's serving as a chemical template. Jerne's passing mention of Holt's hypothesis therefore triggered an immediate response from the professor of general pathology, K. A. Jensen, at the university: "But not from previously formed antitoxin molecules, however. Is this clearly worded?" asked Jensen. Jerne did not go into a polemic, and for the time being the hypothesis was removed from his research agenda.[11]

Even though all these musings were still only speculative and minimally expressed, they meant that Jerne took a step toward identifying not only a new set of scientific problems but also a new disciplinary identity for himself—from biometrician and serologist to an immunologist thinking in terms of the immune response in the living organism. "There can be no doubt," he wrote in the concluding theoretical argument, "that a closer study of avidity will be an indispensable step towards understanding the mechanism of immunity response." Until that time he had directed his scientific passion toward finding errors in the serological measurement methods. Now, for the first time, he began to orient himself toward a more substantial, immunobiological phenomenon. In one of his autobiographical sketches thirty-five years later, he characterized these years working on his dissertation with the phrase "I enter immunology through a study of probability." But he omitted the logical corollary, that is, "through a study of serology and chemistry." Given the fact that by 1985 he was considered the doyen of immunobiology, the omission is perhaps more understandable.[12]

In the middle of August 1950, Jerne's final manuscript, titled "A Study of Avidity Based on Rabbit Skin Responses to Diphtheria Toxin-Antitoxin Mixtures," was submitted to the medical faculty. The evaluation committee, Maaløe and Linderstrøm-Lang, read it rapidly and had few negative comments. They pointed out that the thesis contained "many new and fundamentally confirmed observations" that had been treated "with an awareness of elemental and essential problems" and concluded that it should be accepted to be printed and publicly defended (according to Danish academic tradition). Maaløe remembers that "there was a consensus that the thesis was exceptionally exceptional" because of its theoretical orientation and its sophisticated statistical treatment of the research material.[13]

The committee's judgment stood the test of time: Jerne's Ph.D. became a standard international reference on avidity as a physical-chemical phenomenon. The theoretical part was especially esteemed by younger scientists. Viggo Faber, then at the Serum Institute, remembers that he became "fantastically inspired" by it, that "there were many of us saying: 'If Jerne thinks this way, why can't this way [of thinking] be applied to what we're working on?'" One of the Ph.D. candidates whom Jerne met at the California Institute of Technology a few years later was impressed "precisely because of the quantitative treatment . . . the idea that you could take what to me seemed such a sloppy, messy system and look at it in [a quantitative] way." Another Cal Tech scientist remembers that he thought that the permanent value of Jerne's thesis lay in its "very nice quantitative studies." Nobody, however, seems to have paid much notice to the biological aspects of his work.[14]

Since the end of 1947, Jerne had been intensively occupied with the avidity phenomenon and the theoretical foundation of the standardization problem. These were decisively important years in his life. When he began work on his thesis, he had been an anonymous Danish physician; at its completion, he had put himself on the map as a sharp critic among biometricians and in standard- ization circles. Seen from outside, his dissertation marked his scientific com- ing-of-age, his entrance as a member of the scientific community.

Questioned whether he had spent a lot of effort on the thesis, Jerne believes that *"there was a lot of time, but not a feeling."* He remembers the approaches taken and the results obtained, but not when or how he got there: *"I must admit I don't remember, I have a hole in my memory there."* Apart from the conversa- tions with Maaløe, Rasch, and Weis Bentzon, he did not retain many recollec- tions of his life at the institute at the end of the 1940s: *"I am really at a loss if you ask me which people at the Serum Institute I talked to,"* adding: *"I can't quite dis- tinguish in my memory between these years and the later years."* Neither did he have much to tell about his life outside the institute; neither his relationship with Adda nor his time with the children enters his spontaneous autobiograph- ical story. "It is as though a curtain [is drawn] between me and my experiences during the years after Tjek's death," he later wrote to an acquaintance; in an in- terview he remarked that *"I have great gaps in my memory . . . especially after Tjek's death. I only remember my scientific work, nothing of my personal life,"* which he *"probably repressed . . . in a Freudian sense."*[15]

Jerne's lack of personal recollections corresponds to a gap in the archive. There is no diary preserved from these years, no notes about literature, art, or philosophy; the few extant documents contain no evidence of his thoughts or emotional state. Neither is everyday family life visible in the documents of the late 1940s, as they were in the 1930s. The children emerge now and then in drawings and sporadic messages about school or the Boy Scouts. "Won't you help me with the dumb, awful, important, smarty stuff of arithmetic and men- tal calculation? . . . Please do, for the sake of my health" is one of the few written signs of life from Ivar, who was finding school harder and harder. Donald, on the other hand, seems to have handled school without any serious problems. Jerne's relationship with Adda, which in the beginning bore the imprint of al- most demonic passion, seems gradually to have become a routine, especially af- ter they got married in the summer of 1948 (Adda had divorced her former husband, who had taken custody of their single child). Ivar remembers Niels and Adda being "in love" at the end of the 1940s and that Adda was "very happy," but this may well be a teenager's wishful thinking, for others have a less positive picture of their marriage. "This much, I've understood from him," says Rostock, "that it was some kind of a misunderstanding, that marriage. . . . I have the impression he got shanghaied into it." Noll remembers that Jerne seemed to have a "detached relationship" with "that woman," who appears gradually to have been reduced to a stepmother and housekeeper.[16]

A decade earlier, Jerne had been able to satisfy an essential part of his intellectual needs with Tjek, but now he seemed to spend most of his time away from home. Half of his life was devoted to the Serum Institute; he went in every day ("he was hardworking"), even if he arrived a little late in the mornings. Late, because the other half of his life took place in Copenhagen's pubs and wine bars; he "knew a lot of people down there." Hans Noll remembers that Jerne "liked to leave [the institute] at four or five in the afternoon and then take a leisurely walk to the Hotel d'Angleterre and sit on the terrace and drink a coffee or tea or whatever and watch the pretty girls. . . . He liked to have a certain lifestyle." Evenings and nights he sat discussing politics, art, and poetry at his favorite place, the Café Royal, the source of his only major memories of that time, memories that later entered into his self-image as an intellectual bohemian: "*There, I met interesting people,*" he says, mentioning in particular the Danish poet Jens August Schade, whom he says he had "*quite an attachment to.*" In what way? "*Meaning that neither of us had any interest in going to bed, we drank red wine together all day, all evening. . . . And we discussed interesting things . . . the use of subjunctive in the Danish language and such things.*" The anecdotes about Schade are a part of Jerne's romanticized self-image—he was eager to give the impression of having lived a bohemian life in Copenhagen, and Schade, like Asger Jorn and Egill Jacobsen before him, contributed perfectly to that image.[17]

The lack of archival material about Jerne's personal and family life in this period might be an artifact. But it is also tempting to imagine that the abundance of experimental laboratory notebooks about the avidity experiments, as contrasted with the paucity of personal notes and correspondence, reflects the fact that "peripheral abstractions" had begun to take over his existence, that he was compensating for the gap in "standing for a firm position on significant problems" through "taking a position on detailed problems." It was, to use his own word, "fun" to write a doctoral thesis. But the area of study he had chosen so far allowed little room for his longing for the sublime.[18]

12   *"Antibody This, Antibody That, They Weren't Really Much Interested"*

W hile Niels Jerne was beginning to identify himself as an immunologist, Ole Maaløe was heading full-speed into a study of bacteriophage, that is, viruses that infect and replicate in bacterial cells. Max Delbrück and other geneticists used the tiny phage as a model organism to understand the molecular mechanism of heredity, and during his stay at Cal Tech in the spring of 1949, Maaløe had been seriously bitten by the "phage bug." He returned to Copenhagen full of energy and ideas and with Ørskov's indulgence established his one-man branch of the internationally dispersed phage group in the Standardization Department. The following spring he started a series of experiments on how changes in temperature affect the reproduction of phage in the bacterial cell.[1]

In October 1950, two young American phage researchers unexpectedly arrived. Twenty-six-year-old Gunther Stent had a Ph.D. in physical chemistry and had spent a couple of years on a fellowship with Delbrück. James D. Watson, four years younger, had just completed his Ph.D. in genetics with Salvador E. Luria and, like Stent, had received a grant to travel to Copenhagen to deepen his biochemical knowledge with Herman Kalckar, an internationally known expert on the metabolism of nucleotides, a class of molecules supposedly crucial in the hereditary mechanism. For various reasons the stay with Kalckar

Staff and visiting scientists at the Department of Standardization, known as "the cockpit," Danish State Serum Institute, 1950–51. *From left to right:* Gunther Stent, unidentified technician, Ole Maaløe, Jens Ole Rostock, Niels Jerne (standing), and James D. Watson. (Medical History Museum, University of Copenhagen)

turned into "a complete flop," and instead Stent contacted Maaløe, the "Danish paragon of elegance and microbiological savoir-faire," whom he had gotten to know at Delbrück's phage course in the spring of 1949; without any major formalities, Stent got a place to work in the Standardization Department—and "Watson came along."[2]

The two young Americans quickly made themselves at home in the Serum Institute. Stent remembers that he thought it was "fantastic . . . wonderful, everything. You just said 'I want this, I want that,' and they would have five girls who came with everything." Within a couple of weeks they not only set about looking for girlfriends but were also fully occupied in experiments with Maaløe. Every day the small attic laboratory was filled with bacterial cultures, phages, petri dishes, and the heavy, sweet odor of broth. Stent remembers his first meeting with Jerne as "sort of surrealistic": "We were there in the lab, and all of a sudden a man walks in, behind him, a technician, and they were carrying a board on which a rabbit was stretched out. . . . I'd never seen this before . . . and I thought it was horrible to torture animals like this. . . . Like Christ, they were crucified on the board."[3]

Had Stent been more familiar with serology, he might have thought this intriguing. But for phage biologists, the serological reaction was just a simple tool used for identifying phages by type, so the only thing Stent noticed in Jerne's work was that two parameters were needed to characterize a serum, which he "thought was OK." Otherwise, he did not consider Jerne's avidity work especially significant; it was a contribution to standardization, "that's all." In contrast to Hans Noll, who says that he was "absolutely convinced" that Jerne was "the brightest" person in the Serum Institute, Stent remembers that, in the beginning, he did not think Jerne was an especially interesting conversationalist. Of course Jerne was smart, but no smarter than many others Stent had met. "I must say I didn't really appreciate him," he says, "I didn't realize that he was really something extraordinary. . . . The only thing in which he was special, as far as I remember, was, you know, he had an in with literary and artistic circles in Copenhagen." Jerne could not avoid noticing the visitors' somewhat condescending attitude; they thought that serology and immunology were *"too complicated,"* that one ought to concentrate on *"the most essential"* instead. They had *"a much greater"* scientific goal: *"They wanted to find the gene. . . . So, I mean, I didn't have a great auditorium. Here you are, antibody this, antibody that, and so, what the hell. They weren't really much interested."*[4]

Jerne had hoped to defend his Ph.D. publicly by the end of the year, but for bureaucratic reasons the evaluation committee's report was delayed for several months, giving him extra time to make the dissertation as attractive as possible with regard to language and presentation. At the end of January 1951, he got the proofs from the printer. Every detail was important to him: the cover was printed in two colors, and the paper was the best obtainable. Stent did not understand why Jerne went to so much trouble over the form; he thought it "a little bizarre" to have an artist design the cover of a dissertation. Had Stent had a similar aesthetic bent (or known Jerne better), however, he would surely have understood that this care reflected Jerne's self-image. Decades before, Jerne had learned that people value not only one's inside but also one's outside, that a sharp brain is better accepted if it has a good-looking exterior.[5]

His aesthetic requirements satisfied, the manuscript went to press, and at the end of May he received formal notification that the faculty had accepted it for publication and public defense in the early fall. The list of those to receive copies included everybody of importance to him. Aside from a long line of

Danish physicians and colleagues at the Serum Institute, foreign names dominated: the standardization scientists who had been his target during his four
years' work; the biometricians who had been his allies; a few colleagues of his
newly acquired American phage friends, including Max Delbrück; the immunochemists Linus Pauling, Felix Haurowitz, Michael Heidelberger, and
John Marrack; and those immunologists who represented his newly acquired
professional identity: William Boyd, Macfarlane Burnet, and Alvin Pappenheimer. In addition to professionals there were also old Dutch comrades and
artist friends from the years with Tjek, people who had glided out of his life,
and of course, family and new friends and acquaintances. All together the list
amounted to nearly two hundred persons who composed his intellectual and
emotional network. Although he had earlier maintained that he preferred solitude, he apparently wanted to share his life's biggest achievement thus far with
the rest of the world.

During the winter, even before Jerne's dissertation had been formally accepted
and defended, he was offered a permanent position at the Serum Institute. As a
government official, and with his doctor's degree within reach, Jerne had come
to a point where many paths were open to him. There are no documents preserved from the spring of 1951 that give a direct insight into how he looked
upon his future research opportunities. Much suggests that he was in the same
situation as so many times before—that is, he had talent for numerous things,
but difficulty in making up his mind.

    With his fundamental theoretical and methodological contributions to
standardization research he could have developed further the practical conclusions of the dissertation and continued his work in international standardization. The WHO assignment, which was part of his official duties, was still a
viable research option. But he had begun to distance himself from the standardization business. During the winter of 1950–51, for example, he was invited to write an article on the topic for the *Annual Review of Microbiology*; he
accepted, but the project did not seem to have interested him much, because he
shelved it for a year.

    Another possibility was to engage in bacteriophage research. Stent and
Watson had little interest in serology, but conversely, Jerne became fascinated
from the beginning by what they were doing. In fact, phage had already for
some time been *"among the most discussed subjects of Ole Maaløe and myself,"*
and they had already *"deeply discussed . . . the experimental work of Delbrück,
Luria, and others."* One of the experiments that he remembers best was Del-

brück and Luria's famous "fluctuation test," showing that penicillin-resistant bacterial cells can arise spontaneously through mutations, an elegant experiment that became one of the decisive nails in the coffin of early twentieth-century neo-Lamarckism; a couple of years later it would become one of Jerne's starting points for his own showdown with the prevailing instruction theories of antibody formation.[6]

Phage was also fascinating because of the aura of international science and the regular seminars held by the department—which sometimes included the visiting Max Delbrück and occasionally even Niels Bohr. During the fall and winter of 1950–51 the cockpit was boiling over with scientific discussions (*"the level of conversation was very high"*), and the four scientists soon fused into a lively little group who got together both at the lab and in Copenhagen's restaurants and inns (*"We often spent Saturday nights in pleasant pseudo-intellectual cafes"*). Jerne felt his spirits awaken. He bought Erwin Schrödinger's *What Is Life?* (1944)—the essay that had such influence on the phage group's understanding of the physical foundations of biology—and followed that with *Science and Humanism* (1951). Later in life he had few reminiscences of the four previous years, but from the moment Watson and Stent stepped through the door, he got *"a whole cloud of memories of people and events"* (which, however, *"have left no echo"* in the archive).[7]

So, having just finished the avidity manuscript, Jerne tried out some phage experiments on his own. His attention was drawn not to hereditary problems, however, but to serological properties of phage and antiphage serum. Like bacteria and toxins, phage can function as antigen, too. If a horse or a rabbit is immunized with a specific phage strain, it produces an antiphage serum that can inactivate (neutralize) the specific phage, in the same way as an antidiphtheria serum can neutralize diphtheria toxin. But was the kinetics of inactivation of phage similar to the neutralization of diphtheria toxin? Jerne remembers noticing that the inactivation curve in a logarithm diagram became perfectly straight through almost the entire sequence, that is, the inactivation proceeded according to a simple exponential function. This was entirely in agreement with the experiments Alfred Hershey and his coworkers had done nearly ten years earlier, indicating that phage is inactivated irreversibly.[8]

Jerne also observed, however, that the curve was not *entirely* straight. In fact, at its very end, it *"bends off after about 30 minutes and becomes horizontal,"* meaning that *"one phage in a million . . . is reactivated."* This last bending of the curve was generally known among phage researchers, but because it had no practical significance for the genetic experiments they were doing, for all practical purposes they retained the idea that the process was irreversible. But why should the phage-antiphage reaction be irreversible, Jerne wondered, when his own experiments had indicated that the reaction between diphtheria toxin and diphtheria antitoxin was a reversible equilibrium between formation and dissociation of an antigen-antibody complex? He remembers unequivocally asserting that *"the general conclusion that phage inactivation by antibody is irreversible must be wrong"*; he also talked with Stent and Watson about the matter, though his viewpoint was considered *"a bit far-fetched."*[9]

Jerne does not seem to have had a clear vision of what he wanted to achieve through these inactivation experiments. There is no archival material from the spring of 1951 to indicate that he saw any connection between these experiments and the avidity problem; this would be established later. He seems to have experimented with phage-antiphage-neutralization out of sheer curiosity. In fact, the third career option, biometrics and mathematical statistics, seems to have filled more of his time that spring than the phage experiments. He spent much time in conversation with Georg Rasch and had *"many happy evenings"* at Weis Bentzon's home studying statistical mechanics. While finishing the proofreading of his thesis, he was notified of his election to the board of the Biometric Society, and for the rest of spring 1951 he involved himself in organizational work; for example, via his contacts in Scandinavia and the Netherlands, he set up a Scandinavian-Dutch section of the society.[10]

Jerne might therefore have continued his biometrical career. But some time, probably during that spring, he made an unexpected phage observation. Stent remembers that one day his lab mate was standing by the bench and watching them as they were "doing experiments with phages. . . . We used antisera, antiphage sera, and we were diluting broth." The routine procedure was to do all experiments in regular bacterial growth medium (broth), which is said to have led to an argument. "Why are you neutralizing in broth?" Jerne asked. "Well, everybody does it," was the answer. "It's crazy, you should do the neutralization in a well-defined medium, a buffer or so," Jerne allegedly replied. The two Americans snubbed him with "Get lost!" They did everything in broth and apparently did not think there was any reason to change their procedures. Jerne got irritated. "I think that he got angry, or something like that, furious that we had told him to get lost," says Stent, who has a clear impression that Jerne began to experiment with the culture medium so as to "show that here were two bunches of jerks who don't know anything about immunology, that they don't use proper procedure." Jerne, for his part, remembers that he was irritated because he thought it was *"unreasonable to let inactivation proceed in nutrient broth medium."* There were no bacteria involved in the inactivation, and therefore no need for a bacterial growth medium.[11]

Instead, Jerne began to study the kinetics of inactivation of phage in well-defined salt solutions of different concentrations, "and finally, for some crazy reason," in distilled water. *"Normally, you work with physiological salt solution, but then I thought 'Why do we do that, really?' and so I began to work with distilled water, and then the process went much faster,"* he remembers. Rostock clearly recalls the day when Jerne got the idea: "We sat around the table in the Serum Institute, eating lunch and chatting, and we were talking about what people had used for reagents with different things . . . and then he says: 'Why hasn't anyone tried ordinary water?' . . . So everybody just smiled, ordinary water, yes, it's almost idiocy to think of it, now that we've got all those other good things." Everybody smiled, but the results were surprising. When neutralization is carried out in broth or in a physiological salt solution, an antiphage serum of high avidity can inactivate bacteriophage with a velocity of 500–1000/min. But in distilled water, the reaction occurred many times faster, 100,000/min or more. For the inactivation to take place so rapidly, however, he had to add small quantities of normal serum to the reaction mixture. Very small quantities (20–1000 ppm) were sufficient; at higher concentrations the inactivation was inhibited once again. Conversely, if he worked with a heavily diluted solution of the antiphage serum, no inactivation occurred at all. The easiest interpretation was that the reaction between phage and antiphage required the presence of a factor in normal serum.[12]

This unexpected result modified Stent's skeptical attitude toward Jerne. He became impressed with Jerne's style in the laboratory (it was "different, really. . . . He works slow, I would say. By the standards of the then molecular biologists he was very slow, but he was very deep so, in the end, he didn't make any mistakes"), hence he got more interested in Jerne as a person, and "finally," he "only talked to Jerne, because . . . I found it more interesting to talk to him than Maaløe." In the beginning Stent experienced Jerne as reserved and got no particular insights into his private life or personal background; he thought for a long time that Jerne had studied law in Leiden, and he assumed, observing his nocturnal habits, that he must be a bachelor. It was a good while before Stent realized that Jerne was married and had children; it was quite a long time later that he found out that Adda was his second wife. Nor was Stent ever invited to the Jernes' home. Jerne may have been inhospitable during this time because Ivar, then fifteen, was experiencing worsening psychological problems—probably originating in the trauma connected with his mother's suicide six years before—and had been admitted to a clinic.[13]

In the middle of August, Jerne received an encouraging reaction to his phage experiments; he had sent a notice about the water effect to the phage group's mimeographed newsletter, *Phage Information Service,* distributed from Cal Tech, and Delbrück had obviously become interested. Because the newsletter was not a real publication but merely a personal communication, Delbrück suggested that Jerne "immediately" send a note to *Nature* "to avoid priority problems." As one of the phage group's young members points out, Jerne's finding "was not in itself a great discovery," but Delbrück is said to have been impressed that it was possible to find out something new about such a talked-to-death matter as the phage-antiphage reaction and that the discovery was an example of someone actually being able to make interesting observations without starting from a theoretical problem; it was a serendipitous discovery, one that had "showed up" unexpectedly. Encouraged by Delbrück's quick and positive reaction, Jerne rapidly summarized his results in a short manuscript for *Nature.*[14]

When Jerne looked back on his initial experiments with bacteriophage, he said that they *"were given no importance."* It is true that the brief notice in *Nature* did not attract great attention (there were only nine citations in the scientific literature between 1955 and 1974), but it had considerable personal and social importance for him, like his rarely noticed work on the rankit method eight years before. Just as working out the rankit method had enhanced his self-confidence and scientific status and had marked his *"essential departure"* into science as such, the little article in *Nature* marked his entrance into hot international biomedical science. He never forgot what Watson told him: *"Taj, now you are a scientist. The definition of a scientist is someone who has got a paper published in Nature."* The rumor of his discovery spread quickly, and within a week of the word getting out, the French bacteriophage scientist André Lwoff invited Jerne to take part in a bacteriophage colloquium planned for the following summer.[15]

Delbrück went to Copenhagen in early September 1951, to deliver a lecture at the Second International Polio Congress, on which occasion Jerne arranged for a small party. Two weeks later it was again time for a party, this time to celebrate the public defense of his doctoral dissertation. In his after-dinner speech, Jerne thanked all the opponents and others involved with small anecdotal insights into his scientific life: "I get my best ideas standing on the back of the streetcar," he related, for "there you can meditate so wonderfully

Niels Jerne and two of his opponents (Ole Maaløe and Georg Rasch) at the public defense of his dissertation in September 1951. (Medical History Museum, University of Copenhagen. Drawing: Hans Carl Jensen)

undisturbed and free. So I no longer bicycle at all," and so on, nice and chatty. But he was not entirely able to curb his sharp tongue. Quoting Watson, who allegedly had said he had never "been in a place where so many people do so little," as at the Serum Institute and that the intellectual level there "of course" lay "far below" what he was used to in the United States, Jerne demonstrated, once again, that friendliness and politeness can be united with sharpness and arrogance.[16]

The self-confident speech reflects Jerne's newly acquired status in the Danish medical research world. By 1950–51 he could justifiably regard himself as one of the few theoretically oriented biomedical scientists in the country. Most of his colleagues at the Serum Institute were clinically oriented; they thought in concrete and descriptive terms and "regarded what he was working on as almost a curiosity." Jerne himself had the impression that most of his colleagues were quite indifferent: *"Antibodies and immunology were, at that time, sort of esoteric ideas. . . . It had nothing to do with biology or something that medical doctors were to worry about."* It was probably these descriptively oriented colleagues inside and outside the Serum Institute that Jerne had in mind when he wrote the following poem, under the title "Virus and Phage":

> Not even the sharpest of sharp eyes
> can spy a virus or a phage.
> You still encounter many lies
> about those animals today.
> Some poor guys still remain,
> they are the mathematophobes,
> who think they can see miracles
> in electron microscopes.
> But no, the splendor of the virus
> manifested everywhere and everywise,
> only in numbers can be recognized
> through logarithms and functions.
> It's evident from probit 5
> the bacteriophage has 16 tongues
> each with a split tip that projects
> each time it nourishes its young.
> With 117 rows of teeth
> its smile to some seems somewhat shy.
> That it has 9 legs at either end
> is simply derived from dx/dy.
> Each of its 27 tails
> glowing with a golden light
> is, as the integrals reveal,
> decked out with feathery plumes.
> The pattern of a virus' back
> (striped purple on glaring green,
> I think) distinguishes between a virus and a phage
> as can be seen from matrix calculation.
> Just one parameter is all we lack
> to finish our virus-almanac,
> sending the biological simpleton off once more
> after new subjects to explore.

The sophomoric and slightly sarcastic poem (rhymed in the Danish original and hardly translatable) expresses something fundamental about Jerne's view of science, namely, his strong emphasis on a mathematical and abstract approach to biological phenomena and, conversely, his condescending attitude toward those "mathematophobes" who did not understand statistical reasoning and who wanted more solid proofs of the existence of things.[17]

Jerne's attitude toward the "biological simpleton" was no impulse of the moment. Ten years later he would refer to the "usual spectrum" of biologists, "at the one extremity, those who are enthralled by the ease with which nature brings forth and reproduces a multitude of remarkable structures and forms . . . and who look with mistrust on the introduction of mathematical symbols— at the other extremity, those who are trying to diminish the entropy in our biological Big Picture, who use, for that purpose, modes of observation that have already created law and order in other branches of natural science, and who are impatient to conclude their own work before one of their colleagues has solved all the essential puzzles." Of course he felt he was one of those who wish, impatiently, to diminish the entropy and create law and order in the biological Big Picture.[18]

Jerne's newly won self-confidence as a scientist was also reflected in the brief autobiography he prepared for the university's annual Festschrift. New recipients of a Ph.D. usually wrote half- to full-page entries about their earlier connections and their scientific work and interests, both great and small. Jerne's laconic summary was notably the shortest in many years: "NIELS KAJ JERNE, b. Dec. 23, 1911, London. Son of Tech. Dr. Hans Jessen J. and Else Marie Lindberg. H.S. grad. Rotterdam 28. M.D. Copenhagen 47. Intern R.H. and asst. Danish State Serum Institute. Laboratory head 51." Evidently this was everything he thought necessary to convey to the Danish academic world for the present. Even in his first official autobiography he tried to diminish the entropy in the Big Picture.[19]

*"These People Don't Know
What They're Doing"*

*T*he local Copenhagen phage group dissolved in the summer of 1951. Watson left for Cambridge and the Cavendish Laboratory, where he was going to meet Francis Crick and begin the work that would lead to the elucidation of the double helix structure of DNA; Stent left for Paris with an Icelandic woman he had met at the Serum Institute to work with André Lwoff at the Pasteur Institute; and finally, Maaløe departed to California for a year to deepen his insights into the physiology of bacteria with Cornelius van Niel at Hopkins Marine Station.

Jerne was left solely responsible for the work of the department. In his letters to Maaløe during the following months he complained regularly that the obligatory international standardization work took too much of his time. He would have had little time for his own experiments had Providence not sent Lis Skovsted, a master's student in biochemistry, to the department in October 1951, for her final year of laboratory training. While Jerne spent most of his time preparing the WHO Expert Committee in Biological Standardization, to be held in Geneva the first week in December, she was employed at the laboratory bench with a new series of experiments on the unknown serum factor, now dubbed the "third factor."

Skovsted would soon show that it was thermostable, "*not* dialyzable" (that is, not such a small molecule) and gave a reaction rate exceeding one million. It was difficult to obtain reproducible results, though. "Small differences in the test conditions that are not under my control must be involved," Jerne reported to his friend and colleague in Pacific Grove on the California coast. In November and December, he became more and more "obsessed with the third factor" and worked with it "incessantly." Skovsted remembers him in these moments as a very concentrated person, giving a picture of him that echoes those of his older sister Karen and his fellow students in Leiden: "He was very pleasant and nice, but [seemed] very much like a scientist who went around in his own world and thought very, very much. . . . He was a kind of . . . loner, to some extent, a kind of classic scientist, not the absent-minded kind but one who thought and brooded over things."[1]

After returning from Geneva and taking a short detour to a phage colleague in Göttingen in the middle of January 1952, Jerne identified a possible factor candidate in "chemically pure" form, "effective in very small concentrations, even less than *1 gamma pro liter*." He was "of course, very excited" about his factor and "somewhat hectically occupied with this detective work." But he did not know whether the time was ripe to disclose what substance was involved. He did not want to "enable others to beat me to publication," he wrote to Maaløe, adding: "What I'm in deepest doubt about is, how it is smartest, from the standpoint of research politics, to present it." Should he write a preliminary paper at once, or keep the results secret for the time being while he worked out the details, publishing a more comprehensive article later? This was the first time in his career he expressed tactical awareness in scientific matters.[2]

Eventually he revealed the news to his friend: "So—it is lysozyme." A biochemist at the institute had proposed this relatively low-molecular-weight basic protein; it later turned out that protamine, too, was effective, making Jerne conclude that these kinds of substances could "replace a serum component that is necessary for the inactivation of bacteriophage." Watson, too, heard the news. Normally there was not much that could impress the self-assured young American, but now he showed his immediate admiration: "Your recent letter was most exciting—a really incredible discovery!!—in a way, the most Moewus like fact yet discovered in phage," Watson wrote, in a mocking reference to the German bacterial geneticist Franz Moewus, whose experimental results were stunning but considered impossible to reproduce.[3]

One more small discovery. Would he get a pat on the shoulder from Delbrück this time, too?

Maybe it was this small breakthrough on the third factor that led to Jerne's finally getting it all together and revising Maaløe's and his manuscript on standardization for the *Annual Review of Microbiology*. It was an excellent occasion to summarize differing opinions on the difficulties and limitations of serological standardization, but the article gave him no intellectual challenge, just stylistic problems. "Here it comes at last, the damned piece about standardization," he wrote to Maaløe at the beginning of February 1952. "I have been completely desperate for the last 14 days, and it has been sheer hell to get it finished in acceptable form." Neither did the exhilaration over having solved the third-factor problem last very long. It turned out that he and Skovsted could not reproduce the experimental results in the lowest range of concentration: "I don't really know what to believe." Three weeks later, he had not found anything "essentially new." Instead, for a time he turned his attention once more to the biometric discussion club and called the members to a first meeting in the middle of February 1952.[4]

At the end of the month, the problem of poor reproducibility was still unsolved. Watson was willing to bring up the results at a virus meeting at Oxford in April, but Jerne declined. "Sad to say, the specificity got away from me, and so, too, much of the interest it could have for the phage problem. Immunologically, it still has a certain significance, but I have lost some of my enthusiasm," he told Maaløe. "I miss having someone to talk to," he confided to his absent friend and complained again about having been "excessively busy" since Christmas. He would soon "have no time at all to carry out experiments myself, I find this very disturbing."[5]

The salt-effect experiments were interrupted when Skovsted concluded her training year in June 1952. The few remaining documents have little to say about Jerne's work and his family life during the summer of 1952. His younger son, Donald, took the entrance examination for the Sorø Academy, one of Denmark's few private boarding schools, and the elder son, Ivar, who had been released from the hospital in March, moved to the country with Adda's sister and brother-in-law in order to recover and to begin learning horticulture. "He has perhaps gotten a trifle better and is now a little freer," Jerne wrote to Maaløe, now the only person with whom he could, at least partially, share his family problems. But Ivar's newly acquired religious interests worried him. His son was turning toward the Jehovah's Witnesses, quoting the Bible in his sporadic letters, and sometimes enclosing a copy of the sect's paper, *The Watchtower.*[6]

Jerne had his own sect. The great event of the summer was the first international bacteriophage colloquium at Royaumont, outside Paris, which gathered together the fifty-odd scientists who constituted the front line in bacteriophage research, "everyone who counted for anything in the world of the phage." In retrospect the meeting in the old monastery was one of the milestones in the history of emergent molecular biology, with presentations such as Alfred Hershey's report on his and Martha Chase's "blender experiment," the elegant work that seemed to confirm what many in the bacteriophage circle already suspected, namely, that the genetic information lies in the nuclear DNA, not in the protein, as commonly believed. In this context, Jerne's contribution about the salt effect and the serum factor was somewhat peripheral. Nevertheless, it was received with a certain interest, not least by Delbrück, who later mentioned it in his report from the colloquium as "The Jerne Effect" and hired a student to work further on the results.[7]

Jerne himself regarded the Royaumont meeting as "very successful." It was the first time he had taken part in a conference on basic science, and he was "glad to see all those people in person," he reported to Maaløe. He met his old bacteriophage friends from Copenhagen and Göttingen, witnessed Watson's eccentric behavior, and formed a number of friendships that would endure the rest of his life, with Salvador Luria, André Lwoff, and Jacques Monod. He also got a number of constructive suggestions on the serum factor effect that he tested on his return to Copenhagen later in the summer. He was convinced that the differing results from the flask and test-tube experiments were caused by the antiphage molecules becoming adsorbed to the walls of the reaction vessel. "My experiments fit with the theory [that] phages are neg. charged, like the surface of the antiphage," he told Maaløe. Because the protamine had a strong positive charge, the chances increased that the antiphage molecules could be bound to the phages; the strongly positive protamine molecules "are adsorbed to the glass-liquid interface and therefore disappear from highly thinned serum dilutions," he explained. He wrote the results down, put Skovsted's name on it, apparently without even asking her to read it over, and submitted it to *Annales de l'Institut Pasteur,* which published it several months later.[8]

The article in the *Annales* did not become a classic either—receiving only thirty-four citations in the scientific literature between 1955 and 1974. Even so, it could have become the next step in the career of a molecular biologist, rather than an immunologist. With his presentation at Royaumont, Jerne began to be known and respected in the phage circle. He points out how important these contacts were for his *"self-assurance . . . the inner conviction that you are as good as they are."* The meeting with the phage group *"and the world they represented"* was, as he expresses it, like *"an earthquake, a catapult into higher and deeper regions of ongoing science."* Through the phage group, he first became acquainted with broader-gauge scientific problems: *"The target of their thinking was far more ambitious"* than the problems he had worked on so far. He feels that it was only after meeting Stent, Watson, Delbrück, and the others that the *"dark middle ages"* of his life finally ended. Now his life had entered its Renaissance phase: he had at last encountered sublime science.[9]

It would have been natural for Jerne to join the ranks of the expanding group of scientists who were working on DNA and on bacterial and viral genetics. During the 1950s many chose that road, so many that, a decade later, molecular biology became established as an independent scientific discipline with its own journals, professorates, and departments. But Jerne did not choose to throw in his lot with them. Why? No reasons are to be found in his letters or diary entries of the time, but he later provided a retrospective explanation: *"I didn't want to go over to them,"* he says, *"because there were already a multitude of people working on it, and who were a lot better at it. So I didn't have it to myself. And they knew much more about DNA than I did."* Better to be alone and unusual than one among the sublime multitude. "Göttingen, Royaumont: I never belonged to the group to which I belonged," he wrote in a note many years later, echoing his self-image of someone who always lived his life on the threshold, at *"an interface."*[10]

But if Muhammad would not come to the mountain, the mountain could come to Muhammad. During the fall and winter of 1951–52, Jerne began to realize that, instead of using serological methods and immunological reactions as a routine tool in bacteriophage research, he could stand the situation on its head. The rabbit-skin method he had used in his earlier studies of avidity could demonstrate antigen concentrations only between 10^9 and 10^{10} molecules/ml, so in order to follow the reaction between antigen and low-avidity antisera, he needed a method of demonstrating an excess of antigen in the lowest concentration ranges. The phage group had, by default, provided him with the method he needed, namely, the plaque assay technique. This technique, which had been worked out at the end of the 1930s, was now the most important routine tool for studying bacteriophage. It goes like this: at time t_0, phages and serum are mixed in a test tube and the inactivation of phage begins at once. Then, at various times $(t_1, t_2 \ldots t_n)$, a small sample is taken out of the reaction mixture and diluted 1/100 or more in a dilution tube to halt serum activity and thereby the inactivation. To count the number of surviving phages, a sample from the dilution tube is mixed with bacteria and soft agar and the mixture poured onto a petri dish with a layer of hard agar on the bottom. After incubation overnight, each virulent, surviving phage particle and its offspring have infected so many bacteria on the petri dish that the results can be seen as a clear round spot (a plaque) on the agar plate around the phage particle. Because the number of plaques is proportional to the number of surviving phage particles in the reaction tube, the number of phages at different time points during the inactivation can be determined.

By using the plaque assay, the inactivation of bacteriophage with antiphage serum was not only a phenomenon that could be studied just to show what "jerks" the phage researchers were but also an utterly sensitive biological assay with which Jerne could deepen his investigation of the avidity phenomenon. So he *"decided no longer to pursue these problems [serum factor, etc.] which had deviated me from my plan of looking for 'avidity,' that is, for reversibility of the attachment of antibody to phage."* By using a bacteriophage system and the plaque assay method, he could increase the sensitivity a billionfold: "every single virus particle that is not inactivated can be made to show up." The system was in principle as sensitive as a Geiger counter, which is able to detect the decay of a single atomic nucleus.[11]

In May 1952, Jerne began to inject a new horse (called 2550) with T4 phages in order to produce a hyperimmune antiphage serum that could be used as standard serum. However, he did not immediately return to the reversibility experiments; the serum from horse 2550 seems to have been literally put on ice. "Just now, I'm filled with anxiety," he confided to Maaløe at the beginning of September 1952. He drove himself hard; in the late spring he had had pneumonia, and now he had too much to do with "the terribly increased correspondence about standardization" and his serum experiments. "These days, it's completely crazy," he wrote.[12]

His stressful situation was not improved, either, by his having been "rash" enough to promise that he would take part in a WHO meeting about vaccine production, process control, and the evaluation of vaccination results in Dubrovnik in the middle of October. During the cocktail parties and dinners at the Adriatic Sea he broadened his circle of acquaintance, now paying special attention to an Indian scientist, Dhiren Lahiri, a physician from Bombay who, like Jerne, "found it nice to drink soup and beer in the 3rd class station restaurant." Lahiri took an immediate liking to Jerne, at least the "real Jerne," whom he characterized as a person who was "bubbling with humor, though serious to the core, extremely helpful though severely critical, soft and sensitive like a string galvanometer yet as hard and devastating as an atom bomb."[13]

If Lahiri had accompanied Jerne back to Copenhagen, perhaps he would have understood that Jerne's need to deviate from WHO practice by drinking beer in third-class restaurants was motivated by alienation from normal and established scientific procedures. Why not try ordinary water? Jerne had asked a year earlier when he had seen Stent and Watson stand at the bench neutralizing bacteriophages in broth. "How much dist[illed] water does a person take out of a beaker with a 0.1 ml pipette?" he now wrote in a note. He measured the weight of a beaker before and after he had taken out water with the pipette and varied his way of taking out the liquid: through dipping the pipette in at the beaker's inner wall, through dipping it in at the liquid surface, and so on. He evidently did this because he did not feel at home with the usual procedures: "*I had great difficulties in pipetting. I mean you have to dilute this fluid here one to ten, which for ordinary people poses no problem,*" he recalls. So what was the problem? "*The problem was that I was not convinced that this here really contains one milliliter, and that this thing here contains really nine milliliters, and that if I put it in there I have a dilution one to ten. . . . There must be lots of errors involved. For instance . . . shall I just let this one milliliter run out of my pipette, or shall I blow it out, or shall I perhaps suck it up a few times. It can't be the same. There must be some differences. . . . I was worried.*"[14]

This worry and insecurity—a feeling of lack of control, as it were—not only attached to pipetting but accompanied him wherever he went in the laboratory: "*So I was in terrible trouble. . . . I said, 'How can I do experiments if I can't even dilute.' . . . I was always suspicious of what we were really doing in that laboratory. . . . I said, 'What the hell are you doing?' . . . And, this is perhaps irrelevant, but it always followed me. I did not believe what they were saying unless they were clear about the manipulations they actually did.*" He declared that this insecurity followed him all through life, even when he became director of the Basel Institute for Immunology in the 1970s: "*I thought it's absolutely impossible what they are doing. . . . They told me they diluted it one to ten thousand or so, and they then injected into a frog and then and so forth, and next day they took a sample and so. And I always felt 'let's forget about it, these people don't know what they are doing.'*" When Jerne says "*these people don't know what they are doing,*" it may be interpreted as contempt for people who simply follow the norms without questioning them. That was how his Dutch girl friend Truus had understood him twenty years earlier ("He always knew better, he really knew everything, and he knew he knew better, he was aware of stupidity in other people"). But a distaste for people who do not know *"what they're doing"* can also be interpreted as an expression of cultural marginalization, insecurity, and lack of control. When fellow workers in the laboratory do not understand what sources of uncertainty exist, for example, when one is measuring with a pipette, the whole meaning of existence in the laboratory, at its very roots, is threatened.[15]

"Give me a laboratory and I will raise the world" is how Bruno Latour summarizes Pasteur's scientific strategy. The laboratory, however, is not only a workplace or a microcosm from which you can manipulate the rest of the world; it is also the setting of the sublime in science, a place where normality can sometimes yield to the greatest aesthetic experiences when experiments succeed and where the vision of a theoretical world beyond everyday reality manifests itself. On one condition, though: that you can depend on the pipettes! If not, you cannot trust the laboratory offering you contact with the sublime. Then a fantasy trip to Prospero's island is probably a better life strategy.[16]

After the vaccination meeting in Dubrovnik, Jerne traveled on to Geneva to take part in the annual meeting of the WHO Expert Committee on Biological Standardization. Such meetings had begun to be routine, and Jerne complained to Lahiri about having to "spend so much valuable time on rather dull aspects of biology." Even so it was more interesting to be in Geneva than to stay at home and standardize in Copenhagen. If nothing else, it kept him busy, and "since it is my philosophy that any action, even if in some ways deplorable, is better than no action, I have, on the whole, been quite happy," he wrote in his usual, lightly ironic style to his Indian friend.[17]

A further attraction in Geneva was the new head of the Section for Biological Standardization at WHO, E. M. Lourie, who had taken charge a few months earlier. He proposed that Jerne make an inspection tour of Southeast Asia during the following spring and summer. The League of Nations had established a number of National Control Centers several decades ago to collect and disseminate the international standards and to produce their own national standards. WHO had confirmed the list of centers but wanted to check which ones were really functioning; hence, the Expert Committee decided, in 1951, to send out inspectors to a number of national and local centers, beginning with Southeast Asia.[18]

Why did Lourie want Jerne as an envoy? Jerne himself thinks it was because he had helped Lourie *"with the solution of a problem during one of my visits to Geneva. It was a problem with standardization Lourie couldn't solve, and so I sat down and solved it in two hours and wrote it out for him."* The interpretation is not far-fetched—to evoke the admiration and trust of others by solving their intellectual problems is a recurring theme in Jerne's unprompted life's narrative. The story of how he had solved calculation problems for Johannes Ipsen, Erna Mørch, and other Danish medical scientists was part of his standard narrative repertoire, like the stories of how he helped his siblings with their lessons and his female schoolmates with their math assignments.[19]

Whatever the reason, however, Jerne faced a choice. Should he continue the reversibility experiments or accept Lourie's offer? True, he had a serum from the immunized horse 2550 in the freezer waiting to be used in the new bacteriophage system. But he did not yet know how to proceed experimentally. In addition, India, Thailand, Burma, and Indonesia enticed him with their exotic cultures; this was a unique opportunity to see an exciting part of the world, a chance he might never have again. Horse 2550 could wait. The decision in favor of Lourie was also made easier by the fact that the trip would be economically very advantageous. WHO paid a handsome, tax-free salary—a large plus, considering his appreciable accumulation of unpaid bills. So Jerne said yes, right on the spot, to Lourie's request.

When Jerne returned to Copenhagen at the end of October 1952, Maaløe had returned from his sabbatical in California. Now it was Jerne's turn to make travel plans. A few months later he claimed that he had "really not desired this trip, I am a Jutlander and it is there I want to live in years to come," but for the moment he looked forward to his Asiatic spring and summer. He hoped that the regional office in New Delhi would not overorganize his journey so that he would have some time free to study the people and to "listen to the beatings of the hearts"; he bought textbooks on Hindi and opened his next letter to Lahiri with a phrase in the language. Adda and the boys, however, were not included in his travel plans.[20]

At the end of February 1953, Jerne reported to WHO headquarters in the Palais des Nations in Geneva, where "an exasperating and confusing atmosphere" prevailed. At the Serum Institute he had become accustomed to free and brief working hours; he noticed the contrast at WHO: "You work from 8:30 a.m. to 6:00 p.m. in the Palais and get bone-tired," he reported to Maaløe. After a week's paper exercises in Geneva, he went to London to be briefed on the work of the English standardization institutions, visiting the Ministry of Agriculture and the Fisheries Veterinary Laboratory in Weybridge and spending a day at the Central Enteric Reference Laboratory and Bureau to study standardization methods and an afternoon discussing "units" with Ashley Miles at the Lister Institute. At the National Institute for Medical Research, he got the chance to talk about the phage-antiphage reaction with the deputy director, C. H. Andrewes, whose studies on the subject he had cited in the serum factor papers a year earlier. There he also met John Humphrey, "the very best man I have met here. . . . Reminds me a little of Jim [Watson], same eyes but handsomer, and with a very comprehensive store of knowledge," who "writes only seldom and has a great deal of unpublished material." Humphrey would come to be one of the leading British immunologists of the 1960s and 1970s and one of Jerne's closest scientific allies during his Basel years.[21]

The "uninterrupted stream of new people and conversations" was tiring. "Drank wine and later, in a bar, still another bottle" and "got drunk enough," Jerne wrote in his diary. Presumably the wine was not only a relaxer but also functioned as his soma in the city that symbolized so much happiness and so much pain in his life. Seventeen years earlier, he had wandered the streets of London with Tjek in his thoughts, daydreaming of having her there beside him. Right after the war, a few weeks before she took her life, he had returned to the city of his birth, this time "branded with infidelity" and with betrayal on his mind. Wandering the streets again, he likely relived these open sores in his soul. His alcohol consumption had gradually increased with the years and begun to be a part of his personality ("Jerne loved to drink," says an old scientific acquaintance). Wine, like prime numbers, was on the way to becoming a continual means of escape from his guilt and his painful memories.[22]

After yet another week in Geneva Jerne flew to New Delhi in the middle of March 1953 to begin his Southeast Asian mission. He had three working assignments: to report to the regional headquarters in New Delhi on how the centers in the region were functioning; to inform these centers of the current developments in biological standardization; and to recommend measures to improve efficiency and possible changes in the choice of national centers. He also planned to give lectures on his bacteriophage studies. During the first month in India—traveling from the edge of the Himalayas to hot and humid Calcutta—Jerne met hundreds of scientists. He became impressed with the level of research there and concluded that biological standardization in India was "quite on the level of an average European country"; at the same time he noted the widespread "administrative frenzy" that far exceeded anything he had previously encountered. Life outside the laboratory and the administrative offices also made a mixed impression on him. In one of his letters to Maaløe, he described India as "Americanized": the middle class talked only of money, and far too many were enthralled by "fountains with colored lights." Meanwhile, he romanticized the poor population as "the last rampart of the culture." Although Calcutta's streets were full of "millions of gaunt, starving, miserable beggars who sleep in rows on all the sidewalks," at the same time he thought the poor had "much inborn culture, handsome features, and a gracefulness and dignity of bearing."[23]

He continued to Burma for ten days. The inspections were not encouraging, because the laboratories were still suffering the aftereffects of the Japanese Occupation: equipment had been wrecked or stolen, the libraries had been plundered. There were hardly any trained laboratory workers. As if in compensation, the people on the streets were "cheerful and seem happy." Perhaps, he thought, science was not the source of happiness here on earth. Then on to Thailand, where the standardization situation was somewhat better, with regard to both production and regulation, but he was struck by the fact that, in spite of good laboratory equipment, there was an extreme lack of experienced doctors and assistants. Thailand is "more itself" than India, he thought, "but gives an impression of infinite weakness in its skeleton." In Bangkok Jerne found mail from home waiting for him. Adda missed him, Donald missed him, and the staff of the Standardization Department missed him "so terribly," the secretary declared, "that some of us, on this day of sorrow, have descended to (borrowing your style of expression) peeing in our pants." From Maaløe he also received the big scientific news of the spring, "Jim's and Francis Crick's DNA structural model, that has been inspected and, apparently, fully accepted by the highest authorities, including [Linus] Pauling." The diary gives no hint, however, of what thoughts Jerne might have had about the "situation in Cambridge."[24]

In Indonesia, he gave lectures on the fundamentals of biological standardization at the famous Eijkman Institute in Djakarta. He was almost on home ground in this country. In his youth he had gained a certain insight into Dutch colonial culture through Multatuli's *Max Havelaar,* and even if most Dutch had left the country after the declaration of independence in 1949, the European influence was still evident: he was much more comfortable in Djakarta than in Rangoon and Bangkok. He traveled on to the veterinary research institute in Bogor, the public health institute in Jogjakarta, and the Pasteur Institute in Bandung, all of which lacked competent workers, as in Burma and Thailand, though there existed an urgent desire on the part of the public health authorities to better the situation with the help of WHO.

After another three weeks, Jerne left Indonesia, made a week's side tour to Colombo, Ceylon (now Sri Lanka), and then returned to India. The Pasteur Institute of Southern India, in Coonoor, became one of the high points of the trip. Up in the clear mountain air he found the best fruits of the British imperial era: well-equipped laboratories with great quantities of experimental animals maintained under first-class conditions and, not least, an attentive and well-trained staff who appreciated his views. He gave a lecture on bacteriophage, with "animated discussion" afterward, and was invited to a reception given by the governor of Madras. He could imagine making his home there! Perhaps WHO could establish a regional center in Coonoor, to which all countries concerned could send substances for testing, he wrote to Lourie. And if someone was needed to direct such a center for several years, well, Jerne would "consider the job." Presumably it was only the impulse of the moment, but it is nevertheless tempting to interpret his proposal for a regional standardization center in the southern Indian mountains as another symptom of the old need to escape; as a new and more international variant of the old dream of sitting and playing chess and discussing Shakespeare with the local tax inspector.[25]

Jerne's joy over the Indian mountain paradise did not last long. The itinerary took him to Bombay, where he spent several days at the Haffkine Institute, the largest bacteriological and serological institute of the subcontinent, and thereafter back to New Delhi, where he spent a couple of days collecting his impressions. The professional exchange of his trip had been almost nil. Of course he had given some lectures, but from a scientific standpoint he had "not experienced anything." He had not truly been able to engage himself in the work, he explained to Ørskov; he thought he sensed "a hint of humbug" in the whole project. Life was "too short to occupy oneself with such things too long without being injured by it." But what he wouldn't do for "those golden shekels"![26]

A couple of days later, in August 1953, Jerne stopped over in Rome. "Europe again how beautiful here Rome is paradise" he telegraphed home. Later, he repeated that his "greatest experience" of the trip was to step off the plane from Delhi. "O brave Old World, I mean Europe, it was like coming from some highly viscous liquid into a crystalline thing containing individual discrete persons interacting like music." His European identity became, from then on, an increasingly prominent feature of his persona.[27]

14   *"I Suppose I Should Do Something, Maybe an Experiment or Something"*

*L*ate in the summer of 1953, while Jerne was on his way home to the "brave Old World," a new research fellow arrived in the Standardization Department from the new world. Twenty-two-year-old Karl Gordon Lark had just completed his Ph.D. with one of America's leading immunologists, Alwin Pappenheimer, at New York University. A couple of years earlier Lark had attended the bacteriophage course at Cold Spring Harbor Laboratory and had met Ole Maaløe, who had told him that Copenhagen was a nice place to spend a couple of years if one had a Rockefeller fellowship in one's pocket.

Lark arrived at an auspicious time. Maaløe had left his studies of bacteriophage in favor of the host cell and, inspired by recently published studies of phases in the division of eukaryotic cells, had decided to explore the synthesis of DNA during the division of bacterial cells, something that required access to a bacterial colony in which all the cells divided synchronously. Here, Lark could help. After a few attempts, they succeeded in synchronizing the culture by subjecting it to rapid temperature changes, thereby laying the methodological foundation for the so-called Copenhagen school of bacterial physiology.[1]

The new fellow remembers the department as "very nice," "wonderfully comfortable," and "very informal." He also remembers that one of the recurrent subjects of conversation was Jerne, or Taj, as he was still called among his friends and close colleagues: "They all kept talking about Taj. That was really interesting, I mean, they would say: 'Oh, wait until you meet Taj.'" Lark also has a clear and lively recollection of the day, at the beginning of September, when Jerne returned after his Asian tour: "And so, one day I was doing something in the lab and there were these screams from the women in front of the lab and Taj walked in and everybody was almost prostrate . . . you know, lying there in front of him. I mean he was really loved, I mean he was adored, it was not that he was just liked. . . . Ole Rostock sort of stood next to him, sort of hovering. . . . I mean you could see . . . deep, deep affection . . . a feeling not of fear, not of respect, although a lot of respect, but of real love. And, you know, you feel there's an ambience, you feel it right away. And Ole came in and took out his cigar and . . . tried to keep somewhat detached . . . with Taj." Lark remembers being swept off his feet at once by the returning Jerne. His portrait supports the statements of many contemporary witnesses: "Taj was irresistible, his charm was unbelievable. Just as a person, you wanted him to like you, desperately. I mean he had that kind of impact. . . . The trouble with Taj is that he . . . has that young boyish aspect, so appealing. . . . One just gets sucked into Taj, 'do with me what you will' . . . and I see him and I see his charm. When he smiles everything in the world is just wonderful." When Jerne came up the stairs to the department in the morning he "made them all feel that, you know, Taj has come to spend the day with his family." He liked to open a bottle of wine late in the afternoon; and if it was a good wine he liked to share it, not necessarily with the person he knew best "but with the person who would most appreciate the wine" and afterward he often went out to have a drink in town. Lark's impression was that Jerne drank "an inordinate amount, all the time."

It was Jerne's intellect, however, that fascinated Lark the most. Never before (or since), he declares, had he met such an "intellectual giant"; it felt like "one of God's gifts." You could go into Jerne's little room, and "whenever one talked [with] him about any problem that one had, he would always sort of penetrate all the foolishness and ask a few, very precise, analytical questions," though the tone was "always friendly." Lark remembers that one of Jerne's favorite conversational subjects was the relationship between science and art—"he used to talk endlessly at the lab about how science was all nonsense, that painting is the real thing"—and he also remembers how Jerne returned again and again to "how Kierkegaard was the most important thing for him." Lark did not really understand what that meant, but drew the conclusion that "he certainly was very much in earnest about [it]." The young American also admired Jerne's special unsnobbish sort of elitism, which became apparent in his critical attitude.

Jerne could be "very crushing," but his criticism was always delivered in "a somewhat endearing way," which was reflected in his humor. As Lark saw it, Jerne combined this elitism with an interest in what was going on inside other people: "he loves gossip, he just loves it, and . . . it contributes to his charm tremendously."

Yet, as Lark came to know Jerne a little better, he became aware that this charm entailed a risk. It was as if the intellect was detached from the rest of the man. He realized that Jerne could easily seduce and manipulate other people with his social talents and thereby make life into "one social conquest after another." The interest in people and their doings and sayings could sometimes be replaced by indifference: "Taj would get very thoughtful and very strange" and at times did not seem "to really care for people"; they became "like objects to him." This indifference applied, Lark thought, even to his relationship with Ivar and Donald: "it was as if he was very distant from the kids, I mean, there is no way I could talk about his two sons as being real sons to him." And sometimes, at parties—fantastic parties with "lots of wine and lots of laughing and talking about everything"—Jerne could suddenly become "very depressed and disappear." He always wanted to be alone when he was feeling low.[2]

When his first fascination had subsided, Lark also began to be interested in the content of Jerne's scientific work. "Oh, he works on avidity," Maaløe is supposed to have replied. The laconic answer suggests that Jerne's previously announced plans to return to immunology and the avidity problem after his two-year excursion into the salt and serum effects were serious. The statistical calculations that had occupied him for so many years were on their way out of his life now. He was no longer passionate about finding defects and uncertainties in the treatment of experimental data. He took no part in the Third International Biometrical Conference in Italy in September, nor did he attend meetings of the Scandinavian-Dutch section of the Biometric Society or run for reelection to its board.

Jerne's loss of interest in statistics may have been strengthened by the nonchalant attitude often taken by the bacteriophage scientists toward statistical treatment of experimental results. He felt they did not regard statistics as an especially *"esteemed activity"* and remembered once criticizing Delbrück for his sloppy use of statistics. The answer had *"deeply affected"* him: Delbrück had in fact declared that he treated his data statistically *"because some people had recommended this"* and that he thought statistical methods were *"boring and unin-*

teresting." Jerne remembers that his *"own thought gradually drifted in the same direction"* and concludes that *"all this mathematical and statistical stuff, it still doesn't solve these fundamental problems of antibody formation."* Thus Max Delbrück gradually replaced R. A. Fisher as Jerne's scientific role model.[3]

As with biometrics and statistics, the standardization problem was no longer a source of intellectual satisfaction either. Now standardization simply meant routine tasks. Jerne spent all of September and October 1953 on more or less tedious issues, and in the middle of October he and Maaløe drove to Geneva in Lark's big American car to prepare for the annual session of the WHO Expert Committee on Biological Standardization. Among other matters discussed at the meeting was his travel report from Southeast Asia, which was positively received and was entered in the minutes. But his proposal for a regional control center was rejected. So Jerne's dream of moving to Nilgiri Hills—if it had been serious—went up in smoke.

The two returned to Copenhagen in the beginning of November. Lark remembers that Jerne was a little hesitant about getting started in the laboratory after his nearly year-long hiatus from experimental work and that he lay smoking on the couch in his little office, "sometimes for three, four hours during the day." Now and then he went into the laboratory and said, "'Aha, we should be doing something, I suppose . . . I suppose I should do something, maybe an experiment or something, but, you know, what should I do?' And didn't do anything for a while and he would come in every day." The few extant laboratory notebooks from this period show that he did do a couple of experiments, injecting phage into rabbits to follow the development of the early immune response in vivo. He could not "foresee any interesting developments," however, and never published the results.[4]

Immediately after New Year 1954, Providence acted again by sending a newly graduated Italian microbiologist into Jerne's scientific life. Perla Avegno had received a fellowship to work with Maaløe for six months, but her letter of introduction had been delayed, so she arrived unannounced in the department at the beginning of January "as a surprise" to everyone. Because Maaløe had plenty to do with his own and Lark's work, he could not or would not take care of her, so Jerne, who otherwise had no laboratory help (Rostock was wholly occupied with Maaløe's synchronization experiments), was offered an assistant. Avegno's arrival seems to have broken the spell. "Reluctantly," Jerne turned back to "antiphage serum and plaque-counting," and Lark, for the first time, had the chance to witness Jerne as an experimenter: "Rostock used to go home by four,

four-thirty, and at four o'clock, Taj would suddenly jump off the [couch and say] 'Let's do an experiment.'"[5]

But what kind of experiment? During his salt- and serum-factor studies two years earlier, Jerne had realized that a bacteriophage-plaque assay system allowed the measurement of such low antigen concentrations that the phage-antiphage reaction could be followed in the lowest concentration range, thereby enabling one to chart the course of immunization from the start. His observation, in 1951, that the inactivation curve bent off at the end of the reaction had indicated that the phage-antiphage reaction is reversible (even though the phage scientists asserted the contrary), and during his short visit to London in the spring he had briefly discussed that possibility with C. H. Andrewes, who, twenty years before, had observed that "phage, which has been completely coated by antiserum may be reactivated by dilution." But all this was indirect evidence; during his experiments in 1951–52 Jerne had not been able to give any hardcore evidence for reversibility.[6]

Therefore he now planned, with the help of Perla Avegno, to prove the reversibility of the phage-antiphage reaction. "At the beginning, Jerne wrote the protocols and worked with me at the bench," Avegno remembers, but "after a while I was able to do it by myself and Jerne supervised the results and discussed with me the next experiment." Jerne was not enthusiastic, however, about her accuracy in the lab, not fully trusting her dilutions, "since she does not take a sufficiently serious interest in choosing the correct size pipettes." But he otherwise liked his "little signorina" who fluttered around the laboratory "like a butterfly" and taught him to appreciate Italian baroque music; she also tried to teach him Italian by reading Dante, but he got no further than the "first page."[7]

The old trotter produced the requisite raw material. Two years before, horse 2550 had produced 8-day serum of very low avidity, so low that days went by before the reaction was completed, and now, after having been pumped for three months with T4 phages, it provided large quantities of a hyperimmune, 120-day serum of high avidity, suitable for use as a standard serum reference. In the first experiment, in mid-January, a 1/2500 dilution of 120-day serum was mixed with 10^{10} T4/ml. In barely one hour, the number had declined to about 2×10^5 T4/ml. If the neutralization mixture was heated to 65°C for five minutes (thereby shifting an assumed equilibrium reaction in the direction of antigen and antiserum), the number of plaque-forming phages increased five to ten times. The results suggested that a thoroughgoing reactivation of phages took place, primarily in low-avidity neutralization mixtures, but to some extent even in hyperimmune serum. So "what sort of 'survivors' are we counting on the plates if reactivation comes so easily?" he wrote to Stent. True, there were no signs of reactivation at 37°C, the temperature at which neutralization was usually carried out. But since reactivation occurred at 65°C, "perhaps things happen in the 45° agar or on the plates," that is to say, at the temperature people were using to make agar flow easily into the petri dish. Without a doubt this was "a little disturbing" for the well-tried plaque assay technique.[8]

The initial experiments had shown that what happened from the moment one took a sample out of the reaction mixture to the moment when plaques began to form in the petri dish was crucial to solving the phage-antiphage reaction problem. But how would he be able to follow the progress of reactivation? The plaque assay technique did not distinguish between reactivated phages and noninactivated ones; one could merely see the final outcome, not study the reactivation at any given point. If one looked only for surviving phages, one saw nothing, he wrote later, paraphrasing Kierkegaard: "just as a picture of the Red Sea won't show you the Jews that got over nor the Egyptians that were drowned."[9]

The lack of any laboratory notes for the two first weeks of February 1954 suggests that Jerne was thinking out the solution to this problem. Avegno remembers that he was "in a sort of 'contemplative' state" and did not wish to be disturbed. But in mid-February he hit upon a solution. He inserted two extra steps in the usual plaque assay procedure: first, the sample from the dilution vessel was mixed with bacteria in a "decision tube"; hence the particles that had fastened onto an antibody molecule but had not yet been inactivated got a chance to infect a bacterium. Then, after ten minutes (that is, before a new generation of phages had time to form), a concentrated serum of high avidity was added, incapacitating all surviving free phages. The phages that had "decided" to infect a bacteria were, on the contrary, unaffected and could give rise to plaques.[10]

The results of this "indirect plating," as Jerne called it, were dramatic. It turned out that the inactivation curve for the reaction between T4 and early anti-T4 serum was significantly steeper when he used the indirect method in place of the normal method. Since the indirect method reduced the number of plaques by only 10 to 20 percent compared with the standard method ("direct plating"), he assumed that the higher number of phage particles in direct plating mainly depended on reactivation. "These are, as you will see, very solid effects," he wrote to Stent, "and excellently reproducible."[11]

For the rest of the winter and spring of 1954, Jerne and Avegno carried out almost daily experiments under various conditions to determine the reaction constants and their dependence on salt concentration and temperature. At the end of February something unexpected happened that would soon prove to be important. So far, they had used *undiluted* 8-day serum to get any inactivation. If they added *diluted* 8-day serum, no activation took place. But this diluted 8-day serum proved to have another effect: the addition of tryptophane to the medium was no longer required for the phages to remain active and able to infect bacteria (the T4 strain with which all their experiments were carried out required the presence of small quantities of the amino acid tryptophane to become adsorbed to and attack bacterial walls). "Anti-T4 serum, in dilutions that do not cause observable inactivation, can stabilize the tryptophane-activated state of T4," Jerne wrote later.[12]

Where did Jerne get the idea of trying a tryptophane-free medium in the dilution vessel? Even though the answer is not found in the extant laboratory notes, it is easy to imagine that he systematically varied experimental conditions using the diluted 8-day serum. He might have used a tryptophane-free medium by mistake, but it is more probable that he introduced it as a control: without tryptophane in the decision tube, the phage particles ought to remain inactive and therefore constitute a control experiment. This interpretation is strengthened by a letter to Stent in which Jerne writes that "if the washed fresh bacterial B/1 culture is resuspended in saline (no tryptophane) free phage controls can no longer adsorb, but 'inactivated' T4 can!" (When, forty years later, I confronted him with the problem, he studied the laboratory protocols and concluded: "*I must have said, 'Let's have a control without tryptophane.'*") Whether control or mistake, the natural conclusion was that a factor in the 8-day serum can stabilize phage in an active stage—a "P-star" stage, as Jerne called it—without the presence of tryptophane.[13]

Soon after the unexpected discovery of the P-star effect, and while continuing with detailed studies of the kinetics of the reactivation, Jerne once again was faced with a choice of futures. In the middle of March, he received the offer of a contract position as Lourie's closest associate in WHO's Section of Biological Standardization in Geneva. Then, a few days later, when Delbrück arrived in Copenhagen for one of his irregular visits with Niels Bohr, he invited Jerne on the spot to go to Cal Tech for a year. Within the space of a few days, Jerne faced a decision "between the desk and the lab."[14]

Geneva was surely attractive from a financial standpoint. Jerne was still energetically living beyond his means; in the winter of 1954 he was forced to take out a bank loan to catch up with his debts. He did not complain—"it is probably reasonable that those who work every day with money get hold of more of it than those who fill their time with virus particles and molecules, from which nobody makes a direct profit"—but he had nothing against a monetary injection, either. To say yes to Lourie, "a respectable salary, and the association with a number of very nice people" was tempting. Jerne consequently expressed a strong inclination to accept Lourie's offer but nonetheless asked that he be allowed to postpone his decision till after the approaching phage meeting in Göttingen.[15]

Delbrück's offer of a year's stay in California, on the other hand, would bring him into the center of international biomedical science. Again, he expressed a certain anxiety. True, working in the laboratory gave him "the pleasures of designing your own experiments," he explained to Lourie, but he was also all too well aware of the difficulties involved, of "the depressions" that came "because [the experiments] won't come off" and "everything is more complicated than you hoped." Science involves "continuous speculations" and concentration on a problem "to the exclusion of everything else"; research meant an existence in which "you are neglecting life with your family," often while knowing you probably "are not much good as a scientist after all." Was it really worth it, he added, "the writing and rewriting of papers" that "will be little read and forgotten in less than 20 years"? Maybe it was just an attempt to excuse himself to Lourie, or maybe just one of his affectations, but his uncertainty about the Cal Tech position reminds us of his earlier doubts about a career in science. His anxiety was surely not allayed by Delbrück's opinion that the latest results with the P-star effect were "a big mess" and that the earlier salt- and serum-factor experiments were more interesting.[16]

Delbrück's reaction "disencouraged" Jerne "a little." He suspected that the experimental results could have "some consequences," but he was uncertain what they were, nor did he know how to proceed with either the reversibility experiments or the P-star effect. "Serum is and always was a big mess," he wrote to Stent, echoing Delbrück, "I sometimes wish I never were mixed up into it." Nevertheless he immediately applied for a Rockefeller travel stipend. Despite Delbrück's support, however, the foundation was not forthcoming. "I am not fond of begging anybody for support," Jerne responded, informing Delbrück that he should not make too great an effort for his sake: "I am thankful for what you have done already, and the phage-antiphage reaction will manage to remain a mystery even without my interference." This may have expressed a sincere uncertainty, but it is natural to suspect that Jerne wanted to assure himself that Delbrück was in earnest. Sure enough, his reply did not suit Delbrück, who obviously thought Jerne was too concerned for his economic security and too little concerned for science. "I won't take 'NO' for an answer, and you should not either," Delbrück wrote back; "the problem is not where you get a little more money, but that you have made a first rate discovery which is only half out of the bag and if you drop it now, nobody may pick it up." For the time being he asked Jerne to "hold your horses, please."[17]

At the small phage meeting (attended by only seventeen people, including Jerne, Maaløe, and Lark) in Göttingen in the middle of June 1954, Jerne presented for the first time the results of the spring's experiments with P-star kinetics done with Perla Avegno. He remembers *"clearly"* his talk because he felt *"so happy that Delbrück was much impressed"* and because he was *"gratified by the attention that Delbrück devoted to this story"*—in fact, when looking back on his life in science, he thought that these reversibility and P-star experiments in the spring of 1954 were *"the most beautiful experiments I have ever done."* It also turned out that Delbrück had managed to get some extra money from the National Foundation for Infantile Paralysis to offer Jerne a year's postdoctoral fellowship. "This, I cannot resist," Jerne wrote to Lourie, continuing: "I think I am doing the right thing in continuing my basic research while I still have the enthusiasm, and drive (at times), and hope to contribute something useful along this line. . . . I feel now that I must continue for a while—in a less remunerative sphere—my struggle with some research problems which, though restricted in scope, are a great challenge." Jerne's choice of American laboratory science over a desk at WHO prompted Lourie to express his doubts that Jerne would ever return to Europe: "he may be swallowed up permanently in the USA, once he gets there." Many European scientists had stayed on; after all, it was there, as Jerne had earlier pointed out, that "everything" was going on.[18]

Before returning to Italy in late June 1954, Perla Avegno finished the last details of the P-star kinetics, while Jerne proceeded on his own with his "first-rate discovery." What was the factor in 8-day serum that enabled it to stabilize tryptophane-dependent T4 phages in a tryptophane-independent condition? Even in the early stages of the P-star experiment series, he seems to have suspected that a specific antibody was involved, for he designated the presumed factor as "A" and wrote to Stent that P-stars are formed only after "contact with antiphage." He was also able to show that in an electrophoretic field the factor migrated with the gamma globulin fraction (that is, the fraction of serum proteins that contains antibody activity), a result that further supported his suspicion.[19]

It was not self-evident that he was dealing with an antibody, however. In

Silhouette of Niels Jerne done in the Tivoli Gardens, 1954. In the spring and summer of that year Jerne worked intensively with the P-star phenomenon. (Medical History Museum, University of Copenhagen. Silhouette: Inger Eidem)

serological and immunological usage, the term *antibody* was used for a subclass of gamma globulins detectable after the organism had been subjected to foreign substances ("antigens") and capable of binding to them and possibly of inactivating them. The existence of antibodies was therefore connected with defense against intruding exogenous substances; by definition, antibodies were "anti" what came from outside. The anti-T4 antibody (which Jerne called antibody "B") was a typical antibody, since it inactivated T4. But Jerne's A-factor did not seem to be inactivating; on the contrary, it took part in stabilizing T4 in active form. Truly a peculiar kind of antibody.

However, the fact that the A-factor was pro instead of anti did not keep Jerne from thinking of it as an antibody. Here his earlier chemical and serological training—the fact that for many years he had accustomed himself to thinking of the antigen-antibody reaction in pure chemical terms—paradoxically came to be pivotal for what would soon become his seminal contribution to a biological (Darwinian) understanding of antibody production. In Jerne's view, an antibody was quite simply a molecule that exhibits a specific chemical affinity for another molecule that is called an antigen. In other words, in spite of his burgeoning immunobiological orientation, he rejected the traditional biological defense criterion of what constitutes an antibody—he thought in biomechanical, not bioteleological, terms. Hence, even though it could be demonstrated that the factor was part of the gamma globulin fraction in electrophoresis, it was by no means obvious to him that the factor was a conventional defense antibody.

This reasoning made it decisively important for him to demonstrate that the A-factor bound specifically to the particular kind of phage. Accordingly, two weeks after his return from Göttingen, Jerne immunized a new horse with a strong dose of T4 phages. Daily blood samples showed a steep increase in the P-star forming factor during the early course of immunization, suggesting that the serum factor did in fact consist of specific antibodies "because they appear in large numbers in serum only after specific immunization of the animal with

T4 phage," as he wrote in the published paper a year later. Retrospectively, he emphasizes as a *"most important point"* that the P-star forming serum factor *"multiplied a thousandfold . . . immediately upon immunization"* and that *"they were not* the ordinary well-known T4-*in*activating antibodies!!" He "made *very sure"* that the P-star-inducing property of these early sera "was the property of an anti-T4 antibody."[20]

To have identified a specific factor in early serum that, chemically and physiologically, behaved like an antibody, but in its action increased the antigen's effect, was surprising in itself. But even more surprising was another discovery, namely, that the presence of antibody A, in small quantities, could be detected in the horse even *before* it had been immunized, even if in low concentrations, of the order of 10^{-6}–10^{-8}. The occurrence of an antibody in normal serum "deeply impressed me," Jerne recollected. Lark, too, remembers clearly when Jerne found antibody activity in normal serum: "The most surprising thing was that there was absolutely specific antibody activity in the normal serum. . . . He said: 'it's got activity,' and he disappeared, and two or three days later, working with Perla Avegno, he said: 'it looks like the activity is specific.'" The concentration of antibody A in normal serum sank by half twenty-four hours after immunization, which Jerne interpreted as the adsorption to the injected T4 particles of the normally occurring antibodies. On the second day the content of antibody A rose again to the original concentration and then continued to rise quickly thereafter. Beginning on the fourth day, he could detect traces of the normal anti-T4 activity (antibody B), and on the seventh day the antibody B activity was so high that it masked the occurrence of antibody A.[21]

It was possible to draw two entirely different conclusions from this experiment. One, as Jerne wrote a year later when summarizing the experiments in print, was that "practically all normal animals have been exposed to and have responded to T4 antigen." The other was that the antibodies are *spontaneously* produced in small quantities. The first conclusion was natural, inasmuch as T4 is a commonly occurring virus on a commonly occurring intestinal bacterium (on an earlier occasion, the closely related bacteriophage T1 had contaminated the whole laboratory). This conclusion "cannot be disproven," Jerne continued, "but [I] prefer the hypothesis of spontaneous production," meaning that, in normal serum, gamma globulin molecules are spontaneously produced that by chance happen to have a specific A-type configuration. The latter interpretation immediately became one of the most important prerequisites for formulating his selection theory of antibody formation.[22]

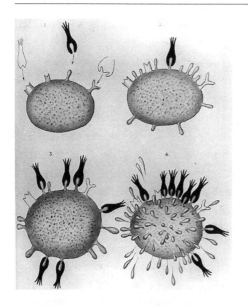

Schematic representation of Paul Ehrlich's side-chain theory, 1900. (Ehrlich, "On immunity," 1900. Library of the Royal Society of London)

On 1 July 1954, right after having immunized the new horse in order to follow the increase of antibody A activity during the early course of immunization, Jerne wrote to Stent, summing up the experiments of that spring and summer. "Only if some of this could lead to an attack on antibody production there would be something . . . of central importance," he declared.[23]

This is the first time the question of antibody formation turns up in Jerne's notes since his having touched on it in his dissertation manuscript in spring 1950. But it was certainly not the first time in history. The formation of antibodies had been the central and classical problem of immunology for more than sixty years. After the discovery by Emil Behring and Shibasaburo Kitasato that the injection of diphtheria toxin leads to the formation of a specific diphtheria antitoxin in serum, Paul Ehrlich had proposed, in 1897, that all the cells in the body carry preformed molecular groups, so-called side-chains (Seitenketten, that is, what today would be called receptors), that were assumed to play a part in the adsorption of specific nutritional substances. Ehrlich further assumed that certain foreign substances, such as toxins, resembled nutrient molecules and therefore could be recognized by these specific side-chains. Under the influence of the toxin, the cell would produce an excess of side-chains, which were then released in the form of specific antibodies, which neutralized the toxin. Thus immune defense was, Ehrlich thought, a secondary function of nutrition.[24]

Ehrlich's side-chain theory was a first attempt to explain the formation of antibodies. After Karl Landsteiner's experiments with synthetic haptens (a hapten is a small molecule coupled to a large molecule, such as a protein, that changes the specific antigenic properties of the protein), started in 1914 and continuing in the 1920s and 1930s, it was generally concluded that almost any foreign substance could constitute an antigen against which the organism could produce specific antibodies. It was therefore considered unlikely that the cells of the body could carry the nearly infinite number of preformed specific side-chains that would be needed. As a result, Ehrlich's theory fell into disrepute. Chemists like Jerome Alexander, Stuart Mudd, and Felix Haurowitz proposed instead that the specificity of antibodies was determined by the intruding antigen, which was assumed to act as a template for the formation of complementary antibody structures. From the middle of the 1930s, the template theory (later coined "instruction theory" by Joshua Lederberg) was completely dominant among serologists and immunologists. The last and, for its time, most sophisticated variant of the template-instruction theory was put forward by Linus Pauling in 1940. According to him, specific antibodies were formed when normal, unspecific globulin molecules that had not yet received their final configuration wrapped around antigen molecules and so took on a specific complementary tertiary structure.[25]

Two or three weeks after having observed specific antibody activity in normal serum, Jerne formulated his alternative to the template-instruction theory of antibody formation. The first extant draft, a single page of stationery dated 9 August 1954, includes the following five basic propositions:

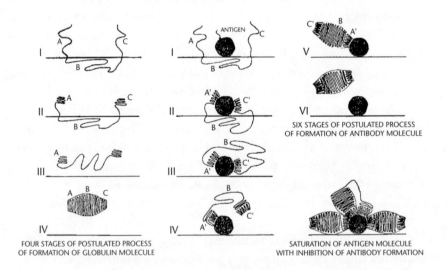

Schematic representation of Linus Pauling's theory of antibody formation, 1940. (Pauling, "A theory," 1940. © The American Chemical Society)

1. Globulin molecules exist in normal serum in a variety of configurations of the amino acid chain.
2. One or several of these configurations fit, by chance, a given antigen.
3. The antigen, therefore, after injection into the organism *selects* such globulin molecules, and transports these molecules to the cell in which these molecules are prepared for multiplication.
4. In the antibody producing cell the antigen need not enter: the selected molecules are there reproduced, perhaps via a nucleic acid translation.
5. The configuration reproduced contains the selected "site" and a random stretch. Among the reproductions there can therefore appear better fitting molecules.

He also sketched some arguments for the theory; first and foremost that it was "nice that the 'foreign' antigen" does not participate in the production of antibodies but "is only need[ed] for selection" of already existing antibodies.

Within a decade, this theory—especially the modified version proposed by Macfarlane Burnet three years later—would eventually come to revolutionize immunology and form the basis for Jerne's career as the discipline's leading theoretician. At the moment, however, he kept it to himself. He said nothing to anyone, neither Maaløe, nor Lark. Instead he laid the draft in a desk drawer in his office—as a kind of "testament" addressed to Maaløe and Delbrück, his two most important scientific mentors and also his would-be scientific executors, in case he should die before he had time to publish the idea.[26]

Looking back, ten years later, in an article that has become a classic in the repertoire of modern eureka stories (published in the famous 1966 Festschrift to Delbrück), Jerne claimed that the selection theory was revealed to him in a brief moment of insight. The idea "occurred to me one evening . . . as I was walking home in Copenhagen from the Danish State Serum Institute to Amaliegade," he wrote. It took around twenty minutes to stroll through the Christianshavn district, and "the framework of the theory was complete" before he "had passed the Knippel Bridge." He remembers *"clearly"* that he came into the laboratory on the day after and declared that he had had *"a marvelous new idea about the mechanism of antibody formation."* He also remembers that he did not want to tell them immediately; he first wanted to *"think it over more carefully in my own mind."* He decided to "let it mature" a while: *"I thought I wanted to wait and describe it to that fellow Delbrück, he was so intelligent, so with him I ought to be able to discuss the matter."*[27]

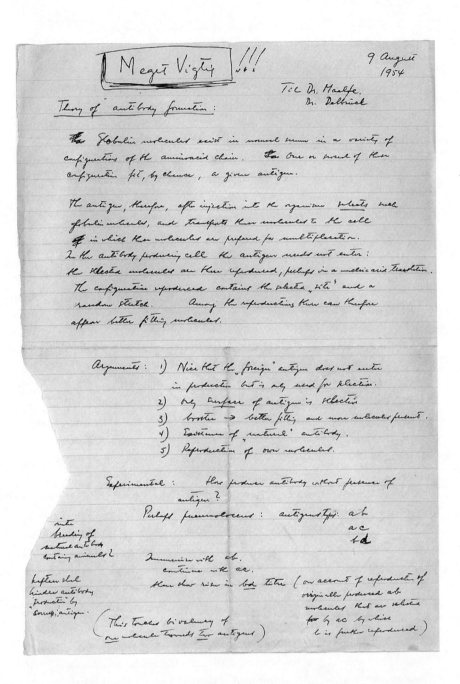

The first outline of the natural selection theory of antibody formation. Niels Jerne called it his "testament" and headed it "Very Important !!!" (Jerne Collection, The Royal Library, Copenhagen)

Unfortunately, no contemporaneous notes tell us when or how the construction of the selection theory took place. In fact, the dating in itself is problematical. In his retrospective eureka account, Jerne wrote that he came up with the theory "in March 1954." But the first extant sketch in the archive—the one that went into the drawer—is dated 9 August. Is it possible that Jerne had already arrived at the selection theory in March, without the idea leaving the least trace in the files until five months later? Or is the sketch misdated? Or is his eureka story incorrect? The answer is not a matter of indifference—if the theory was formulated as early as March, it may have guided his experimental series during the spring; but if the theory was first formulated during the summer, this suggests that data from the P-star experiments were instrumental. Dating the construction of the selection theory therefore has consequences for the perennial philosophical discussion of whether experimental data are guided by theory, or scientific theories are data-driven.[28]

Confronted with the dating problem, Jerne said he was absolutely sure that he had made an error concerning March and that he was quite sure that he hit upon the idea at the end of July *"or maybe even one of the first days of August, 1954.... By that time I had finished the P-star experiments (with Perla) and was occupied with the final arrangements for my trip [to Cal Tech]."* There are several good reasons to think that Jerne's revised date (that is, summer of 1954) is correct. First, as mentioned, there are no contemporary items in the archive that suggest that the idea came to him in March. Second, and more important, in our discussions Jerne admitted that he consciously antedated the event in the Festschrift article so that no one would suspect that he had been inspired by Delbrück or anybody else at Cal Tech and hence that he might not have been the sole and independent constructor of the selection theory: *"I was writing this in Pittsburgh, for the 'Max Delbrück Festschrift.' This was ten years after the 'event,' and all my old papers I had left in Europe. I now think that my objective was to emphasize, that the idea of the natural selection theory did not arise during my stay in Delbrück's department at Caltech, but in Copenhagen before I left for the USA."* Jerne concludes that *"all this speaks against March"* and gives a couple of other good reasons why the events took place in the summer of 1954: *"Moreover, I walked home from the Institute, which (knowing me as well as you do) I would not have done in the Danish March weather. Also, I would not have been able to keep the idea secret from Maaløe and Lark during March, April, May, June and July, but would obviously have discussed it with them. Therefore it must have been shortly before my departure."*[29]

So Jerne knew that he had come up with the selection theory before his departure to the United States, but his contemporaries did not. They knew, on the other hand, that he had spent a year with Delbrück at Cal Tech before the theory was published, and they knew that it was Delbrück who had communicated the paper to the *Proceedings of the National Academy of Sciences.* So it is easy to imagine that Jerne, ten years later, when he began to be famous for his selection theory, and when he sat down to write about its conception for the Delbrück Festschrift, may have thought it necessary to forestall any possible rumors disparaging his originality. A slight antedating was all that was required.

Parabasis

The Selection Theory
as a Personal Confession

It has gradually become clear to me what every great philosophy up till now has consisted of—namely, the confession of its originator, and a species of involuntary and unconscious auto-biography.

—Nietzsche, *Beyond Good and Evil*

There is no reason to disbelieve that Niels Jerne had a eureka experience as he crossed the Knippel Bridge in Copenhagen one afternoon in the summer of 1954. But among historians of science the belief is widely held that eureka experiences, on closer inspection, are the result of complex and extended cognitive and cultural processes. I therefore wish to take time out from the narrative to analyze more systematically the background of the selection theory. Which theoretical traditions and cognitive resources did Jerne draw on? What role did his own experimental findings play? And is knowledge about the scientific and intellectual context and his own experimental practice all that is needed to give a satisfactory understanding of why he became the theory's "onlie begetter," as Burnet later called him, with a nod to his favorite poet? Or do we also need to have recourse to the begetter's personal life-story, his emotionally colored worldview and life experience? In other words: Was there also a personal context for the selection theory?[1]

The Theoretical Tradition in Immunology

There were a number of common intellectual prerequisites for Jerne's selection theory of antibody formation. One was the prevailing tradition of template-instruction theories already referred to. Jerne had read the first edition of Boyd's *Fundamentals of Immunology* (1943), which devoted a couple of pages to theories of antibody formation, and Johannes Ipsen recalls that he gave Jerne a photostat of Pauling's paper to read during the war; Jerne says that *"from the very beginning"* he found it *"laughable,"* even "extremely distasteful." Hans Noll remembers that Pauling's paper lay on Jerne's desk when he visited the department in 1949 and that Jerne discussed the theory with Maaløe: "What I remember distinctly is that he was questioning this [theory]. . . . I have a clear recollection that he disagreed." In one of our conversations Jerne said that by the late 1940s he was musing over the question *"How the hell are they made, these antibodies?"*[2]

It was not only Jerne who disagreed with the template-instruction theories, including Pauling's latest version of them. "I think most people knew that [they] didn't fit the facts," asserts Lark, who had a good overview of the American immunological theater in the beginning of the 1950s: "Mark Adams and [Alwin] Pappenheimer and [Colin] McLeod and so on . . . they knew the instruction theory isn't going to work." One stumbling block was how the organism can produce antibodies long after the antigen template has disappeared from the body. Macfarlane Burnet thought he could solve this problem by analogy with the theory of adaptive enzymes, namely, that the cell could modify its enzymatic activity as external conditions changed, and proposed that the antigen stimulated an adaptive modification of the enzymes involved in the synthesis of globulin. But not even Burnet's modified-enzyme theory could explain such anomalous phenomena as the increase in avidity during the immune response or the so-called booster effect—and therefore did not solve the fundamental problems of the template-instruction theories.[3]

One reason Jerne thought the template-instruction theories were laughable was their implicit assumption that there can be infinitely many antigens and hence that the body can make infinitely many kinds of antibodies. Landsteiner had used the fact that an organism can form antibodies against any synthetic antigen as an argument against Ehrlich's theory; a relatively small number of side-chains could not cope with an, in principle, infinite number of antigens. Jerne disagreed: "Having studied some thermodynamics [in Leiden] I became irritated at [Landsteiner's] conclusion that the potential to produce antibodies is 'infinite,'" he claimed retrospectively. In a television interview, he explained that his aversion to the argument of infiniteness functioned as an important source of inspiration: "For quite a while I had been brooding over the possibility of finding a flaw in the reasoning the instruction theories are based on. And one evening, when I was walking home from the Serum Institute to Amaliegade, I think it was on the Knippel Bridge, it suddenly struck me that the basic flaw in the reasoning had to be the word infinite, that there are infinitely many antibodies. And, as an old mathematician, I had thought for a long, long time it was irritating whenever people used the word infinite. Nothing is infinite." He adds: *"I have always hated the word infinite,"* thereby reinforcing the characterization of him by Anne Marie Moulin, a historian of immunology, as "le chevalier du fini." Perhaps Jerne had in mind his studies at the end of the 1930s, when he had summarized the dimensions of the cosmos, based on Eddington's *The Expanding Universe.* There he had learned that there are both extremely small and extremely great dimensions and, above all, that even if there are almost inconceivably many protons, there are not infinitely many.[4]

Correspondingly, Jerne reasoned, neither is the number of antigens infinite; it is only very large: "Even if (what I think very unlikely) as many haptenic groups of different specificity could be synthesized as there are names in the New York telephone directory, this would amount to only about one million, whereas the number of globulin molecules in the blood of a rabbit is more than a million times a million times a million," he wrote to Felix Haurowitz, one of the most outspoken advocates for the template approach. His avidity studies had further taught him that an antibody does not have to fit precisely to the antigen to exhibit affinity, and so it is sufficient to have a finite number—maybe on the order of a million—of different specific antibodies to cope with the very great number of different antigens.[5]

In later discussions he often used a key-in-the-lock metaphor: a key doesn't have to fit 100 percent to open a lock (he had apparently not experienced modern digital hotel key cards!), so even if there exists a very large number of locks (antigens), the number of keys (antibodies) needed to open any given lock is only a fraction of the total number of locks. He also liked to use the analogy of a puzzle to illustrate the idea that should there be sufficiently many kinds of preformed specific antibodies, one of them is always going to fit a given antigen: *"If I make a puzzle with 10 million pieces, then certainly [at least] one piece will fit."* To the leading question of whether the puzzle analogy should be seen as a cognitive resource in the formulation of the selection theory at the time, Jerne answered: *"Yes, I thought in puzzle terms, in three-dimensional puzzles, of course."* He tried, too, to explain the puzzle metaphor autobiographically by referring to his early experiences. *"As a child, I was always interested in these [jigsaw] puzzles where you make pieces stick together."* He described these experiences in emotional terms: *"I loved these puzzles."*[6]

The template-instruction theoretical tradition, with its assumption of infiniteness, therefore seems to have functioned mainly as a negative context for the gestation of the selection theory—this was the kind of theory Jerne was *not* looking for. So, where did his positive theoretical stimulus come from? What role did Paul Ehrlich's old side-chain theory play, for example?

After Jerne's theory was published, in November 1955, assertions came from several quarters that he had only resurrected Ehrlich's theory, an allegation against which Jerne reacted stiffly. When, after the publication of the paper, one of his colleagues at the Serum Institute remarked at a seminar that Jerne's theory in essence was a repetition of Ehrlich's, Jerne is said to have become "very upset and offended." The critic allegedly declared that "he had never seen the like, that Jerne shut up and got surly and offended." A little later, Haurowitz wrote to Jerne, expressing the opinion that Jerne had simply taken over Ehrlich's "way of looking at preformed receptors in a new form." Jerne replied that he was "indeed sorry" not to have mentioned Ehrlich, since several had commented on the similarity between the two theories, but he firmly maintained that he had not "consciously" derived his ideas from Ehrlich. With limited space at his disposal, he explained, he had only dealt with current theories, among them Haurowitz's own and Burnet's. Besides, he wrote, it had never occurred to him that there was any "close conceptual similarity" between Ehrlich's theory and his own. Of course Ehrlich assumed that antibodies were preformed. "But is this a sufficient reason to call his theory 'very similar' to mine?" For example, his own selection theory of antibody formation did not assume that antibodies had any other function in the organism, as Ehrlich's did. Some years later, he asserted that demanding that he make reference to Ehrlich was as inappropriate as claiming that Einstein should have referred to Newton on the grounds that the theory of relativity "undoubtedly is an elaboration" of Newton's theory.[7]

Despite Jerne's objections, it is "peculiar," remarks Arthur M. Silverstein, a historian of immunology, that he made no reference to Ehrlich in his selection-theory paper. Questioned directly, Jerne denied that he had thought of Ehrlich while writing the manuscript: "Let me first give you the simple and true answer: it did not even occur to me! In retrospect, you may find this hard to believe. In 1956, I went to WHO, Geneva, and it was only a year or so later that someone pointed out to me (perhaps it was Talmage) that my theory was similar to that of Ehrlich. However, don't forget that I did not (as Burnet did) place [antibody] receptors on cells, which was the crux of Ehrlich's side-chain concept." So much for Jerne's memory. But, according to archival sources, while writing the manuscript in the fall of 1954, a few months after the Knippel Bridge incident, Jerne was indeed highly conscious of the similarity between his and Ehrlich's theories, at least regarding the preformed antibodies and the antigen's limited role in antibody formation. In one of the early manuscript drafts, he devoted a paragraph to Ehrlich's side-chain theory: "The most radical view is the original Ehrlich side-chain theory which assumed that antibodies of all kinds were already present on the cells. . . . Though since long regarded as obsolete, this theory has the advantage of radically dismissing any direct inducing action of the antigen. . . . [Similarly, the selection theory] is remarkable because it does not entertain the later notion of the active role of the antigen." It is one thing, however, that Jerne ignored Ehrlich in the published paper. It is another thing to find out whether Ehrlich's selection ideas and his thesis of preformed antibodies inspired him to his own theory in the summer of 1954. Jerne later assured Haurowitz that he "did not *consciously* derive" (my emphasis) the selection idea from Ehrlich, and his assurance is not falsified by the archive: there is indeed a total lack of references to Ehrlich in the documents before the fall of 1954, that is, before the construction of the theory. Nevertheless, it cannot be ruled out that Jerne did in fact derive the idea from Ehrlich, especially since he himself refers indirectly to the possibility that he may, at least unconsciously, have done so.[8]

In conclusion, it is tempting to see Jerne's emotionally charged denial of Ehrlich as a manifestation of what Harold Bloom has called the "anxiety of influence," namely, that "strong poets" make history by "misreading one another," thereby clearing "imaginative space for themselves." Jerne's reply to Silverstein suggests that he (even if unconsciously) may have creatively misread Ehrlich—making the side-chains, and not the selection mechanism, the crux of the theory—rather than forgotten his great German predecessor. The episode suggests that he was a strong scientist who expressed anxiety over being under the influence of another thinker, that he wanted to be unique, that he opted for originality rather than displaying his connectedness with tradition.[9]

The Darwinian Context

Ehrlich's theory had been inspired by Darwinism. Jerne's theory, too, had, as he himself expressed it later, "Darwinian overtones," because the selection mechanism constitutes the central and most radical feature of the theory. One of the reasons why Burnet—who was interested in natural history and an early adherent of neo-Darwinian ways of thinking—reacted so positively to Jerne's paper in the late 1950s was probably that it stood in such sharp contrast to the Lamarckian overtones of the template-instruction theories and his own, not very successful modified-enzyme hypothesis. Was Darwinism therefore an intellectual resource that Jerne drew upon in the construction of the selection theory?[10]

Retrospectively, Jerne expressed the view that Darwinism was not important in understanding the origin of his theory. *"Of course I thought of Darwin, I called it natural selection theory,"* he says, and adds that *"everybody was aware of Darwin, so it is not a clue."* If Jerne meant by "everybody" the general scientific community of the day, he is right; knowledge of Darwin and natural selection was part of the general education of the day. But after the neo-Lamarckian reaction around the turn of the last century, biologists and not least microbiologists were still skeptical of Darwin's selection theory; the neo-Darwinian synthesis of the 1930s had not yet been accepted outside a small group of geneticists and evolutionary biologists.[11]

If, however, Jerne meant by "everybody" those scientists he respected the most at this time, Darwinism indeed becomes an essential background factor for the selection theory of antibody formation. As already mentioned, one of Jerne's early intellectual models was R. A. Fisher, who, with his theoretical studies of natural selection in the 1920s, was one of the inventors of the neo-Darwinian synthesis. Jerne had studied Fisher's statistical work closely in the early 1940s, and the two men had met at the Second International Biometric Conference in 1949. And so there is good reason to believe that Jerne knew Fisher's principal theoretical work, *The Genetical Theory of Natural Selection* (1930). Fisher wrote expressly from a physicist's standpoint—among other things, he strongly emphasized the similarity between the fundamental theorem of the selection theory and the second law of thermodynamics—and, since Jerne had launched his attack on the avidity problem from the perspective of physical chemistry and thermodynamics, one may reasonably assume that he was positively inclined toward Fisher's treatment of the concept of natural selection. The fact that Jerne, in both the manuscript drafts and the published paper, used concepts from population dynamics as metaphors—for example, "globulin population" and "population pressure"—strengthens the impression that he was aware of the neo-Darwinian synthesis.[12]

Among the scientists in Jerne's social circle who were influenced by Darwin were members of the phage group. Delbrück had lectured on *The Genetical Theory of Natural Selection* as early as the mid-1930s and had tried to set up a collaboration between German physicists and biologists based on Fisher's ideas before he emigrated to the United States. With Delbrück's and Luria's famous fluctuation experiment, the emerging science of molecular biology seemed to be purged of Lamarckian thought. By the end of the 1940s, Jerne was thoroughly familiar with this experiment, and when looking back it struck him that *"the Delbrück-Luria fluctuation test, which had so deeply impressed me, prior to 1950, probably prepared my mind for the selection theory of antibody formation. The fluctuation test showed that penicillin does not teach bacteria to become penicillin resistant. In a deep sense of analogy, there is a similarity to the assumption that antigen does not instruct or teach [the] cell to make specific antibodies, but that these antibodies are already present before the antigen arrives."*[13]

Besides that, Jerne had special cause to direct his attention to the Darwinian selection theory during the spring and summer of 1954. The March issue of the journal *Biometrics*—to which Jerne had subscribed and contributed—contained a debate between Fisher and a group of English statisticians on transformation methods for variance analysis, a subject that impinged on some of the standardization problems with which Jerne had worked some years earlier. The footnotes of Fisher's paper referred to earlier *Biometrics* papers on natural selection (a subject otherwise rarely discussed in the journal), and therefore it is tempting to draw the conclusion that the subject was touched on when Jerne met Delbrück a few weeks after.[14]

Of course all this is simply circumstantial evidence. But since Fisher and Delbrück were two of Jerne's intellectual heroes and both were enthusiastic selectionists, since Delbrück and Jerne had a mutual interest in Fisher's ideas, and since Jerne was probably aware of the debate in *Biometrics* in the spring of 1954, there are many indications that, in the months preceding the Knippel Bridge incident, the Darwinian selection theory had an active place in Jerne's awareness. His personal contacts with the phage group and its orientation toward Darwinism and natural selection were therefore probably an essential backdrop to the selection theory of antibody formation.

One should also note the strong element of chance in the theory. While the template-instruction theories are strictly deterministic, the natural selection theory is stochastic. As Jerne wrote in his draft of 9 August 1954, one of the variant globulin configurations fits a given antigen "by chance." In the Delbrück Festschrift article ten years later, he put no special emphasis on the random element, but in later reminiscences he identified the chance (or random) aspect as a decisively innovative feature of the theory. He thought he was "the first to point out the importance of a *random* element" in the formation of antibodies and that this was "the most important departure from earlier paradigms." *"The essential thing [is] not selection, but chance,*" he asserted during a conversation.[15]

Jerne's stressing the importance of chance to the theory is probably not coincidental. He was well trained in statistics and biometry, and his later autobiographical statement that he came to immunology at the age of forty "steeped in fantasies about randomness and diversity" is, therefore, not without foundation. His well-grounded biometrical experience in the late 1940s and his habit of thinking in terms of chance can therefore be seen as a cognitive resource ready to be mobilized in the construction of the selection theory of antibody formation. In fact, over forty years later, he declared in a letter to the statistician David Finney that their conversations and correspondence at the end of the 1940s "played a considerable role in my further career" and that his selection theory was a "good example" of Finney's influence.[16]

The Avidity Problem

Another crucial cognitive element in the construction of the selection theory was the avidity problem. The selection hypothesis provided the answer to a number of immunological questions, but especially the avidity problem. In interviews Jerne gave contradictory testimony as to the significance of his earlier avidity studies to his theory. Sometimes he maintained that they were important, "*in the sense that the idea of avidity convinced me that the animal can make many different antibodies to the same antigen . . . so the diversity was greater than most people thought.*" On other occasions he minimized their importance for the gestation of the theory: "I do not think that this theory really had much to do with my experiments on antibody avidity."[17]

For an outside observer, however, there is no doubt the avidity phenomenon did indeed play a central role. The constant purpose of Jerne's research, from the late 1940s right up to the summer of 1954, was to understand the avidity phenomenon and the course of early immunization. It was the search for an understanding of avidity that had provided him with the experimental system that led (even though by pure chance) to the demonstration of P-star phages, the specific P-star generating serum factor, and the specific antibody A in normal serum. It was also the avidity phenomenon that supplied a continually unsolved scientific mystery: Why did antibodies become more avid after a second immunization? Why were late sera better able to inactivate the antigen than early sera? The question of avidity improvement had haunted him ever since writing the fourth chapter of his doctoral dissertation in 1950. The change in a serum's avidity during the course of immunization constituted a problem for the template-instruction theories and remained a puzzle—a phenomenon in continual need of explanation.

Furthermore, when the idea of the selection mechanism had once been established, Jerne's experiences in his avidity work strengthened his belief in the theory. The selection mechanism gave an immediate logical explanation for the rise in avidity in the course of immunization. At the primary stimulus, the antigen finds only a few natural antibodies with varying affinity. When the selected molecules have been reproduced in greater numbers, the antigen can, at a later stimulus, "find a larger concentration of globulin molecules fitting all its surface patterns and will preferentially carry those which show the highest combining capacity to the globulin-reproducing cells." In the first sketch of the selection theory Jerne referred to "better fitting" as one of the most important arguments for the theory, and in his later recollections he points out that "avidity observations" strengthened his "faith in the truth of antibody selection."[18]

Natural Antibodies: An Empirical Finding?

Jerne's selection theory therefore had a number of important preliminaries. First, his negative attitude toward the template-instruction theories and their assumption of an infinite number of antigens stimulated him to find an alternative theory. Second, his close contacts with the phage group and their selectionist way of thinking indirectly offered him a Darwinian frame of reference for the interpretation of antibody formation. Third, his lifelong fascination with probability reasoning and his fundamental training in statistics inclined him to see the formation of antibodies in terms of chance. And fourth, the avidity rise during immunization was a problem in search of a theory. All these experiences and ideas enter as essential elements in the construction of the theory.

In addition, Jerne claims that a decisive role was also played by the observation that freely circulating antibodies exist spontaneously in the organism before it has been subjected to antigen influence. The last documented experimental result preceding the first sketch of the theory from 9 August 1954 was the unexpected discovery, two months earlier, of antibody A activity in normal serum, a result that, in Jerne's words, had "deeply impressed" him. A year after the Knippel Bridge incident, he wrote that these observations "led to speculation about the mechanisms of antibody formation." As he later expressed it, *"the important [thing] was the idea that they are already there."* In a philosophical reconstruction of the origin of the selection theory based on Jerne's published papers and correspondence with Jerne, Kenneth Schaffner concludes, too, that the discovery of a natural antibody was "the major empirical finding impelling Jerne to his theory."[19]

But the existence of a natural antibody was not an *empirical* finding, as Jerne and Schaffner claim. It was an *interpretation* of an empirical finding, namely, the discovery of antibody A activity. For, as mentioned, two utterly different conclusions could be drawn from this discovery. The experiments took place in the 1950s, long before bacteria-free animal stalls had been introduced, and the Standardization Department was highly conscious of how easily phages could infect whole laboratory environments; among other countermeasures, they used special mutant phage and *E. coli* strains because the laboratory was infected with the wild-type strains. The most natural conclusion was therefore not that antibody A was a natural antibody but that the animal had already been exposed to T4 phages. Jerne was aware of this interpretation, because, several months later, he wrote to Maaløe that "sad to say, the objection can always be raised that the horse has earlier encountered T4." Later, when he was presenting his ideas publicly, he often had to hear just that objection: "*They said the animal has, most likely, been exposed to that antigen without our knowing of it.*"[20]

Even if this conclusion could not "be disproven," Jerne nevertheless "prefer[red]" the other possible conclusion, "the hypothesis of spontaneous production," that is, that "normal sera contain among their γ globulin molecules a fraction of less than one to one million that happens spontaneously to have a specific configuration of the A type." Furthermore, he generalized the alleged spontaneous presence of this deviant antibody in normal serum into the idea that *all* antibodies are spontaneously produced before the arrival of the antigen. Why?[21]

To be sure, the preferred interpretation had some support in the scientific literature. The existence of preformed antibodies in the form of side-chains had been postulated already by Ehrlich, and now and then they had cropped up in the serological literature; for example, they were mentioned in Robert Doerr's textbook *Antikörper* (1949). But they were a marginal phenomenon, because when Ehrlich's theory lost favor, in the first decades of the century, to various versions of template-instruction theories, according to which antibodies are formed de novo on the arrival of the antigen, natural antibodies were rejected as "theoretical impossibilities." As Silverstein points out, "their provenance [was] mysterious and their very existence neglected, in the main, by the proponents of instruction theories" from the 1920s through the 1940s. And even if some serologists still asserted they were real, or at least real artifacts (Jerne remembers from his first years at the Serum Institute, that "the serological diagnosticians told me that they 'started' with serum dilutions 1:10 [because] 'if we start with undiluted serum we get too many false positives!'"), they were mainly consigned to footnotes in the serological and immunological literature. It was Jerne who restored these theoretical impossibilities to the immunological agenda—by interpreting the empirical finding of antibody A activity during the P-star experiments in the early summer of 1954 as the existence of a spontaneously produced, preformed natural antibody.[22]

Jerne's point was that natural antibodies and gamma globulins are identical. This idea did not come out of the blue. In the early 1940s, another scientist at the Serum Institute had found experimental proof for the formation of antibodies in plasma cells and had shown that the concentration of antibodies rises at the same pace as the globulin concentration, drawing from this the conclusion that "the antibody formation is composed exclusively of extra production of globulin." Jerne maintains that these results *made a great impression* on him. Thus the difference between antibodies and gamma globulins exists only in the mind of the immunologist. "It seems useless to envisage a special mechanism for the synthesis of antibody, and to place it in opposition with [a corresponding mechanism for] the globulins called 'normal,'" he later wrote in a note, and continued: "No known property, with the exception of the given specificity under consideration, distinguishes the antibodies from the globulins of an animal that we consider as normal, because it has not been sick, or in the hands of an immunologist. It seems, on the contrary, that all these chemical, physical, immunological . . . and physiological . . . properties are identical."[23]

The Personal Context: Preformation as Jerne's Emotional a Priori

So, if the interpretation of the presence of antibody A as a preformed natural antibody did not have much support in the immunological literature— why, then, did Jerne prefer this interpretation? When reporting the results of his experiments a year later, he didn't give any reasons for his preference, and unfortunately, there are no documents that cast direct light on his reasoning in the summer of 1954. But, drawing on a number of letters and notes from Jerne's prescientific years, I suggest that his preference for the natural antibody interpretation had its foundation in his emotionally charged self-understanding and life experiences, and particularly his view of himself in relation to the social world.

In retrospect Jerne describes the gestation of the selection theory as intuitive, more like an act of faith than a rational event. As mentioned, he asserted that he experienced the template-instruction theories as "extremely distasteful," adding: "I somehow knew inside myself that this [theory] must be wrong." Conversely, he states that he had *"an inner knowledge"* about the selection theory: *"This selection theory, I was convinced it was true."* And the theory did not grow logically and rationally, he felt; instead he got "a sudden feeling" that the theory "*must* be true" and that it was "not only useless but abhorrent to consider any other solution." Besides, as he wrote in the "testament," it was "nice" that the foreign antigen had no active function.[24]

Why did Jerne feel so sure about the selection theory? Where did this inner knowledge come from? In his autobiographical recollections in the Festschrift to Delbrück, Jerne gave a hint of the metaphorical background of the selection theory. In paraphrasing the opening lines of *Philosophical Fragments* (1844), in which Kierkegaard refers to the Socratic doctrine about the learning of virtue being a recalling from the memory of already existing knowledge, he stressed the importance of the preformation concept to the selection theory: "Can the truth (*the capability to synthesize an antibody*) be learned? If so, it must be assumed not to pre-exist; to be learned, it must be acquired. We are thus confronted with the difficulty to which Socrates calls attention in *Meno* . . . namely, that it makes as little sense to search for what one does not know as to search for what one knows; what one knows, one cannot search for, since one knows it already, and what one does not know, one cannot search for, since one does not even know what to search for. Socrates resolves this difficulty by postulating that learning is nothing but recollection. The truth (*the capability to synthesize an antibody*) cannot be brought in, but was already inherent." And so, Jerne continued, if one replaces the word "truth" with "the capability to synthesize an antibody," the Socratic statement can "be made to present the logical basis of the selective theories of antibody formation." Just as the truth is not imposed from without but is latent and can be recalled from the memory, all the antibody specificities exist latently, preformed, and can be recollected by the antigen.[25]

The reference to Plato's *Meno* (as quoted by Kierkegaard) as a source of inspiration for the selection theory was made a good ten years after Jerne's stroll across the Knippel Bridge and as such may well be a construction after the fact. Neither are there any notes about the maieutic theory of learning in the archive before 1965. But Jerne's general devotion to preformationist thinking dates from considerably earlier. His stress on the echo of Socratic thinking in fact agrees with a view of the self that can be traced back several decades. In a number of letters and diary entries from the 1930s and 1940s he expressed, often in very emotional terms, his view on the autonomy and primacy of his self. For example, in a note from the winter of 1932–33 he discussed how people position themselves in relation to life. Most people, "the really ignorant, those [who are] ignorant on the grounds of insight, the utterly bored, the lovers, those who have given up all hope, those who are wracked with problems, the lonely, the indifferent, people who comport themselves with propriety," fall outside his analysis. But, beyond them, four categories of people exist. Some have "one viewpoint from which they regard whatever comes before their eyes"; they are "very narrow-minded." Others take two points of view: "They stand by turns on the one and the other point of view and are very rushed because they have to jump back and forth all the time." This way of regarding life he called "hopelessly boring." Closely related to these are people who have "a very broad attitude" that "comprehends all proper small viewpoints": "They are the renowned objective [people] who are so dumb, they do not even know they [are] fatalists." To none of these categories was young Jerne sympathetic. He believed, however, that there was a fourth type, namely, those who "by no means occupy any point of view" but who are "so clever that they always have a set of viewpoints in stock, which can be put to use on different occasions." Such a person he characterized as "a useless nihilist." Because he had labeled himself as both useless and a nihilist on several occasions, he apparently felt most akin to this category.[26]

The note about "viewpoints in stock" is no isolated phenomenon. In fall 1935, when Jerne worked for a Copenhagen publishing company, he wrote home to Tjek and characterized himself—in words that stir associations to Robert Musil's *Der Mann ohne Eigenschaften*—as a wrench that fits all kinds of bolts (in Jerne's understanding "screws"): "I feel like a monkey wrench [Englischer Schlüssel]. That's the kind of tool mechanics use; it fits all screws. I do, too. I am more or less of the same opinion as all the people I talk with and so also as Arthur Jensen [the publisher]. It's very easy, you only have to exercise your memory a little bit in order always to remember which opinion fits which screw." On another occasion, he had stressed his "unusual intellectual flexibility"—a character trait that turns one's thoughts to the Cyrenaic philosopher Aristippus, who, according to Diogenes Laertius, "was capable of adapting himself to place, time and person, and of playing his part appropriately under whatever circumstances."[27]

The isomorphism (to borrow a term from Lewis Feuer) between these expressions of Jerne's chameleonic idea of himself and the natural selection the-

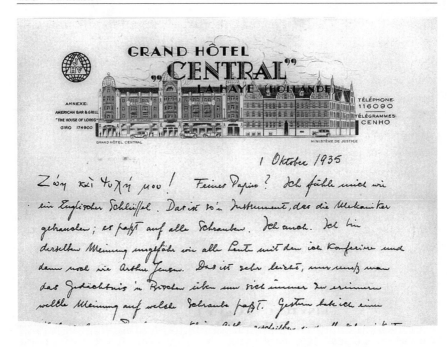

A letter to Niels Jerne's first wife, Tjek, written 1 October 1935: "I feel like a monkey wrench." ("Ich fühle mich wie ein Englischer Schlüssel."). Jerne described himself as a person who has a number of opinions, one of which will always fit another person's. This understanding of self was later utilized as a metaphor for the construction of the selection theory of antibody formation in the summer of 1954. (Jerne Collection, The Royal Library, Copenhagen)

ory of antibody formation is interesting. In choosing phrases such as "viewpoints in stock," feeling himself like "a monkey wrench," and displaying "unusual intellectual flexibility," Jerne was expressing a central aspect of his self-understanding, namely, that the self has a number of given mental states or conditions in stock that one can draw on to cope with one's relations with the outer world. Although Jerne's opinions and viewpoints may have been triggered by outside interventions, the repertoire was clearly located in an autonomous self. His self was given from within, not from without. Others, in a similar way, described him in selection terms, as a person who did not take initiatives but allowed himself to be seized by passing events before expressing his opinions. It is therefore tempting to draw the conclusion that Jerne preferred the hypothesis of preformed, natural antibodies to explain the presence of antibody A because it corresponded with his understanding of himself.[28]

Even the comparatively subordinate role of the antigen in the selection theory (as a passive selection agent) has its counterpart in Jerne's romantic world view and self-understanding. It was more reasonable to assume, he wrote a few months after the walk over Knippel Bridge, that the organism reinforces a stimulus it has itself produced rather than making functional use of all kinds of foreign substances: "As nothing is actually known, however, about the mechanism of antibody formation, it seems to me equally or more reasonable to assume that an animal can translate a stimulus by protein molecules which it has itself produced into an increased synthesis of the same type of molecules than to assume that the animal can utilize all sorts of foreign substances . . . and build them semipermanently and functionally into the most intimate parts of its protein synthesizing cells."[29]

For a person who, like Jerne, had a deep-seated distaste for being dominated by others (remember that in the beginning of the 1930s he complained that Jeanine put her soul at the midpoint of everything and forced him to revolve around her and later criticized Tjek because she dominated everything with her "strongly egocentric personality"), it must have been "nice" to be able to construct a theory in which the antigen did not thrust into the cell's "most intimate parts" but which stated that the antibody repertoire has its origin in the organism itself. Jerne's emotionally tinged argument against an instructive role for the antigen is also reminiscent of one of his earliest childhood memories, the incident when he and a playmate had stuck twigs into their anuses, "quite deeply, back and forth," and then had connected the idea of sickness (appendicitis) with this forbidden game. Jerne's distaste for the antigen's thrusting into the body's "most intimate parts" is therefore isomorphous with several earlier life experiences, including one of his most anxiety-laden childhood remembrances.[30]

Isomorphisms between different domains of experience have been discussed by Mark Johnson in terms of "metaphorical projection." Drawing on Johnson's cognitive-emotional approach to the understanding of origin of concepts, I suggest that in the summer of 1954 Jerne projected, metaphorically, entrenched patterns in his emotionally charged self-understanding and life experience to structure the puzzling experimental evidence he was confronted with in the laboratory. Such a metaphorical projection is, of course, not unique in the history of science. For example, Ronald N. Giere has proposed that Alfred Wegener used his long experience of working in the Arctic region as a cognitive resource for his continental drift theory: the South American and African continental plates drew apart "like floating icebergs, drifted farther and farther apart."[31]

But whereas Wegener metaphorically projected his experiences of the *outer,* natural world (Arctic icebergs) to a scientific domain (geotectonics), Jerne, I suggest, constructed his theory by utilizing his experiences of his *inner* life, his understanding of *himself.* In other words, shortly after he had found antibody A activity in normal serum, Jerne chose that interpretation of his experimental results—preformed, natural antibodies—that agreed best with his view of himself in relation to other people. He was thereby able to insert the last piece into the cognitive puzzle that led on to the selection theory of antibody formation. It was for that reason, I suggest, that Jerne preferred the natural antibody interpretation without further argument and that he had an "inner knowledge" that the selection theory must be true.[32]

In another sense, too, the (most probably unconscious) process of metaphorical projection must have been deeply emotionally satisfying to him. In a letter to Tjek, he had once said that he wanted "to impress his personality like a stamp in colors and form; to be able to let nature reflect in the depths of my own soul." And to Adda he had explained that "our surroundings . . . only gain the value we ourselves are able to confer on them; they are like empty shadows that are colored and animated by what we ourselves contain of thoughts and emotions, and are tinged by our moods." In the summer of 1954 he got his chance. The natural world on the petri dish was suddenly in accordance with his inner world: it now reflected "in the depths of my own soul." He now had the opportunity to impress his life experience onto the petri dish with antibody A activity. His self-understanding and life experience was therefore in a double sense an "emotional *a priori*" for his new immunological theory. His life's most important scientific contribution was the confession of *ib begetter,* a species of involuntary and unconscious autobiography.[33]

III

A Man, His Theory, and His Network (1954–1994)

15

"My Hopes and Failures Are Within Myself"

After locking up his scientific "testament" in a desk drawer in mid-August 1954, Jerne made the last travel arrangements for his visit to California. Adda was accompanying him, but the children, now aged twelve and eighteen, would remain in Denmark, and the apartment on Amaliegade would be rented out. His many books and Tjek's paintings made the apartment Jerne's umbilical cord to Denmark and a reflection of his life history: "Don't let it catch fire," he allegedly said when leaving, "because if it catches fire I don't come back—this is my life."[1]

He had looked forward to discussing his selection theory with Delbrück during the transatlantic crossing, but nothing came of it. "Unfortunately, the atmosphere did not seem to permit rather far-fetched theories of antibody formation to get more than scant attention," he recalled later. Delbrück is supposed to have defended himself by saying that he could not discuss immunology because he didn't know anything about the subject, at which point Jerne began to ask himself why Delbrück wanted him in California at all. In the middle of September 1954, the Jernes arrived in Pasadena with its endless rows of bungalows and streets "as boring as they were long," where "pedestrians had long since ceased to exist," and where whoever did not drive "risked arrest for loitering." An apartment was waiting for them near the campus. A few days

Adda and Niels Jerne before their departure to California in August 1954. (Medical History Museum, University of Copenhagen)

later, Jerne began his daily routine at the California Institute of Technology. Adda got a job as a laboratory assistant soon after.[2]

The Biological Division at Cal Tech, situated in the Kerckhoff laboratory building on campus, contained seventeen full professors and more than sixty research fellows, who worked within a large variety of research groups, including one for virus research and biophysics that had been established when Delbrück was appointed professor seven years earlier. During the academic year 1954–55 the virus group had thirty scientists connected with it: two professors (Delbrück and Renato Dulbecco), twenty research fellows, and eight graduate students.[3]

The virus group socialized a lot, sometimes at parties but especially on the (in)famous excursions to the nearby California deserts, which were "the favorite means of entertaining visitors." For Jerne—who loved to see himself as an urban intellectual strolling on the rue de Rivoli, drinking a Pernod at Le Dôme or rooting through secondhand book stalls on Fiolstræde in Copenhagen—this was a barbaric activity. And directly injurious: "What a shame you hit your knee so badly, father, during your exciting desert excursion," Ivar wrote sympathetically after his father's first and probably last such outing. Later, with light sarcasm, Jerne characterized the essence of this desert philosophy: "Delbrück arranged frequent expeditions to the desert, which was even more desolate than Pasadena. By sheer will-power, he would make everyone climb nameless mountains strewn about in the hot sand. Here I gained a deeper insight into pure randomness." Jerne was not alone in thinking these social get-togethers in the California sand were meaningless or perfectly repulsive; it was said that some people, like Luria, would not come to Cal Tech "unless guaranteed immunity from camping."[4]

Jerne already knew some of the virus group: Delbrück, Watson, the Lwoffs, and the Swiss physicist and bacteriophage scientist Jean Weigle, who customarily spent the winter months in California. The rest of the group consisted of entirely new acquaintances, several of whom became lifelong friends—for example, Renato Dulbecco, who had worked out a plaque assay method for animal viruses and was then studying, along with the Lwoffs, the process by which polio viruses left infected cells; George Streisinger, who had been at Cal Tech for a year, developing a corresponding plaque assay technique for plant viruses; and Werner Reichardt, who was going to analyze the light adaptation in the sensory cells of a slime mold, *Phycomyces,* a research field Delbrück had picked up after tiring of bacteriophage.[5]

At the Serum Institute Jerne had had high academic status, but at Cal Tech he was just one among many research fellows, a few of whom, like Watson, were already world famous. His status as one in a multitude may have reinforced his individualistic and rebellious tendencies during his ten months in Pasadena. Harry Rubin, a graduate student who shared a basement laboratory with Jerne, remembers his new colleague not only as "a real intellectual" but also as an "iconoclastic" person, "sort of an outlaw," "very individualistic," and "very European." As a result, Jerne soon got "a coterie of admiring graduate students" tagging along after him at the coffee breaks, among them Gordon Sato, who also worked with bacteriophage and would eventually become one of his close friends, and Charley Steinberg, who had just joined the group to write his Ph.D. Both Jerne and Steinberg were perceived as "rebels against Delbrück." Jerne remembered being impressed by the young Steinberg and considered him one of the few at Kerckhoff whom he respected.[6]

Jerne was apparently willing to set the scene at Kerckhoff: "There was no question that he was always the star of the show," remembers Marcel Baluda, a graduate student with Dulbecco. "When Taj is around, he's bound to say something that is going to alert your ear, your attention." He loved to give miniseminars on the political and social problems of the day and "had a lot of acuity in his analysis." At the same time many had good reason to dislike him, in that he did not like Americans' habit of always smiling. He could be very "intolerant to phoneyness." Did this cause people to think him arrogant? No, says Baluda, "haughty," instead. Jerne was not contemptuous of others; "he just thought that he knew best, which is different." As the evenings grew late and the wine really began to flow, Jerne became "somewhat opinionated" in his beliefs, Baluda recalls. He never appeared seriously drunk, however. Whereas others fell under the table, Jerne drank till he reached a certain level of intoxication and then remained there all evening, all night.[7]

Yet behind this mask of European urbane conversationalist and detached intellectual, many could see another man. One fellow's clearest memory of Jerne was as "a rather sad person." Steinberg believes that Jerne had a strong ego and was highly involved but that he did not wish to "show it to other people" and that he wanted "to maintain the distance, and to play the dispassionate scientist." Was Jerne a man with strong feelings? "Yes, but he conceals it"—a characterization that calls to mind the younger Jerne's admiration of Hemingway, whose greatness, he thought, lay in his ability to capture an emotion by distancing himself from it. Maybe it was this Hemingwayesque mask that caused others to describe Jerne as a rather self-enclosed person who did not talk much about himself or his personal life.[8]

The virus group at Cal Tech constituted an active, internationally prominent hotbed for experimental biology, where people "rarely read [published] papers" for the simple reason that the authors either "sent preprints or came and spoke at the seminars." The laboratories were busy day and night. The young scientists in the virus group were not uninterested in theoretical questions, but it was so easy to work with phage and the results came so quickly that they were continually tempted to do new experiments, which might not always be well thought out. "The urge to do experiments was always so strong that we could not get ourselves to sit down and write up the results," recalled Seymour Benzer, one of the graduate students. Delbrück is said to have insisted that at least once a week everyone have "one pipetteless day during which one was obliged to think."[9]

Pipetteless days were wholly to Jerne's taste. Back home in his Copenhagen cockpit, he would allegedly lie on the sofa and smoke for hours before starting an experiment. He later came to be considered very theoretical and "extremely economical" in his experimental planning; it is said that he thought intensely before going into the laboratory, after which he carried out "one or two critical experiments." But this was based on his having the Serum Institute's infrastructure at his disposal, so that he could bypass mundane details. Cal Tech had no ground-support personnel, however, which meant that if one had no grant to employ research assistants, one had to organize any practical matters oneself. He apparently even complained to his mother, who wrote back and evinced sympathy that "[your] work is such heavy going and you get too little done."[10]

Jerne declares that he *"did absolutely nothing"* during his year at Kerckhoff: *"I couldn't do anything. I just walked around, a whole year."* He explains that *"you had to make [everything] yourself, you had to find your rabbits somewhere, you have to sterilize your plates in a sterilizer and all that. I wasn't used to that. In Copenhagen ... I just picked up the phone in Serum Institute and said, 'I want twenty sterilized plates with agar and twenty mice and a rabbit and so forth, this afternoon at two o'clock.' And everything was there. But Cal Tech wasn't like that. 'So you need some sterilized plates, well then make them.' I didn't know how to make sterilized plates. And I didn't know where to find the rabbit, or twenty mice, I didn't know anything. . . . I just sit at my desk and think about life in general."* Did Delbrück know? Oh yes, *"I said to him I can't work here, because there's no-body who provides me what I need."* How did Delbrück react to that? *"He didn't mind that, it's funny enough."* Delbrück confirms the picture of a Jerne who maintained that it was "a waste of time for him to do experiments," since he did not have the usual staff of assistants around him.[11]

Several of the graduate students also draw the picture of a person who either avoided doing experiments or considered them a little superfluous. Rubin has no memory of his ever working at the bench ("My impression is that he was always talking to somebody"), and Steinberg remembers that Jerne, half in jest, said that "all possible experiments in immunology had already been done" and was convinced that Jerne had never before injected rabbits with phages. "I remember [Jerne] wanted to inject a rabbit to make antiserum," Steinberg recalls, "and he asked me what you did, and I said: 'Well you go, there is a store room and you can get a syringe and some needles.' And he came back with this huge needle about that diameter [indicates with his hands]. Even for a horse it would have been rather big. . . . He was going to, you know, you inject into the eye vein of the rabbit, it was obvious that he had never, never injected a rabbit before." Steinberg's anecdote contributed to the myth of Jerne as a person living in the world of theory, elevated above practical existence, a myth that was later canonized as an "open secret," namely, that "Niels Jerne has never seen a rabbit in his life."[12]

The autobiographical claim of an idle year at his desk—which, for both Jerne and his young admirers, may have been a criterion of genius—has a certain support, therefore, in the retrospective statements of contemporary witnesses. But it should not to be taken too literally. The archive gives a different picture. Among the papers left from the year at Cal Tech are bundles of laboratory records of P-star experiments whose main purpose was to confirm the preliminary results from the preceding spring. A week or so after his arrival, Jerne was already at work with his T4 strain and the serum samples he had brought along, and in a letter to Avegno just before his return to Denmark in the summer of 1955 he wrote that he had done "quite a large number of experiments" during the preceding year.[13]

If Jerne exaggerated his experimental inactivity during his year at Cal Tech, his theoretical work was not pushed aside. The selection theory was developed further. Apart from a seminar on his inactivation experiments, a couple of lectures delivered in Ray Owens's immunology course, and the supplementary P-star experiments, he worked hard, right through the fall and winter of 1954–55, to develop and extend the argument for his theory. The drafts and notes of this work are preserved, making it possible to reconstruct the rhetorical development of the theory from the testament of 9 August 1954 to the final manuscript.

Now he needed to share his ideas with others. "My theory is as follows," he wrote to Maaløe a month after his arrival in Pasadena:

> Antibody specificity depends on the amino acid sequence in the globulin molecule. The globulin molecules in normal serum consist of all possible kinds of amino acid sequences, and therefore, among the 10^{17} globulin molecules/ml in normal serum, there already exist a small fraction of molecules with specificity to all antigens. When the antigen is introduced into this population of molecules, it binds to just that small fraction that has the necessary configuration. The molecules that are selected in this way out of the large heterogeneous distribution are carried, together with the antigen, and become phagocytosed, for example, or in some other way taken inside a cell. The antigen is *not* taken inside, but the specific collected globulin molecules are sent further to *reproduction*. The antigen is thrown away.

Among the molecules reproduced, some have better specificity than the original ones, he continued: "These gain advantage, on a second antigen stimulus → avidity increase. There are many more [molecules] of the necessary kind when the secondary stimulus is applied → booster phenomenon. Only the antigen's surface is important, therefore, and only for selection." This reasoning means that "'natural' antibodies" must exist "against everything," and such is the case, he thought, "when you look very very carefully."[14]

Jerne's letter exploded like a bomb on the Standardization Department. "For weeks, Ole and I discussed the model in all of its aspects," Lark wrote back, adding that the theory had "tremendous sex appeal." He later describes the letter from Jerne as one of the most exciting experiences of his young life: "I remember going through that [letter], it was a long letter, page by page, and I remember how everything one could think of in immunology fell into place, and it was so exciting, it was so exquisite. I mean it must be like seeing the first great impressionists or something in real life and full color." It was one thing to convince Jerne's admiring friends in the Standardization Department of the excellence of the theory, however; it was something else again to persuade his American colleagues, whose opinions were divided. Some, like the immunologist Ray Owen, were "neutral." Delbrück thought it was "a good idea," Jerne told Maaløe, but otherwise his American mentor did not seem to pay much attention. During a visit to Berkeley in February 1955 Jerne gave a lecture on his theory at Wendell M. Stanley's virus seminar, and he vividly remembers how Stanley came up to him afterward saying that in fact it was *"a very good idea."* Jerne's strongest American supporter was Gunther Stent, who had moved to Berkeley after several years at the Pasteur Institute in Paris and went down to Pasadena now and then. It took "only fifteen, maybe twenty minutes" for him to become convinced that the selection theory was correct. It was crystal clear: Jerne had formulated the right answer "in the face of the entire establishment." What made the greatest impression on Stent was that the theory could explain the rise in avidity, "an obvious proof" that antibody formation was an "evolutionary phenomenon."[15]

Others were much more critical. This was only a couple of years before Francis Crick officially formulated the central dogma of molecular biology— that the hereditary information goes one way from DNA to protein, never the reverse—and most of those in the virus group at Cal Tech had already abandoned the idea that proteins might be able to reproduce themselves. Jerne's theory therefore went up against an emerging consensus in molecular biology, making the selection theory seem like a step backward. It was "difficult for us graduate students," writes Gordon Sato, "to accommodate Jerne's ideas on the selection theory of antibody formation into what we were perceiving to be a golden age of the new biology centered on DNA and phage." And Jim Watson apparently did not like it at all; Jerne later recalled how Watson at an "all-night restaurant" with his "characteristic way of producing a succinct, unambiguous answer to any question" is supposed to have rejected the theory with the comment "it stinks."[16]

The immunologists were not much in favor of it either. In connection with a meeting in San Francisco in April 1955, Jerne had an opportunity to discuss his theory with Elvin Kabat, Alwin Pappenheimer, and other leading American immunologists. One of the regular targets of their criticism was the idea of spontaneous production of antibodies, because Jerne did not know whether his animals had been exposed to the specific antigens. Another counterargument was, *"Why should we produce a thousand times more antibodies than we have any use for? We just don't need ten million, so it's 'a frightful waste.'"* Stent relates taking the ferry between Berkeley and San Francisco with Jerne and Pappenheimer: "So we were trying to persuade Pappenheimer on the ferry [but] he . . . was just shaking his head, thinking this was all baloney . . . all hocus pocus."[17]

Jerne also had the chance to meet Linus Pauling, who had just received news of winning the 1954 Nobel Prize in chemistry, and later recounted several anecdotes about the new Nobelist's reaction. According to one, Jerne presented his idea at a garden party for Pauling, but *"I was just a research fellow, and he said, 'No, I don't believe it.'"* In another Delbrück had arranged for an "audience" with Pauling: "The *maestro* kindly listened to my selective idea for antibody formation; he understood and rejected the thing, probably within five seconds from the start of the exposition, perhaps recalling his own instructive exercises in this field." Pauling was later said to have asserted that the selection theory "wasn't a theory at all since it didn't specify anything about the molecular mechanism."[18]

The question of the mechanism was, of course, crucial. Jerne had not touched it in his testament. Now he found himself in a scientific environment wholly focused on finding molecular explanations for medical and physiological phenomena. Pauling and his coworkers at Cal Tech had shown that sickle-cell anemia is a "molecular disease" caused by a simple molecular alteration in the hemoglobin molecule, a discovery that had made a great impression on their contemporaries. It was therefore clearly insufficient to show only that the template-instruction theories were illogical and that the selection theory could better explain a series of anomalous phenomena. It was also necessary to propose an intracellular mechanism that could explain, in a satisfying way, how the reproduction of the selected globulin molecules took place.[19]

Judging by the surviving notes, Jerne spent quite a lot of time and energy during his time at Cal Tech going through the literature and writing his way into the problem of the reproductive mechanism. As the weeks and months went by, the section on the reproduction mechanism came to fill almost half the manuscript. Like Burnet before him, he initially devoted a great deal of attention to the literature on adaptive enzymes, a hot topic among the molecular biologists, especially in Jacques Monod's research group at the Pasteur Institute in Paris. The reason for Jerne's interest was simple: enzymatic adaptation was a mechanism for increased production of a specific protein. Therefore, in the second manuscript draft, Jerne used a couple of pages to give an account of the latest discussions of adaptive enzymes.[20]

When Jerne presented the first typewritten version of his paper at an internal seminar with the virus group sometime during the winter of 1954–55, he received—judging by his notes—no critical comments about adaptive enzymes. It seems, however, that he himself thought the idea was unsatisfying and "in a speculative stage," and in later versions of the manuscript he reduced the section on adaptive enzymes to a footnote. Instead, he began to speculate about the possibility that the originally selected antibody molecules can function as templates for the synthesis of RNA molecules, which would then in turn be able to function as templates for the synthesis of new antibody molecules: "If these syntheses were coupled," he wrote, "it would seem feasible that the introduction of a protein molecule into a cell could initiate a replication of its specific structure." This was the kind of mechanism that "would be needed" for the selection theory.[21]

But as we have seen, Jerne met with resistance from Watson ("it stinks") and others at the Kerckhoff laboratory on precisely that point, and today we know that he was wrong. The mistake was nonetheless interesting, for in the discussion of a possible mechanism he reintroduced the idea of preformation, now on the molecular level. Either the selected antibody molecule initiates the synthesis of a specific RNA, which in turn synthesizes more antibody molecules (in analogy with the instruction theory), or the selected antibody molecule is combined with "preexisting RNA," followed by synthesis of more antibody molecules. The latter alternative (the preformation approach transferred to the molecular level) required that the cells already contain a large number of different RNA molecules, that is, that "a cell is already potentially capable of synthesizing a large variety of globulin molecules of different specificity."[22]

Jerne also began to speculate about *where* the reproduction of the globulin molecules takes place and thereby took yet another a step away from the reaction-kinetical and immunochemical issues that had informed both his dissertation work and the third-factor and P-star studies. Now the cellular basis for antibody formation came into focus. In the first manuscript versions he wrote that the selected globulin molecule gets "engulfed by a phagocytic cell" and that the introduction of these molecules into the cell signals reproduction. Later he added that "the transfer of these molecules into other cells" might constitute the signal. But what "other" kinds of cells? During discussions in the winter of 1954–55, Jean Weigle pointed out repeatedly that Jerne ought to specify the kinds of cells the reproduction takes place in. Was the phagocytic cell identical with the globulin-producing cell? And if Jerne was unable to answer, he should at least explain why the question of the precise cell type was not critical to the theory and so need not be discussed.

The selection theory did not stand or fall on the answer to Weigle's question. Jerne could easily have satisfied himself by pointing out that the question of cell type did not require this discussion. As Arthur Silverstein points out, "the actual antibody formation would then proceed in some sort of intracellular black box." Jerne nevertheless invested a lot of work in the problem. It was known that the lymphatic tissues are differentiated into three types of cells (plasma cells, lymphocytes, and phagocytic cells), and much evidence pointed toward the plasma cells being responsible for the major part of antibody production, while the lymphocytes, which exist in great numbers in the thymus, among other places, did not play any major role. In one draft, for example, Jerne speculated that phagocytes might be able to convey the signal to the plasma cells, and certain published experimental data suggested that this process might take place in the spleen. In the final manuscript, however, he wrote only in passing that "circulating phagocytes also come into close contact with the lymphoid tissue."[23]

Jerne was therefore prepared to discuss many different intracellular mechanisms for the production of antibodies. But one thing he was not prepared to negotiate: the antigen was nothing but a selection agent; it was not allowed to have any instructive role whatsoever. In his testament he had already written that it was "nice" that the antigen was passive, that it did not take an active part. "Antibody formation is *not* a defense mechanism!" he exclaimed in one of his Cal Tech notes. "This theory thus abandons the idea that an entirely foreign structure should be able to participate in a functional system," he added in another. In a second manuscript draft he crossed out this wording, only to let it bob up again, several drafts later, now in the introductory passages to the paper: the antigen "is solely a selective *carrier* of spontaneously circulating antibody." This wording remained all but unchanged through the final version.[24]

During the winter of 1954–55 Jerne also began to ponder the role of thymus in antibody production. It was commonly believed at the time that this mysterious organ played no role in the immune response. But Jerne thought otherwise. His selection theory was based on lymphoid cells (probably plasma cells) continually producing and reproducing globulin molecules. The production of both normal gamma globulin and antibodies could be reduced to one fundamental mechanism: unselective versus selective reproduction of circulating globulin molecules. Yet sometime the system must have been set in motion: "Somewhere in the beginning, however, we have to postulate a spontaneous production of globulin molecules of a great variety of random specificities in order to start the process," Jerne wrote. To this problem, the thymus might provide an answer: "Possibly a specialized lymphoid tissue, such as that of the thymus, which is most active in embryonic and early independent life and decays soon after, is engaged in this function." This was sheer speculation, however; more than five years would pass before the role of thymus in antibody formation would begin to be elucidated.[25]

In connection with his discussion of the thymus, Jerne also engaged one of immunology's classic mysteries, that is, how the organism's immune system can differentiate between its own molecules and antigens coming from outside. How can the immune system avoid producing antibodies against all the millions of different kinds of molecules the organism itself is composed of, including its own immune system? For Macfarlane Burnet the distinction between "self" and "nonself" was immunology's central problem, both philosophically and practically, and it played a large role in his later modification of Jerne's selection theory into the clonal selection theory. The question of self and nonself, on the contrary, played no great role in Jerne's deliberations. As a matter of fact, the issue was not mentioned at all, either in the testament or in the early manuscript drafts that followed, something that Maaløe and Lark were quick to point out in their response in the fall of 1954: "One thing which is not explained by your theory is the lack of production of antibodies vs. the organism's own constituents." And yet, they wrote, it was probably unfair to criticize Jerne's theory for not being able to explain this, since "no other theory at present explains these things either."[26]

In later versions of the manuscript, Jerne added (perhaps after the discussions with Owen, who, with his studies of chimeras, was one of the pioneers in research into immunological tolerance) a few words on the self versus nonself problem in connection with the presumed role of the thymus in early antibody production. Now he thought that an essential aspect of the selection theory was that it could apparently explain "the absence of auto-antibodies." If there were a spontaneous production of antibodies in the thymus in early embryonic stages, Jerne thought, the antibodies directed against the body's own antigens could be removed. Such a mechanism would also be able to "explain the absence in the blood of specific globulin against antigens of the organism itself, since such globulin molecules, if spontaneously produced, would be removed by attachment to the auto-antigens." But he wrote nothing more than these few lines of speculation about the thymus and the distinction between self and nonself. It would be fifteen years before he returned to the subject, with the somatic mutation theory of the origin of the antibody repertoire: in 1969 he proposed that the normal rate of somatic mutation in the genes that are coding for antibodies can give rise to antibody diversity, if the organism selects, in the thymus, mutants by destroying nonmutant cells.[27]

The whole rhetorical development of the selection theory was therefore a long pipetteless period. Jerne was aware, of course, that a scientific theory stands or falls as the pipettes measure; even as he was writing the testament sketch in August 1954, he was thinking about how the theory could possibly be tested experimentally, and a few months later he wrote to Maaløe that he was brooding over "good possibilities of experimental conclusions." But otherwise he did not invest much effort in proposing experimental tests. In that respect it is true that he did nothing other than sit at his desk and think. The construction of the selection theory in the summer of 1954 and the rhetorical elaboration of it during the year at Cal Tech was sheer desk work, however many extra P-star experiments he may have done. Neither would he, after his return to Europe, engage himself in experimental work to test the theory itself. And why should he? After all, from the very first, he had been convinced he was right.[28]

Others remained unconvinced. The reactions to the selection theory continued to be rejection or skepticism. In the middle of June 1955, after "a happy month together" with Stent in Berkeley (where they worked almost "*like madmen*" on one of Stent's research problems concerning the fate of phosphorus atoms through the phage generations), Jerne set out with Werner Reichardt on a month-long lecture tour across North America, which gave rise to plenty of anecdotes, snapshots, and happy memories. With Reichardt at the steering wheel of an old Studebaker, they drove over the Rocky Mountains and through the Midwest, spending nights in sleeping bags under the open sky or in cheap motels just above the "bedbug threshold." They lived a spartan existence, drank "not a single cup of coffee if it [could possibly be] avoided," and gave "*lectures in the university towns, getting fifty dollars every time.*" Reichardt had a "spectacular lecture" about his research on eyesight, and of course Jerne talked about his

Niels Jerne floating on the Great Salt Lake in the summer of 1955, on his way home from his cross-country lecture tour of America. (Medical History Museum, University of Copenhagen)

new theory. In St. Louis they visited Melvin Cohn, a talented young immunologist who had studied with Pappenheimer in New York and had then spent a year with Lwoff and Monod at the Pasteur Institute to study adaptive enzymes and who, for that reason, probably defended Burnet's modified-enzyme theory. They continued to Baltimore and Johns Hopkins University, then headed to New York, before turning westward once more. Via Denver and a lecture with Theodor Puck, they continued on to Salt Lake City, saw the Mormon Temple, and swam in the Great Salt Lake, returning to Pasadena in the middle of July.[29]

The selection theory did not get an appreciably better reception on this summer tour than it had received in Pasadena and San Francisco in the preceding ten months. Most immunologists seem to have been skeptical: "'Not especially probable,' they said." In fact, Jerne remembers only a single exception to the chorus of wary or critical voices, namely, Colin McLeod, at the New York University College of Medicine, who was said to have uttered some positive words "almost to console me, since there had not really been any reaction." He maintains that it was McLeod's (and, earlier, Stanley's) positive comments that "finally encouraged" him to write up the manuscript. "After my trip through the USA I had three weeks left and then I worked day and night with the last draft of the three papers." He later remembered sitting through the night, writing, while he played Bach's Brandenburg Concertos on his newly purchased gramophone. In a first manuscript he summarized the reversibility experiments he had carried out with Perla Avegno during spring 1954, another concerned the P-star effect and the specific antibody A in normal serum, and the third was the manuscript of the selection theory.[30]

After finishing his writing just before his departure in August 1955, he asked Delbrück to send the two experimental papers to the *Journal of Immunology* and the paper on the selection theory to the *Proceedings of the National Academy of Sciences*. Apart from a trifling change in the P-star paper and a quotation mark in the selection theory paper, Delbrück had nothing to add (one of Jerne's favorite anecdotes is that "I got a postcard on which he wrote that he had *corrected a comma"*); he submitted them for publication and asked the journals to charge the cost of reprints to his own grant: "If you are able to pay me back I will not object," he wrote to Jerne, and added: "Otherwise wait until you get the Nobel prize." Presumably this was meant ironically, a little teasing flick of humor, or maybe it was also evidence of Delbrück's much talked about ability to spot quality. In any case, he did not live to see his words come true.[31]

The final days in Pasadena gave Jerne time to mull over what he had accomplished. A year earlier he had looked forward to meeting some of the leading immunologists of the day and to "benefit in my scientific development." True, compared to the preceding, creative spring and summer of 1954 back in Copenhagen, the year at Cal Tech had only confirmed and extended insights he had already gained. But at the same time he was aware of the importance of his having *"met a lot of people."* In much the same way as he had experienced the first meeting with the phage group in 1951–52 as an *"earthquake, a catapult into higher and deeper regions of ongoing science,"* his lasting impression of the stay at Cal Tech was that it reinforced his scientific self-confidence: *"Once I had met all these people, Watson, Delbrück and so on, they were at the top of the world of biology, I understood that there wasn't anyone in the world I couldn't talk to. This gave me a fantastic confidence, self-confidence."*[32]

But scientific self-confidence does not necessarily match with personal self-confidence, as illustrated by Jerne's fallout with Delbrück toward the end of his stay: *"We became enemies,"* he says, *"I said 'Heil Hitler' on the 20th of April!"* Delbrück never had Nazi sympathies, so presumably Jerne's comment was instead an expression of his rebellious attitude and *puer aeternus* habitus. As regards science, the two men had a lot in common. Both were sharp, abstract, mathematical thinkers, both were accustomed to "drawing conclusions from the shape of curves." In our conversations Jerne mentioned Delbrück time after time with admiration in his voice, and it was probably not just out of politeness that he told Manny Delbrück after her husband's death that "without Max" his life would have "been quite different, and less interesting." When it came to a critical attitude and criteria for scientific standards, Delbrück was undoubtedly influential in Jerne's continuing development: "Whenever . . . I tried to develop a new idea in immunology, my first thought was always: what would Max say to this hypothesis."[33]

But personally, the two men were opposites. Stent thinks that Delbrück was dominating and involved himself in his coworkers' private lives, that "recruiting" people was his intention; he wanted to "convert" them to his scientific outlook, "increasing the world of believers" and "informing the world"; Jerne had, in Stent's opinion, no ambitions whatsoever in that direction. Another well-known source of conflict was the two men's very different views of the New World. Manny Delbrück recalls the contrast between her "tremendously pro-American" husband and the "very anti-American" Jerne, who was full of resentments and "animosity, prejudicity against things in America." In Stent's view, Jerne thought that Delbrück had disowned his European origin, that "he was trying to be a cowboy. Instead of sitting in this stupid desert he should be in a coffeehouse, drinking good wine on boulevards, and so on."[34]

Their differing views of American and European cultural values seem to have been rooted in a much deeper emotional level, however. Manny Delbrück refers to a "love-hate relationship." *"There are many hate parts,"* Jerne comments. All his life he was irritated by what he perceived as Delbrück's exaggerated conceit and narcissism. He remembers several occasions when he felt humiliated by his mentor, for example, at a New Year's Eve he spent at home with the Delbrücks: *"So I go to Max Delbrück with a bottle of, which I'd specially bought, red wine from the Bourgogne. The first insult is that he says, 'Oh that's one of these other bottles' and just throws it into the other thirty-five bottles which he already has."* The anecdote supports the general picture of Delbrück, but, more important, it also reveals how Jerne's scientific ego was accompanied by a substantial lack of personal self-confidence.[35]

A preserved draft of a farewell letter to Delbrück also gives interesting insight, not least in its crossed-out passages, into Jerne's image of himself. He was grateful for all that the Delbrücks had done to get him over to America, he said, but now he was told that they thought the whole visit to Caltech had been "a failure" and that all the hopes they and "a few others" had held out for him had shattered. "Have I failed to realize your hope of finding another admirer of the spiritual vacuum of Southern California?" Jerne responded. Nor did he accept Delbrück "as a competent judge" of his behavior, for "my hopes and failures are within myself. You don't know their shape." Just as he had thought it unreasonable to suppose that foreign molecules could be built into the "most intimate parts," of the cell, so now he rejected the notion that Delbrück's moral values should be allowed to affect his inner life. In another passage he warned Delbrück "against trying any psychological constructions." Twenty years before, Jerne had been furious at the graphologist who had thought himself able to make an objective judgment of his personality. Now he told Delbrück that psychological insight "can only be gained intuitively and not by a sterile approach." "Psychological constructions cannot replace intuitive insights," he declared.[36]

Jerne's emphasis on intuition was no passing whim. Even as a young banana company employee, he had drunk deep of Henri Bergson. Of course he did not reject deductive, rational, logical thinking as such, and he did not believe that nature eludes rational understanding, nor did he depend exclusively on intuition, imagination, poetry, and emotion. But in contrast to many other positivistically inclined scientists of the time Jerne thought that reason alone is not sufficient and that the fundamental ideas of science are reached primarily through intuition. Later notes show that he thought of experimental work as a means for confirming results already achieved through intuitive thinking: "The object of (biological) experiments is to obtain results that sanction and legitimize the conquests of intuition," he wrote a few years later, commenting on the French mathematician Jacques S. Hadamard's view of the relationship between intuition and mathematical rigor.[37]

Jerne's words about the importance of intuition had their effect. Delbrück declared "how intensely" he disapproved of it: "We have both seen the grand idolatry of intuition run his course. If anything, this is of the Devil," he wrote back, without commenting on the other accusations. And Jerne, finally, seemed to want to smooth things over. "I suppose we would disagree on the subject of intuition," he wrote, adding that "it would be fun to discuss this on a rational basis." His wording suggests that he was trying to gain the usual distance to an emotionally tense situation by adding comments and observations on what had transpired. "Quarreling is unsatisfactory," he continued, "unless carried through in a grand style. . . . Considering our meek and gentle dispositions . . . a continued quarrel would suffer from lack of élan vital," so it would be best to end it. "Me thinks there was a Huge Eclipse of Sun and Moon, and it Makes Man Mad," he closed.[38]

16 "This Theory Hadn't Made Much of a Stir, So Now, What Was I to Do?"

With his farewell salute to Delbrück, Jerne was ready to leave Pasadena. Students, visiting researchers, and staff wrote their adieus. "Have a miserable trip; I hate you (but love Adda)," wrote George Streisinger. The next day, the Jernes flew to New York to sail back to Europe. In the week it took to cross the Atlantic, Jerne buried himself in Kierkegaard's *Concluding Unscientific Postscript* (1846), a tract on inwardness that mentally prepared him for his return to Denmark. A week with the "subjective problem" was also, he thought, "a valuable antidote" to the endless suburban streets of Pasadena, to Delbrück and his desert excursions, and, not least, to "the objectivism which is spreading so deplorably among the educated [classes]," as he expressed it in a letter to Stent.[1]

To return to Europe was, wrote Jerne to Delbrück, to go back to "something very special," something that had not yet been uprooted, something hard to imitate or to transfer to the New World, and that was of "tremendous importance": the European soul, a thousand years of European history, "fantastic vitality" and creativity. Culturally, he felt like a fish back in water. But scientifically, his return was anticlimactic. Maaløe had gone the whole way, leaving bacteriophage and devoting himself entirely to bacterial physiology with only a polite interest in serology and immunology; his most enthusiastic home supporter for the selection theory, Karl Gordon Lark, had returned to the United States; and new young scientists, unknown to him and not much interested in his work, were now carrying out the experiments on synchronization of bacterial cultures. Neither did he meet with much interest in the Copenhagen medical community. He recalls that after giving a lecture at the Serum Institute, he *"chatted with one of the chief physicians,"* who *"said that [the selection theory] could not be correct."* Toward the end of October he gave a lecture at a Pathology Association meeting and received another unenthusiastic reception. He sums up the situation by saying, *"I came back to Copenhagen, gave a few lectures about my selection theory, but the immunologists thought it was all nonsense."* He claims that the lack of interest in his theory did not really bother him: *"I didn't care if somebody didn't believe it, that's their own problem."* Do we sense sour grapes here?[2]

The rest of 1955 passed without Jerne's focusing on any clear-cut research project. Between writing letters and giving lectures on his previous DNA work with Stent, he undertook a couple of "useless experiments" in which he injected phage into newborn rabbits, to "see what happens" during the very first immune response. Maybe one could use phage to demonstrate "the antibody formation that takes place within the first few days after the antigen is introduced into the blood stream," he wrote to Stent. He also got somewhat involved in one of Maaløe's projects on the role of RNA in protein synthesis, "fooled around with RNA-ase," and observed that the enzyme had a "striking effect" on the synthesis of proteins in *E. coli*, which indicated that RNA is intimately involved in the process. None of this seems to have aroused his scientific passion, however. "Again I am trying to write you a letter," he wrote to Stent, right after New Year 1956, "and to escape the shirking of the task of producing some shape out of a mind oscillating between states of laziness and frivolity and multitudinous patterns of bewildered thoughts. I have not for weeks been able to focus beneath the surface on a merely scientific object, nor in the face of the chaos of life to preserve any other spiritual dignity than that of stubbornness."[3]

Jerne's "bewildered thoughts" concerned, in part, his future at the Serum Institute. By his own account, he had returned to Denmark with a feeling of *"fantastic confidence, self-confidence"*; but Stent claims that Jerne was "disappointed and angry" that his scientific work was not sufficiently valued in Copenhagen. It was generally expected that Maaløe would get a new chair in microbiology at the university, and everyone assumed that Jerne would then succeed him as head of the Standardization Department, so in order to finance his research during the interim, Ørskov wanted to send an application to the

Danish National Science Foundation. But Jerne was hesitant. He "insisted, God help me," as Maaløe later put it, on getting a permanent research position rather than having his application for a grant evaluated by the Science Foundation. Maaløe accused his friend of "hunting for a recognition" that would impress his elder brother, Thomas, "who scarcely accepts anything but hard, economic success." Stent thinks that Jerne's failure to be offered a top, permanent science job in Copenhagen immediately "really deeply hurt him" and that he feared he might become a sort of "super Ole Rostock or something."[4]

Jerne's bewildered thoughts were not only about pride or vanity as measured in permanent positions, however. Money was again on his mind, as it had been a year and a half earlier when he was wrestling with the choice between Cal Tech and Geneva. He remembers being uncertain whether he wanted to continue at the Serum Institute at all, even if he got a good research job: *"I didn't think I could live properly on my salary. . . . I think it's true that I wanted enough money to go to expensive restaurants now and then. I didn't want to be rich, but . . . I didn't want money to restrict my personal life. I wanted to buy that bottle of wine."* So once again he considered whether he should accept Lourie's nearly two-year-old offer to join WHO in Geneva. Lourie had written him several times over the past year, promising to hold the position open if they could count on getting "a good man." Jerne would get "all the rope in the world." Of course, Jerne knew that it was an administrative job, affording only marginal possibilities for his personal research. A couple of years before, he had painted a dismal picture of the administrative colossus in the Palais des Nations, with all the staff running back and forth in "a maelstrom of papers, letters, documents, and memoranda," a place where there was "no time for quiet meditation, not even on scientific matters." And yet: *"It was appealing, actually, to go to Geneva because this theory hadn't made much of a stir, so now, what was I to do?"*[5]

His memory is selective, though. True, most immunologists in the United States had been dismissive of the theory before its publication, and his Danish colleagues, too, had been rather lukewarm. But in the spring of 1956, soon after it had appeared in press, it got a growing number of supporters, especially among nonimmunologists. The geneticist Joshua Lederberg immediately wrote to "express [his] approbation of approaches that avoided an instructional role for the antigen," and Stent reported that several American molecular biologists were "crazy about" it. Later in the spring one of Jerne's young colleagues at the Serum Institute, Jørgen Spärck, returned from a year with the embryologist C. H. Waddington in Edinburgh with the news that the theory had made "a very strong impression" there. Despite this growing appreciation, Jerne seemingly did not want to take up his theoretical work again, at least for the present. *"I was finished with that theory,"* he says, thinking back; *"I wanted to do something else."* As if he had to legitimize his decision, he adds: *"I've always had a need for change."*[6]

He sounds like an echo of Kierkegaard's satirical description of the typical restless aesthete: "One tires of living in the country, and moves to the city; one tires of one's native land, and travels abroad; one is *europamüde,* and goes to America, and so on; finally one indulges in a sentimental hope of endless journeyings from star to star." As a young romantic aesthete, Jerne had come to Denmark because he was tired of the Netherlands. However, as time passed, he had become more and more Denmark weary; a couple of years earlier, he had even considered the Nilgiri Hills in the mountains of southern India. Up until then he had felt obliged to remain in Denmark for the sake of his eighty-year-old mother— *"I had decided that I did not want to travel as long as she lived"*— but at the end of 1955 Mama fell suddenly ill, was hospitalized, and died a month later. So *"I didn't need to bother about that any more."*[7]

Apparently Adda was not included in these deliberations. There is quite a bit of testimony that, over time, Jerne had become more and more remote from his second wife. On her part, she always remained his "devoted Adda," and it is said that she "clearly adored" him. Occasionally his passion for her revived: after his return from India in the late summer of 1953 he had been "full of longing, love, cruelty, tenderness," all his "nerves and senses" had stretched "their tips and tongues and flames" toward her; she was his "forever." But after that things had gone seriously wrong. Even if, during his cross-country tour in the summer of 1955 he had addressed her as "My beloved girl" and "My dear lonely girl" in his postcards, several persons assert that for the most part he ignored her during the stay at Cal Tech. Manny Delbrück is said to have admired "Adda's being able to stand up to such a person" and his "peculiar cruelties." In Jerne's words *"the trouble really started when I went to Pasadena. . . . All the trouble started right away. I didn't really like this female."*[8]

It is not clear what his problem was. He claims that earlier sexual infidelity on Adda's part was involved; he tells of getting pubic lice at the end of the 1940s, but it wasn't until *"many years later . . . [that I] realized that this woman, Adda, had very simply acquired these beasts. . . . I couldn't understand that this woman would do a thing like that to me. I mean, fucking with a baker's boy, and then fucking with me."* The anecdote is an unshakable part of Jerne's self-justification for not having anything further to do with Adda, but it is difficult to reconcile the story with the statement that the problem between them began "right away" after their arrival in Pasadena. What is crucial in this connection, however, is not when and why the relationship went wrong but that, in the spring of 1956, Jerne felt so free of his marriage that he could, instead, pursue his career interests. All the later anecdotes and stories about lice and so forth can therefore be seen as a legitimation of his flight from Copenhagen. His need for change, too, may well have concerned his wish to leave the marriage without having to decide on a divorce.[9]

Judging by the evidence, the children had no part in his deliberations. After his return from the United States, Jerne, as he himself put it, "rediscovered" his sons. Ivar—who had "not read a single book since he was twelve," who had left school at the age of fourteen, had been admitted to a psychiatric clinic, and finally spent three years as a gardener's apprentice in Jutland—was now twenty years old and startled his father by reading Flaubert and Strindberg and making "original and pertinent remarks about them." Donald, fifteen years old, still attended boarding school, made good progress, and in his correspondence gave the impression of being a well-adjusted boy with sound interests. So Jerne probably thought the boys could very well get along without him.[10]

Accordingly, Jerne notified Lourie that he was now seriously considering accepting his offer but let him also know that he would prefer to avoid submitting a formal application. His eagerness to go to Geneva apparently outweighed his distaste for being openly judged in competition with others, and in mid-February 1956, he sent his application to WHO. In less than a month he was notified that he had been given the job as medical officer in the Section of Biological Standardization. He requested two years' leave of absence from the Serum Institute, probably just to keep the door open for a possible return.

The circumstances surrounding Jerne's decision to take the job in Geneva have given rise to further creative autobiographical rationalizations. Already in our first interview the anecdote came up about his approaching Ørskov and saying, *"I couldn't live on my salary, of which half went into cigarettes, so he had to give me a little more salary, otherwise I wanted to accept a position in Geneva at WHO that had been offered me. Then he only said: 'Have a nice trip.'"* The anecdote illustrates the importance of having a cautious attitude toward interview material. In the first place Jerne had not been offered the position but had applied for it. Second, a Danish public servant couldn't negotiate his salary. And finally, by all accounts Ørskov was not especially positive toward Jerne's travel plans but thought Jerne ought to stick to science, something that Ørskov had expressed through the application to the Danish National Science Foundation.[11]

Maaløe judged the matter in moral terms. In an unusually frank letter, written the day after Jerne's decision, he criticized his friend's way of looking after his family. Maaløe was convinced that neither Adda nor the children "gained anything positive by this"; he thought the boys had greater need for "a father who is there, than of a Santa Claus, who from time to time takes along rare things from the far east or west (even if I fully realize how much fun *that* can be for them—and, not least, for Santa Claus)," and wondered whether Jerne could "find a single person (with the exception of Lourie)" who gained "anything but unpleasant experiences—or even sorrows" by the decision. Such was Ole Maaløe's "brutal but correct" judgment in a nutshell. Jerne later reflected on his choice between following his intellectual and professional interests versus fulfilling his paternal duties. He had a well-developed image of his own father as *"the man who everybody respects, the pater familias"* and was well aware that he himself did not live up to that model: *"I did not inherit that [quality]."* In another conversation, he realized that his success in science had exacted its price: *"There's also a negative aspect of this. It can go together with bad behavior . . . the absolute feeling that what I am going to do is more important than being a nice guy."* Did he become a bad guy instead? *"Yes, I think so. I have a letter from Maaløe in which he says that I was not behaving in a moral way [when] putting the children in a boy's school, saying I wanted to do what pleases me most. . . . I was probably not such a good father or husband."*[12]

Maaløe's critique came at about the same time as Jerne's scientific integrity—that is, his above-mentioned failure to acknowledge Paul Ehrlich's side-chain theory—was attacked by Felix Haurowitz. Maybe the simultaneous moral criticism from Maaløe and Haurowitz contributed to Jerne's writing Stent a little later in the spring of 1956 that he was "depressed about my relation to science, scientists, position, money, atmosphere, and everything" and that he currently had his sights set on Geneva. He expressed the hope that "even without scientific stimulus" he would be able to see what was meaningful in Geneva "surrounded by the wonderful peoples of old Europe."[13]

Thirteen years at the Danish State Serum Institute were about to end. When he looked back on those years, they did not fill much of his memory: *"The time at the Serum Institute seems to be a very short time, three years perhaps."* During his last months in Copenhagen he was occupied with bringing his old work to a close and preparing for the new. With Maaløe he wrote up the ribonuclease experiments in a little paper for *Acta Pathologica* and worked up a catalogue of standard preparations that was later much used in the department. Lourie asked him to think over the program for the development of snakebite serum standards that the WHO section had started a year earlier and assigned him a trip to Brazil in the late summer to present the results of toxicity experiments with snake venom at the Butantan Institute at a forthcoming meeting of the Expert Committee.[14]

Apparently Jerne did not consider Lourie's assignment simply a duty. Even before his trip to Southeast Asia, three years earlier, he had displayed interest in snakes and snake venoms and expressed his willingness to write an outline of the global scope of the problem, to collect material and compare assay procedures, and to study the possibility of a centralized international standardization activity. In the spring of 1954, on a short assignment for WHO, he had begun a systematic study of venoms and the standardization of antivenins, which was later published as a separate report; and finally, in the spring of 1956, the medical faculty of the University of Copenhagen appointed him member of an evaluation committee for a dissertation on South African snake venoms and antiserums.[15]

Because Jerne had shown no more than peripheral interest in practical standardization problems in recent years—after all, he had viewed his Southeast Asia assignment in 1953 primarily as an all-expense-paid tourist trip—it is not so easy to understand why he was so interested in snakes and their venoms. Maybe he thought the production of antisera against snakebite could illustrate some of the general problems with the validity and reliability of standardization he had worked on during the preparation of his dissertation; antivenin standardization might even amount to something like a suitable small research problem. But there may also have existed more personal, partly unconscious motives. Jerne's wish to write a comprehensive outline of the snakebite problem can be seen as an extension of his earlier bent toward writing lists, compilations, and tables of this and that. And just as he had repeatedly expressed the wish to settle down as a general practitioner in a small town in the Danish countryside, to spend his leisure hours in discussions and chess games with the local apothecary, at this point in his life, one may speculate, he could establish a niche for himself as a world expert on snake venoms and spend his leisure hours sitting in cafes in Geneva, contemplating the European soul. Antivenins were a reasonably limited and well-defined research area, a secure place in a new and insecure life situation.

Maybe there is even a deeper connection between this seemingly scientific interest and his lifelong fascination with sadism and "the whip, the rope, the naked struggle." From Roman poetry up to Freud, the snake has been a mystical and sexual symbol; its sinuous movements, sudden attacks, and lethal poison symbolize erotic passion, which attacks the will and social morality. The relationship between erotic life and intellectual willpower was, as I have earlier shown, a recurrent set of problems in Jerne's correspondence and notes. One may therefore imagine that the work with snake venoms and antivenins not only concerned an important standardization problem but also stirred some fundamental elements in his conception of his life. One need not be a dyed-in-the-wool psychobiographer to interpret Jerne's interest in the control of snakes and their venom as an extension of those attacks made, more than two decades earlier, by self-satisfied little Niels, alias Pietje Kleverjong, on Cupid's influence or as an expression of his lifelong attraction to subduing female sexuality. His early dreams of torturing defenseless young women and his sadistic acts (burning his submissive lover's nipples) can be seen as elements in the same basic stance toward life: to exert intellectual power over spontaneous pleasure and sexuality.[16]

"I'd Better Make Sure I Learn a Little about Immunology"

*I*t had been years since Jerne had vacationed with Ivar and Donald, but in the summer of 1956 he took his sons to Italy. By their own account the boys were immensely satisfied to have their father's undivided attention for a while. Their joy did not last long, however. In the middle of July, Jerne sent them back to Adda in Copenhagen, took the train to Geneva, and found a rented room in the center of the city. At the Palais des Nations he familiarized himself with the World Health Organization's multitudinous activities and its complicated system of public documents, reviewed arrangements for impending meetings, and prepared for his upcoming trip to Brazil. He was ready to begin a new career, ready to enjoy the sophisticated nightlife of the capital of international politics. Once again he had turned his back on his roots to live in a country and culture he barely knew. The future lay before him, undoubtedly filled with risks but also with hopes and expectations.

Within a few weeks the scene changed. In the middle of August, E. M. Lourie suddenly and unexpectedly died. Jerne—depressed and in "sagging spirits"—was obliged to take over responsibility for the international standardization effort. In a month he was to replace Lourie at an international meeting of immunomicrobiological standardization in Rome; following that, he had just three weeks to prepare for the annual meeting with the Expert Committee for Biological Standardization. The trip to Brazil had to be canceled, the plans for standardization of antivenins were put on ice. Yet daily work soon drove out the despondency. In the middle of October the rumor spread in his circle of friends that Jerne was "very busy shuffling papers behind a desk."[1]

The rest of the year has left few other traces in the archive. In the beginning of February 1957, Jerne was officially appointed Lourie's successor and began the work of developing a new policy for WHO's standardization of biological preparations. At the Rome meeting he had hinted that the present standardization program was problematic. The traditional principle behind biological standardization was "to define the abstract concept of a unit of biological activity by linking it to a definite sample of a well-guarded substance." The idea was that copies of test substances "should enable all [laboratory] workers to speak the same language and to use the same unit notation." Unit definitions were, Jerne maintained, usually considered "independent of methods," and for this reason no one had wanted to recommend any methods over any others. But drawing from his earlier avidity studies and from his conviction that standards are dependent on the method used (that is, context dependent) and that one cannot therefore, in principle, establish a single international biological unit standard, he thought it better to evaluate methods instead. Particularly because WHO had begun to standardize "such exceedingly complex substances as Vaccines," he felt that the existing negative attitude toward recommending measurement methods had to be changed, "since well defined methods may be absolutely essential for a useful evaluation of such substances."[2]

In his opening lecture at the Third International Meeting of Biological Standardization in Yugoslavia in September 1957, Jerne laid down new guidelines for WHO's standardization procedures. The organization's official policy now supported the development of practical and methodological guidelines for assay methods, so-called "minimum requirements." In October 1957, a Study Group on Recommended Assay Methods and Minimum Requirements met, and the following summer, at the Fourth International Meeting of Biological Standardization in Brussels, Jerne announced that WHO was going full speed ahead on guidelines not only for individual substances but also for general procedures, such as sterility tests, labeling, and so forth. As the secretary for a number of expert groups during the years that followed, Jerne established guidelines for a whole series of standardization fields, including vaccines against smallpox, poliomyelitis, yellow fever, and cholera. The work required diplomatic skills: he had to weigh the opinions of various experts, meld different proposals, and coax the decisions through the bureaucracy. His contribu-

Niels Jerne at a meeting of the World Health Organization, 1956–62. (Medical History Museum, University of Copenhagen. Photo: J. Cadou, Geneva)

tions soon earned praise, both in international standardization circles and within the internal WHO bureaucracy, not least in the eyes of its director general, Marcelino Gomes Candau.[3]

Jerne had only a temporary appointment at WHO. Should he try to stay in Geneva or return to Copenhagen? From time to time he considered returning to take over the Standardization Department after Maaløe. This would mean "almost unlimited freedom to occupy myself with 'interesting' little things in every way," he wrote to Jeppe Ørskov. On the other hand, he had no wish to cut his income in half merely to sit in Copenhagen and do experiments in which he was not "brilliant enough" to make real advances. "Science is getting too difficult for amateurs like me," he complained. "I have understood," he continued, "that the true scientific advances are borne by a very few people, and that you have to attain their circle before the whole thing can gain a significance proportionate to the pains of the permanent one-sided preoccupation with a single detail of life that is required." Maybe it was an affectation—or maybe an evasion, a way to avoid taking a stance on the Serum Institute's and his family's wish for him to return to Copenhagen. But it may also have been a sincere expression of his lifelong distaste for the mediocre. "The air is thin up on the mountain tops, and the masses are wallowing down in the valley," he had said fifteen years earlier. Some might ascend to the higher scientific stratosphere and attain the realm of the scientific elite, but for most people scientific work meant a life spent with "peripheral abstractions."[4]

For the present, however, Jerne had nothing on his mind that would enable him to make a true scientific advance. He had emptied his stock of immunological ideas and so could bide his time in Geneva with "a view of Mont Blanc" and wait for inspiration. At WHO, he was occupied with "a practical, comprehensible contribution." In his spare time, he also involved himself in the little group of bacteriophage researchers at the University of Geneva, with whom he had become acquainted a couple of years earlier: in addition to Jean Weigle, it included the biochemist Valentin Bonifas and the young biophysicist Eduard Kellenberger, who was carrying out electron microscope studies of phage. Jerne began to participate regularly in the group's discussions, though mainly as a "weekend warrior."[5]

The sweet life of Geneva also tempted Jerne—then forty-four. WHO paid him a high, tax-exempt salary and provided substantial fringe benefits, which enabled him to move in the jet set of the international medical bureaucracy. He also became acquainted with an au pair with the Bonifas family, Ursula Kohl, the daughter of a German businessman. She was only nineteen years old, intelligent, spoiled, self-willed, insecure, and looking for reassurance—the best guarantee of an exciting erotic relationship. "Usch" became the spice of his existence and his chauffeur, to boot. Together they began to live the life he had always dreamed of: *"I found it so fantastic to go to three-star restaurants,"* he says: *"I remember . . . we had a fantastic dinner in a star restaurant, and then we drove back again, though it was 200 kilometers or so. . . . And we did that many times, in the evening at six we said, 'Shall we go somewhere, Lyon or somewhere?' And then we drove along."* The wanderer had acquired a companion and could circulate freely among Europe's cultural and culinary centers.[6]

In December 1957, Jerne renewed his contract with WHO for another five years—definitely a bad sign for his family back in Copenhagen. In the summer of 1957 he vacationed with the boys and Adda, and the following summer with his sons alone, but thereafter his contacts with his family in Denmark became sporadic. His relationship with Adda sharply deteriorated. "I was not only superfluous—like any other woman of forty. I was practically in the way—to the point of irritation!" she complained after their last coming together. A year later, Adda—who still seemed to know nothing about the relationship between Jerne and Miss Kohl—demanded that they be reunited in Geneva, if necessary in separate domiciles. At first Jerne did not react to these signals, even though Adda became more and more depressed and in the end broke down from "insecurity—waiting for letters—sleeplessness." The younger son spoke his mind and made demands: his father could not allow himself to forget his obligations and run away from everything, even if that was what he wanted most. Maybe he did not understand, the son thought, that there was something called responsibility.[7]

Oh yes, Jerne knew that well enough—in principle. But in practice, presence and responsibility was something that applied only to his standardization work and his science.

The selection theory of antibody formation came back to mind now and then. Hans Noll, who had ended up in Pittsburgh, reported that the paper had "stirred great interest" and that Jerne had acquired a number of "enthusiastic followers" among the microbiologists there. It also began to be noticed by some of his immunological peers. At a conference on antibody production in Gatlinburg with several of the leading American immunologists in April 1957, Ray Owen referred to "Jerne's ingenious treatment" of the problem of antibody formation, and Mel Cohn took the first step toward their future immunological pas de deux when he referred to Jerne's "very interesting natural-selection theory," although he still perceived it as a variant on Burnet's modified-enzyme theory on the grounds that Jerne's theory assumed that the antigen need not be present for continued antibody formation to take place.[8]

The biggest problem with Jerne's selection theory was still that it could not really give a satisfactory explanation of the intracellular mechanism for the production of antibodies. The mechanism he himself had proposed conflicted with the emerging central dogma of molecular biology. A solution to the problem was apparently suggested to Jerne already a few months after the publication, when his younger colleague at the Serum Institute, Jørgen Spärck, is said to have proposed that the theory would be even better if it was assumed, instead, that it was "cells that are the selection unit." Spärck thought that microscopic evidence indicated that clones of cells were involved. Jerne is said to have listened to the argument but "was evasive and did not accept it," maintaining instead that it was more reasonable to regard freely circulating serum globulin molecules as the selection unit. Thus, even though Jerne was directly confronted with the possibility of letting antigen selection work with cells instead of molecules—a revision of the theory that would have resolved all of Jim Watson's and others' objections in a single blow—he continued to hold on firmly to his original theory.[9]

Jerne soon had reason to regret his evasive answer. In a review article in the *Annual Review of Medicine,* written a few months after the publication of Jerne's paper, David Talmage pointed out, in passing, that the problem with the central dogma could be solved if one assumed that selection works on cells and not on freely circulating antibodies. Simultaneously and independently Burnet came to a similar conclusion. He says he had read Jerne's paper during a visit to Berkeley at the end of 1955, "pondering heavily" why Jerne's theory was "so attractive, though obviously wrong." By replacing the selection of molecules with the selection of clones of antibody-producing cells (lymphocytes) with antigen-specific membrane receptors, "the whole picture fell into shape" for Burnet. As Jerne later expressed it, "I hit the nail but Burnet hit it on its head." Like Jerne's theory it explained a number of immunological phenomena; in addition it could be reconciled with the emerging central dogma. By focusing on antibodies as cell receptors and denying any role for circulating antibodies in the initial phases of antibody formation, the theory was more akin to Ehrlich's side-chain theory than Jerne's; and like Ehrlich's theory it had an almost pictorial simplicity.[10]

In the summer of 1957, Burnet published his new theory in a short paper, "A Modification of Jerne's Theory of Antibody Production Using the Concept of Clonal Selection," in an Australian journal; six months later he developed the idea in a series of lectures at Vanderbilt University; and in May 1958 he completed a book-length manuscript, *The Clonal Selection Theory of Acquired Immunity.* Several groups of researchers set to work immediately to test the theory experimentally. According to Burnet, every individual lymphocyte should only produce antibodies of a fixed specificity, so if lymphocytes that produced two or more specific antibodies could be detected, it would be hard to maintain the theory. In the fall of 1957 one of Burnet's students in Melbourne, Gustav Nossal, in collaboration with Joshua Lederberg, developed a method for the detection of individual antibody-producing cells in microdrops and soon achieved results that supported Burnet's proposal. On the other hand, Mel Cohn and Edwin S. Lennox, who developed a similar method of studying the production of antibodies in individual cells, got results that suggested that upward of 10 percent of the lymphocytes could produce antibodies against at least two distinct antigens.[11]

Even though the experimental results remained contradictory for several years, opinion swung slowly over to the advantage of the selection theory. Time was ripe for a more biological approach to immunology. The chemical approach, which had dominated immunological thinking for the past fifty years, was now being challenged by a rapidly growing number of biological and clinical discoveries, for example, that tuberculin hypersensitivity and tissue-graft rejection are mediated by cells rather than by circulating antibodies, that immunological-deficiency diseases demonstrate much more complex immune processes than previously thought, that many autoimmune diseases indicate the existence of intricate immunoregulatory mechanisms, and that a state of specific immunological tolerance accompanies the development of the immune response system. So, by the mid- and late 1950s, it was becoming increasingly evident that the immune response involved much more than just antibody molecules. The old immunochemical research programs were gradually substituted with more biological, particularly cellular, approaches. In November 1958, in a lecture at Harvard Medical School in Boston, Lederberg summed up the situation as a choice between the "instructive theories" dominant until then and the so-called "elective theories" that Jerne, Talmage, and Burnet had formulated and that Lederberg thought owned the future. The lecture was published soon afterward in *Science* and contributed significantly to establishing selection theories as serious alternatives to the template-instruction theories.[12]

Although Burnet had apparently hit the nail on its head, Jerne was perceived from the beginning as the originator of the modern selection theories and was therefore the obvious speaker at the international symposium entitled the Mechanism of Antibody Formation, arranged by the Czech immunologist Jaroslav Šterzl in Liblice, outside Prague, at the end of May 1959. The symposium was dominated by Eastern European, especially Czech scientists, but even so it was the first international meeting on antibody formation of any importance and Jerne's initial participation in an immunological conference. There he met some of the leading figures in international immunology, including a number of scientists who would be included in his expanding immunological network, and for the first time had the chance to discuss his theory with the assembled experts.[13]

In his introduction to the main session, Jerne emphasized that the theories so far advanced were still "almost entirely speculative" and that for the present no experimental results existed that "permit the elimination of any particular one of these theories." And yet, he added, the lack of experimental evidence need not restrain the immunological imagination. Several years before, there had only been a single theory in existence; now, it seemed as though every participant in the conference had his own theory. That was not so bad, Jerne thought; "since most of this must remain speculative anyway, I should like to encourage everybody here to let himself be carried away by fancy so as to give the discussion with which today's session will finish wings to fly with into the realm of imagination." The reference to the realm of imagination was an unusual suggestion for immunologists, a community of scientists with their feet solidly planted in the messy soil of experimental and clinical chemistry, microbiology, and pathology. But ever since his youth Jerne had expressed a romantic wish to fly on the wings of fancy, to free himself from convention, daily banalities, and the "usual concepts," so as to be penetrated with "a sea of light." A straight line runs from these early thoughts to his first appearance in the international community of immunologists and further on to his criticism in the 1980s of the way immunology had lost its way in inessential, technical, and fragmentary details. Alain Bussard, then best known for his work on immunological tolerance, remembers that his Danish roommate at the conference was "very talkative and very philosophically minded" and that they had deep discussions many nights, leaving Bussard with the conclusion that Jerne was a person who primarily "plays with ideas. . . . He plays in his own mind."[14]

The Prague meeting not only revived Jerne's immunological spirits; it was also his debut as one of the intellectual leaders who, during the post–World War II phase, would turn immunology into a full-scale scientific discipline. Another important step in his immunological ascent was the assignment from *Annual Review of Microbiology* to write an article on antibody formation. Jerne worked on it through the fall of 1959 and the winter of 1960, once he was free from his other WHO tasks. He explained to the editor that because it was not going to be one of "the usual reviews in which scores of experimental papers are surveyed," he was thinking of calling it "Immunological Speculations." The "realm of imagination" into which he now flew had the contours of a theory of the immune system as a linguistic system. Stimulated by a book written by an acquaintance in Geneva, Émile Delavenay, director of UNESCO's documentation department, he developed an analogy between the antibody forming system and the working of an electronic translation machine. He compared "the already spontaneously preexisting accumulation of antibody configurations" with a "random dictionary," a kind of "'lexicon of foreign words' in which the antigen can 'look up' suitable elements."[15]

He saw several analogies between language and immune functions: the possibility of inserting an "interlanguage" between "entry and final translation" reminded him of Jacques Monod's proposal that the antigen may first be recognized by an enzyme; he saw the idea of "pre- and postediting" as a parallel to Burnet's modified-enzyme theory; and, finally, the "polysemic properties of dictionary items" could be seen as analogies to Talmage's "restrictions on immunological specificity." He ended with still another analogy. It was already known that the antibody molecule is divalent; it resembles a rod with a specific combining site on each end. Where else could one find rods with the same "monogram" on both ends? Well, on a typewriter, where a system of rods mediates between the fingers and the typed letters "in selected stimulus chains."[16]

Jerne also proposed a number of innovative terms for the immune system: "epitope" instead of "antigen determinant," "paratope" for the portion of the antibody molecule that determines its specificity, "idiotope" for single antigenic determinants (that is, epitopes) that "the body accepts as identical with its own," as well as "xenotope," "pantachotope," and other more or less exotic words. The new terminology was probably an attempt to find words that emphasized the topological aspects of the immune system as an interactive system, an approach Jerne would develop further in the network theory of the immune system more than a decade later. So far, however, the primordial network vision was restricted to finding new terms: *"I thought it must be possible to improve the terminology,"* he says in an interview. Even though some of his colleagues reacted a little sarcastically to his neologisms ("After having looked at the first few pages . . . I decided to buy a dictionary," one of them wrote afterward), several of his coined terms, for example, paratope and epitope, eventually passed into common immunological usage: *"They're using concepts like epitope today, but nobody knows where they come from,"* Jerne comments.[17]

Although some of the terms found their way into the immunological lexicon, the implicit topological approach went unnoticed. Neither did his readers understand the introductory and concluding sections of his article, in which Jerne made his first appearance as immunology's linguist; for example, his thoughts about the translation machine were totally ignored: *"[I wrote] this 'Immunological speculations' but no one reacted to it, that time."* Nearly a quarter century would pass before, in the fall of 1984, he took up the linguistic theme again in his Nobel lecture. In spite of the lack of response to the speculative aspects of the article, however, his overhaul of the theories of antibody formation was positively received—a "magnificent review" of the research situation, said a telegram from the otherwise critical Mel Cohn—and hence assumed an importance among immunologists of the time as a creative summary, although it never became a citation classic.[18]

In the winter of 1959 Jerne gave in to Adda's complaints and agreed that she and Ivar should move to Geneva. Once there, however, they saw very little of him. Jerne spent most of his time in the Palais des Nations, preparing the meetings of the many study groups and the annual standardization meetings, or traveled to conferences. Entertaining Usch took most of his spare time, and after little more than a year Adda returned to Copenhagen, humiliated. Once more it fell to Donald, who was now studying medicine in Copenhagen, to articulate the neglected family's powerlessness and anger. The son thought his father had lost his wits entirely, that he behaved dishonorably and treated Adda wretchedly. It was a puzzle, Donald thought, why his father always succeeded in making matters so tremendously difficult.

Jerne did not seem to react to such reprimands. Instead, he immersed himself deeper in his immunological career. Through the Prague symposium and "Immunological Speculations," he had made a comeback on the immunological scene. He now belonged to the "select few" within the study of antibody formation, and his work once again began to achieve a significance that might be proportional to "the pains of the permanent one-sided preoccupation with a single detail of life that is required." He began to express the feeling that the work in WHO's standardization section did not give him sufficient scientific satisfaction. Even if the past three years had been "extraordinarily useful," especially in giving him administrative experience, he missed the laboratory, especially "the deeper confrontations with scientific problems."[19]

Where could he continue with immunology? In December 1959 he saw the possibility, some years down the road, of becoming head of one of Europe's oldest immunological research institutions, the Paul Ehrlich Institute in Frankfurt, after Richard Prigge's retirement. Jerne wrote that he would gladly pass along his experience in standardization work but emphasized that he wanted above all to go in for immunological research: "Last but not least, my greatest scientific goal has always been to deepen my understanding of the formation of antibodies." Prigge backed Jerne wholeheartedly as his successor, but the salary that Jerne expected proved a stumbling block. His requirement of keeping the WHO salary level would have made him one of the most highly paid officials in the state of Hessen, and after less than a year's negotiations with the ministry the question was dropped. Another possibility was joining the biophysical research group at the University of Geneva. Jerne remained a weekend warrior with the group, and as a discussion partner he had involved himself in Kellenberger's project on the structure and function of T4 phage tail fibers, a subject he had dealt with during his studies of P-star kinetics five years earlier. Kellenberger was so pleased with the group's "brain" (a pun on the Danish word for brain, "hjerne") that he tried to arrange a position for him at the university; a year later the university hired Jerne as a part-time visiting professor to give a course on biophysics with Kellenberger.[20]

The prospects of getting a permanent position at Geneva were uncertain, and so in the spring of 1960 Jerne chose instead to pin his hopes on an attempt to establish immunology "as a sort of central pivot for WHO research." He had an ally in Burnet, who had been appointed a member of the organization's newly formed Advisory Committee on Medical Research (ACMR) and who declared that "immunology may become the greatest contributor to medicine in the next generation." Because many diseases involve immune defense and because prevention, diagnosis, and treatment often build upon immunological methods, Jerne believed that WHO should give a higher priority to immunology. Although the organization's task was not to support basic research, he believed it should nevertheless contribute by creating an overview of this large and heterogeneous research field. A great need existed for "critical judgment of the importance, or the relative importance, of published experimental findings." He was evidently trying to sell his own talent to WHO.[21]

At the ACMR's second session in June 1960, Jerne was assigned to continue investigating the possibility of making immunology an independent field of activity within the organization. The initiative received an unexpected boost in the fall of 1960, when it was announced that Burnet had shared a Nobel Prize in physiology or medicine with Peter Medawar for their studies of immunological tolerance—the first Nobel Prize awarded for an immunological discovery since Karl Landsteiner's in 1930 for his discovery of blood groups. After this, Jerne apparently judged the chances of continuing with immunology at WHO to be so great that he declined an offer to become head of the Department of Biological Standards at the National Institute for Medical Research in northern London, on the grounds that standardization had turned into an entirely applied research area and that he wanted to concentrate on "the analysis and evaluation of more theoretical research problems."[22]

By this time, the most attractive place for international immunology—as for most other biomedical sciences—was the United States. In the beginning of January 1961, Jerne went to California to meet the "Nouvelle Vogue" of immunologists at the informal Antibody Workshop in La Jolla and then continued on a tour of the United States to discuss plans for the WHO program and to give lectures on the problem of antibody formation. With respect to the selection principle, the attitude of the American immunologists was still divided (Fred Tauber and Scott Podolsky even maintain that "the early 1960s were quite a nadir on the route of [the clonal selection theory] to eventual widespread acceptance"), but Jerne nevertheless felt he was being taken much more seriously now than when he first lectured about it in 1955, when it was considered "baloney." The growing respectability, if not acceptance, of the selection principle certainly also helped him in getting support for the WHO program.[23]

Back in Geneva in February, Jerne tried to convince the WHO bureaucracy that the best way of developing "an orderly WHO programme" was yearly to convene an Expert Committee on Immunological Research. He also placed great emphasis on the organization's opportunities to support international information exchange and personal contacts, including funding an international team that could train immunologists in developing countries. The major research needs would be mapped out in a number of scientific groups. Candau is said to have accepted the plan immediately. *"And when it had all been decided and they had put money in it, I myself got to decide whom I wanted to invite,"* Jerne comments, proudly. The work of putting the scientific groups together and developing action plans for them became his main task for the rest of 1961.[24]

Jerne had set his sights on taking on the leadership of WHO's immunology program. But the winter tour had also raised his profile in the United States. New temptations followed. Soon he was offered a job at a new institute that the virologist Jonas Salk was setting up in La Jolla. After considering it a while, Jerne declined the offer, for as his youngest son said, repeating his father's words, "You can't be inventive on command." Then, a few weeks later, he received yet another, even more attractive offer to chair the Department of Microbiology at the University of Pittsburgh, probably on a suggestion by his old admirer Hans Noll. After a guest lecture in Pittsburgh, Jerne accepted on the spot and it was decided that he would begin his new job the following fall. Why did he choose to move to "what is probably the ugliest town on earth"? It was not for the sake of the money, he claimed, but to "re-emerge as a scientist—o jeh, o jeh, wenn *das* nur gut geht!" Adda reacted negatively to his America plans: "Is it, then, farewell to WHO, is it a guest appearance—or are you sliding into the emigrant 'mentality,' in which everything new is better," she wrote, reminding him that she still was, in fact, "Mrs. Jerne."[25]

The spring of 1962 became one long immunological seminar, with "a mountain of correspondence, paper- and report-editing, etc." Four scientific groups—on immunoprophylaxis and immunotherapy, on immunopathology, on tissue antigens and transplantation, and on immunochemistry—with scores of international experts (the roster reads like a contemporary Who's

Who in immunology, including Ashley Miles, David Evans, Albert Sabin, Jonas Salk, Pierre Grabar, M. F. A. Woodruff, Georg Klein, Hilary Koprowski, Alain Bussard, Morten Simonsen, Robin R. A. Coombs, Milan Hasek, Michael Heidelberger, John Humphrey, Elvin Kabat, Ernst Sorkin, and, of course, Macfarlane Burnet, among others) convened with Jerne as the spider in the web. At the beginning of June, the chairs of the groups met to recapitulate and sum up the work, and in his final report to the ACMR, Jerne emphasized the historical importance of the undertaking. The understanding of immune processes had developed to a stage, he wrote, "where immunology in the broadest sense is more clearly emerging as an autonomous science." By establishing a permanent program, WHO would be able to contribute to making immunology more recognized as an independent scientific discipline, "as an important subject by itself." Jerne's rhetoric was undoubtedly meant to impress the ACMR, but it was not unfounded. The many study groups in Geneva in the spring of 1962 and the week-long discussions among some of the world's leading immunologists were undoubtedly an essential element in the creation of a platform for international cooperation—in retrospect Jerne's work with the WHO immunology program in 1961–62 can be seen as the first step toward a globally organized effort that culminated in the First International Congress of Immunology in 1971.[26]

But the work with the study groups was also of great importance to Jerne's own career. Through the whole spring he had been rubbing shoulders with a significant fraction of the international biomedical research elite. It had been heavy work but also exciting: "After having gotten to know the top layer of scientists, you have an urge to shift into 4th gear—then you notice that there are only 3!" he wrote in his diary. He later came to look on these events as "a sort of turning point" in his career: from having been a "timid, conscientious standardizer" he had now become, in his own retrospective words, "a rather extraordinary person." The work with the WHO immunology groups became the best preparation he could imagine for his budding university career. *"I had an ulterior motive in all that,"* he recollects: *"I thought, 'I'm going to Pittsburgh, so I'd better make sure I learn a little about immunology.' And of course it was a perfect way of getting everything first-hand."*[27]

The company of other immunologists also gave him ideas for his personal research. As the months passed, he gradually filled his pocket notebook with ideas of what he should be able to undertake in Pittsburgh. "Millipore filter chambers containing insoluble Ag could be inserted in organism to take out all specific Ab molecules, in good time," he wrote in one note; "inject the same

Niels Jerne at a meeting with one of the five scientific groups he convened at the World Health Organization in the spring of 1962. *At the table, from left to right:* Ole Maaløe, Jerne, and John Humphrey. (Medical History Museum, University of Copenhagen. Photo: J. Cadou, Geneva)

mixture of a number of antigens into a population—see whether there are individual differences in the titer spectrum," he wrote in another, adding the possibility of using an isotope labeling technique to show the presence of low antibody concentrations. These were broad sketches of experiments whose purpose is not perfectly clear. The note about the millipore filter suggests that he wanted to try to demonstrate free circulating antibodies before immunization. It is possible that his motivation came from a critical remark that Felix Haurowitz had made six months earlier. Haurowitz could, at a pinch, accept Burnet's clonal selection theory, but Jerne's theory was "purely speculative," for no one had succeeded in detecting preformed circulating antibodies, even using the most sensitive methods. Of course Jerne supported Burnet's clonal selection theory, but—as he had pointed out in the "Immunological Speculation" article two years earlier—he added a reservation in favor of his natural selection theory, namely, that "the mediation of antibody formation" might occur through "circulating antibody molecules." Jerne was not convinced that Burnet's clonal selection theory was the only possible answer to the question of antibody formation. In a lecture at the Eighth International Congress for Microbiology in Montreal in the summer of 1962, he spoke of Burnet's theory as "one of the selective theories." But still only one of them: he had apparently not given up on his own theory of preformed circulating antibodies.[28]

The summer of 1962 was quiet. Jerne wound down his involvement in the Palais des Nations and began to train his successor. His thoughts rotated around the future in Pittsburgh. He hired one of their new Ph.D.s, Albert Nordin, as a postdoctoral fellow and asked his old colleague Jens Ole Rostock, who had moved on with Maaløe to the new microbiological department in Copenhagen, to come over to Pittsburgh later in the fall to build up his laboratory there. His summer notes show that he was thinking almost daily about his impending experimental work. He had several experimental irons in the fire. In June, for example, in discussions with John Humphrey, he got the idea of an experiment to disprove the template-instruction theories. One of the participants in the spring seminars had told him that immunologically inert latex and bentonite particles can adsorb up to 20 percent of their weight in globulin molecules. Bovine gamma globulin adsorbed to latex acquires different antigenic properties than it would have if adsorbed to bentonite. That fact should make experimental use possible, Jerne wrote to Nordin later in the summer, since the globulin had to remain adsorbed to the particles to function as a specific antigen. If the template-instruction theories of antibody formation were correct, "the globulin plus the particles should be present in the antibody producing plasma cells. If the particles are large enough their presence should be directly visible within such cells, or their absence might be demonstrated." If the complex could not be demonstrated within the cells, "the stimulus [for antibody formation] must be outside! [the cell]." The summer passed thus, in the making of experimental plans.[29]

By September 1962 Jerne was ready to leave Europe. He wrote to Adda that he wanted to dissolve their marriage, and in the middle of the month he took the boat from Le Havre to New York. Tjek's paintings went along, but Usch (or Alexandra, as he had begun calling her) and most of his books had to remain in Geneva for the time being. The extant notes from the trip mostly concern the phage tail-fiber experiments with Kellenberger, but there is every reason to believe that Jerne's thoughts were also orbiting around the existence he was leaving and the one that awaited him. Twice before he had left a life behind him. Nearly thirty years before, he had left the Netherlands to study medicine in Copenhagen. Six years before, he had left pancake-flat Denmark for the international atmosphere in Geneva. Now he turned his back on Europe's "narrow old streets," "agreeable inns," and "dusty bookshelves" in favor of the energetic and vital American immunological scene. Immunology had finally taken the highest priority in his life.[30]

18

"Finally, My Precious, I Have to Be Brilliant and Make Antibodies"

*L*ike a social atom, fifty-year-old Niels Jerne arrived in the United States to begin a new and unknown life. He was going to a country whose science he admired, though he scorned America in many other ways. Once again, he was assuming the role of foreigner in another culture. It is significant that the first person he wrote to after his arrival in Pittsburgh was another immigrant and foreigner, Gordon Sato, the young Japanese American he had met at Cal Tech, who had now established himself as a respected molecular biologist.

Jerne was housed in one of the apartment complexes at the University of Pittsburgh, and in a few days was ready to take on his new assignment as head of the Department of Microbiology, one of the medical faculty's larger departments. The microbiologists were active in a multitude of research areas, including organ regeneration, protein synthesis in ergosomes, virological studies, and bacterial genetics. Besides Jerne, who was the only real immunologist in the department, there were two full professors and four tenure-track professors, five postdoctoral fellows, and six graduate students, as well as a number of instructors and laboratory technicians. Although Jerne was well acquainted with the American research scene, he was nevertheless impressed. Pittsburgh was bubbling with intellectual activity, the department offered "excellent" working conditions, and "many daily seminars" were held, so that you could keep "*à jour* of the latest." For the first time in his life he faced the task of teaching students; during that first fall, however, he gave only a lecture or two.[1]

One of Jerne's explicit purposes in taking the job in Pittsburgh was to get back to experimental work. His postdoc, Albert Nordin, has the impression that Jerne "was probing and casting around for something that could work," but that he had nothing more specific in mind than trying to get a look at the early immune response. Judging by his correspondence and notes, in October Jerne was still occupied with the bentonite and latex particle experiments. For unknown reasons he did not show "much enthusiasm for those experiments," however, and soon gave up the idea. He briefly considered studying the early immune response in more primitive vertebrates like frogs, but this, too, was rejected. Nordin also remembers that Jerne was inspired by the sedimentation technique that three of his new, younger colleagues, Hans Noll, Felix Wettstein, and Theophil Staehelin, were using, so that when Jens Ole Rostock arrived at the beginning of November they spent more than a month trying to develop a system for detecting small quantities of antibodies through studying the difference in sedimentation properties of free antigen (phage T2) and antigen-antibody (anti-T2) complex: "We did one experiment, at least one," Nordin remembers, "but it didn't work." Jerne's lack of orientation toward a specific goal is reflected in a letter to Alexandra from the beginning of November 1962: "Beloved Rabbit-Down, I am feeling really low, like a wounded rabbit who has hidden away in an odd corner. I really don't know how I am going to get through the next four weeks. . . . Darling, I love you so, I feel so alone, as if some empty machine were operating automatically here in my body, while my spiritual content remains with you. Finally, my precious, I have to be brilliant and make antibodies, our antibodies."[2]

How to become brilliant? Among his notes from the preceding spring is the sketch of a method for detecting the existence of individual antibody-producing cells. The idea was to combine the plaque assay technique he had used in Copenhagen in the early 1950s with the well-known principle of complement-mediated immune hemolysis, discovered by Bordet in 1901 and further developed by August von Wasserman and his coworkers for the diagnosis of syphilis in 1906: "E.g., lymphoid cells from animals immunized against red [blood] cells could be forming plaques on plates with red cells, [and it would be possible to show that] the antibodies they produce . . . hemolyze the neighbouring red cells. . . . Can *single* [antibody] molecules be shown this way, by a method which would *magnify* the action of one molecule[?]" Nordin remembers that Jerne took up this idea in their discussions in the beginning of December 1962: "And we talked about what to do. And that's when he was taking this

[note]book and says that 'this will work.'" And what was it? "This was the plaque assay . . . [in] pretty good details." They started it "almost casually" before Jerne traveled to Geneva in December where he would be consultant to the Expert Committee on Biological Standardization and celebrate Christmas and New Year with his Rabbit-Down. "By chance," however, Nordin happened to have a few real rabbits that had been immunized with the red blood cells of sheep. He tried out the recipe and two weeks later got the first positive results.[3]

The method was simple. A rabbit was injected with sheep red cells, the lymph nodes were removed, and the lymphoid cells (including cells producing antibodies against sheep red cells) were teased out into a tissue-culture medium. One million of these cells were mixed with sheep red cells (that is, antigen) in fluid agar, and the whole mixture was poured onto a supporting bottom layer of agar in a petri dish. After incubation at 37° for an hour (whereby antibodies secreted from the antibody-producing cells diffused out and attached to the red cells), the dish was covered with complement (in the form of diluted guinea pig serum), causing hemolysis of the red cells immobilized in the agar around the antibody producers. Further incubation for fifteen minutes "revealed about 100 clear plaques of about 0.25 mm diameter that stood out sharply against the uniformly red background."[4]

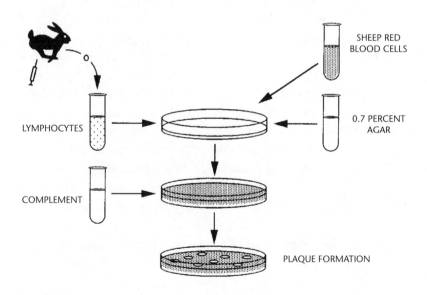

Reconstruction of the hemolytic plaque assay. (Drawing: Mikael Larsen)

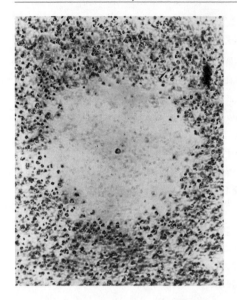

Microphotograph of a "Jerne plaque." A single antibody-producing cell in the center of a clear (lysed) area. (Medical History Museum, University of Copenhagen)

Right after New Year 1963, when Jerne returned to Pittsburgh with a bad cold, Nordin was standing in the door with the first plaque on the petri dish. Then followed an intense period of writing, and in the beginning of February they submitted to *Science* a two-page manuscript, which, after minor revisions, was published in the middle of April 1963. "I believe that this technique may prove very useful, and less cumbersome, than putting single cells into microdroplets [as Nossal and Lederberg had done]," Jerne wrote to Burnet, who replied that the new method would come to be "the most powerful weapon in Antibody formation studies." The reactions from the rest of the immunological world were equally overwhelming: "Bravo! . . . It's all very pretty and surely an excellent way to go on with single cell analysis," wrote Edwin Lennox from Paris. "Experimental brilliance and analytical thinking in the finest combination," "elegant," "quite exciting," "most ingenious," "truly ingenious" were some of the superlatives. People were "impressed" and "terribly impressed" by the "simplicity and ingenuity" of the new technique. "The idea . . . is a most ingenious one, and the photos are beautiful," wrote the old veteran Michael Heidelberger.[5]

Nobody questioned Jerne's and Nordin's priority. Yet the plaque technique is a good example of multiple discovery (or rather multiple construction). Only a few weeks after Jerne and Nordin had sent in their manuscript, the American physiologist Joseph Ingraham, who had been trying since the end of the 1950s to construct a plaque method for detecting antibody-producing cells, succeeded in doing so during a stay with Alain Bussard at the Pasteur Institute; his paper came out three months after Jerne and Nordin's. Furthermore, Gustav Nossal in Melbourne claims that he and Joshua Lederberg, when they were developing the microdrop method in 1957, had also considered trying "a sheep red cell hemolysin system" but that it "did not work," perhaps because they did not use enough complement. There is no reason to believe that Jerne and Ingraham ever exchanged ideas. Whether any exchange of information ever took place between Nossal and Lederberg, on the one hand, and Jerne, on the other, is harder to say. At least two independent successful constructions were involved—and Jerne and Nordin's happened to come first.[6]

An initial problem with the method was that it required great quantities of guinea pig serum to supply the necessary complement. This problem was solved within a few weeks, when Claudia Henry, a young Australian virologist, joined the group. Henry—who had just finished her Ph.D. in Pittsburgh with Jerne on her committee—suggested that they use a specific substance, DEAE-dextran, to neutralize the anticomplementary effect of agar. This made it possible to decrease the amount of guinea pig complement in the system and thereby make the method less expensive, and thus more useful. Another colleague in the department, Aaron Stock, suggested staining the cells on the dishes dark blue so that the plaques stood out like stars in a dark August sky. So improved, the technique was presented by Jerne at a conference on Cell-Bound Antibodies in Washington, D.C., in the middle of May 1963.[7]

The aesthetic effect certainly contributed to the method's quick breakthrough. Several groups announced that they would immediately begin using it: in one lab, the method was in use as early as a week after the conference. A couple of months later, Nossal wrote from Melbourne, thanking Jerne for sending the reprint on "what we are popularly terming in the Institute 'Jerne-plaques'! You cannot imagine how much pleasure this elegant technique has given to all of us!" And the pleasure was long-lasting—in the next two decades, the two methodological papers by Jerne and his coworkers were cited some four thousand times in immunological literature. During roughly this same period the short paper in *Science* was among the journal's three most cited and soon became one of the most cited papers in modern biomedical literature. It is no exaggeration to say that the significance of the plaque technique to cellular immunology in the 1960s corresponded to that of the precipitin method to immunochemical research during the period between the wars. The method itself was not modified to any degree worth mentioning during the next few years; the Pittsburgh group's own improvements consisted of an automated, transistorized plaque-counting machine. Later, however, A. J. Cunningham combined Ingraham's and Jerne's methods by enclosing a single closely packed cell layer in a chamber on a slide.[8]

During the spring and summer of 1963 Jerne gathered four persons in two small laboratories overlooking the university's football stadium. Nossal, Henry, and the technician Arthur Park were joined by Jerne's first, and only, Ph.D. candidate, Aurelia Koros. During the following three years the little group concentrated on using the new technique for studies of the early immune response. Utilizing the method to test the clonal selection theory was obvious. Five years earlier, the Cohn-Lennox group had obtained preliminary results that suggested a lymphocyte can synthesize antibodies against two different antigens, an outcome that, if true, created a problem for the clonal selection theory, since the theory stipulated that a clone of cells makes specific antibodies against one kind of antigen only. At the conference in Washington, D.C., the nuclear physicist Leo Szilard, who had become interested in immunology late in life, had proposed that the plaque technique could be used to test the double-production hypothesis, something that Jerne did immediately on his return to Pittsburgh. In principle, the experiment was simple to carry out: antibodies against sheep red blood cells and antibodies against rabbit red blood cells were produced and plated onto a mixture of sheep and rabbit red blood cells. If all the plaque-forming cells were single producers, the plaques should be a little opaque, but if double producers exist, all plaques should be completely lysed. The result appeared unambiguous: "We saw none that were entirely clear and that could be identified as a plaque resulting from a double producing cell," Jerne reported to Szilard.[9]

Despite this satisfying result, however, Jerne was not especially interested in continuing to test the clonal selection theory. He assumed that antibody-producing cells arise out of multipotential cells through cell division and differentiation, and that now and then "two potentialities" can be "expressed simultaneously." Even if double producers should later be detected, he thought, that would not be any problem for the clonal selection theory, and he thereafter showed no interest in the question. He was already convinced that the clonal selection theory was correct in principle—the problem that continued to haunt him was rather what role circulating, spontaneously produced antibodies might have. His nearly ten-year-old natural selection theory still had, in his own view, a place alongside Burnet's theory.[10]

In the fall of 1963 the cell biologist Hiroshi Fuji joined them as a postdoc to perform cytological studies of the plaque-forming cells. Through different staining methods Fuji could eventually establish that the plaque-forming cells were members of the plasma cell series; immature (precursor) plasma cells and blast cells predominated in the early course of immunization, while mature plasma cells predominated later on. As they developed their research routines, more and more visitors arrived in Pittsburgh to learn their technique. It took a good deal of kitchen know-how to get it to function; for example, it did not work if one tried to produce plaques with fresh red blood cells: "red cells are better the older they are, short of showing spontaneous hemolysis."[11]

During the next two years Jerne followed to a great extent the same research strategy he had developed in collaboration with Ole Maaløe at the Serum Institute more than fifteen years earlier, that is, to produce empirical dose-response curves and try to construct a theoretical model to explain the empirical curves. The dose-response reaction had then consisted of diphtheria toxin (dose) versus the size of the skin reactions (response); it now concerned the amount of red blood cells (dose) versus the number of plaque-forming cells (response) in the course of early immunization. They were able to establish that the mouse spleen contains small quantities of plaque-forming cells against sheep red blood cells. They found an average of one hundred specific plaque-forming cells in a normal mouse spleen, but the individual variation was great: "We were immediately impressed by the variability between mice," Henry recalls. New questions arose: Were the plaque-forming cells the direct targets of the antigen, or were the cells affected indirectly? Did the quick increase of plaque-forming cells depend on cell division? If so, when did these cells arise, and from where were they derived? Which type of antibody (IgG or IgM) did the cells produce? What was the relationship between dose and response during the early course of immunization? How much antigen was necessary to set the immune reaction going? "I am now waiting for brilliant ideas to come," Jerne wrote to his friend Stent.[12]

Through "hard work and the mass slaughter of mice" the group produced empirical dose-response curves, and by intense concentration at the blackboard Jerne tried to frame mathematical models. For Art Park it seemed as though Jerne "would always have the answer before we did the experiments, like he almost knew intuitively." Even so, the mysteries grew faster than the insights and the dose-response curves became the source of continual "challenge and torment." In letters to colleagues, Jerne referred to "puzzling data" and "puzzling results."[13]

Among the puzzling observations was the possibility that antibody production might be regulated by a negative feedback: "It appears, then, when few cells are stimulated, they can each reach a larger offspring than is the case when almost all competent cells are initially stimulated, *as if there were a feedback factor* which restricted the maximum yield of antibody-producing cells." He wrote around to his colleagues ("What I would need most at present would be some intellectual support") and took every chance to discuss his results: he gave lectures at Emory University and at the Rockefeller Institute, and after a two-week

Niels Jerne at the blackboard, ca. 1964–65. By "hard work and the mass slaughter of mice" the Pittsburgh group tried to understand the kinetics of the early immune response. (Medical History Museum, University of Copenhagen)

break in Geneva to discuss the new WHO program for immunology, which was starting under the direction of the American immunologist Howard Goodman, he made a lecture and conference tour of Oak Ridge, Tennessee, Duke University, and the Institute for Cancer Research in Philadelphia. The titles of his guest lectures during the late fall of 1963 and the year to come were variations on the same basic theme: "Antibody Producing Cells in the Mouse Spleen Before and After Experimental Antigenic Stimulation."[14]

Toward the end of the year, the experimental work came to a stop. "Our research work hasn't progressed very much," Jerne wrote to Burnet. In the beginning of March 1964, Nossal arrived on a quick visit with dynamite in his baggage: proof that antigen could not be detected in the antibody-producing cells and that phagocytic cells take up foreign antigens. It was a convincing experimental blow to the template-instruction theories, and Jerne was enthusiastic. But the refutation of the instruction theory did not necessarily confer a clear-cut advantage on the *clonal* selection theory, so Jerne once again sensed an opportunity: "Things are looking up a bit even for the old 'Natural' selection theory," he wrote to Stent. In a lecture in Copenhagen in May 1964, he asserted that the observed saturation of the system might well depend on "circulating specific antibodies." The antigen's immediate target could as well be macrophages or "a limited number of pre-formed specific antibody molecules." In other words, once again he saw the possibility that the natural selection theory might be able to coexist with Burnet's clonal selection theory. "Influenced by the natural selection theory . . . we entertained the possibility that a specific event involving 'natural' antibody might precede stimulation of the specific precursor cells predicted by clonal selection," Henry recalls.[15]

Alongside his guest lecturing and brain work at the blackboard, Jerne was given many more administrative duties; his days as chair of the department were filled with various committee activities, budget work, and personnel questions. He also became incorporated into the American immunological research community as a referee for the National Science Foundation and a member of the National Institutes of Health's Study Section for Immunology. He continued to be affiliated with WHO, now as a member of its Advisory Committee on Medical Research. He judged applications for grants from the world's leading immunologists but was not impressed with the development of the subject. "Socially, the whole field seems to be moving rapidly upwards, though scientifically it is still much in the dark," he wrote. His judgment may seem unfair: this was shortly before the elucidation of the distinction between variable and constant regions of the antibody molecule, a distinction that would once again alter fundamentally the scope of the question of antibody diversity. Then the whole immunological scene would change, and the conditions for Jerne's scientific work as well. But at the moment (early February 1964) his verdict was not beside the point.[16]

Jerne also became more involved in teaching in Pittsburgh. During the fall term of 1963 he worked hard at reorganizing the courses in microbiology and immunology for medical students. It was the first time in his life he had taught, but he declared retrospectively that he enjoyed it, *"as long as it didn't become too much."* Evidently the students liked his teaching so well that two years later they awarded him their teaching prize, the Golden Apple, as the best lecturer on the faculty. One reason for this surely was his well-known ability to explain things in a simple way; but his mildly iconoclastic attitude toward his subject may also have influenced the choice. During a lecture in the fall of 1963, for example, he claimed that immunology had nothing whatever to do with defense mechanisms. Neither, in his view, did complement belong in immunology, since the complement researchers did not have to take the specificity of antibodies into consideration. "In my personal opinion," he explained to the students, "it would be useful to regard all responses and phenomena that involve *antibodies* as immunological—and conversely, to regard all phenomena that have nothing to do with antibodies as falling outside the subject of immunology."[17]

Such a categorical definition of immunology suggests a certain scientific self-confidence. Aside from the puzzling experimental results, nearly everything was in fact going well for Jerne. He had made a scientific success with the new plaque technique and had good working conditions in the department. Apart from sitting and conversing in the evenings over a beer or a bottle of wine at a bar or in one of the local jazz clubs, he lived and breathed his scientific work. Tjek's paintings remained in their wrappings, and he said he still felt "like

Select staff at the Department of Microbiology, University of Pittsburgh, ca. 1964. Among them are Albert Nordin (*standing second from left*), Aurelia Koros (*in the middle*), Claudia Henry (*standing second from right*), and Niels Jerne (*sitting second from left*). (Medical History Museum, University of Copenhagen)

a passenger" in life. "But then, we are all passengers," he confided to Stent. Evidently it did not matter so much that he traveled through life as a passenger as long as he was confirmed as a successful scientist. "Nothing can be more pleasant than to be a person of good reputation living in Pittsburgh," he wrote in a later reminiscence.[18]

It was also pleasant to be able to play the part of a scientist with somewhat broader interests than most in the immuno-business. One of the areas that fascinated Jerne the most was the operation of memory. He had corresponded with Stent for several years about this subject; once he had summarized his views in a long and playfully worded letter dispatched from a fictive "Kaiser Wilhelm Institut für Gedächtnisforschung." Like one of the heroes of his youth, Henri Bergson, he felt that memory is a prerequisite for consciousness but that science did not seem to have anything sensible to say about the matter: "As soon as one enters this field it becomes obvious that it is a scandal: nobody seems to know how memory functions, nor where it is located. It is very difficult to stay clear from Behavior, Psychology, Semantics, and Philosophy—I think all this should be avoided as far as possible." There was more to be gained, he thought, in introspection, novels, and belles lettres—it is probably no coincidence that Proust was still one of his favorite writers.[19]

Jerne's fascination with memory did not entirely lack points of contact with his interest in the immune system. The cognition theme from his "Immunological Speculations" article came up again: "There is a trace of immunological flavour about memory (long term immunity that wears off, reinforcement doses, recognition)," he explained to Stent. A rumor about his speculations on memory spread among his acquaintances, and Karl Gordon Lark got him invited to a symposium, The Role of Macromolecules in Complex Behavior, at Kansas State University at the end of April 1964, where Jerne presented a lecture entitled "Antibody Formation and Immunological Memory." The analogies between the immune system and the central nervous system seemed to be "quite superficial," he thought, and even if one could not exclude "functional similarities," the comparison lay more on the metaphorical level: in both the immune system and the central nervous system the organism builds upon knowledge it already possesses. The selection theories of antibody formation start from the idea that "the organism acquires no *new* knowledge by the exposure to antigen"; in a corresponding way, Jerne maintained, again referring to Socrates (in Plato's *Meno*), "understanding must be preceded by recognition, and all learning, therefore, must consist of a 'recollection' of knowledge already present in the soul." The discussion was a trifle marginal in relation to the conference theme: Jerne felt himself to be "a lone immunological bird among psychologists, neurologists and perhaps several cyberneticists," nor did he get anything special out of listening to the others. The time was not really ripe for a dialogue between immunologists and cognitive scientists. "What scientists at the present time know about memory is hardly worth knowing," Jerne concluded.[20]

Despite his success with the plaque technique and his growing celebrity in the United States, Jerne had begun to entertain plans to move back to Europe. He remembers that he *"had some nostalgia for Europe. . . . One yearns for Europe if one cares for old traditions, old cities, if one cares for some history."* His chance came as early as the fall of 1963, when the professorship in general pathology and bacteriology in Copenhagen was advertised. Jerne sent in an application and, six months later, was unanimously rated first by the search committee, who referred to his "unusual sense of essential and biologically fundamental questions, combined with a rare capacity for experimentally approaching difficult areas." But when Jerne realized the disadvantages of being a university professor in Copenhagen (comparatively low salary and many students to examine), he became "tormented by indecision." "It's always hardest," he wrote to Maaløe, who was hoping to get his old friend home again, "making decisions that deeply involve one's personal activities." After having tasted, as he put it, the "bitterness of the world" he was afraid that it would be too "pleasant" to settle down again in Denmark. Besides, he told Stent, he felt it disconcerting to return to the "scene of one's earlier life." He concluded that he "could not face it," and declined the offer.[21]

Also on the scene of his earlier life were Adda and the children. His wife was living alone and abandoned in Copenhagen; contact between them had completely broken off since his move to Pittsburgh. Both children were living independent lives, exchanging letters sporadically with their father, who in return sent them money now and then—"undeserved gifts," as Ivar called them. In the summer of 1964 Jerne's divorce from Adda was finalized, and a few months later he married Ursula Kohl, who moved in with him under the name of Alexandra Jerne, thereby finally becoming part of his public life. From that moment, Jerne removed Adda completely from his life's narrative. Biographical dictionary articles often mention his first and third wives, but not Adda—"nobody talks about Jerne's second wife." She continued to live in Copenhagen, had occasional contact with the children, but never remarried, and died in a home for retired hospital workers in 1993.[22]

Later in 1964 Jerne received two new career offers. On the occasion of a lecture on antibody formation and primary response at the Massachusetts General Hospital in the beginning of November, he was informally asked by Albert Coons, Salvador Luria, and Herman Kalckar whether he would consider moving to Harvard Medical School. At about the same time, Richard Prigge renewed his efforts to get Jerne to take over the Paul Ehrlich Institute in Frankfurt. The salary requirements that Jerne had set four years earlier were no longer a problem. At the end of January 1965, he received an official invitation from the state of Hessen to be director of the Paul Ehrlich Institute and to be professor of experimental therapy at the Wolfgang Goethe University. "They're looking forward to you as the Israelites the Messiah," Prigge explained.[23]

During spring 1965 Jerne negotiated simultaneously with Hessen and Harvard. He wanted guarantees that basic immunological research in Frankfurt would not be put in jeopardy, and he demanded an enlargement of the staff by three or four scientific positions, plus a budget for guest researchers. Harvard, for its part, promised a commensurately big laboratory, and Jerne responded that he was "overjoyed at the prospect of being able to devote more of my time to immunological thought and experiment." His presumptive colleagues had great expectations of him: "At the present the community [of immunologists] divides itself between those who are interested in the detailed chemistry of antigens and antibodies and those who deal with more general biological phenomena. The kind of work which interests you would clearly fill the gap which exists between these two camps and perhaps bring us all closer to one another," wrote Edgar Haber, as if predicting Jerne's "Waiting for the End" paper two years later.[24]

As Jerne weighed his choices, thousands of new mice were being sacrificed in the laboratory. The work of writing up the experiments with plaque-forming cells kept being postponed because of unclarified issues and new speculations. The question of feedback mechanisms had become the permanent agenda on the blackboard. At that point it was not only "as if" there was a feedback factor; it became clearer and clearer that "this must be provided by antibodies," remembers Henry. "We are much interested now in the fact that antibody (maybe of a certain molecular type) specifically inhibits the proliferation of antibody-forming cells in the primary response," Jerne wrote to Mel Cohn, so "we are once more repeating and consolidating our findings."[25]

In the winter of 1964–65 Jerne got busy writing up the past two years' experimental work. At least two other groups—E. A. McCulloch's in Toronto and Göran Möller's in Stockholm—were on the heels of the Pittsburgh group. "Practically all your data agree well with our findings," Jerne told Möller. The writing was interrupted by a month's inspection trip for the Pan American Health Organization of South American immunological research institutions. But matters of interpretation and style also delayed the manuscript—Jerne was choosing his words with great care. In March 1965 they had hoped to have finished the project within a couple of months, but the only thing that got past Jerne's self-censorship were two short and preliminary conference presentations. At the end of August he said that the goal was to write "three extensive papers" but that for the moment the group could only produce "a synopsis of these papers." A week later they had completed a comprehensive manuscript, "The Agar Plaque Technique, the Target of the Antigen, and Clonal Selection," which they arranged to distribute in mimeographed form through the newsletter of the Information Exchange Group on Immunopathology.[26]

A month later Jerne made his decision, and in the middle of October he was officially appointed full professor in "experimental therapy" at the university and director of the Paul Ehrlich Institute. None of his American colleagues understood his choice. Why reject Harvard? Why move to Europe when practically all immunological research of any importance was going on in the USA? *"'The guy [Paul Ehrlich] is dead,' they said."* At the same time a certain baffled admiration was expressed that Jerne had chosen a lot of administrative chores over "a minimum of formal responsibilities." Jerne's official motive was that he wanted to "develop and modernize immunological research in a region [that is, Europe] where this has been comparatively neglected during the past decades." He declared that there was "a much greater need for strengthening a modern approach to immunology" in Frankfurt than at Harvard. He wanted to restore the "worldwide reputation" of the Paul Ehrlich Institute, and since he considered himself "one of the most widely known immunologists of our time," he felt called upon to assume the task.[27]

But he also had more private reasons to go to Frankfurt. Alexandra wanted to go back to Germany. Furthermore, just as Jerne a couple of years earlier had declined the offer to join the Salk Institute on the grounds of having to be creative "on command," he found the thought of moving into the Boston hothouse a trifle unsettling. Of course it was flattering to be sought after by one of the world's leading medical research centers, but it was also *"a little overwhelming"* to be wise and brilliant among all *"these Harvard-arrogant people."* Immunologically lagging Frankfurt was more secure, and the expectations imposed on a messiah, lower. There he could earn a princely wage for supervising others' standardization work while thinking his own large immunological thoughts in peace and quiet. There, too, the consequences of not living up to the role of an immunological genius were less frightening. And there would always be a *Kneipe*, or bar, around the corner to which he could repair—or "a little 'pied-à-terre' in the Provence."[28]

Perhaps it was Jerne's decision to choose Frankfurt that liberated his energies to reflect on his ten years in international immunology. In an article for the Festschrift to Max Delbrück's sixtieth birthday, Jerne looked back on the genesis of the selection theory in summer 1954. The Festschrift genre fitted him perfectly. He could give free rein to the style he had hitherto expressed only in letters to friends and colleagues, he could alternate between irony and dispassionate description of experimental results, and he could be personal and spice his writing with anecdotes. At the same time he was able to get his version of the origin of the selection theory included in the book *Phage and the Origins of Molecular Biology*, which was going to be the cornerstone of the molecular biology clan's own heroic historiography.[29]

Jerne took the occasion to tell the story about his way to the selection theory, how it came to him in a flash when he was walking home from the Serum Institute across the Knippel Bridge in Copenhagen. As already mentioned (in the Parabasis), Jerne's literary favorite, Søren Kierkegaard, and his *Philosophical Fragments* were allowed to play a major role in the Knippel Bridge eureka story. Maybe, Jerne wrote, "reverberations of Kierkegaard" contributed to the formulation of the natural selection theory. His story has so far been uncritically accepted among historians and philosophers of science. If it were true, it would be analogous to the suggestion that Niels Bohr was inspired to his theory of the quantum structure of the hydrogen atom by lectures of the Danish philosopher Harald Höffding on Kierkegaard and by reading *Stages on Life's Way*. As we have seen, however, Jerne's ideas about learning as recollection are not Kierkegaard's but Socrates'. Kierkegaard's view of learning in *Philosophical Fragments*—"If the learner is to obtain the truth, the teacher must bring it to him [and] provide him with the condition for understanding it"—is actually the opposite of Socrates' and resembles more the template-instruction theories.[30]

True, a pervasive pattern of thought throughout Kierkegaard's authorship is the centrality of the free agent, that is, it is not the social surroundings that form and instruct the individual. In that sense Kierkegaard indeed reverberates throughout Jerne's life and work. This is not what Jerne specifically referred to in the Festschrift article, however, so why did he make a specific reference to Kierkegaard instead of to Socrates? Perhaps because he was in a hurry and did not have time to check the quote (the passage was obviously quoted from memory), but also, and perhaps more important, "because I found the passage so beautiful." When he later read this paragraph in draft, he confirmed: *"I only used the quotation from the 'Smuler' [Fragments] because it fitted so nicely in a Festschrift."* In another conversation he admitted that he often read and quoted Kierkegaard to suit himself: *"I often attributed opinions to Kierkegaard which he never said."* So even if Kierkegaard's writings were a general source of inspiration for Jerne in his life and work, purely aesthetic considerations and even intellectual snobbery seems to have been involved, too. Everybody knew of Socrates, but few had read Kierkegaard—so what could better impress his peers when he contributed to the canonization of the molecular biology revolution.[31]

By spring 1966 Jerne was well on his way out of Pittsburgh. He and his small group continued to struggle with the manuscript of the definitive and comprehensive account of the plaque technique but did not have time to complete it.

Niels Jerne with his "delightful 'brat' of a bride," Ursula, alias Alexandra. (Medical History Museum, University of Copenhagen)

As Henry says, they wanted to postpone publication until they had interpreted all the results to their satisfaction, a goal that "perpetually eluded us." And satisfaction took its time: the results of the three Pittsburgh years were not published until a decade later.[32]

At the beginning of March, Niels Jerne boarded the SS *Olympia* in New York, together with his "delightful 'brat' of a bride," Ursula, (alias Usch, alias Alexandra), a chessboard, forty-four boxes of books, and twenty boxes filled with Tjek's paintings. After a week's participation in the annual Antibody Workshop in Rehovoth, Israel, Jerne arrived at Naples to pick up his big American car. They drove up through Italy and southern France, stopping here and there to admire charming houses in charming villages, and arrived in Frankfurt after Easter, ready to, as Jerne put it, "stir things up a bit in German immunology."[33]

"Like a Log Coming Slowly to the Surface of a Lake"

*T*he Paul Ehrlich Institute was, in Jerne's recollection, an *"ancient institute"* where most people went home at four o'clock in the afternoon and almost nobody carried on any research alongside the work of standardization and testing: *"They didn't want to do science at all."* He therefore set to work on a major housecleaning—to throw aside the traditional German academic hierarchies and rituals that stood in the way of his mission to modernize European immunology. He wanted to establish an institute where, as a younger assistant expressed it, you "could ask any question" and where "nothing was considered stupid." The memorial hall, devoted to the memory of Paul Ehrlich, was converted to a seminar room where Jerne held an "antibody workshop" with his new colleagues under the heading "Continuation of the Discussion, Opened by Professor Ehrlich, on Antibodies and Their Formation."[1]

In June 1966, shortly after Jerne was installed as a professor at the Wolfgang Goethe University, Claudia Henry and Hiroshi Fuji arrived from Pittsburgh to set up the plaque technique. While they fine-tuned the experimental routines, he took a one-month, well-paid intellectual vacation in Boulder, Colorado, to participate in the great neurobiology event of the summer, a meeting organized by the MIT Intensive Study Program in Neuroscience, which assembled some of the greatest stars in science of the day. In his talk, Jerne continued the theme of his Kansas lecture two years earlier, that of the analogy between the immune system and the nervous system, now expanded to include a discussion of the relationship between the template-instruction and selection theories. When describing an organism as a whole, perhaps one could say that both systems "learn" through "responding to" external stimuli (antigens and sensory impressions, respectively). But evolutionary biology, molecular biology, and immunology show us that what looks like a learning process (instruction) is instead due to a selection mechanism. So, perhaps cognitive "learning," too, is a "selective process." He called on the heritage of philosophy. Against Locke's "instructive theory of learning" he contrasted the Socratic "selective theory of learning." Although his analogy between the immune and nervous systems and selectionist learning had certain basic features in common with the evolutionary epistemology being developed at the time, his ideas made no immediate impression. A decade later, however, Gerald Edelman, who was also present at the meeting, would leave immunological research to undertake the further development of Jerne's argument in a Darwinian theory of the nervous system.[2]

After Boulder, Jerne took part in a ten-day summer school in Frascati, outside Rome, on the Structure and Synthesis of Antibodies and returned to Frankfurt in mid-September feeling that he was "up-to-date with the subject." His duties as professor were confined to a couple of lectures per term to the medical students; furthermore, he declared that he did not want to teach microbiology, since it had nothing to do with immunology (*"bacteriophages don't make antibodies"*). He was therefore free to devote almost all his time to research. He held seminars twice a week at the institute and took part regularly in the immunology discussions organized by one of his few friends in Frankfurt, Adolph Wacker, a professor of therapeutic biochemistry. He laid plans for the rebuilding and expansion of the Paul Ehrlich Institute and spent much time in negotiations with government officials. He was entrusted by the Deutsche Forschungsgemeinschaft with evaluating applications for grants and became a member of the editorial committee of *Current Topics in Microbiology and Immunology,* where he took the initiative of commissioning survey articles on various immunological topics. During the fall he was invited regularly to European conferences and seminars, delivering talks on various topics, among them "New Frontiers in Immunology" at the Second International Biophysics Conference in Vienna; the regulation of antibody synthesis at an international symposium on organ transplantation in Bad Homburg; "Genetic and Cellular Diversity in Antibody Formation" in Brussels. He talked about the antibody problem at the Max Planck Institute for Experimental Medicine in Göttingen, and gave the opening lecture of the Tenth Anniversary Meeting of the British Society for Immunology in the beginning of November. Through the winter and spring of 1967, the lecture tour continued: "The Antibody Problem" in Geneva in the middle of January; "The Diversity of Antibodies and the Problem of Antibody Formation" in Leiden in the middle of February; "Origine cellulaire des anticorps" ("a subject of which I think I understand less and less as time goes on") at the Collège de France a few days later; and "The Problem of Antigen Competition" at the International Symposium on Combined Vaccines in Marburg at the end of March. Jerne had become a seasoned lecturer who captured his audience with simple and clear presentations. The extant manuscripts testify to his sticking to the big picture, with emphasis on the theoretical problems.[3]

Jerne solidified his standing as immunology's leading intellectual when, in the beginning of June 1967, he took part in the annual Cold Spring Harbor Symposium on Quantitative Biology on Long Island. For the first time the prestigious symposium series had an immunological theme on its agenda, namely, "Antibodies," and Jerne had been asked, with Nossal and Edelman, to draw up the invitation list. As John Cairns, director of the Cold Spring Harbor Laboratory, wrote, the subject of antibodies was a fitting theme a year after the epochal Genetic Code meeting in 1966, now that sequence analysis of immunoglobulins "was providing an ever more detailed picture of the end-product of immunogenesis" and the mechanism of antibody formation "was about to develop its own dogmas." Most historians of immunology have characterized the 1960s as a period when a cellular approach to immunology superseded a chemical; few have given appropriate attention to how the traditional chemical and serological approach gave way to molecular immunology. The program of the Cold Spring Harbor meeting reflected this duality of basic immunology of the mid-1960s. Approximately half the presentations dealt with the biosynthesis of immunoglobulins, cellular differentiation, and other cellular events in the immune response, whereas the other half was concerned with the molecular structure of immunoglobulin molecules and the genetic basis of antibody variability. The recent great breakthrough in molecular immunology was the proposal that each of the chains of the immunoglobulin molecule contains two regions, a variable and a constant, and that the specificity of antibody function is due to the high variability of the amino acid sequence in the former.[4]

In his introduction to the nearly three hundred participants, the elder statesman of the field, Sir Macfarlane Burnet, reflected on the clonal selection theory; no longer considered merely hypothesis, it had become an established scientific fact, in particular through the recent elucidation of antibody structure, and would soon be considered the central dogma of immunology. As Mel Cohn later wrote: "The bandwagon was rolling, instructionism was being swept away." Jerne, the selection theory's "onlie begetter," had been asked to conclude the meeting, and so he did, in his own way. He summarized the many contributions in the form of a choice between research strategies, in short, should one go molecular or biological? To understand the origin of antibody specificity, one could either, as modern molecular immunochemists were then doing, begin with the structure of antibodies, a strategy he dubbed "trans-immunology." Or one could follow the lead from the biologists and begin with the effect of antigenic exposure, a strategy he dubbed "cis-immunology." The two kinds of immunologists seldom talked with one another, he declared, or rather "a cis-immunologist will sometimes speak to a trans-immunologist; but the latter rarely answers." The problem of which strategy would best lead to the elucidation of antibody diversity was central to Jerne's concerns, but the purpose of the paper was presumably also to get the molecular people to take a greater interest in functional questions, especially in the problem of the regulation of the immune response. Should such a rapprochement be achieved, Jerne thought, the "definitive solution" of the antibody problem would be close at hand, whereupon he and his generation of "older amateurs" would be able to sit back, "waiting for the End." Jerne's colleagues were delighted: "excellent," "masterful summary," were the reactions from his two fellow organizers.[5]

The title of Jerne's talk, "Waiting for the End," was probably inspired by a book of the same name that the "wild man of American literary criticism," Leslie A. Fiedler, had published several years earlier. At the Boulder conference the previous year, Jerne had already discussed the end-of-science theme with Stent, and during the past year they had exchanged letters and manuscript drafts, in fact intending to publish a book together. There were, however, certain differences in their perceptions of this "Forbidden Subject," as they called it. Jerne did not believe in Stent's prognosis of a general extinction of knowledge and art. Of course there are "limitations to the growth of knowledge and art within the framework and styles at present practiced," and so it might look as though all styles of art were already discovered and as though the number of scientific problems was limited. For example, one could imagine the basic problem of immunology being solved within fifty years, and then all that would remain would be to discuss some "curious anomaly in the immune system of the penguin," as he put it a couple of years later. Yet new opportunities for the development of knowledge on new levels of complexity would always arise:

"The growth of knowledge will lead to a step-up in complexity whereby properties will come to light that are unpredictable from our present elementary
viewpoint." When all the arts and styles had exhausted their possibilities, one
could imagine new styles on a higher level of complexity, "for instance an attempt at interaction between artists and public: 'Participation,' as the new slo-
gan has it." Scientific and artistic progress was still possible, but now on a level
"that includes 'consciousness,' instead of leaving it out"—a train of thought
that has striking similarities to the ideas about a second-order cybernetics that
emerged during the 1960s among neurobiologists and anthropologists, like
Gregory Bateson and Margaret Mead.[6]

Jerne's own experimental work, however, offered no hope of reaching an end. A
new generation of cellular immunologists was building further upon the clonal
selection theory, and the plaque technique, in its original or modified form, had
become one of their standard instruments. The number of papers utilizing the
new method in cellular immunology grew rapidly; one had to come up with
something really new to avoid being relegated to the mass of scientists. Aurelia
Koros, who remained in Pittsburgh, expressed her fear of being left behind:
"Unfortunately more and more plaque papers keep appearing and . . . I hate to
even look at journals these days."[7]

Jerne's thoughts were drifting increasingly toward the regulation of the immune response. As early as 1960, in "Immunological Speculations," he had suggested that the clonal selection theory did not exclude his own selection theory,
and during the years in Pittsburgh he had become more convinced than ever
that free circulating antibodies did play an important role in the regulation of
the immune response. Around 1965 he received experimental results indicating that the "regulatory system" consists not only of cells "but also of circulating
proteins—that is antibodies interacting to keep everything in balance," an idea
that foreshadowed a central aspect of the network theory. Together with Claudia Henry, he continued to test the idea that the primary antigen response is
regulated by "preformed specific 'natural' antibody molecules." Henry experimented with injection of specific molecules of different immunoglobulin
classes and found that very small quantities of the IgG (7S) class gave a marked
inhibition of the primary response, whereas another class of immunoglobulins
(IgM, or 19S) appeared stimulating—an outcome that "did not fit into current
immunological thought" and that Jerne therefore hesitated to publish at first.
On short notice, however, he chose to present the preliminary results at a Nobel
Symposium on antibodies in Stockholm in June 1967, and after Henry had

asked him several times to suspend his usual "desire for perfection" he sent in their joint manuscript for publication in the *Journal of Experimental Medicine*.[8]

The title of the paper—"Competition of 19S and 7S Antigen Receptors in the Regulation of the Primary Immune Response"—might sound "a little odd," he explained to the editor, because normally the term *receptor* was used for a molecule bound to a cell membrane. But Jerne chose to conceive of even free antibody molecules as kinds of receptors: "It is because I want to stress that the antigen, when passing through the events towards eliciting an immune response, will meet with antigen-receptors, both those that are receptors on the surfaces of cells and those which are freely circulating as antibody molecules." That is to say, even those antibody molecules that had "arisen spontaneously as 'natural' antibodies" were, as Jerne saw it, potential antigen receptors. The use of the receptor concept was odd, indeed, but it should not come as a surprise when one considers that he was stubbornly convinced that the natural selection theory still had a role to play alongside the clonal selection theory. In hindsight, Jerne's unusual definition of receptor can also be seen as a precursor to what would later become the network theory of the immune system, in which he made equivalent the variable region on circulating antibodies and lymphocyte receptors; both can "recognize" other paratopes in the immune system.[9]

In August 1967, Germany experienced an outbreak of so-called Marburg disease, a highly contagious affliction that proved to be caused by a filovirus (closely related to the Ebola virus discovered later) that had been brought in with some of the African green monkeys that were used in the institute's serum and vaccine production. The virus caused several deaths among animal caretakers in Marburg, Frankfurt, and Belgrade, and also, as Jerne put it, "much sadness" and "a great uproar" in the media and the Hessen government. A large portion of the rest of 1967 went into committee work and reports about the Marburg incident.[10]

Later in the fall, Jerne gave a postgraduate course on the characterization of antibody-producing cells with support from the newly established European Molecular Biology Organization (EMBO). He recruited a number of leading immunologists to be the instructors, among them Benvenuto Pernis, Ruggero Ceppellini, Göran Möller, Alain Bussard, Guido Biozzi, Denise Mouton, Morten Simonsen, and Diego Segre. His original ambition was to contrast his plaque technique with Biozzi's method of detecting antibody-forming cells through so-called rosette formation, but when he heard the news of Richard W. Dutton's and Robert I. Mishell's system for induction of antibody formation in spleen cells in vitro, Dutton, too, was invited to demonstrate the new method.

Niels Jerne writing (scientific notes or a letter?) on a stone bench in a church somewhere in Europe. (Medical History Museum, University of Copenhagen)

The EMBO course was a success, with hard work during the day and an intensive social life in the newly established Jerne home on Schumannstrasse in the evening. Möller thanked him for "an excellently organized course and outstanding social activities" and complimented Jerne's ability "to stay up late at night and appear fresh and healthy in the morning," one of many testimonies to Jerne's tirelessness and working capacity, an ability to stretch his powers that, from time to time, was broken by brief periods of illness and pessimism.[11]

Jerne had been hailed as a coming messiah in biomedical West Germany. But he soon realized that the task was more difficult than he had imagined. It was not so much the backward German immunology that stood in his way but, instead, the Paul Ehrlich Institute ("a classical rigid institute, with all these Staatsangestellte [civil servants]") and the West German federal bureaucracy, where every minor matter gave rise to "unbelievable quantities of documents." When the chairman of the Paul Ehrlich Foundation complained of Jerne's lack of willingness to cooperate in the awarding of the annual Paul Ehrlich prize, Jerne replied that he had "scant sympathy" for his colleagues, who put aside weeks of work in order to prepare the annual celebration, and refused henceforth to attend meetings of the foundation: "I make short work of intrigues," he added. He was also increasingly frustrated by the fact that "despite every effort" his small research group had become relatively isolated from the rest of the institute. Right after the EMBO course, Claudia Henry left Frankfurt to seek her fortune in the United States; some months later Fuji disappeared, too. Jerne's grandiose plans to give back to the institute its "world renown" faded. He came to the conclusion that it was "very hard" to combine standardization and testing operations with a "pure research operation" in a single institution. The testing work took such a large part of the institute's collective capacity that it would require a long time to create a sufficiently strong research group. He believes that his efforts "*were a great fiasco; it was an old institute and the people were useless.*"[12]

At the end of February 1968 Jerne got a new and better chance. The multinational pharmaceutical company F. Hoffmann-La Roche had advanced plans to establish the world's largest institute of immunological research to date. Roche had made preliminary contacts with the American immunogeneticist Baruj Benacerraf and the German immunopathologist Hans Müller-Eberhard, but both had turned down the company's invitation. The bid then went to Jerne. The overall budget and the size and location of the new institute—a two-story building on the Rhine less than a mile from downtown Basel, close to company headquarters—had already been decided upon. But beyond that, there were no limitations worth mentioning. The institute would get complete freedom to choose its areas of research and organization; the only condition the company imposed was the right to reserve for itself any possible patents. Money was no object: Roche was prepared to toss in what was needed, and Jerne would consequently be able to offer his associates internationally competitive salaries and generous funds for travel, instrumentation, animal facilities, and the like—all in all, resources capable of attracting the best young immunologists in the world and therefore of making the planned institute the leading immunological research organization in the world. Academic freedom, great financial resources, no unwieldy bureaucracy—this was an ideal and unique offer.[13]

At the end of March 1968 Jerne began serious negotiations with Roche, and during the month that followed he invited three leading European immunogeneticists for a small planning group; two of them, Benvenuto Pernis and Andrew S. Kelus, accepted immediately. The third invitee was Klaus Rajewsky, a Cologne geneticist who worked on one of the newest and hottest topics among immunologists in the late 1960s—namely, cellular cooperation and the so-called carrier effect—and who had recently written a joint paper with Jerne that further indicated that two cell types needed to come together to trigger an antibody response. (From this and other strands of research emerged a picture of the interaction between thymus- and bone-marrow-derived lymphocytes in the immune response. A year later the two cell types were dubbed T-cells and B-cells, and soon one of the fundamental principles of modern immunology— that the immune response involves cell cooperation—became firmly established.) Although Rajewsky never joined the planning group as an active member, he remained in close intellectual contact with Jerne for many years. It is probably no coincidence that Jerne chose three immunogeneticists. Even though he did not do any immunogenetical research himself, he was clearly aware of the fact that genetics, and particularly molecular genetics, was the key to the enigmas of immunology in the future. The end of immunology apparently had to be postponed for the time being.[14]

Between the negotiation sessions and talks with his advisory group Jerne stood once again at the blackboard, developing mathematical models to describe the dynamics in the formation of plaque-forming cells in the mouse spleen after stimulus. Meanwhile Alexandra was traveling in the Mediterranean area in search of a summer residence—in the end, she found a cheap, if rundown, stately villa in Castillon-du-Gard in Languedoc. In May Jerne left on a lecture tour of Denmark and then continued on to an immunopathology conference in Amsterdam to speak on the problem of the generation of antibody diversity. He was plainly entering a new life phase: "Please do not tell me that you want a complete manuscript of my lecture," he forewarned the organizer of the Amsterdam meeting; "I have written so many repetitive papers on the antibody problem during this year that I do not want to publish more variations on this theme, for the time being."[15]

In early summer of 1968 Jerne finally decided to accept Roche's offer. The decision roused consternation and dismay in German immunological circles. Otto Westphal, at the Max Planck Institute for Immunobiology in Freiburg, thought that Jerne's leaving the country was "a disgrace and a catastrophe for immunology in Germany (which has just begun to develop)" and tried to attract him with a new Max Planck Institute instead. But in vain, if for no other reason than the salary: the Max Planck Gesellschaft had no chance of competing with Roche. Jerne would be paid about one hundred thousand dollars a year, about double the salary of a full professor in Germany.[16]

The following year the planning for Roche's new institute in Basel took most of Jerne's time and energy. At the end of 1968 he left Frankfurt. His household goods, including books and paintings, were transported to the newly acquired villa in Castillon-du-Gard, where Alexandra soon set to work placing orders with the local craftsmen to create the future Château de Bellevue. Jerne moved by himself into a little bachelor apartment in Basel so as to be able to participate in the sometimes daily consultations with the Roche administration, the institute's architects, and the planning group. Most of the practical work was delegated to Kelus and to a young Czech refugee microbiologist, Ivan Lefkovits, who had participated in the EMBO course two years earlier. Lefkovits asked his former boss for advice before accepting the assignment as Jerne's assistant in Basel, and the answer conveys a common attitude toward Jerne among his European colleagues at the time: Lefkovits would be exposed to a mixture of "typically European education . . . and the liberality of a Danish-American scientist." The only risk the young man would take was to be "too much influenced by [Jerne's] mathematical-philosophical views." Lefkovits took the risk and became Jerne's stout squire for the years to follow. He and Kelus had to take charge of furnishing the laboratories, purchasing the major instrumentation, and planning the animal facilities. Jerne devoted his chief efforts to recruiting a nucleus of well-established researchers. His first great catch after Pernis was yet another immunogeneticist, Ruggero Ceppellini, who had specialized on the human-tissue antigen system; a few months later, Jerne referred to Pernis, Ceppellini, Kelus, and (for a short time) Rajewsky as the scientific nucleus team.[17]

A major problem was how the institute should be organized. Roche had originally conceived of a conventional research institute with departments, sections, and units, a model that had been applied a couple of years earlier to the Roche Institute of Molecular Biology in New Jersey. But Jerne apparently did not want to copy an existing system. At an early stage he rejected "rigid departments" and decided that all the scientists (with the exception of himself and his deputy) would have the status of "members" and be grouped into research units that could be "rearranged from time to time according to the progress made and the strategy decided upon." In the beginning he visualized an institute with nine (later twelve) units, each having two senior scientists, one postdoc, and three laboratory assistants. The unit heads would make up a "strategic command" (or "central intelligence") that, together with the director, would be located in a "small central tower." (The Benthamite idea of a Panopticon comes to mind.) At the beginning of 1969, Jerne was still thinking along these Panopticon lines and played with various models of the relationship between unit heads and the representation of the units in the strategic command. "It is my intention," he wrote to Stent, "to make younger people 'heads' of the 'Units,' with each Unit having a second man who will reside in the tower, as part of the 'Central Intelligence.'"[18]

In the course of the following year, however, Jerne broke completely with the hierarchical concept and introduced a horizontal structure, somewhat like that at Rockefeller University, which was known for its flat organization, composed of "members" and without departmental structure. He alone would choose new members, but otherwise all the scientists in the institute would be of equal position and allowed to choose their research projects freely. (A distinction between temporary members and a small number of permanent members was nonetheless introduced.) Since the number of laboratory assistants was limited, Jerne is said to have thought that "the realities of experimental science would force Members to collaborate with each other."[19]

It is not perfectly clear just when and why Jerne decided on this nonhierarchical organization plan. According to Lefkovits, the decision was made late in the spring of 1970 after a meeting of some forty presumptive members at the Hotel Krafft in Basel. "In addition to discussing science," Lefkovits remembers, "the participants argued until long into the night about how the Institute should be organized." Inspired by the student movement, the younger scientists are said to have sought "assurances that they would not be repressed" by the unit heads; "the 'spirit of the times' called for a new form of research organization," Lefkovits thinks. But Lefkovits—who later took on the task of writing the heroic early history of the Basel Institute and who associated himself with the group of young scientists—has probably overvalued the importance of the student movement. Jerne had changed his organization plan long before the Hotel Krafft meeting; a year before, Kelus had reacted strongly against plans to reduce his planned unit to a laboratory: "Democracy which is too far going does not appeal to me very much," an irritated Kelus wrote to Jerne. This suggests that even then the unit concept was already out the window. Neither is it probable that Jerne would have accepted being influenced by radical young left-wing scientists' references to scientific democracy. All his life, he had had the same elitist attitude toward science as toward art, an activity that, in his view, was "aristocratic par excellence." His purpose could hardly have been to introduce democracy into the institute. Rather, he intended to recruit the very best: "One good man is worth more than any number whatever of mediocrities," he proclaimed to the Roche headquarters.[20]

In that case, why did Jerne want to introduce a more horizontal organization? Lefkovits himself suggests another answer. Jerne is said to have voiced worry, even at an early stage, that the planned two-floor building would bring with it a "floor syndrome, that people from one floor would not talk to those from another floor," and decided for that reason to install a number of spiral staircases between the levels. The motive for the horizontal structure, then, was not to introduce democracy but to facilitate conversation and informal contacts between the scientists. For the same reason, Jerne consciously tried to overpopulate the institute "because crowding promotes interactions among scientists." It worked: during the first years the institute hummed like a beehive. The "horizontal structure," or "network," as it was later called in laboratory jargon, came to be one of the Basel Institute's chief characteristics.[21]

In Frankfurt Jerne had already left most of the experimental work to his assistants. With his decision to opt for Basel he brought his own experimental research to an end for good, concentrating instead on the evaluation of others' research and on theoretical syntheses.

One of the fundamental immunological problems at the close of the 1960s was understanding the genetic basis for the origin of the antibody repertoire, that is, the many different possible specific amino acid sequences in the variable region. It was evident, as the selection theory predicted, that the specificity was genetically determined. The only question was, how? Does all the information for the coding of all the specific immunoglobulin chains exist in the genes, as stated by the so-called germ-line theory, or does the final repertoire, as suggested by somatic mutation theories, arise through mutations during the differentiation of the antibody-producing cells? The problem with the germ-line theory was that the organism had to use an apparently disproportionate share of its aggregate genetic material to code for the large number of different specific antibodies. Conversely, the problem with the somatic mutation theory was that one had to imagine some mechanism through which a small number of genes could give rise to the whole spectrum of specific antibodies during the differentiation of lymphoid cells.[22]

Jerne caught up with the moving frontier. He had discussed the problem of the genetic background of antibody diversity in his Brussels lecture in October 1966, and in the years that followed he returned to it more and more often, for example, in his Leiden lecture in February 1967 and in a lecture on the genetical and cellular diversity of antibody formation at the German Society for Hygiene and Microbiology in May 1967. His correspondence during the spring of 1967 testifies to his great interest in developments in sequence studies, most of each letter being devoted to the latest scientific results, as if he was honing his ideas by writing letters to his colleagues. By the end of 1968, Edelman and his collaborators had mapped the entire primary structure of an immunoglobulin chain. The expectations were high. Even so, Jerne was not convinced of the excellence of the sequence studies. It was "both frustrating and fascinating," he wrote to Edelman, that knowledge of the amino acid sequence did not seem to give especially great insight into the cause of variability.[23]

Jerne was also troubled by a seemingly insignificant anomaly in the clonal selection theory. Several years earlier, the Danish experimental immunologist Morten Simonsen, well known for his studies of the so-called graft-versus-host reaction (whereby a transplant tissue rejects the host), had demonstrated that a small number (between fifty and one hundred) of randomly chosen lymphocytes could give rise to a specific reaction in the host organism. This argued against the clonal selection theory, Simonsen thought, for if a lymphocyte really produces only *one* kind of antibody (the basic postulate of the clonal selection theory), then one should expect a specific graft-versus-host reaction only after having transplanted a fairly large number of cells (for example, ten thousand or more), but not after as few as one hundred. The results suggested instead that every lymphocyte is able to produce several kinds of specific antibody molecules.[24]

The Simonsen phenomenon troubled Burnet greatly, and it troubled Jerne, too, who tried to find a way to incorporate the phenomenon into the clonal selection theory. Could the phenomenon of self-tolerance be combined with the problem of the origin of the antibody repertoire? Maybe diversification could occur during embryonic development through somatic mutation in the antibody genes? The answer came in mid-July 1969. It lay, Jerne explained to Stent, in the fact that "the normal rate of somatic mutation in antibody genes can give antibody diversity, if we select rare mutants by killing non-mutant cells": "To get self-tolerance you have to kill cells that make antibody against self. Ergo: (and this was the most difficult thought to dig up) the antibody genes in your germ-line code for antibodies against self! That is how they are selected in evolution. By suppressing cells expressing these genes you get self-tolerance *and* mutants generating antibody diversity."[25]

Just as Jerne had experienced the selection theory as an intuitive insight on the Knippel Bridge, he described the emergence of this new theory as a similarly intuitive occurrence. "I was hit by a spell of creativity that lasted until the day before yesterday," he told Stent: "Being aware, I followed my own behavior quite carefully; I felt that all the chores (such as farewell speeches in Frankfurt, etc.) were merely nothingness. I had the feeling that I had a good idea somewhere though I did not quite understand what it was. Fact is, that I was very nervous, stopped eating, writing, etc. until 20 July like a log coming slowly to the surface of a lake, I knew what I wanted to understand." The discovery process was experienced as slower and more painful this time, but in both cases it was heavily fraught with emotion. Of course Jerne is not alone in having that kind of experience. Several scientists and creative artists have described the intense feelings that can accompany their work; Iris Murdoch refers to the "passion or desire which is increased and purified in the process"; the creative artist "attends the dark something out of which he feels certain he can, if he concentrates and waits, elicit his poem, picture, music."[26] "Like a log coming slowly to the surface of a lake," as Jerne put it.

Jerne completed his manuscript in the beginning of August 1969 and circulated it to his peers. At the same time, and probably for reasons of priority, he had it published as a semiofficial WHO document. The reactions varied. Burnet thought the idea was "most attractive"; Max Delbrück was "delighted and excited" and promised to send it on to the *Proceedings of the National Academy of Sciences;* and Richard T. Smith considered it such a "marvelous synthesis" that he invited Jerne straight away to the Brook Lodge Symposium (a series of small, exclusive immunological meetings organized in the United States in the late 1960s and early 1970s) the following year to "clarify the hypothesis and bridle overextrapolation." At the opposite extreme, David Talmage did not allow himself to be convinced. Jerne's theory could admittedly explain the Simonsen phenomenon, but when it came to explaining the origin of the antibody repertoire, he and the young molecular geneticist Leroy Hood had come to "quite opposite conclusions." Even though Talmage did not want to exclude somatic models altogether, he felt that the germ-line theory fitted the multitude of sequence data much better. It was not until the middle of the 1970s that this conflict approached resolution, when, among others, Susumu Tonegawa at the Basel Institute for Immunology was able to show that somatic recombination does play an essential role in the development of the antibody repertoire and the immune response.[27]

After the enchanted summer of 1969, Jerne took an almost three-month-long trip to Australia and the United States to recruit members. He had no problem attracting good immunologists. Roche's financial resources were a magnet in themselves, and Jerne's intellectual powers had begun to be legendary; in addition he is said to have had an "extremely good judgment" and "wisdom" in handpicking the "right individuals" for the institute—in fact, he was very much aware of his "good sense" for recognizing "the best among the good people."[28]

During his trip to the U.S., Jerne continued to develop his new somatic mutation theory, by reviving one of the dormant ideas from his own work on the selection theory in 1954–55, namely, that in the thymus a spontaneous production of antibodies might take place in early embryonic stages and that these antibodies directed against the body's own antigens are thereby removed. In the mid-1950s this had been sheer speculation; in fact, as late as 1963 Peter Medawar had asserted that the presence of lymphocytes in the thymus was "an evolutionary accident of no very great significance." In the meantime, however, the role of this previously mysterious organ had changed: in 1961 Robert Good and Jacques Miller had independently shown that the removal of the thymus had severe immunological effects on young mammals, and in following years the thymus was put on the immunological agenda.[29]

In contrast to 1955, the time was clearly ripe to accept new and bold speculations about the role of the thymus in the generation of antibody specificity. Couldn't it be imagined, Jerne wrote to Simonsen, that both the origin of self-tolerance and the generation of antibody diversity takes place in the thymus? The thymus might play a central role in the process of eliminating self-recognizing lymphoid stem cells and preserving those that recognize foreign membrane antigens: "the thymus and other organs may be considered as breeders of mutant cells." Whereas the germ line produced lymphoid stem cells, the thymus could, he thought, be involved in selecting the "bad" cells (which turned against self) from the "good" cells (which did not). The analogy with the institute's proposed central intelligence tower is striking—the thymus might act as the organ of GOD (Generator Of Diversity) in the same way as Jerne intended to sit in the tower and select good scientists and ideas and discard the bad ones.[30]

Passing through California he also resumed intimate contact with a woman he had met on the East Coast six years earlier. Nine months later she gave birth to his third child. Jerne continued to be in touch with both her and her son, and over the years they exchanged almost weekly letters. The American woman stirred—at least in the form of epistolary rhetoric—his longing for closeness and sensuality: "I miss you so profoundly—as Adam banished from paradise—as a bird in a dark cave . . . my loneliness can only be abolished by *your* magic—only with you everything becomes natural, beautiful, full of mirth and gentleness. You belong to me—I miss you so deeply that all other experiences lose quality. Why do I have to accept this cruel fate, this separation from joy and light? I have never loved anyone as I love you, my love. I shall accept all if I can see you a few times per year." The biographer's suspicion always lies in wait when one reads Jerne's letters; it is especially difficult to take seriously the letters he wrote to women. Did he mean what he wrote, or did he not? (Or did he mean it only when he wrote it?) But even if the tone was theatrical, as in many of the love letters of his youth, the letters to the American woman diverged from most of what he had written earlier. He was no longer ironic, nor was he talking about love in abstract or general terms. Instead, he talked in these letters (even though sentimentally) about himself and his own longing in a concrete way, with no hints of the "spiritual spider web" he had spun around Adda a quarter of a century earlier. Was this a step in the direction away from cynical word games toward sincerity? Should this be regarded as one of the rare "screams" from his "innermost secret" that he had drawn attention to three decades earlier?[31]

Hard work seems to have held Jerne's feelings in check following his return to Basel after New Year 1970. The whole spring was spent in the planning of

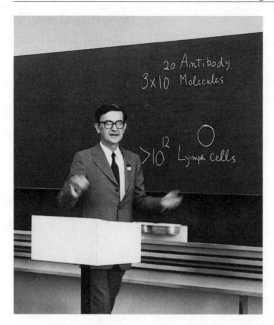

Niels Jerne at the official opening of the Basel Institute for Immunology in June 1971. (Medical History Museum, University of Copenhagen)

great and small matters and in the first meeting of the international advisory board for Roche's institute. He worked tirelessly on the thymus aspect of the somatic mutation theory and presented his ideas at a small specialist symposium in the United States in mid-May, where they were thoroughly discussed by Cohn and Simonsen, among others; Simonsen thought the theory "extremely elegant" and "the most impressive" that had been proposed, but Cohn delivered an extensive critique. Despite Delbrück's enthusiasm, the *Proceedings of the National Academy of Sciences* refused Jerne's original manuscript on the grounds that it was too long. In summer 1970, after several reworkings, Jerne completed the manuscript and sent it off for publication in the first issue of the new *European Journal of Immunology*.[32]

Later that same summer, the buildings on the bank of the Rhine were finished, and the following year the newly recruited immunologists gradually moved into the laboratories. The official opening of the Basel Institute for Immunology—what a colleague called the "world's first truly international center devoted wholly to immunology"—in June 1970 was a triumph for the fifty-eight-year-old Jerne, but the sweetness of victory was soon followed by depressive thoughts and feelings. During the summer of 1971 he was completely at the end of his tether and even called off his long-planned participation in the First International Congress of Immunology in Washington, D.C.—an event that finalized the institutionalization of immunology at the international level. Perhaps the hard work of the past three years had at last taken its toll, or perhaps his unhappy love and longing, and the separation from "joy and light," were closing in on him. We do not know. Delbrück recommended that he read

Samuel Beckett's *Molloy* "for the night-side of our lives," whereas his old friend Ernst Sorkin—whom he had come to know at the Serum Institute in the beginning of the 1950s—promised to stand by him if needed, for, as he said: "While things may go outwardly quite splendid[ly], there are internal commotions in all of us, which can terrorize or torture us."[33]

20   *"I Still Think That My Original Natural Selection Theory Was Better"*

Jerne had invested enormous efforts in setting up the Basel Institute for Immunology. Did he feel like going on? Some doubted it: "You are and always will be a 'gypsy,'" his friend Sorkin had declared. Others questioned whether Jerne would be able to continue without establishing a more hierarchical organization. John Humphrey thought his friend was running the institute as "a scientific commune," with the Taborites and the Levellers as models, and imagined, as an inevitable outcome, that "sooner or later a pyramidal structure will evolve."[1]

But Jerne was to remain in Basel almost ten years and would hold firmly to his vision of the communicative network in which everyone was to participate in the intellectual life. For many years, even the laboratory technicians took part in the research seminars and were generally given significantly greater responsibility for their work assignments than was customary, especially in comparison with their Roche counterparts. The place is said to have been like one great big seminar, with "a lot of talking, a very nice atmosphere," a kind of Epicurean scientific garden on the outskirts of the wealthy canton: "One didn't have much contact with people outside the institute." Most of the scientists and quite a few laboratory technicians were foreigners who lacked the ties of family or friendship in Switzerland, so their colleagues became their family and the institute their home, even in the night hours.[2]

Not only was the Basel Institute a communicative beehive, but it also produced good, sometimes outstanding research that Jerne meticulously summarized in a series of *Annual Reports*. The responsibility for the reports was later taken over by his friend from Cal Tech, Charley Steinberg, who joined the institute as a permanent member in 1970 and would come to play a significant role in its intellectual life as a "mentor" and "guru." The Basel Institute therefore rapidly established itself as the organizational and intellectual center for European immunology. It also developed into the largest of its kind in the world, with a total personnel of about one hundred and fifty, including some sixty scientists and about as many laboratory technicians. The turnover of members was deliberately high: Jerne recruited many younger, talented scientists, gave them full freedom and almost unlimited resources for a couple of years, and thereafter made room again for new ones. As a consequence, in the past two or three decades a large portion of the world's leading immunologists have spent some of their scientifically formative years in Basel. The institute became a place where young scientists could raise their scientific credentials in a very short time. Whoever had a good idea might soon gain recognition. "The first feeling was a feeling of enormous power," says a scientist who arrived in 1971: "One could do anything in terms of ideas and putting them into practice, it was like going into a cathedral of thinking. . . . You could breathe thinking in the air [and experienced] a wonderful climate of tolerance."[3]

The most spectacular scientific event during the 1970s was undoubtedly Susumu Tonegawa's contribution to the discovery of the mechanism for the generation of the antibody repertoire, a finding for which he was awarded the Nobel Prize in 1987. Tonegawa—a clever young molecular geneticist who came to Basel in the spring of 1971 on the recommendation of Jerne's old Caltech friend Renato Dulbecco—knew nothing about immunology but was introduced to the discussion about somatic generation versus germ-line theories by Steinberg. Five years later, in 1976, his group, in hard competition with other groups, was able to show that separate gene segments code for one and the same immunoglobulin chain and that the variation in the antibody repertoire arises through somatic recombination of genes so that a comparatively small number of genes can code for millions of specific antibodies—a kind of "gene lottery." Jerne endorsed Tonegawa's findings at a Cold Spring Harbor Symposium later in the summer: "It seems clear to me," he wrote in his introduction to the proceedings volume, "that the proponents of a germ-line theory are fighting a losing battle."[4]

Although not everyone at the meeting jumped on the somatic bandwagon, Jerne had now taken Burnet's role as the chieftain of the immunological tribe.

Niels Jerne, director of the Basel Institute for Immunology from 1969 through 1980. (Medical History Museum, University of Copenhagen)

He did so from a secure home base. Housed in the institute's central tower, he followed activities in detail. It is said that he was always ready to receive anyone who wanted to talk about any problem whatsoever, scientific or cultural, and that he could sit for hours in such discussions. He states that he always *"asked very simple questions. When somebody said he had made a finding, I asked him: 'Please, show me in detail what you are doing: You have a pipette in one hand, a test tube in your other, what kind of mouse did you use,' so we went through the whole procedure."* Yet he rarely went to the bench. During his ten years at the institute, he is said to have gone to the laboratories only twice, "once with a visiting scientist, once to pick up his wife, who had gone astray." Lefkovits remembers asking Jerne to accompany him to the animal facilities (the design of which was one of the great problems during the first years), whereupon Jerne answered that he would prefer to study the problem on "a map, plan, blueprint of the space," for, as he said, "I don't want to go down [to the animal facilities], the reality would confuse me." He displayed the same attitude when, fifteen years later, as a retiree, he was going to rent an apartment in Basel. When the owner wished to show him around in the apartment and point out its facilities, Jerne is said to have become troubled and asked: "Do you have a plan of this [place]? Couldn't we just sit down and you show me this apartment on the plan, [then] I don't need to go to each [room], I want to sit by the plan."[5]

Immunological reality confused Jerne, too. The complexity in the immune system grew each year, with new cell types and new factors. As already mentioned, one of the big news events at the end of the 1960s had been that the immune response requires two types of lymphocytes, T-cells and B-cells. But despite his (albeit limited) role in the elucidation of cellular cooperation, Jerne was not especially interested any more in finding new cell types or even in studying the genetic versus somatic basis for antibody diversity. He asserted that the antibody problem was essentially solved and that he was heading toward new hunting grounds.

Jerne's scientific impulse had always been to reduce complexity, to find a few principles, a blueprint of the immune system. The selection theory had been one such principle, the somatic mutation theory another. As discussed earlier, he had, as early as 1965, developed the idea that freely circulating antibodies could hold the immune system in balance, and in Frankfurt he had been working with Claudia Henry on the regulation of the immune response. Now he took their studies a step further in the form of a general theory for the regulation of the immune system as a whole. In a talk in London in 1971 he suggested that the clonal selection theory needed broadening with "a set of basic concepts" concerning the way in which the antibody repertoire arises and the elements that control the repertoire's "maintenance and variation." One such basic concept was self-regulating cybernetic systems, a line of thinking that Norbert Wiener had transferred, in 1948, from the study of computing machines and information theory to biology and the social sciences and that was propelled still further by Ludwig von Bertalanffy in his popular book *General Systems Theory* twenty years later.[6]

Another basic concept was the idiotype. In the early 1960s two groups of investigators—Henry Kunkel's at Rockefeller University and Jacques Oudin's at the Pasteur Institute—had independently described antigenic determinants unique to particular immunoglobulin molecules. Oudin later termed these determinants on antibodies (that is, regions that can elicit an antibody response) "idiotypes." Implicit in this definition of idiotypy was that the antigenic determinants were localized to the variable, antigen-binding region of the antibody molecule. As Jerne later put it: "The variable region of an antibody molecule constitutes not only its 'combining site,' but also presents an antigenic profile (named its idiotype) against which anti-idiotypic antibodies can be induced in other animals."[7]

Jerne now began to merge the two concepts of cybernetic systems and idiotypy into a theory of the immune system as a self-regulating system of idiotypic relations. Unfortunately the archive contains only a few documents that can illuminate the cognitive process leading to the theory. In a letter to a Swiss colleague in the summer of 1971, he speculated about whether or not a "larger cyclic system or network system could be thought to describe the total potentiality of the immune system." He imagined that limited sections of the variable region (the paratope, in his 1960 terminology) in every antibody molecule are able to function as a specific antigenic determinant (epitope) for other antibodies. And further: if the antibody repertoire is modulated with the aid of idiotopes, the system would be "more autonomous and self-contained and less dependent on encounters with foreign antigens"—a theme reminiscent of his testament of 9 August 1954, namely, that it was "nice" that the antigen did not participate in the production of antibodies.[8]

Two years later, in 1973, Jerne further developed his idea of the immune system as an idiotypic network simultaneously in a popular article for *Scientific American* and in a colloquium on immunogenetics at the Pasteur Institute. He introduced at this time a third basic concept, namely, that the reaction between antibodies and antigens can be regarded as "recognition." This concept (and by default the concept of cognition) was not in itself new; it had existed implicitly in immunology from the very beginning and was also an element in Burnet's understanding of the relation between self and nonself. But it was Jerne who made explicit a cognitive model of the immune system, for example, when he compared, in 1960, the antibody-forming system with "an electronic translation machine" that recognizes words and sentences. At the symposium on neurological science in Boulder in the summer of 1966, Jerne had emphasized the analogy between the nervous system and the immune system and again proposed that the immune system be seen as a molecular recognition system. "I am convinced," he wrote in the *Scientific American* article, "that the description of the immune system as a functional network of lymphocytes and antibody molecules is essential to its understanding, and that the network as a whole functions in a way that is peculiar to and characteristic of the internal interactions of the elements of the immune system itself." The system "displays what I call an eigen-behavior," he added (*eigen* in German means "peculiar to," or "characteristic of," that is, the immune system's behavior is the result solely of its own internal, repeated operations). Every paratope functions as an epitope that is recognized by a number of paratopes that in turn function as specific epitopes, that in turn are recognized by still another number of paratopes, and so on, as in a "hall of mirrors." In this way "ever larger sets" are achieved that "recognize and are recognized by previously defined sets within the network."[9]

He regarded the immune system as a system continually seeking "a dynamic equilibrium"—and by dynamic he meant that "a vast number of im-

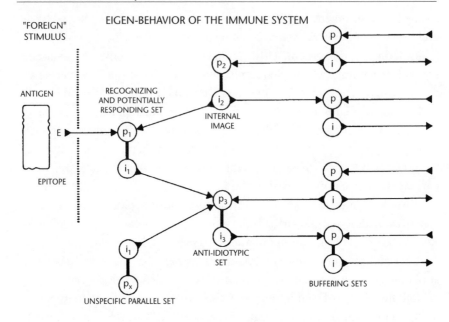

Niels Jerne's schematic representation of the network theory of the immune system. (Jerne Collection, The Royal Library, Copenhagen)

mune responses are going on all the time, even in the absence of foreign antigen." He did not actually like the term "immune response," since it gave the misleading impression that "the system is 'at rest,' waiting to 'respond.'" Instead he visualized the system as "continuously active, interacting with self-antigens, idiotopes, factors, etc." The external world with its antigens was of subordinate importance to the regulation of the immune system, he thought; the immune response was a result of mutual stimulations and inhibitions within the self-regulating network: "In the *eigen*-behavior of the immune system these opposing forces result in a balanced suppression which must be overcome in order to obtain an immune response." As if echoing the romantic, and later structuralist, idea that language is self-referential and establishes a world in itself, Jerne assumed that the immune system is nonreferential.[10]

Jerne's formulation of the network theory not only involved a creative use of the concepts of cybernetic systems, idiotype, and recognition. It was also the culmination of his more than fifteen-year-long argument that freely circulating antibodies played an essential role in the immune system. As emphasized repeatedly in previous chapters, even long after Burnet had modified the selection theory into the clonal selection theory (in which free antibodies do not play any role at all), Jerne stubbornly maintained that freely circulating, pre-formed, natural antibodies play an independent role alongside the lympho-cytes. In the network theory, these freely circulating antibodies play a leading role, because they constitute the major part of the total quantity of "internal images" in the idiotypic network. The network theory can therefore be re-garded as Jerne's way of uniting his own earlier natural selection theory with Burnet's clonal selection theory. He even thought that the network theory in-corporated the selection theory, "without sacrificing it," as a special case, and he continued to hold on to his natural selection theory. As he wrote two years be-fore his death: "Even with a repertoire of 10^7 different antibodies, there should be an average of 10^9 antibodies of every specificity in every ml. of blood. There-fore, every antigen will immediately be covered by recognizing antibodies, be-fore it enters antibody presenting cells, and before T-cells get involved. I there-fore *still* think that my original 'Natural Selection Theory' was *better.*" Jerne's mature scientific work in the 1960s and 1970s, including his idiotypic network theory, can thus be seen as a kind of extended postscript to his selection theory of antibody formation—his life's major conceptual achievement, his personal confession.[11]

Just as the selection theory had been able to explain a number of puzzling sero-logical phenomena in the mid-1950s, Jerne believed that the network theory could explain phenomena such as low-zone tolerance, antigen competition, and unspecific immune response. The theory also apparently explained the re-sults he and Claudia Henry had obtained a few years before, that is, that the im-mune system can be regulated with the help of small doses of immunoglobu-lins. The ability to form auto-anti-idiotypic antibodies was demonstrated experimentally shortly after the theory was made public, and in the years that followed other studies showed that even nanogram quantities of monoclonal anti-idiotypic antibodies had regulatory (inhibitory or stimulatory) effects on antibody production. At the close of the 1970s the network theory was im-mensely popular among immunologists, triggering "its own network of theo-retical and experimental activity." Anne Marie Moulin even calls it a "Coperni-can revolution."[12]

Not all immunologists saw a new Copernicus emerging, however. Some American immunologists called it a European phenomenon, which cut no ice with Jerne, who replied that in the Soviet Union it was surely a "bourgeois phe-nomenon." The most vociferous of the critics, Mel Cohn, conceded that the theory was almost universally accepted but asserted that it was theoretically untenable: it was unscientific, even "absurd," since it was incapable of being tested empirically. He was not alone—Göran Möller claimed that "the network hypothesis lacks . . . an element necessary to all hypotheses, namely, to be able to be verified experimentally," and concluded that the fact that "this hypothesis has been such a hit tells you something about the intellectual standard in today's immunology." It was probably the network theory Cohn had in mind when he later asserted that Jerne thought "instinctively" yet did not follow through his theoretical alternatives logically and systematically: "[In Jerne's thinking] there is the failure to acknowledge and confront competing concepts in analyzing phenomena. The best way to evaluate a given concept is to weigh it in the light of alternative formulations. This is often difficult to do." Cohn concluded by saying that "there is no such thing as instinctive knowledge," echoing Max Delbrück thirty-five years earlier.[13]

Jerne was aware that there were those who thought that the "whole network is a fairy tale and that I am like the emperor in his new clothes." But he was deeply convinced that the theory reflected the essence of the immune system. Asked whether he wished to contribute to a plenary discussion pro and con the existence of an idiotypic network, he replied that he could not understand how anyone could argue against the idea of a functional network: "Maybe some dislike the idea, but surely there cannot be any experimental data *against* it." He rejected point blank the requirement of falsification and accordingly spoke out against its leading philosopher, Karl Popper, who, he thought, spoke "a lot of nonsense, and too much." In wording reminiscent of his recommendation to the immunologists at the Prague conference in 1959 to fly "into the realm of imagination," Jerne pointed out that "science is not just an accumulating series of falsifiable propositions which experimentalists try to falsify, but also, and mainly, imagination: a development of concepts and new perspectives that change the outlook and the *type* of propositions, discussions, and experiments." He felt he had much more in common with William Blake: "If a fool would persist in his folly he would become wise."[14]

Cohn, who, at least privately, was the first to admit that Jerne earlier had "inspired and influenced [his] thinking more than anyone," nevertheless wondered what "philosophical" or "psychological" reasons lay behind Jerne's persisting in the idea of the self-recognizing network. Cohn's question is unusual (scientists rarely ask for biographical explanations), but nevertheless sensible. Why was Jerne so absolutely sure that the network theory was correct? His certainty brings to mind his conviction, twenty years earlier, that the natural selection theory must be right, too. In the Parabasis I argued that in that case this confidence had its foundation in Jerne's emotionally laden life experience and understanding of himself, that the selection theory was the "confession of its originator." Can the idiotypic network theory, too, be seen as a metaphorical expression of a kind of (to use Nietzsche's words again) "involuntary and unconscious auto-biography"? And if so, which biographical traits?[15]

"Every individual," Jerne declared in his argument for the network theory, "must start with self." He advised those immunologists who were always looking for "exterior pressures" (antigens) to explain the evolutionary origin of variability in the antibody repertoire; they "would do well to turn their vision towards the interiors of themselves, and there discover the mystery . . . of the immune system." It is advice that sounds as if it was taken from one of the early nineteenth-century Romantic scientists, for example, the Danish-German geologist Henrik Steffens, who asked: "Do you want to know nature?" and answered: "Turn your glance inwards and you will be granted the privilege of beholding nature's stages of development in the stages of your spiritual education."[16]

If Jerne had followed his own advice and turned his vision inward, he, too, would probably have been able to recognize important features of his personality and life experience in the network theory. To begin with, the mirror metaphor resonated with his self-understanding and emotional experiences. "The things, our surroundings, have no value in themselves," he once had told Adda. But, he added, nature and its things "can become gratifying to us because we ourselves have animated them, they are like mirrors reflecting something of ourselves." More important, perhaps, were his lifelong individualism and feeling of being culturally alienated. Attraction to the individual and the idiosyncratic—and vice versa, distaste of collectivity—was a pervasive feature not only in Jerne's personal lifestyle and philosophy but also in his scientific work: his interest in statistics was primarily directed at individual variations and distributions; for example, when he planned the experimental series in 1948 for his doctoral dissertation he emphasized the importance of studying antidiphtheria sera from individual guinea pigs instead of pooling them, and in 1950 he interrupted his work on the dissertation manuscript to write a polemical article to the Danish medical journal in which he argued for individual dose-effect curves. Later in life, this attraction to the individual and the idiosyncratic can be found in his seeking a method of detecting individual antibody-producing cells. His attraction to the individual coexisted with his feeling of being culturally alienated. In correspondence, in diary entries, and in interviews Jerne appears consistently as a Byronic hero, or a Simmelian stranger, a socially and culturally liberated individual condemned to live out his life as a wanderer. He was drawn to separateness in railroad station coffee shops, where he could sit as an anonymous individual, not having to be responsible, among other anonymous individuals and watch people pass like ships in the night.[17]

It is therefore probably not coincidental that Jerne had been so fond of Beatrice Harraden's book *Ships That Pass in the Night*; and it is exactly this image of the individual and alienated wanderer that returns as a central metaphor in his immunological thinking in the form of the network of individual, freely circulating, colliding antibody molecules. In notes from the 1930s he had explained that society could be described as an equilibrium, the men and the women being attracted to one another "like molecules." He declared that one of his favorite subjects *"then and even now"* is *"collision frequence,"* that is, *"how often do these molecules meet each other in a solution, and, when they meet, do they then stick, and, if they stick, how long do they keep stuck before they loosen again?" That's my favorite,"* he adds, thereby emphasizing that the image of chance collisions between individuals was a metaphor not only for life experience but also for scientific work—one of the metaphors by which he lived both his private and scientific life. After having read a draft of this chapter, Jerne agreed with my interpretation—that "collisions" were *"a lifelong metaphor for the need to use chance and randomness for scientific explanations (and for fun!)"*; he thought, too, that the collision metaphor was even more *"deeply buried in my soul"* than the preformation idea. Similarly, in Jerne's vision of a cybernetic immunological network, billions upon billions of molecules and lymphocytes collided randomly, some recognizing one another and some freeing themselves from one another, as if they were molecular ships chancing to pass each other in the wine-dark sea of bodily fluids.[18]

A personal, rather than cultural, context for the network theory is also suggested by the striking structural similarity between the idiotypic network theory and the vision that lay behind the organization of the Basel Institute. Jerne's ultimate vision of the organization of the institute was closely related to—and, indeed, isomorphic with—his vision of how the immune system was organized. The use of the word *network* both for describing the new kind of social organization and for denoting his new theory of the immune system was hardly coincidental. The social network as well as the idiotypic network was based on the idea of recognition: the social network of the institute was envisioned as a conversational network of scientists. Jerne wanted it to be a self-regulating equilibrium system, a dynamic network of intellectual discourse, where even the architecture was conducive to chance meetings. The Taborite community was supposed to regulate itself through discussion and criticism in its internal seminar activities. Similarly the idiotypic network of the immune system was envisioned as a network of molecular recognition.

The analogy should not be forced too far, but it is nevertheless thought provoking that two such similar visions arose consecutively in the mind of a single man. It is difficult to understand this coincidence in terms of the cultural context, for example, the general interest in cybernetics or structuralism at this time. Cultural contexts can explain why certain intellectual resources are available but not why a specific person puts them to use in a local setting at a given point in time. Because both the network theory and the Basel Institute were one individual's unique accomplishments, it is perhaps more telling to search for the origin of these two visions, the organizational and the theoretical, in Jerne's self-understanding and practice.

One personal trait that comes up again and again, both in the archive and in talks with Jerne, his friends, and his colleagues, is his lifelong passion for conversation. It was one of his great talents, at the center of his social existence. Any time he got the chance, he engaged in conversation, not only about immunology, not only about science, but about everything conceivable: literature, art, politics, sex. "What makes me happy is to talk with other people" is how he opened his first long interview with a journalist after the Nobel Prize. He "likes to talk," he could talk "for hours," he "loves the gossip" and was well aware of his passion, say some of his close colleagues. Even though Jerne had started with thinking in terms of a centralized Panopticon model for the organization of the Basel Institute, he soon replaced it with a network model that maximized social interaction and discourse. A circulating network structure would heighten the chances that scientists would meet and interesting conversations occur. The step from a network model for the Basel Institute to a network model for the immune system was a small one and rested on the same basic idea of individual meetings, exchanges, and recognitions. One man's vision of communication and recognition therefore had a great effect—both organizationally and theoretically—on European immunology in the next three decades.[19]

21   *"Immunology Is for Me Becoming a Mostly Philosophical Subject"*

*A*fter more than a decade as director of the Basel Institute, Jerne decided to retire in 1980. Roche asked Fritz Melchers, who had been at the institute almost since its start, to take over the post. Jerne was sixty-eight years old, and despite two or three packs of cigarettes a day and ever increasing alcohol consumption, he was still in full vigor. For about a year he functioned as *conseiller général* of the Pasteur Institute's new Department of Immunology, but he was not comfortable there: "Paris was cold, wet and noisy, and I couldn't get accustomed to the Pasteur's somewhat complicated and smug way of 'doing research.'" Instead he moved permanently to his summer residence in Languedoc with his young wife, Alexandra, who for many years had lived alone for long periods in Château de Bellevue. In France, he had more time to read, as usual on the most diverse subjects—everything from Marshall Berman's Marxist critique of modernity, *All That Is Solid Melts into Air* (1982), to Nicolas Schöfer's *La théorie des miroirs* (1982), a book that reinforced his vision of the immune system as an endless hall of mirrors.[1]

By that point in his life, he considered himself a "theoretical immunologist." Even though he was aware that a theoretician is, fundamentally, dependent on experimental discoveries, he believed that the future relationship between theoreticians and experimentalists in immunology ought to be as in physics, where it is the theoreticians who guide new experiments: "The theoretical immunologist should tell the experimentalists what type of data are needed." Jerne's first theoretical work after his retirement was the result of discussions with two scientists at the Pasteur Institute, Pierre-André Cazenave and Jacques Roland, who seemed to have experimentally confirmed the network theory. Jerne took their results as his point of departure to "reconsider our orthodox distinctions between 'combining site' (paratope) and idiotype, or, 'sets of idiotopes,'" and arrived at the conclusion that "there is no difference between 'recognizing' and 'being recognized,' and therefore no difference between combining sites and idiotopes. They are all 'combining sites.'"[2]

Jerne's view of the idiotypic network therefore did not undergo any major modifications. Even if his identity as immunologist emeritus currently rested on the network theory, he was not satisfied with all the talk about networks. The word had quickly become popular among immunologists, but Jerne disliked its being used so loosely. They were talking about networks of suppressor cells, helper cells, B-cells, inductive signals, and other things "which have nothing to do with the idiotypic network that some of us feel is at the center of our attempts at system analysis," he wrote. For Jerne the network was not an accumulation of interacting material factors of all those kinds, but an abstract principle, a complex recognition system. He increasingly spoke of the immune system as a cognitive and semiotic system.[3]

His retirement was also followed by scientific prizes and other marks of distinction. In 1981 he was chosen a foreign member of the Académie des Sciences and a Fellow of the Royal Society (he was still a British subject), and in December of the same year, on his seventieth birthday, his Basel colleagues, convened by Charles Steinberg and Ivan Lefkovits, honored him with a two-volume Festschrift. In 1982 he received the Paul Ehrlich Prize, a year later he was elected an honorary member of the British Society for Immunology, and in 1984 and 1985 he had honorary doctorates conferred on him by Erasmus University in Rotterdam and the Weizmann Institute of Science in Israel.[4]

The greatest mark of honor, however, was the Nobel Prize in physiology or medicine in 1984. On Monday, 15 October 1984, while on one of his occasional visits to Basel, where he still occupied an office as an emeritus, Jerne received the news that he had been awarded the prize, together with Georges Köhler and César Milstein at the British Medical Research Council's laboratory in Cambridge. The next day the newspapers carried short reports from telephone interviews and a photo of Jerne and Köhler (who had returned to his alma mater) toasting each other in champagne in the cafeteria of the institute. Whereas the fifty-seven-year-old Argentinian-born César Milstein was described as a work-aholic who had bought a new house in Cambridge two minutes away from his laboratory in order to work all night, and the thirty-eight-year-old wunderkind, Köhler, was quoted as being a little anxious about possible pressure in the future, seventy-two-year-old Niels Jerne was portrayed as a Danish "farmer's son" who wanted to "enjoy the money and enjoy his life."[5]

Formally, the prize was awarded jointly "for theories concerning the specificity in development and control of the immune system and the discovery of the principle for production of monoclonal antibodies." But in reality the prize was more divided. Köhler and Milstein got it for their discovery a decade earlier of the hybridoma technique for the production of monoclonal antibodies, that is, chemically identical antibodies obtained from a single, genetically identical clone of lymphocytes. Jerne, on the other hand, was cited for his accumulated theoretical work over the preceding thirty years: the natural selection theory, the somatic mutation theory, and the network theory. In his introductory speech at the ceremony in Stockholm a few months later, Hans Wigzell, professor of immunology at the Karolinska Institute and an admirer of Jerne's work, explained that Jerne received the prize for his "visionary theories" that had enabled modern immunology to make "major leaps of progress."[6]

The decision to award the prize to Köhler and Milstein was unproblematic. Monoclonal antibodies were generally considered one of the major methodological innovations in the biomedical sciences in the 1970s. With few exceptions, there had not yet been any entirely new clinical applications—but since monoclonals are chemically pure and can be produced in large amounts, they were replacing conventional sera and thereby, as Köhler pointed out, "contributing to a worldwide standardisation of antibody-mediated reactions." Moreover, Köhler's and Milstein's work had resulted in a paradigmatic discovery of a kind that fully satisfied the original intentions in Nobel's will, namely, that the prize should be given to those that had made "the most important discovery within the domain of physiology or medicine."[7]

Jerne's achievements did not immediately satisfy the donor's will, however. In the 1920s, a similar clause concerning "discovery" had caused some controversy about the justification for awarding the physics prize to Albert Einstein (who got it for the photoelectric effect but not for his theories of relativity). The Nobel Committee for Physics soon changed their view, but the medical committee was slower to change their empiricist understanding of what constitutes

Niels Jerne and Georges Köhler celebrating in the Basel Institute cafeteria after receiving news of their Nobel Prizes in October 1984. (Polfoto, Copenhagen)

a "discovery." Hence the decision to give the prize to Jerne signaled a change in practice. In a private letter to Jerne, Wigzell pointed out that "it was good that we are also able to reward theories; actually, this is the first time [in medicine], as far as I know."[8]

The Nobel archives covering the 1984 events have not yet been made public, and so it has not been possible to substantiate rumors about the deliberations for and against Jerne. But one can nevertheless make an informed guess about the committee's reasoning. A possible chain of argument might have run like this: as one of the most eminent theoreticians in the biomedical sciences of the post–World War II period and undoubtedly of Nobel caliber, Jerne was surely repeatedly nominated for the prize. Yet he had not made an empirical discovery in Nobel's sense, and since theoretical contributions by tradition played a minor role in the biomedical sciences, as compared to the physical sciences, the nominations for Jerne probably had less effect on the committee members than nominations for equally eminent experimentalists. Further, given that the nomination of Köhler and Milstein for their highly innovative and clinically useful invention of monoclonal antibodies was unproblematic in the eyes of the committee, they may have felt an obligation to award those who had laid the theoretical basis for it, namely, Jerne (the natural selection theory) and Burnet (the clonal selection theory). Burnet had already received a Nobel Prize in physiology or medicine (although not for the clonal selection theory), however, and could not receive it again. Jerne, therefore, was probably given the prize as a corollary to the award for monoclonal antibodies. If this reconstruction is correct (and we can only get a clear answer in 2034, when the Nobel Foundation opens its 1984 files), Jerne got the prize by default.

Some members of the press made a similar interpretation of Jerne's prize. "It has long been expected that the Swedish Nobel Committee at Karolinska Institute would give the Nobel Prize to the originators of the hybridoma technique," wrote a well-informed Swedish journalist the day after the announcement; "now this being the case, the Swedish prize committee also, although less expectedly, chooses to honor the theoretician and visionary behind the practice, namely, Niels K. Jerne." In other words, had not Köhler and Milstein invented the hybridoma technique, Jerne would probably not have received the prize at all.[9]

Some press reports even removed the distinction between the theoretician and the two others. A follow-up story two days later in the *International Herald Tribune* focused entirely on the invention of monoclonal antibodies and portrayed Jerne as the third member of a monoclonal triumvirate. Maybe the hints that he was nothing but an appendix to the monoclonal story prompted Jerne to put some distance between himself and his cowinners: he "had no part in this monoclonal invention," he wrote in a note, his interest in science had always concerned "synthetic ideas," and he had tried to "read road-signs leading into the future." Jerne's attitude to the hybridoma technique calls to mind his youth, when he distanced himself from everything that "had . . . practical purpose," everything that "could . . . be *used*," and, correspondingly, his fascination with what is "only existing for its own sake." In a later interview he says that as early as the 1930s, during his Leiden years, he had been impressed by the fact that there was a difference in status between *"science, and then there's a second class of science, called engineering."* He kept firmly to this distinction throughout his life. "Monoclonal antibodies don't interest me that much," he told a colleague: "our Immune System does not produce monoclonal antibodies."[10]

Jerne also put distance between himself and the public interest in immunology that was fueled by the emerging AIDS epidemic. Monoclonal antibodies had been used to recognize the first cases of AIDS three years earlier, and the expectations were high that the hybridoma technique would help in the struggle against the new scourge. "Their research helps diagnose AIDS," reported the *International Herald Tribune* in its coverage of the prizewinners. Jerne was indifferent. The AIDS epidemic was unimportant, he said to the astonished representatives of the press, particularly when compared with infectious tropical diseases, such as malaria. Neither would a virus ever be able to wipe out the human species: "Viruses can kill people, but not humanity; otherwise, they would have done so long ago." He did not consider AIDS an immunological problem at all: "The destruction of lymphocytes is a virological problem." He had no professional interest in the new syndrome.[11]

For most immunologists, however, the finer details in Alfred Nobel's will or Jerne's provocative and—from the point of view of biomedical politics—counterproductive remarks on the uses of immunology were of minor importance. Other leading immunologists of the postwar period had already received their share of prizes: Macfarlane Burnet and Peter Medawar had been honored in 1960 for the discovery of acquired immunological tolerance; Gerald Edelman and Rod Porter in 1972 for their studies of the chemical structure of antibodies; Baruj Benacerraf, Jean Dausset, and George Snell in 1980 for their immunogenetical discoveries. Now it was Jerne's turn. Few questioned that he was the equal of, or even superior to, these laureates; he was an obvious prize recipient who should have been chosen many years before: "What took them so long?" one of them wrote. "The king of theorists has finally been crowned!" exclaimed another theoretician, the evolutionary geneticist Susumo Ohno. "Your name is synonymous with modern immunology," added the leading thymus researcher, Jacques Miller. The immunogeneticist Bernard Amos congratulated Jerne as "a person who has made us all *think*," and Mel Cohn wrote that even though they had seldom agreed on how the immune system should be analyzed, Jerne's ideas had "catalyzed most" of his thoughts and influenced his view of the way creative science should be done: "Rarely is the prize so well-deserved," Cohn added.[12]

The news of the prize also opened a Pandora's box of unexpected voices from the past, petitions for help, and apocalyptic visions. An Australian woman wrote to tell him that the news reports had reminded her about her childhood years in Assen and the neighbors' small boy Niels. People who thought that his theories about the immune system and his co-winners' invention of monoclonal antibodies might save themselves or a dear relative from a serious illness saw him as a prospective savior (Jerne answered most of these letters, invariably referring them to their general practitioner). A Nobel Prize is also an excellent opportunity for the cranks of the world to express their views: one letter writer told Jerne that she had "*scientific* proof that rebirths are occurring," went on to offer a number of "new psychological theories . . . a new religion, a new political party, new weapons, a new energy source, new evolutionary theories, etc.," and finally asked Jerne to hasten to New York to read the manuscript that would save the world from the coming nuclear catastrophe. There is no airplane ticket receipt in the archive to indicate that Jerne ever accepted the invitation.[13]

Being aware of his adversary's ambivalent attitude to pomp and his talent for provocation, Mel Cohn expressed the hope that Jerne would drop his "cynicism" and appreciate the award ceremony in Stockholm. What Cohn did not know was that Jerne had long been fascinated by royalty and so did not need to be instructed as to the Nobel protocol. It also tickled Jerne's vanity that, as the oldest laureate of the year, he was seated with Queen Silvia of Sweden at the banquet in Stockholm after the ceremony in December.[14]

The event in Stockholm also gave Jerne an opportunity to turn back, in his Nobel lecture, to the subject of his article in the *Annual Review of Microbiology* a quarter of a century earlier, that is, the analogy between the immune system and language. Terms such as *immune response* and *immune recognition* suggested, he said, "some more or less superficial though striking analogies with human language." When a person is vaccinated with cowpox vaccine, antibodies are produced that also fit, more or less well, with smallpox and other closely related pox diseases, that is, "the normal I[mmune] S[ystem] does not interpret, but simply covers a range of more or less overlapping [interpretive] possibilities." In this, Jerne thought, there exists an analogy to the understanding of language. The immense repertoire of the immune system could be seen as "a lexicon of sentences which is capable of responding to any sentence expressed by the multitude of antigens which the immune system may encounter." Drawing from Noam Chomsky's theory of generative grammar, Jerne also suggested that the immune system was governed by a set of grammatical rules that allowed the formation of new sentences. Just as Chomsky's grammar allows an open-ended number of sentences, Jerne's grammar allowed the generation of the "'completeness' of the antibody repertoire."[15]

Apart from a single humanities scholar who pointed out that there was no "rigorous analogy" between Chomsky's generative grammar and the generation of the antibody repertoire, Jerne met with no opposition. This absence of

Niels Jerne with Queen Silvia of Sweden at the Nobel dinner in December 1984. (Pressens Bild, Stockholm. Photo: Jan Collsiiö)

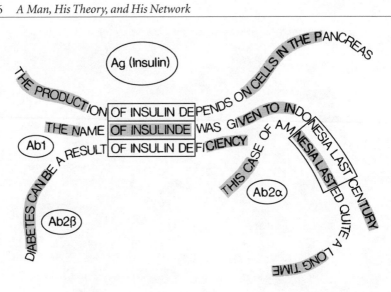

In his Nobel lecture, Jerne illustrated the analogy between language and the immune system: "The sentences representing antibodies possess partial mirror images of an antigenic sentence." Playing with language was something he had enjoyed since childhood. (Jerne, "The generative grammar," 1985. © The Nobel Foundation)

critical views does not necessarily imply that immunologists agreed with him but rather that they took the analogy between the immune system and language to be entertaining and thought-provoking, though without any significance for experimental research. Whatever could not be implemented in experiments, one had no need to oppose. They respected and honored the "king of theorists," but now, as a quarter-century earlier, they were guided by his imagination only when it could be put to work in the laboratory.[16]

Jerne's interest in language indicates, like so much else in his life and work, a romantic undercurrent. I have already mentioned how both the selection theory of antibody formation and the idiotypic network theory can be regarded as an expression of a romantic conception of the self. With his theory of the immune system as a semiotic network, Jerne introduced still another romantic topos: nature as an organic, self-organizing whole. It is difficult to find any holistic ideas in Jerne's earlier research; right up to the beginning of the 1970s he believed that biological phenomena could be reduced to physical laws. During the 1980s, however, his thought developed more and more in antireductionist and holistic directions, and he began to question the epistemological and ontological bases of current immunology: "When, in the 1940s, I began to focus on the subject of immunity, reductionism was clearly needed: what are the cells that make antibodies, that reject transplanted tissue, etc.[?] Now, in the 1980s, antibodies are well-known, and also the lymphocytes that produce these molecules, and those that produce 'factors,' and that kill target cells. Even many genes, gene-segments, and other elements are known. Clearly what is now needed is the opposite of reductionism, let us call it inductionism," he wrote in a note. Reduction requires logic and experiment, he continued, while induction requires "imagination" as well. He compared the situation in immunology with a chess game: "Even if you know all the pieces, and all the rules, the essence of the game escapes you; why does the master defeat you? Because he has induced a more true complexity from the elements than you." Evidently he thought himself immunology's grand master.[17]

"Immunology is for me becoming a mostly philosophical subject," he wrote to a friend in the winter of 1983; in his view, it was impossible to describe or explain complex systems by "studying the elements involved." On the other hand, he defended studies of the "elements involved" against philosophers who were all too ignorant of science. His younger colleague Antonio Coutinho had recommended to him a book about autopoietic systems written by the Chilean-French biologist and philosopher Francisco Varela. Jerne was impressed at first, but after rereading it "found that he says the same thing dozens of times, and finally leaves you almost empty-handed." He was irritated at philosophers who had not done their homework: "This is all very beautiful and profound, but without antibody molecules and lymphocytes discovered by scientists in the street, the philosophers would never have known that there *exists* an immune 'system.' They are good at pointing out the essence of what we have been doing, but it is not they, but *we* who must decide what to do *next*."[18]

Jerne's questioning of reductionism, his more and more explicit holism, and his emphasis on emergent properties, cognitive structures, and semiotics began to sound increasingly like an echo of his neo-Romanticism of the 1970s and 1980s. He stressed that reductionalism (or "Carthesialism" as he also called it) had failed to "'explain' the properties of complex systems." He found immunology increasingly unsatisfactory in that it was becoming "too complicated" and too "technical." He felt "put off," he admitted, when he read papers "about T_{3+4-8-} cells, and the like," and sought an approach that provided some connection to what had once again become "a fragmented field of research." The direction research was taking toward molecular genetics did not interest him. Of course he admired Tonegawa's work, but the molecular geneticists could yield only limited insights into the functioning of the immune system: "The DNA technologists are doing astonishing work, but it does not really help the proper physiological description of the immune system all that much." All these reductionist analyses had not yielded anything "more than CRAP."[19]

Even such a celebrated discovery as that in 1983 of the T-cell receptor, which gave the clue for the mechanism of T- and B-cell interaction in the immune response, left Jerne cold. Detailed functions of the immune system were being revealed, and the genetic coding of antibody variability had in principle been elucidated. But Jerne thought that none of this—"including the T-cell receptor and all 'factors' and accessory cells"—could explain the Immune System, which he now increasingly capitalized. "Biochemistry can't explain networks," he asserted. Instead, immunologists ought to study a large network's properties "as one whole thing," or study analogous and better-known systems, for example, ecological, or linguistic systems. He was also critical of the prevailing research policy, which stimulated young scientists to sequence a bit of a gene but prevented them from taking on more theoretical tasks. The prevalent "DNA-tide," with its mapping of nucleotide sequences, could not go on forever, he thought; "within ten years or so," interest would be renewed in how the system as a whole functions: "At that time, the idiotype people will be back on top—I hope."[20]

In the years following the Nobel Prize, Jerne withdrew to his home in Castillon-du-Gard. "All these science people and their lectures are becoming scarcely endurable," he complained to his old friend Ole Maaløe after having attended a symposium in Copenhagen in 1985. From his large villa he corresponded with his old colleagues in Basel and the immunologists who were fighting for the idiotypic network theory. He sat with his beloved prime numbers through the long winter evenings and spent many warm summer days with Alexandra conversing with family members, friends, and old colleagues who dropped by from time to time. The wine flowed copiously; except for drying-out periods, both husband and wife were rather alcoholic.[21]

Encouraged by the Sloan Foundation, Jerne thought a while about writing the history of recent immunology but soon gave up the idea. In the past thirty years, "dozens of Ehrliches, Bordets and Landsteiners" had appeared, so how could anyone write anything worthwhile about these hundreds of good scientists? Instead, he started making notes for an autobiography, which got no further than scattered observations and two short drafts of chapter heads. One of the drafts has already been mentioned (Chapter 1); in the other draft—comprising sixteen chapter headings in the classic "in which" format that makes the autobiographical self speak more directly to the reader—Jerne devoted a third of his chapters to his formative years in Holland, another third to his twenty years in Copenhagen, and the final third to his international career:

1. In which my mother tells me [admits] that she does not know whether or not God exists.
2. In which I tell my father that a roulette has no memory.
3. In which I become the youngest baccalaureate of the Netherlands in 1928.
4. In which I am an office boy in the Rotterdam branch of the United Fruit company.
5. In which a group of scientists tell me that philosophy without science is nonsense.
6. In which, instead of studying thermodynamics, I brush up my Greek and Latin.
7. In which, instead of studying medicine, I marry a paintress in Copenhagen.
8. In which I am given a half-day job in the Danish State Serum Institute, and finally discover (suddenly) that I am a scientist. Spätzünder.
9. In which I discuss with James D. Watson, Gunther S. Stent, Ole Maaløe, Niels Bohr, Max Delbrück, and Jeppe Ørskov [and] Georg Rasch.
10. In which I discover the random element in the structure of the Immune System.
11. In which I travel [hike] across the US in an old Studebaker earning 50 $ per lecture.
12. In which I join the WHO, but actually join Eduard Kellenberger and Werner Arbor [and] marry Alexandra.
13. In which Hubert Bloch and Jonas Salk make me chairman of the Department of Microbiology of the Medical School of the U[niversity] of Pittsburgh.
14. In which of three offers I choose the worst.
15. In which arise the Basel Institute of Immunology and my suggestion of an Immune network.
16. In which I look back upon 100 years of immunology.

Thus in reconstructing the chronology of his life, however witty or self-indulgent—as in understanding the development of the immune response—Jerne was apparently most interested in the early developmental stages.[22]

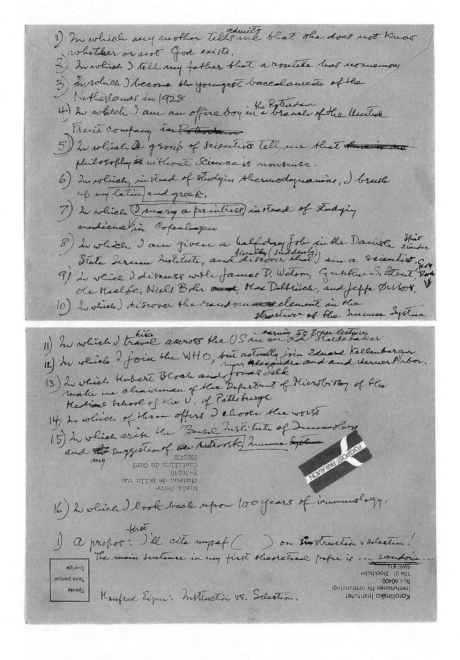

List of chapter headings for Niels Jerne's planned autobiography, written on an envelope, 1984 or 1985. (Jerne Collection, The Royal Library, Copenhagen)

Fall of 1985 passed mostly in similar autobiographical musings. He noticed that his childhood and youth were becoming clearer in his memory, whereas the forty years on the world stage after Tjek's death were becoming more diffuse. "It is as though a curtain [is drawn] between me and my experiences during the years after Tjek's death," he wrote; "it makes me lose confidence in all my other memories, too." Of course he had his large archive to turn to, but at the same time he felt "a bit of horror at delving into those old stacks of paper!" He found it hard to concentrate and was always tempted to write about something else. Where should he draw the line between the relevant and the irrelevant? "I feel a bit like playing chess against myself."[23]

He occasionally expressed uncertainty about the value of what he had busied himself with in his life: "Maybe I should have stayed at home instead of meeting hundreds of new people I have forgotten, once again, all around the world," he wrote to an old acquaintance from Copenhagen. Such doubts were rare, however, and might have been, as so often before, merely affectations. Throughout his life Jerne had remained a *puer aeternus,* a man without *Heimat,* a kind of stranger wherever he found himself, a *thēoros* who preferred contemplating the world from a distance to taking practical action, someone who got his life energy from conversations but who had no fixed moorings in everyday reality.[24]

For Niels Jerne, both art and science were means of creating order in a chaotic world ("everything is chaos," he repeatedly observed). As Rita Levi-Montalcini points out, scientists are often satisfied with discoveries that reveal only small sections of the world, whereas artists are more intent on formulating and transmitting their own worldview. Jerne never took satisfaction from small discoveries—in this respect, he resembled an artist more than a biomedical researcher—and he struggled to formulate theories of great breadth, wishing to impose his own worldview and his personality on nature. Perhaps it was this preoccupation with himself and his own creations that made it difficult for him to show loving concern. He had been in love several times, now and then to the brink of obsession; at times he was driven by a strong and sentimental longing for love—and by love for the feeling of being in love—but he never seems to have realized that this eternal longing could be dispelled only by surrendering himself to love for another.[25]

EPILOGUE
"WHAT STRUGGLE TO ESCAPE"

*I*n December 1986, a few weeks before he turned seventy-five, I met Niels Jerne in Castillon-du-Gard and proposed that I write his biography. He was intrigued at the prospect, but also hesitant, and it took him almost two years to accept the idea. During intense evenings and nights, as I interviewed him in his flat in Basel, he told me about some of his most emotionally vivid memories and experiences. On the fifth night, he interrupted the "confession" and demanded to see how the material would be used before continuing and before giving me access to his papers.

He got his sketch. He wrote me that it was *"quite strange"* to read about himself *"in the third person,"* but it was also fascinating: *"I seem to have reacted in a similar way to many situations in life: perhaps a basic element of my character."* During the years that followed I visited him a couple of times a year to go through the files and discuss his life and science, often using documents from the collection as our point of departure. We sat for hours at a stretch, sometimes with a tape recorder between us, at the long desk in his study on the second floor of the Château de Bellevue; our conversation continued at lunch, over Alexandra's soups and fine pâtés, and often went on, accompanied by a bottle of wine or two, till the sun set over the Pont du Gard, the old Roman aqueduct. Jerne spoke mostly about himself and his life but did not neglect

Niels Jerne in the garden of his home in Languedoc, ca. 1990. (Medical History Museum, University of Copenhagen)

comments on the progress and pitfalls of immunology; for example, to a Danish medical student he aired his mistrust of emerging psychoneuroimmunology, "which is as boring as the word is long." In that respect he was a true Cartesian: he didn't believe for a minute that the immune system could be influenced by the central nervous system. He warned the young fellow—a relative, as it happens—against going into the field for fear he would risk losing his reputation and end up among "hypnotizers, Zen Buddhists, Taoists."[1]

As time went by, I was allowed to borrow more and more from his papers, and at last, in the summer of 1992, Jerne donated virtually the entire archive to the Royal Library in Copenhagen. It gave him great satisfaction to be included among the cultural elite of Denmark rather than being reduced to one of many figures in the archives of the history of science, and he especially liked the fact that Søren Kierkegaard's papers were in the library, too. Nor was he ever in doubt that his papers should end up in Denmark, for although he loved to present himself as a European, he felt himself a Dane, he said. Nevertheless, he did not fail to manifest contempt for what he perceived to be the mediocre tradition of Danish popular culture. He often quoted the popular nineteenth-century poet Hans Vilhelm Kaalund's "Paa det Jevne" (On the

Ground), which expressed what he disliked most about the country's mentality:

> On the ground, on the ground!
> Not in skies above!
> 'Tis where life has summoned you
> To prove your worth.
> Every wondrous thing,
> Every lofty thing your soul may reach
> Must take root in life
> Firmly, down below.
> On the ground! On the ground!
> Sounds the paean of existence!

Some years later, his older son, Ivar, confirmed my impression that Jerne "hated mediocrity" and had always had the opinion that one "should be something exceptional" if one was involved with culture: "If you're not an exceptional ballet dancer," he once said, "just be a spectator. If you are not a brilliant writer, just read books." Ivar also told me about an incident on his eighteenth birthday. In the small hours, when both father and son were a little drunk, Jerne is said to have remarked that "Tjek was a genius" and, after a long pause for thought, added: "And I am unusual." Ivar remembers the moment well: "Then I said, 'And you are also a genius.' Then he [Jerne] interrupted me, saying, 'And I am unusual. And if you can't be somebody, you can go to hell.'"[2]

Once the archive had been transported to Copenhagen, our contacts were limited mostly to occasional telephone calls and letters. Jerne hoped that his comments and opinions would fill *"around 10%"* of the book but realized in the end that his contribution would amount to little more than *"a few remarks."* He declared that he never got his autobiography written because he was more interested in the memory function itself than in the contents of his memory: *"I now see that I never (or hardly) would have been able to write my 'erindringer' [memoirs], because my mind seems to be so structured that the first thing, that occurs to me, is to analyse the composition of 'erindringer' instead of focussing on telling my own memoirs."* I sent him drafts of several chapters for comment, and our conversation turned increasingly to how The Book was going to look. He did not seem concerned about how I portrayed his character; he never tired of pointing out that many times during his life he had been driven by money and his need for success. Nor did he fail to mention his lack of desire to do

Niels Jerne ca. 1992, at the age of eighty-one. (Medical History Museum, University of Copenhagen)

something for humanity. And, apart from his incessant feeling of guilt at having contributed to Tjek's death, he never evinced any pangs of conscience about anything else he had done in his life. The most important thing was that the biography become a contribution to literature, that it be unique. He was afraid of having "*wasted our time*" on something that might turn out to be average.[3]

He also expressed anxiety that I might not wish or be able to complete the work. In the summer of 1993, after undergoing several months of radiation treatment for an evil-looking tumor in his mouth, he wrote me that he had begun to be "forgotten by the young crowd of immunologists"; and, as if to remind me that it was important for the book to be published, he sent me several clippings, one of which touted him as "one of the [most] famous immunologists of all times, possibly also the greatest."[4]

Later that summer the doctors found an adenocarcinoma in his right lung. During the year that followed, we had only sporadic contact, but it seems that the question of his posthumous reputation was still gnawing at him, for at the beginning of August 1994, Alexandra suddenly called me up. "Niels doesn't like the title of the book," she proclaimed in her usual direct way. Two years earlier I had suggested calling it "What Struggle to Escape"—as a way to summarize Jerne's troubled life, as an oblique reference to his romanticism, and as a contextual play on the title of Francis Crick's recently published autobiography. Jerne had accepted it then. Now he apparently did not.

I asked to speak with Jerne, and a few minutes later he came to the telephone.

"What do you mean?" I asked. "Why don't you like the title of the book?"

There was a silence. *"You want to call it 'What struggle to escape,' right?"* he replied at last. *"Isn't that from a poem by Keats?"*

"*Yes,*" I answered.

"And the line before it is 'What mad pursuit'?"

"*Yes,*" I answered again.

"Which is also the title of Francis Crick's autobiography?"

"*That's right,*" I answered, still not sure just what his drift was.

Then out it came, loud and clear, without any uncertainty in his voice: *"I don't want to be second to Francis Crick."*[5]

That was our last conversation. Just over two months later, on 7 October 1994, Niels Kaj Jerne died in his home in Castillon-du-Gard.

ABBREVIATIONS USED IN NOTES

AJ   Adda Jerne (previously Sundsig-Hansen)
CS   Charles M. Steinberg
EJ   Elsa Falkner (born Jerne)
EM   Erna Mørch
EML   E. M. Lourie
GS   Gunther Stent
GW   Gertrude van der Schalk (born Wansinck)
HN   Hans Noll
IJ   Ivar Jerne
JI   Johannes Ipsen
JOR   Jens Ole Rostock
JR   Jeanine Reyss
JØ   Jeppe Ørskov
KGL   Karl Gordon Lark
KJ   Karen Guldbrandsen (born Jerne)
MB   Marcel Baluda
MD   Max Delbrück
NKJ   Niels Kaj Jerne
OM   Ole Maaløe

RP   Richard Prigge
ThS   Thomas Söderqvist
TJ   Thomas Jerne
TjJ   Tjek Jerne

Short References to Correspondence

Letters to Jerne

Hans Wigzell to NKJ, 15 October 1984. (Note that all letters to Jerne are in Jerne's collection.)

Letters from Jerne

NKJ to GS, 1 July 1954. (If no qualification follows, the letter from Jerne is in the recipient's private collection.)

NKJ to OM, 28 February 1983 (copy) and 3 March 1983 (copy). (A copy of the letters is in Jerne's collection.)

NKJ to EML, 8 May 1954 (original). (The original letter was later retrieved from the recipient and is now in Jerne's collection.)

NKJ to EM, 15 February 1942 (draft). (A draft of the letter is in Jerne's collection.)

Short References to Interviews

NKJ, 5 May 1987; JI, 17 March 1988, and 7 August 1989.

NOTES

Introduction

1. Jerne, "The generative grammar," 1985, p. 157.
2. Wigzell, "The Nobel prize," 1985, p. 24; Burnet, *Changing Patterns,* 1968, p. 249; Bibel, *Milestones,* 1988, p. 190; Pernis and Augustin (Review), 1982, p. 3; Cohn, "Foreword," 1989, p. xxxiv.
3. Jerne, "The natural selection theory," 1966, p. 303.
4. Burnet, "The impact," 1967, p. 2; Tommaso Meo, 19 June 1992.
5. E.g., Hilary Koprowski calls Jerne "an intellectual giant" because "he had discovered the Network Theory" (Vaughan, *Listen,* 2000, p. 267).
6. Woolf, *Three Guineas,* 1977, p. 131.
7. Yeats, "The choice," 1957.
8. On being one's own archivist, cf. Shortland, *Hugh Miller,* 1996, p. 232. A large correspondence with an American woman who gave birth to his third child in 1970 was burnt in 1993 (cf. Chapter 19, this volume). Pletsch, "On the autobiographical life," 1987, p. 415.
9. NKJ, 2 May 1989.
10. The interview notes, tapes, and transcriptions are presently in my personal files (see further "Unpublished Sources" at the back of this book).
11. Lively, *According to Mark,* 1984, p. 147. E.g., he once said: *"What I'm saying on this tape recorder . . . it's not necessarily true, because I'm also playing games with you,*

with myself and so . . . I'm not sitting here like a witness for the prosecution or something. I'm just saying what suddenly occurs to me as appropriate at this moment" (NKJ, 11 February 1988). In another setting, when we were discussing his reasons for moving to Denmark in 1934, I confronted him with the possibility that his motives might be a rationalization after the fact, and he answered, without consulting his sixty-year-old notes and letters: *"Oh yes, surely, that's what I am saying now. If you had asked me on that occasion, I don't really know what I would have answered"* (NKJ, 17 October 1988). Had similar questions been asked about all his reminiscences, similar answers might have followed.

12. Cassidy, *Uncertainty,* 1992, p. x; Hamilton, *In Search,* 1988.

13. Cf. Nye, *The Invented Self,* 1983, and Tonkin, *Narrating Our Pasts,* 1992.

14. NKJ, 28 August 1989.

15. See Söderqvist, "Biography," 1991. For a systematic critique of the poststructuralist view of the subject, see Burke, *The Death,* 1998.

16. Rorty, *Philosophy,* 1980, p. 366.

17. See Söderqvist, "Existential projects," 1996.

18. Undated note (mid-1980s); NKJ to ThS, 8 July 1993.

19. Kierkegaard, *Stages,* 1988, p. 10.

20. E.g., Tuchman, "Biography," 1986, p. 103; Edel, *Writing Lives,* 1984, p. 14, and "Confessions," 1987. See also Smocovitis, "Living with," 1999.

21. Moraitis, "The psychoanalyst's role," 1985.

22. For a summary of the genre of biographies of scientists, see Shortland and Yeo, *Telling Lives,* 1996 (especially the editors' introduction), and Söderqvist, "Existential projects," 1996.

23. For a review of the rise of immunology as a scientific discipline in the post–World War II period, see Söderqvist and Silverstein, "Participation," 1994, and Silverstein and Söderqvist, "The structure," 1994.

24. Like Desmond and Moore, *Darwin,* 1991, a "defiantly social portrait." (p. xviii).

25. Like Holmes, *Hans Krebs,* 2 vols, 1991–92.

26. For a recent summary, see Hunter, "Psychoanalysing," 1999.

27. Shapin, "Essay review," 1993, p. 337; for narrative unity, see MacIntyre, *After Virtue,* 1984, esp. chap. 15.

28. Skidelsky, "Only connect," 1988, p. 14. This territory has been to some extent explored in recent biographies of scientists, e.g., in Walter, *Science,* 1990, and of philosophers, e.g., in Miller, *The Passion,* 1993, Monk, *Ludwig Wittgenstein,* 1990, and Monk, *Bertrand Russell,* 1996–2000. See also Hunter, *Robert Boyle,* 2000.

29. For details, see Söderqvist, "Existential projects," 1996; cf. Eriksson, 1997, pp. 106–7.

30. Kierkegaard, *Søren Kierkegaard's Journals,* vol. 1, 1967, pp. 408–9 (# 928).

31. Franz (*Puer aeternus,* 1981) discusses the Peter Pan complex.

32. Cf. Söderqvist and Stillwell, "Essay review," 1999; Söderqvist, "How to write," 1993. The most ambitious undertaking focusing on the rise of molecular immunology is Podolsky and Tauber, *The Generation,* 1997.

33. Jerne thereby transcended "the polarization of the personae of artist and scientist," which Lorraine Daston ("Fear and loathing," 1998, p. 74) suggests characterizes science since the mid-nineteenth century.
34. Nietzsche, *Beyond,* 1989, p. 11.
35. See further Söderqvist, "Virtue ethics," 1997, and "Immunology à la Plutarch," 2001; Skidelsky, "Only connect," 1988, p. 13; Rorty, *Philosophy,* 1980, p. 360.
36. E.g., Smiles, *Life,* 1876; Heilbron, *The Dilemmas,* 1986, p. viii; Duff, *Plutarch's Lives,* 1999, pp. 243, 69.
37. MacIntyre, *After Virtue,* 1984, p. 213.

Chapter 1: "I Have Never in My Life Felt I Belonged in the Place Where I Lived"

1. Undated note (1985).
2. NKJ to his siblings, 2–21 August 1978 (copy); undated note (1985).
3. Undated note (1985). The narrative of the family history and Jerne's childhood years is based on NKJ to Campbell Moses, 20 September 1973 (copy), NKJ to his siblings 2–21 August 1978 (copy), interviews with Jerne, his father's small collection of documents (now in Jerne's estate), and official documents in the Twello City Archive, the Assen City Archive, and the Rotterdam City Archive. For a genealogy of the Jerne family, see Grønnegaard, *Sønderhoslægter,* 1988.
4. *Berlingske Tidende* (Copenhagen), 2 July 1937.
5. NKJ, 16 October 1988.
6. Ibid.
7. For parental loss, see Price, *Little Science,* 1963, p. 109; Silverman, "Parental loss," 1974 (for a critical view, see Woodward, "Scientific genius," 1974); Raphael, *The Anatomy,* 1983, p. 126. For psychobiographical accounts of scientists' lives, see, e.g., Manuel, *A Portrait,* 1968; Bowlby, *Charles Darwin,* 1990; and Hunter, "Psychoanalysing Robert Boyle," 1999.
8. Undated note (probably summer 1933); NKJ, 16 October 1988; Marth H. Smith-Frijda to ThS, 11 September 1991.
9. Undated note (probably 1985); NKJ, 29 April 1989; diary entry, 28 September 1938; undated note (probably summer 1933); diary entry, 3 August 1985.
10. NKJ, 9 February 1988; undated note (on the rear side of NKJ to TjJ, 13 July 1938; original); KJ, 1 June 1988; quoted in Louis Du Pasquier to ThS, 27 November 2001.
11. NKJ, 12 February 1988. He was quoting the song from memory, cf. Dal, *Danish Ballads,* 1967, p. 236.
12. NKJ, 11 February 1988; *Berlingske Tidende,* 2 July 1937; NKJ, 11 February 1988.
13. NKJ, 12 February 1988.
14. Undated note (1984 or 1985); NKJ, 15 October 1988; quoted in [Sigg], "Ich höre," 1985, p. 6.

15. KJ, 1 June 1988; Eiduson, *Scientists,* 1962, p. 50; NKJ, 11 February 1988 and 8 December 1986. Frank Sulloway has suggested (*Born to Rebel,* 1996) that later-born children are the most creative.

16. Undated note (after 1932, probably 1933); NKJ, 12 February 1988; KJ, 1 June 1988; note, November 1927.

17. NKJ, 12 February 1988; undated note (after 1939, probably 1940s).

18. NKJ, 12 February 1988 and 5 May 1987.

19. NKJ, 5 May 1987; undated note (1985); NKJ to Miep, Paul, and Daaf van den Hoek, 14 September 1934 (draft); NKJ, 5 May 1987. For his immunological sentence playing, see Chapter 21, this volume.

20. NKJ, 5 May 1987 and 15 October 1988; undated note (probably late 1980s).

21. NKJ, 25 February 1989 and 15 October 1988. Stevens quoted from Kermode, "Strange," 1994, p. 9.

22. NKJ, 15 October 1988 and 5 May 1987.

Chapter 2: "Stylistically, I'm Best at Irony"

1. Diary entry, 23 April 1928; undated note (1928).

2. Willy Boer to NKJ, 24 November 1930; NKJ to JR, 2 June 1928 (draft), and undated (1928; draft); note, 14 June 1928; NKJ to JR, undated (1928; draft); NKJ to JR, 2 June 1928.

3. NKJ, 12 February 1988; NKJ to JR, 12 July 1928 (draft) and 30 September 1928 (draft).

4. NKJ to JR, 3 September 1928 (draft) and 30 September 1928; undated note (January 1929).

5. KJ, 1 June 1988; NKJ to GW, 13 January 1930 (draft); GW, 10 November 1990.

6. NKJ to GW, 24 January 1930 (draft); GW to NKJ, 14 October 1930.

7. GW, 10 November 1990; diary entry, 22 June 1932; NKJ, 2 May 1989.

8. NKJ, 16 October 1988.

9. NKJ, 16 October 1988; NKJ to ThS, 11 January 1991.

10. NKJ to JR, 25 May 1930 (draft); Biddis, *The Age,* 1977; Herf, *Reactionary Modernism,* 1984; undated note (around 14 January 1931).

11. NKJ to GW, undated (later dated 15 June 1930; draft).

12. NKJ to JR, 17 December 1929 (draft); Jeanine quoted in NKJ to JR, 27 January 1930 (draft); NKJ to JR, 30 January–16 February 1930 (draft).

13. NKJ to JR, 30 January–16 February 1930 (draft). For detachtigers, see Weevers, *Poetry,* 1960.

14. Undated note (later dated December 1929 on the reverse side); For Schiller, see Peckham, *The Birth,* 1986, p. 56. For a discussion of the roots of Modernism in Romanticism, see Peckham, p. viii.

15. NKJ to JR, 25 May 1930 (draft) and 12 July 1928 (draft). He is also said to have claimed that "what I really like is being alone, to close the door and being alone"

(Manny Delbrück, 17 January 1988). Klein (*Cigarettes,* 1993) suggests that smoking is a way of getting in touch with the sublime.

16. Undated note (probably September 1930); undated note (probably summer 1933); note, 28 September 1938; NKJ to GW, undated (1930; draft); undated note (probably September 1930).
17. Undated note (probably September 1930).
18. NKJ to JR undated (probably December 1930; draft); undated note (probably late fall 1931 or spring 1932); NKJ to Johan Witkam, undated (probably January 1931; draft); Multatulti, *Minnebrieven,* 1951, p. 47; NKJ, 9 December 1986.
19. Undated note (probably summer 1933); NKJ to JR, undated (later dated 12 December 1930; draft); undated note (probably summer 1933).
20. NKJ to JR, 26 July 1931 (draft) and 1 January 1931 (draft).
21. Diary entry, 28 September 1938; NKJ to ThS, 13 May 1994.
22. Undated note (probably September–November 1931).
23. JR to NKJ, 2 November 1931.
24. Diary entry, 22 June 1932.
25. NKJ, 11 February 1988 and 21 July 1990; for "soma" in physics, see Segré, *Enrico Fermi,* 1970, p. 90; TJ, 17 November 1988; Ray Owen, 17 January 1988; undated note (1985).
26. Bergson, "Introduction," 1903.
27. Pilkington, *Bergson,* 1976; diary entry, 19 January 1932; diary entry, 18 January 1932.

Chapter 3: "I Wanted to Study Something That Couldn't Be Used"

1. NKJ, 16 October 1988; diary entry, 22 June 1932; undated note (probably summer 1933); NKJ to AJ undated (September 1945; draft); NKJ to Papa, 25 October 1933 (original); NKJ, 5 June 1991.
2. NKJ, 7 May 1987 and 11 February 1988.
3. E.g., in NKJ to AJ, undated (September 1945; draft); admittance protocol, Universitetsarchief, Leiden.
4. NKJ, 11 February 1988 and 25 June 1992.
5. NKJ, 5 May 1987, 11 February 1988 and 5 May 1987 (the conversation spanned two long evenings and was influenced by alcohol; perhaps these circumstances contributed to focusing his memories on the alcohol consumption fifty-five years earlier); undated note (probably summer 1933); NKJ, 11 February 1988.
6. NKJ, 11 and 12 February 1988. For the political situation, see Jong, *Het koninkrijk,* 1969.
7. NKJ, 11 February 1988; Piet Swart and L. W. Sluyterman van Loo, 18 November 1988.
8. Undated note (probably summer 1933).
9. NKJ to Papa, 25 October 1933 (original); NKJ, 11 February 1988; NKJ to Papa, 25 October 1933 (original); NKJ, 11 February 1988.

10. NKJ to Papa, 25 October 1933 (original).
11. Kierkegaard, *Either/Or*, vol. 1, 1944, p. 245; quoted in [Sigg], "Ich höre," 1985, p. 8; NKJ, 9 December 1986.
12. NKJ, 11 February 1988; NKJ to Jacques [?], 18 January 1934 (draft); NKJ, 5 May 1987.
13. NKJ to Aage Henriksen, 15 January 1934 (incorrectly dated 1933; draft); undated note (probably fall 1933).
14. Undated note (probably summer 1933).
15. NKJ to Papa, 25 October 1933 (original).
16. Diary entry, 20 July 1934; NKJ, 17 October 1988.

Chapter 4: "I Have the Feeling That Everything Around Me Is Enveloped in a Mist"

1. NKJ to Mama and Papa, 3 September 1934 (draft and original), and 9–11 September 1934 (original); NKJ to Kurt Dym, 12 September 1934 (draft).
2. NKJ to Mama and Papa, 3 September 1934 (draft and original).
3. For Copenhagen science, see Söderqvist et al., *Videnskabernes København*, 1998.
4. NKJ to Mama, Papa and KJ, 12 October 1934 (draft and original).
5. Diary entry, 28 April 1936; quoted in [Sigg], "Ich höre," 1985, p. 7.
6. NKJ to Mama and Papa, 9 November 1934 (original).
7. Diary entry, 22 April 1933; NKJ, 9 December 1986; NKJ to TjJ, 30 May 1945 (original); Kierkegaard, *Repetition*, 1983, p. 170; e.g., NKJ to Thijs[?], 1 October 1934 (draft).
8. NKJ to Kurt, 31 October 1933 (draft); NKJ to Thijs[?], 1 October 1934 (draft); NKJ, 9 December 1986; undated note (around 1936); NKJ to Thijs [?], 1 October 1934 (draft); undated note (probably 1936 or 1937); Ivar Jerne, 21 March 1993.
9. NKJ to Mama and Papa, 21 January 1935 (original).
10. NKJ, 17 October 1988. Tjek's early life story draws upon Zibrandtsen, "Malerinden," 1945, and "Jerne," 1949, on Jerne's diary entries for 1940, and on an interview with Inge Fussing, 31 March 1989.
11. NKJ to EJ, 22 March 1935 (draft); NKJ, 5 June 1991; diary entry, 16 February 1935; NKJ to TjJ, 17 September 1936 (original).
12. NKJ to AJ, undated (September 1945; draft; self-presentation may have been influenced by the fact that the letter was written to impress his mistress, Adda); NKJ, 25 February 1989.
13. Papa to NKJ, 30 May 1935 (draft and original); NKJ 18 October 1988; NKJ to Papa, 7 September 1935 (original).
14. NKJ to Emilie and Robert Wahl, 19 December 1935 (draft).
15. NKJ, 18 October 1988 and 5 June 1991.
16. NKJ to Gerhard[?], 12 February 1936 (draft).
17. NKJ to TJ, Good Friday 1936 (draft); Inge Fussing, 31 March 1989.
18. NKJ to TJ, Good Friday 1936 (draft).

19. Papa and Mama to NKJ, 11 May 1935; NKJ to EJ, 7 March 1936 (draft); EJ to NKJ, 19 March 1936; NKJ to TJ, Good Friday 1936 (draft); undated note (probably early March 1936).
20. Undated note (probably summer 1933); NKJ to EJ, 7 March 1936 (draft).
21. Edith Permin, 11 June 1989; Louis Du Pasquier to ThS, 27 November, 2001; NKJ to Mama and Papa, 2 May 1936 (draft and original).
22. TJ to NKJ, 4 March 1936. The following account of Hans Jessen Jerne's bacon experiments is based on a large number of documents from the years 1936–39 (in Jerne's collection).
23. NKJ to Mama and Papa, 2 May 1936 (draft and original).
24. NKJ to TjJ, 23–24 June 1936 (original).
25. NKJ to TjJ, 28 June 1936 (original).

Chapter 5: "When I Look at Other Scientists . . . None of Them Have Wasted as Many Years as I Have"

1. See Jørgensen, *The Development,* 1951, pp. 45–46; Jørgensen, *Bertrand Russell,* 1935.
2. NKJ to TjJ, 21–22 August 1936 (original), 29 August 1936 (original), and 4 October 1936 (original).
3. NKJ, 25 February 1989.
4. Breton quoted in Gascoyne, *A Short Survey,* 1935, p. 59. For the similarity between sadism and science as two related ways of exercising dominance and power, see Keller, *Reflections,* 1985, chap. 6.
5. NKJ to Mama and Papa, 15 April 1937 (draft and original).
6. NKJ to TjJ, 17 June 1937 (original); NKJ, 20 October 1988; NKJ to TjJ, 2 September 1937 (original).
7. NKJ to TjJ, 23 September 1937 (original).
8. NKJ to TjJ, 4 May 1938; HN, 12 September 1989; JI, 17 March 1988; NKJ to ThS, 4 April 1992; NKJ, 18 October 1988.
9. NKJ to TjJ, 23 September 1937 (original) and 4 May 1938 (original).
10. TjJ to NKJ, 17 May 1938, 11 May 1938, 5 June 1938, and 13 June 1938.
11. NKJ to TjJ, 30 June 1938 (draft); NKJ, 11 February 1988.
12. NKJ to TjJ, 13 July 1938 (draft).
13. TjJ to NKJ, 30 June 1938; Inge Fussing, 31 March 1989.
14. TjJ to NKJ, 13 June 1938, 20 June 1938, and 8 August 1938; NKJ to [J. W.] Palludan, 27 August 1938 (draft).
15. NKJ to TjJ, 15 August 1938 (original); diary entry, 1 September 1938; TjJ to NKJ, 18 August 1938; Inge Fussing, 31 March 1989; Ellen Byström, 23 March 1989.
16. NKJ to TjJ, 24 September 1938 (original).
17. Diary entry, 28 September 1938.
18. Diary entry, 7 July 1941; NKJ, 9 December 1986.
19. Edith Permin, 11 June 1989; Marianne de Loes, undated (fall 1994).

20. NKJ, 18 October 1988; Mama to NKJ, 17 November 1938.
21. NKJ to TjJ, 23 January 1939 (original); diary entry, 7 June 1941.
22. Undated note (probably 1985).
23. Kierkegaard, *Either/Or*, vol. 2, 1944, pp. 112–13.
24. NKJ, 20 October 1988 and 25 February 1989.
25. NKJ to ThS, 25 September 1992.

Chapter 6: "Now I Think Nobody Can Keep Me from Becoming a Doctor"

1. NKJ to TjJ, 17 January 1939 (original).
2. NKJ to Mama and Papa, undated (around 15 June 1939; draft); NKJ to TjJ, 14 June 1939 (original).
3. NKJ, 18 October 1988, 15 October 1988, and 18 October 1988.
4. NKJ, 9 December 1986, 5 June 1991, 17 October 1988, and 1 May 1987.
5. Undated note (probably 1985); diary entry, 9 April 1940 (in Jerne's collection); undated note (probably 1985).
6. Else and Ejnar Møller Nielsen to NKJ, 16 August 1940.
7. Diary entry, 1 October 1940 (in Jerne's collection); undated (probably 1985).
8. NKJ, 4 May 1989.
9. Diary entry, 8 July 1941; diary entry early September 1940; quoted in [Sigg], "Ich höre," 1985, p. 9; NKJ to AJ, undated (September 1945; draft).
10. Undated note (probably fall 1940); undated note (late 1940 or early 1941).
11. Undated note (late 1940 or early 1941).
12. Undated note (probably 1942); TjJ to NKJ, 14 January 1942.
13. Simon Krause and Gudrun Madsen, 8 August 1989.
14. Ibid.; Ane Brügger, 11 April 1989; NKJ, 21 October 1988 and 9 February 1988.
15. NKJ to Mama and Papa, 19 February 1936 (draft); undated note (probably 1980s); quoted in [Sigg], "Ich höre," 1985, p. 7; NKJ, 7 May 1987.
16. Undated note (probably 1938); undated note (probably summer 1940).
17. Atkins, *Jorn*, 1968, p. 33.
18. [Sigg], "Ich höre," 1985, p. 8 (Egill Jacobsen says, 5 June 1989, that it was he who gave Jerne this piece of good advice); Jerne quoted in [Sigg], p. 8 (the spatial metaphor, of course, is not to be taken literally, and so it is not entirely clear what the expression "stand it on its head" actually means in a scientific context; and on another occasion, NKJ to ThS, 21 January 1987, he asserted that "my association with artists, before and during the war, was entirely irrelevant to the way I handled immunological problems"); Jorn quoted in Andersen, *Asger Jorn*, 1994, p. 8.
19. Undated note (around 1940–41).
20. Ibid.; undated note (late 1930s); NKJ to TjJ, 12 July 1943 (draft).
21. NKJ to TjJ, 5 July 1944 (original); MB, 4 September 1989; NKJ to Alfred Pletscher, 10 March 1968 (draft).

22. NKJ to Mama and Papa, 10 March 1941 (draft); NKJ to Papa, 19 May 1941 (original); Paludan, "Sommerdage," 1941.
23. Diary entries, 14 July 1941, 7 July 1941, and 8 July 1941.
24. Undated note (probably late fall 1941; cf. Croce, *Guide*, 1995, p. 25).
25. NKJ to Mama and Papa, 21 January 1942 (draft).
26. NKJ to TjJ, 20 May 1942 (original).
27. NKJ to TjJ, 3–4 June 1942 (original).

Chapter 7: "To Be Able to Let Nature Reflect in the Depths of My Own Soul"

1. NKJ to EM, 15 February 1942 (draft).
2. NKJ to EM, 21 June 1945 (draft); Mørch, *Serological Studies*, 1943; faked newspaper clipping produced in connection with Erna Mørch's thesis defense (1943); NKJ to TjJ, 27 July 1945 (original).
3. Tonny Bundesen, 15 April 1989; Edith Permin, 11 June 1989; Tove Olafsson, 22 September 1988; NKJ, 10 February 1988; undated note (1980s); Louis Du Pasquier to ThS, 27 November 2001.
4. NKJ to TjJ, 6 August 1942 (original), 13 August 1942 (original), 25 August 1942 (original), and 15 August 1942 (original).
5. Undated note (in Jerne's collection; later dated 1942 by Jerne); TjJ to NKJ, 3 September 1942.
6. Undated lecture notes (probably 1942).
7. Diary entry, 14 February 1943 (in Jerne's collection); Preben Torp to NKJ, 26 January 1943.
8. NKJ, 9 February 1988.
9. NKJ, 27 April 1987; diary entry, 18 April 1943 (in Jerne's collection).
10. Madsen, *Statens Seruminstitut*, 1940.
11. JI, 17 March 1988; [Fredrik], "Seruminstitutet," 1952; NKJ, 25 August 1987.
12. Madsen, *Statens Seruminstitut*, 1940, p. 87; Madsen, *Experimentelle Undersøgelser*, 1896; "Biological standardization," 1948.
13. For a general review of international biological standardization before 1945, see Cockburn, "The international contribution," 1991; for a review of the research that was carried on within the framework of the League of Nations up to 1945, see "Bibliography of technical work," 1945; Jensen, *Die intrakutane*, 1933; Ipsen, *Contribution*, 1941.
14. TjJ to NKJ, 9 July 1943; NKJ to TjJ, 15 July 1943 (original) and 12 June 1943 (original).
15. JOR, 22 March 1988; NKJ to TjJ, 2 June 1943 (original); NKJ, 5 May 1987; JI, 17 March 1988; NKJ, 4 May 1987; undated note (probably around 1940).
16. NKJ to TjJ, 12 June 1943 (original) and 12 July 1943 (draft).
17. NKJ to TjJ, 12 July 1943 (draft).

18. NKJ to JI, 6 August 1943 (draft) NKJ, 5 May 1987; The probit method had been known among statisticians since the turn of the century but was rediscovered in the 1930s by Fisher and C. I. Bliss (Hald, *Statistiske Metoder,* 1948, p. 127); Fisher and Yates, *Statistical Tables,* 1938.

19. NKJ to JI, 6 September 1943; NKJ, 5 May 1987.

20. Ipsen and Jerne, "Graphical evaluation," 1944 (according to *Science Citation Index,* it was cited only fifteen times, 1945–74); NKJ, 28 August 1989. I'm grateful to Anders Hald, Ole Olsen, and Michael Weis Bentzon for the interpretation of Jerne's rankit work.

21. NKJ, 5 May 1987 and 10 February 1988 (the expression "Watsonistic" refers, of course, to the molecular biologist James D. Watson, whom Niels got to know as a supremely self-confident person when he spent the year 1950–51 at the Serum Institute); undated note (1985).

22. JI, 17 March 1988; NKJ, 11 February 1988.

23. NKJ to TjJ, 12 July 1943 (draft); Kierkegaard, *Soren Kierkegaard's Journals,* vol. 3, 1975, p. 250 (#2820); Schrödinger, *Nature and the Greeks,* 1954, p. 93.

24. NKJ to TjJ, 12 July 1943 (draft); NKJ to GW, undated (later dated 15 June 1930; draft).

25. Frye, "The drunken boat," 1963, p. 11. For Romantic science, see Cunningham and Jardine, *Romanticism,* 1990. Jerne apparently contradicts Lorraine Daston's suggestion ("Fear and loathing," 1998) that Western culture since the mid-nineteenth century has been characterized by a growing gulf between factual science and imaginative art.

Chapter 8: "I Am Branded with Infidelity, and See That Open-Eyed"

1. EM to NKJ, undated (probably 1943–44); undated note (spring or summer 1945).

2. Edith Permin, 11 June 1989; TjJ to NKJ, 9 June 1943.

3. NKJ to TjJ, 12 July 1943 (draft); undated note (spring or summer 1945); NKJ to TjJ, 12 July 1943 (draft).

4. Diary entry, 18 November 1943; TjJ to NKJ, 18 November 1943; Poul Cramer to NKJ, 20 November 1943; TjJ to NKJ, 30 June 1943; diary entry, 25 March 1944 (in Jerne's collection).

5. Papa to NKJ, 29 April 1944; NKJ, 4 May 1989; JI, 17 March 1988.

6. NKJ, 9 December 1986; JI, 17 March 1988 and 7 August 1989.

7. NKJ to TjJ, 7 June 1944 (original) and 23 June 1944 (original).

8. Ipsen, "A standard," 1944.

9. Jensen, *Die intrakutane,* 1933; Jerne and Maaløe, "Standardization," 1949, p. 55.

10. Quoted in [Sigg], "Ich höre," 1985, p. 8; NKJ to TjJ, 18 June 1944 (original) and 12 July 1944 (original); Jerne, *A Study,* 1951, p. 57; undated lecture manuscript (probably 1949).

11. NKJ, 26 May 1989 and 15 October 1988.
12. Boyd and Hooker, "The influence," 1939, p. 290; Kraus, "Ueber ein akut," 1903; NKJ, 5 May 1987, 25 August 1986, and 27 April 1987; G. Rasch, "Bemærkninger til Principper for Standardisering af Toxiner, Antitoxiner og Anatoxiner," unpublished manuscript, 24 September 1938 (in Jerne's collection); Jerne, *A Study,* 1951, p. 10 (cf. Ipsen, "Systematische," 1943); undated note (around 1946); Jerne, *A Study,* 1951, p. 50.
13. NKJ to Papa and Mama, 12 December 1944 (original); undated note (spring or summer 1945).

Chapter 9: "Letters Are a Spiritual Spiderweb in Which You Snare the Dreaming Soul of a Woman"

1. NKJ to TjJ, January 2, 1945 (draft; the two spouses lived together at the time, so the draft "letter" may rather be a diary entry); undated note (late spring 1945).
2. NKJ to TjJ, January 2, 1945 (draft; cf. note 1).
3. Undated note (spring or summer, 1945); NKJ to TjJ, 27 July 1945 (original).
4. NKJ to EM, undated (March 1945; draft); undated notes (spring 1945 and mid-June 1945).
5. NKJ to TjJ, 22 March 1945 (original); Margrethe Gade, 27 January 1994; NKJ to EM, undated (March 1945; draft).
6. NKJ to TjJ, 30 May 1945 (original), and 23 June 1945 (original).
7. NKJ to TjJ, undated (around 20 May 1945; draft); Edith Permin, 11 June 1989.
8. TjJ to Edith Poulsen, 2 August 1945 (in Jerne's collection); TjJ to NKJ, 25 July 1945.
9. Diary entry, 21–22 May 1945; NKJ to TjJ, 24 May 1945 (original); NKJ to TjJ, undated (around 20 May 1945; draft); diary entry, 21–22 May 1945. After reading a draft of this chapter Jerne protested against my description: *"Tjek, she didn't dominate me, but the house was full of her friends"* (NKJ, 5 June 1991). I had probably touched a tender spot in his image of himself—the repugnance toward being dominated and directed from outside, a feeling that, in a metaphorical form, became the emotional a priori for the selection theory of antibody formation (see Parabasis).
10. NKJ to AJ, 10 September 1945 (draft); NKJ, 10 February 1988 (note that Jerne corrected "*orgons*" to "[*or*]*gasms*"; wilhelm Reich was popular in certain Danish medical circles in the 1930s, so there is much to indicate that he was conscious of Reich's ideas); undated note (1980s).
11. Diary entry, 31 July 1945; NKJ to AJ, 3 August 1945 (draft); AJ to NKJ, 17 August 1945.
12. NKJ to AJ, 10 September 1945 (draft).
13. Edith Permin, 11 June 1989.

14. NKJ to AJ, 15 November 1945 (original); Tove Olafsson, 22 September 1988.
15. TjJ to NKJ, undated (3 October 1945).
16. NKJ to Ingeborg Andersen, 21 December 1945 (draft); diary entry, 26 July 1945.
17. Edith Poulsen to NKJ, 11 November 1945; NKJ to Ingeborg Andersen, 21 December 1945 (draft).
18. NKJ to Lisbeth[?] and Theo[?], 8 July 1946 (draft); NKJ to Mama and Papa, 24 January 1947 (original); JOR, 22 March 1988; NKJ to Mutting and Vatting (i.e., Emilie and Robert Wahl), 31 October 1945 (draft); Inger Goldmann to NKJ, 28 February 1946.
19. Quoted in Berg, "I virkeligheden," 1984, p. 84.
20. Olmsted and Olmsted, *Claude Bernard,* 1952, p. 238.
21. NKJ to Ingeborg Andersen, 21 December 1945 (draft).
22. TjJ to NKJ, 8 August 1938; NKJ to TjJ, undated (around 20 May 1945; draft).
23. NKJ to Ingeborg Andersen, 21 December 1945 (draft); AJ to NKJ, 9 January 1946 (wrongly dated 1945); NKJ to AJ, 9–10 January 1946 (original).
24. NKJ to AJ, 9–10 January 1946 (original).
25. NKJ to Daphne Ipsen, 19 October 1946 (draft); NKJ to Mama and Papa, 26 December 1946–2 January 1947 (original).
26. NKJ to Mama and Papa, 24 January 1947 (original).
27. Ibid.

Chapter 10: "The Happiness of Feeling Superior to a Lot of People"

1. NKJ to Mama and Papa, 6 February 1947 (original); NKJ, 29 April 1989; and 7 May 1987.
2. Maaløe, *On the Relation,* 1946; OM, 2 December 1986; see Maaløe, "Pathogenic-apathogenic formation," 1948; Maaløe, "How it all began," 1981, pp. 1–2; NKJ, 29 April 1987 and 11 February 1988; Anne Edel Adolph, 4 March 1988.
3. Crick, *What Mad Pursuit,* 1988, p. 93; Maaløe, "How it all began," 1981, p. 4; Viggo Faber, 24 March 1988; HN, 12 September 1989.
4. Undated note (20 September 1951); NKJ to ThS, 24 January 1991.
5. "Expert committee," 1948.
6. NKJ, 29 April 1987.
7. OM to JØ, 1 October 1948 (copy in Jerne's collection).
8. NKJ, 28 August 1989.
9. Maaløe, "How it all began," 1981, p. 2; Viggo Faber, 24 March 1988; NKJ, 26 May 1989 and 27 April 1987.
10. NKJ, 7 May 1987.
11. Arrhenius and Madsen, "Physical chemistry," 1902; e.g., Marrack, *The Chemistry,* 1938, Heidelberger, "Chemical aspects," 1939, Pauling, "A theory," 1940, and

Kendall, "The quantitative," 1942; Glenny and Barr, "Dilution ratio," 1932 (cf., Boyd, *Fundamentals,* 1943, p. 189).

12. Boyd and Hooker, "The influence," 1933; Teorell, "Quantitative aspects," 1946.

13. Pauling, "A theory," 1940, Pappenheimer et al., "Studies," 1940, Marrack, *The Chemistry,* 1938, and Heidelberger, "Chemical aspects," 1939; Jerne, *A Study,* 1951, p. 99.

14. Jerne, *A Study,* 1951, p. 6.

15. NKJ to Mama and Papa, 24 January 1947 (original).

16. Jerne and Maaløe, "Standardization," 1949, p. 56; Jerne and Wood, "The validity," 1949, p. 273; NKJ, 5 May 1987.

17. Jerne, *A Study,* 1951, pp. 65–67, table 13 and fig. 8–9

18. Ibid., p. 60; NKJ, 11 February 1988.

19. JOR, 22 March 1988; HN, 12 September 1989.

20. Reconstructed from NKJ to OM, 24 January 1949, 15 February 1949, 18 February 1949, 9 March 1949, 4 April 1949, 19 April 1949, and 16 May 1949.

21. NKJ to OM, 16 May 1949.

22. NKJ, 5 June 1991 and 27 June 1992; Jerne, "Matr. nr. 11," 1949, pp. 49–50; JOR, 22 March 1988; Jerne, "Matr. nr. 11," 1950.

23. NKJ to OM, 18 February 1949; Michael Weis Bentzon, 24 March 1988; HN, 12 September 1989.

24. Viggo Faber, 24 March 1988.

25. JOR, 22 March 1988.

26. David Finney, 25 July 1989; [name withheld], 23 February 1988.

Chapter 11: "I Think the Work Has Principal Application to Immunology"

1. Jerne, *A Study,* 1951, pp. 101, 17.

2. NKJ, 27 April 1987.

3. Jerne, *A Study,* 1951, pp. 176, 177; Jerne, "Matr. nr. 11" 1949, p. 49.

4. NKJ to Kai Linderstrøm-Lang, 27 June 1950 (copy).

5. See, e.g., Silverstein, *A History,* 1989; Moulin, *Le dernier langage,* 1991; Silverstein and Söderqvist, "The structure," 1994.

6. NKJ to OM, 15 February 1949.

7. Jerne, *A Study,* 1951, pp. 62, 134; NKJ, 29 April, 1987; Jerne, *A Study,* 1951, pp. 135–39 (particularly fig. 24); lecture manuscript, 20 November 1950.

8. Jerne, *A Study,* 1951, pp. 139, 135, 139.

9. The notion of an immunobiological revolution has been suggested by Silverstein, e.g., "The dynamics," 1991.

10. Jerne, *A Study,* 1951, pp. 135, 140.

11. Quoted in undated note (probably fall 1950). Jerne did not mention Holt's hypothesis in "The natural-selection theory," 1955.

12. Jerne, *A Study,* 1951, p. 140; undated note (1985).
13. The Medical Faculty Archive, University of Copenhagen, file nr. 21/49–50; OM, 2 December 1986.
14. See, e.g., Talmage, "Allergy and immunology," 1957, and Uhr, "The heterogeneity," 1964; "It is known [from Jerne] that the avidity of antibody increases with duration of immunization," wrote Pernis et al., "Specificity," 1963; Viggo Faber, 24 March 1988; CS, 9–10 February 1988; Ray Owen, 18 January 1988.
15. NKJ, 29 April 1989, 4 May 1989, 9 December 1986, and 29 April 1989; NKJ to Ejnar Tassing, 20 December 1985 (copy); NKJ, 25 February 1989 and 29 April 1989.
16. IJ to NKJ, 11 February 1949; IJ, 21 March 1993; JOR, 22 March 1988; HN, 12 September 1989.
17. Anne Edel Adolph, 4 March 1988; JOR, 22 March 1988; HN, 12 September 1988; NKJ, 21 October 1988.
18. NKJ to Daphne and Johannes Ipsen, 8 July 1946 (draft).

Chapter 12: "Antibody This, Antibody That, They Weren't Really Much Interested"

1. Watson, "Growing up," 1966, p. 245; Maaløe, "Some effects," 1950.
2. Watson, *The Double Helix,* 1988, p. 30 (see also Kalckar, "Autobiographical notes," 1990); Stent, "The Copenhagen spirit," 1985, p. 378; GS, 12 July 1989.
3. GS, 1 November 1988 and 12 July 1989.
4. GS, 12 July 1989; HN, 12 September 1989; GS, 1 November 1988 and 12 July 1989; NKJ, 11 February 1988.
5. GS, 12 July 1989.
6. NKJ to ThS, 8 January 1991; Luria and Delbrück, "Mutations of bacteria," 1943. For an evaluation of the "fluctuation test," see Keller, "Between language and science," 1992.
7. NKJ, 24 April 1987; NKJ to ThS, 24 January 1991.
8. Hershey, "Experiments," 1943. This description of Jerne's first phage experiment during the late fall of 1950 is a reconstruction based on his recollections forty years later; only fragments of archival material exist to confirm the sequence of events.
9. NKJ to ThS, 22–23 January 1991.
10. NKJ to ThS, 19 January 1991.
11. GS, 1 November 1988 and 12 July 1989 (cf. Stent, "The master," 1996); NKJ to ThS, 23 January 1991.
12. GS, 1 November 1988; NKJ, 29 April 1987; JOR, 22 March 1988.
13. GS, 1 November 1988 and 12 July 1989.
14. MD to NKJ, 13 August 1951; CS, 9–10 February 1988; Jerne, "Bacteriophage," 1952.

15. NKJ, 29 April 1987 and 10 February 1988; NKJ to ThS, 23 January 1991.
16. Note, 20 September 1951.
17. Viggo Faber, 24 March 1988; NKJ, 10 February 1988; undated note (1951).
18. Jerne, "Arrhenius," 1960, p. 18.
19. *Festskrift*, 1952, p. 188.

Chapter 13: "These People Don't Know What They're Doing"

1. NKJ to OM, 2 November 1951, 28 November 1951, and 18 January 1952; Lis Skovsted, 1 May 1990.
2. NKJ to Carsten Bresch, 18 January 1952 (draft); NKJ to OM, 18 January 1952.
3. NKJ, to OM, 18 January 1952; lecture manuscript, March 1952; James D. Watson to NKJ, 13 February 1952; on Moewus, see Sapp, *Where the Truth Lies*, 1990.
4. Maaløe and Jerne, "The standardization," 1952; NKJ to OM, 6 February 1952; NKJ to OM, 18 January 1952 and 6 February 1952.
5. NKJ to OM, undated (before 6 April 1952) and 4 March 1952.
6. NKJ to OM, undated (before 6 April 1952).
7. Jacob, *The Statue Within*, 1988, p. 265 (see further the papers from the Royaumont meeting in *Annales de L'Institut Pasteur* 84 (1953): 1–318); Hershey and Chase, "Independent functions," 1952; Delbrück, "International Phage Symposium . . . 1952," mimeographed report to National Foundation for Infantile Paralysis, 1952 (in Jerne's collection).
8. NKJ to OM, 6 September 1952 (original); Jerne and Skovsted, "The rate," 1953.
9. NKJ, 29 April 1989; NKJ to ThS, 15 January 1991; NKJ, 29 April 1989; NKJ to ThS, 17 December 1988.
10. NKJ, 5 May 1987; undated note (probably 1985); NKJ, 25 February 1989. For the early history of phage genetics and molecular biology, see, e.g., Olby, *The Path*, 1974; Stent and Calendar, *Molecular Genetics*, 1978; Judson, *The Eighth Day*, 1979; Fischer and Lipson, *Thinking about Science*, 1988; and Gaudillière, "Molecular biologists," 1996.
11. NKJ to ThS, 24 January 1991; NKJ to Mollie Barr, 1 April 1952 (copy).
12. NKJ to OM, 6 September 1952 (original).
13. NKJ to Dhiren Lahiri, undated (probably late November 1952; draft); Lahiri to NKJ, 19 May 1953.
14. Note, 20 November 1952; NKJ, 12 February 1988.
15. NKJ, 12 February 1988; GW, 10 November 1990.
16. Latour, "Give me a laboratory," 1983.
17. NKJ to Dhiren Lahiri, undated (probably late November 1952; draft).
18. Cockburn, "The international contribution," 1991, p. 166.
19. NKJ, undated (the problem was probably identical with that in Jerne, "The 'unit,'" 1954).
20. Diary entry, 1 March 1953; NKJ to Dhiren Lahiri, 3 March 1953 (draft).

21. NKJ to Dhiren Lahiri, 3 March 1953 (draft); NKJ to OM, 7–10 March 1953 (original) and 14 March 1953 (original).
22. NKJ to OM, 11 March 1953 (original); Hilary Koprowski, quoted in Vaughan, *Listen to the Music,* 2000, p. 267.
23. Report to director-general, WHO, 27 April 1953 (copy in Jerne's collection); NKJ to OM, 2 May 1953 (original), 19 July 1953 (original), and 2 May 1953 (original).
24. NKJ to OM, 2 May 1953 (original) and 19 July 1953 (original); Anne Edel Adolph to NKJ, 4 March 1953; OM to NKJ, 29 April 1953.
25. NKJ to EML, undated (around 10 July 1953; draft).
26. NKJ to OM, 19 July 1953 (original); NKJ to JØ, undated (around 15 July 1953; draft).
27. NKJ to AJ, 23 July 1953 (original); NKJ to GS, 31 March–10 April 1954.

Chapter 14: "I Suppose I Should Do Something, Maybe an Experiment or Something"

1. Lark and Maaløe, "The induction," 1954. For an overview of the Copenhagen school, see Schaechter et al., *The Molecular Biology,* 1985.
2. KGL, 17 September 1989.
3. NKJ, 28 August 1989; NKJ to ThS, 18 January 1991; NKJ, 5 May 1987.
4. KGL, 17 September 1989; NKJ to MD, 18 December 1953 (draft).
5. Perla Avegno to ThS, 14 June 1990; NKJ to GS, 31 March–10 April 1954; KGL, 17 September 1989.
6. Andrewes and Elford, "Observations," 1933, p. 383.
7. Perla Avegno to ThS, 14 June 1990; NKJ to GS, 31 March–10 April 1954; NKJ to Luciana Forni, 25 May 1985 (copy).
8. NKJ to GS, 31 March–10 April 1954. The reconstruction of the experimental series of the winter and spring of 1954 is based on a large number of laboratory notes and on Jerne's correspondence with Max Delbrück and Gunther Stent.
9. NKJ to MD, 8 May 1954 (draft) Cf. Kierkegaard, *Either/Or,* 1944, vol. 1, p. 28.
10. Perla Avegno to ThS, 14 June 1990.
11. NKJ to GS, 31 March–10 April 1954.
12. Jerne, "Interaction," 1954, p. 5. For tryptophane requirement, see Anderson, "The role of tryptophane," 1945, and "The activation," 1948; and Wollman and Stent, "Studies on activation," 1950. The T4 used by Jerne was a tryptophane-dependent strain that Stent had brought with him to Copenhagen in 1951.
13. NKJ to GS, 31 March–10 April 1954; NKJ, 25 June 1992.
14. NKJ to EML, 8 May 1954 (original).
15. NKJ to J. W. Palludan, 26 January 1954 (copy); NKJ to EML, 8 May 1954 (original).
16. NKj to EML, 8 May 1954 (original); quoted in NKJ to GS, 31 March–10 April 1954.
17. NKJ to GS, 31 March–10 April 1954; NKJ to MD, 8 May 1954 (draft); MD to NKJ, 15 May 1954.

18. NKJ to ThS, 23 October 1991 and 24 January 1991; NKJ to EML, 26 June 1954 (original); EML to W. Aeg. Timmermann, 28 June 1954 (in Jerne's collection); NKJ to JI, 7 September 1946 (copy).

19. NKJ to GS, 31 March–10 April 1954. For further details concerning the A-factor experiments, see Söderqvist, "Darwinian overtones," 1994.

20. Jerne, "The presence," 1956, p. 214; NKJ to ThS, 8 July 1993; NKJ to [Ed] Goldberg and [Jim D.] Karam, 22–23 February 1992 (copy).

21. NKJ to [Ed] Goldberg and [Jim D.] Karam, 22–23 February 1992 (copy); KGL, 17 September 1989.

22. Jerne, "The presence," 1956, p. 215.

23. NKJ to GS, 1 July 1954.

24. See, e.g., Ehrlich, "On immunity," 1900. For a summary of theories of antibody formation, see Silverstein, *A History,* 1989, chap. 4., and Silverstein, *Paul Ehrlich's Receptor Immunology,* 2001.

25. Landsteiner, *Die Spezifizität,* 1933; Lederberg, "Genes and antibodies," 1959 (I use the slightly anachronistic term "instruction theory" for the period before 1959 as well); Pauling, "A theory," 1940.

26. Jerne used the expression "testament" in several interviews.

27. Jerne, "The natural selection theory," 1966, p. 301; NKJ to ThS, 23 October 1991; Jerne, "The natural selection theory," 1966, p. 302; NKJ, 28 April 1987.

28. Jerne, "The natural selection theory," 1966, p. 301.

29. NKJ to ThS, 23 October 1991.

Parabasis

1. For eureka experiences, see e.g., Rocke, "Hypothesis and experiment," 1985; Caneva, *Robert Mayer,* 1993; Holmes, "Patterns," 1986; Geison and Secord, "Pasteur," 1988; Löwy, "Variances in meaning," 1990; Tauber and Chernyak, *Metchnikoff,* 1991; and Geison, *The Private Science,* 1995. Similarly, several philosophers of science have argued that apparently intuitive discoveries can be analyzed in terms of a logic of discovery, e.g., Hanson, *Patterns of Discovery,* 1958, and "An anatomy of discovery," 1967; and Schaffner, "Discovery," 1980, and *Discovery,* 1993. "As I hope I have always been careful to say, its 'onlie begetter' was Niels Jerne," said Macfarlane Burnet at the Cold Spring Harbor Symposium on Antibodies in June 1967 ("The impact," 1967, p. 2) with reference to Shakespeare's introductory dedication of the *Sonnets,* "To the onlie begetter of these insuing sonnets Mr W. H."

2. JI, 17 March 1988; NKJ, 5 May 1987; NKJ to Kenneth F. Schaffner, 28 March 1978 (copy); HN, 12 September 1989; NKJ, 5 May 1987.

3. KGL, 17 September 1989; Burnet and Fenner, *The Production,* 1949.

4. NKJ to Pauline Hogeweg and Rob de Boer, 29 March 1989 (copy); NKJ in "Outpost of Immunology," produced by Jørgen Rygaard for Danish Radio-TV, 9 September 1981; NKJ, 8 December 1986; Moulin, *Le dernier langage,* 1991, p. 276.

5. NKJ to Felix Haurowitz, 28 March 1956 (copy).

6. NKJ, 29 April 1989.

7. Jørgen V. Spärck, 23 May 1995 (Spärck says that the scientist Viggo Friedenreich told him about the episode in March or April 1956). Haurowitz's letter has not survived, but the argument can be derived from NKJ to Haurowitz, 28 March 1956 (copy), and from RP to NKJ, 5 October 1960, NKJ to RP, undated draft (after 5 October 1960), and RP to NKJ, 14 October 1960; NKJ to Felix Haurowitz, 28 March 1956 (copy); quoted in RP to NKJ, 1 December 1960. Cf. Haurowitz, "Biosynthese," 1959, p. 62.

8. Silverstein, *A History*, 1989, p. 77 (others, too, have wondered why Jerne did not mention Ehrlich, e.g., Talmage, "Allergy and immunology," 1957, p. 247, and Nossal, "Genetic control," 1962, p. 51); NKJ to Arthur Silverstein, 8 June 1985 (copy); undated note (fall 1954); NKJ to Felix Haurowitz, 28 March 1956 (copy).

9. Bloom, *The Anxiety*, 1973, p. 5.

10. Jerne, "The natural selection theory," 1966, p. 303. For a detailed discussion, see Söderqvist, "Darwinian overtones," 1994. Podolsky and Tauber (*The Generation*, 1997, pp. 36, 55) suggest that Burnet's modified-enzyme theory expressed a kind of Lamarckism that contrasted with his otherwise strong Darwinian conviction (Sexton, *The Seeds*, 1991), so Jerne's expressed Darwinian theory may have helped Burnet out of the dilemma.

11. NKJ, 23 April 1987. For the history of neo-Lamarckism and neo-Darwinism, see Bowler, *The Eclipse*, 1983, and Smocovitis, *Unifying Biology*, 1996.

12. Jerne, "The natural-selection theory," 1955, p. 850.

13. On Delbrück, see Fischer and Lipson, *Thinking*, 1988; NKJ to ThS, 19 January 1991.

14. Fischer, "The analysis of variance," 1954; Fischer, "Gene frequencies," 1950.

15. NKJ to Debra Jan Bibel, 8 October 1986 (copy); NKJ, 8 December 1986.

16. Undated note (probably 1985); NKJ to David Finney, 18 September 1990 (copy).

17. NKJ, 29 April 1989; NKJ to Kenneth Schaffner, 28 March 1978 (copy).

18. Jerne, "The natural-selection theory," 1955, p. 850; Jerne, "The natural selection theory," 1966, p. 302.

19. In [Max Delbrück], "Semi-Annual Report to the National Foundation for Infantile Paralysis . . . July–December 1955," mimeographed report (in Jerne's collection); NKJ, 24 April 1987; Schaffner, "Discovery," 1980, p. 196 (cf. Keating and Ousman, "The problem," 1991, p. 245: "Natural antibodies have played a central role [as] a foundation of 'selective' theories").

20. NKJ to OM, 16 October 1954 (original); NKJ, 27 April 1987.

21. Jerne, "The presence," 1956, p. 215.

22. Keating and Ousman, "The problem," 1991, p. 245; Silverstein, *A History*, 1989, pp. 77–78; NKJ to Pauline Hogeweg and Rob de Boer, 29 March 1989 (copy). For the low status of natural antibodies, see also Silverstein, *A History*, pp. 116–17.

23. Bjørneboe, *Studier*, 1940, and "Serum proteins," 1943, p. 233; NKJ, 29 April 1987; undated note (probably fall 1954).

24. NKJ to Kenneth Schaffner, 28 March 1978 (copy); NKJ to ThS, 8 July 1993; NKJ, 20 February 1990; NKJ to Kenneth Schaffner, 28 March 1978 (copy). When reading the quote from his letter to Schaffner in an earlier draft, Jerne underlined "must" (NKJ to ThS, 8 July 1993).

25. Jerne, "The natural selection theory," 1966, p. 301 (cf. Jerne, "Antibody formation," 1966, p. 157). The quoted passage in English was his own translation (from memory) of the Danish original, *Philosophiske Smuler* (1844); cf. Kierkegaard, *Philosophical Fragments,* 1985, p. 9.

26. Undated note (winter 1932–33).

27. NKJ to TjJ, 1 October 1935 (original); NKJ to TjJ, 13 July 1938 (draft; cf. chap. 5, this vol.); Diogenes Laertius, *Lives,* 1953, vol. 1, p. 195.

28. Feuer, "Teleological principles," 1978, p. 378.

29. Undated note (fall 1954).

30. NKJ to TjJ, undated note (probably around 20 May 1945; draft); diary entry, 28 September 1938.

31. Johnson, *The Body,* 1987, pp. xiv–xv; Giere, *Explaining Science,* 1988, p. 230. See also Paul Weindling's (1981) point that Virchow's notion of the cell state as a metaphor of Imperial Germany was put to use in the construction of his cell theory.

32. After I had presented this analysis to him, Jerne declared that he was *"fully in favor"* of the idea that his scientific theories had *"'autobiographical' traits"* (NKJ to ThS, 8 July 1993).

33. NKJ to TjJ, 12 July 1943 (draft); NKJ to AJ, 10 September 1945 (draft); Feuer, "Teleological principles," 1978, p. 380.

Chapter 15: "My Hopes and Failures Are Within Myself"

1. KGL, 17 September 1989.

2. Jerne, "The natural selection theory," 1966, pp. 304–5.

3. "Biology 1955 at the California Institute of Technology: A Report for the Year 1954–1955 . . . ," 1955, pp. 145ff. (mimeographed report in Millikan Library, California Institute of Technology).

4. Benzer, "Adventures," 1966, p. 159; IJ to NKJ, 23 October 1954; Jerne, "The natural selection theory," 1966, p. 305; Benzer, "Adventures," 1966, p. 159.

5. Lwoff, "The prophage and I," 1966, p. 90; Streisinger, "Terminal redundancy," 1966, p. 335; Fischer and Lipson, *Thinking,* 1988, pp. 234ff.

6. Harry Rubin, 8 September 1989; Sato, "Antibodies," 1981, p. 379; Harry Rubin, 8 September 1989.

7. MB, 4 September 1989.

8. Guiseppe Bertani, 16 January 1988; CS, 9–10 February 1988.

9. CS, 9–10 February 1988; Benzer, "Adventures," 1966, p. 158.

10. HN, 12 September 1989; GS, 1 November 1988; Mama to NKJ, 14 February 1955.

11. NKJ, 10 February 1988; Delbrück, "Introduction," 1980, p. 41.

12. Harry Rubin, 8 September 1989; CS, 9–10 February 1988; Kelus, "The ideal rabbit," 1981, p. 284.

13. NKJ to Perla Avegno, 14 August 1955 (in Avegno's collection, quoted in Avegno to ThS, 14 June 1990).

14. NKJ to OM, 16 October 1954 (original).

15. KGL to NKJ, undated (probably mid-November 1954); KGL, 17 September 1989 (cf. Lark, "Selection," 1985, p. 144); NKJ to OM, 16 October 1954 (original); NKJ, 23 April 1987; GS, 12 July 1989.

16. Sato, "Antibodies," 1981, p. 379; Jerne, "The natural selection theory," 1966, p. 306. Jerne's memory was exaggerating, however: according to a contemporaneous record (undated note, probably late fall 1954) from a seminar with the virus group, Watson was not especially negative to the theory.

17. NKJ, 4 May 1987; GS, 1 November 1988. For Pappenheimer's views on antibody formation, see Pappenheimer, *The Nature,* 1953.

18. NKJ, 6 May 1987; Jerne, "The natural selection theory," 1966, p. 306; quoted in GS to NKJ, 27 February 1956.

19. Pauling et al., "Sickle-cell anemia," 1949.

20. Jacob, *The Statue Within,* 1988, pp. 215ff.

21. Undated notes (September 1954–July 1955); Jerne, "The natural-selection theory," 1955, pp. 854–55.

22. Jerne, "The natural-selection theory," p. 855.

23. Silverstein, *A History,* 1989, p. 78; Bjørneboe and Gormsen, "Experimental studies," 1943; Jerne, "The natural-selection theory," 1955, p. 852.

24. Undated notes (fall 1954).

25. Jerne, "The natural-selection theory," 1955, p. 853. For the history of early thymus research, see Stillwell, "Thymectomy," 1994.

26. For Burnet's views, see Tauber, *The Immune Self,* 1994, e.g., pp. 157ff. KGL to NKJ, undated (probably mid-November 1954).

27. For Owen's chimeras, see "Immunogenetic consequences," 1945; Jerne, "The natural-selection theory," 1955, pp. 856, 853–54; Jerne, *The Generation,* 1969, and "The somatic generation," 1971.

28. NKJ to OM, 16 October 1954 (original).

29. Jerne, "The natural selection theory," 1966, p. 307; NKJ, 6 May 1987 (the results were later published in Stent and Jerne, "The distribution," 1955, and Stent, Sato, and Jerne, "Dispersal," 1959); Jerne, "The natural selection theory," 1966, p. 307; NKJ to AJ, 19 June 1955; NKJ, 26 August 1986; Jerne, "The natural selection theory," 1966, p. 307 (cf. Reichardt, "Cybernetics," 1966).

30. NKJ, 23 April 1987 and 6 May 1987; Jerne, "The natural selection theory," 1966, p. 307; NKJ to ThS, 24 January 1991.

31. Later published as Jerne and Avegno, "The development," 1956, Jerne, "The

Notes 319

presence," 1956, and Jerne, "The natural-selection theory," 1955; NKJ, 26 August 1986; MD to NKJ, 14 September 1955.

32. NKJ to EML, 11 June 1954 (original); NKJ, 28 April 1987; NKJ to ThS, 15 January 1991; NKJ, 27 April 1987.

33. NKJ, 26 August 1986; Ray Owen, 17 January 1988; NKJ to Manny Delbrück, 20 March 1981 (copy).

34. GS, 1 November 1988 (for biographical portraits of Delbrück, see Hayes, "Delbrück," 1982, and Fischer and Lipson, *Thinking*, 1988); Manny Delbrück, 17 January 1988; GS, 1 November 1988.

35. Manny Delbrück, 17 January 1988; NKJ, 10 February 1988.

36. NKJ to MD, undated (August 1955; draft).

37. Undated note (probably early 1960s); Hadamard, *An Essay*, 1945. Jerne was not, of course, the only biomedical scientist who emphasized the significance of intuition; Jonas Salk, for example, did the same (*Anatomy of Reality*, 1983).

38. MD to NKJ, 23 August 1955; NKJ to MD, undated (after 23 August 1955; draft).

Chapter 16: "This Theory Hadn't Made Much of a Stir, So Now, What Was I to Do?"

1. George Streisinger to NKJ (undated postcard, summer 1955); NKJ to GS, 18 October 1955.

2. NKJ to MD, undated (after 23 August 1955; draft); NKJ, 23 April 1987, 7 August 1992, and 24 April 1987.

3. NKJ to GS, 18 October 1955; undated note (fall 1955 or spring 1956); NKJ to GS, 28 April 1956 and 7 January 1956.

4. NKJ, 27 April 1987; GS, 1 November 1988; OM to NKJ, 11 March 1956; GS, 1 November 1988.

5. NKJ, 7 August 1992; EML to NKJ, 2 January 1955; NKJ to OM, 7–10 March 1953 (original); NKJ, 30 April 1987.

6. Quoted in Lederberg, "Ontogeny," 1988, p. 177 (Lederberg's letter to Jerne isn't preserved but is mentioned in NKJ to Felix Haurowitz, 28 March 1956 (copy)); GS to NKJ, 27 February 1956; Jørgen Spärck, 23 May 1995; NKJ, 8 May 1987, 4 May 1987, and 30 April 1987.

7. Kierkegaard, *Either/Or*, 1944, vol. 1, p. 239; NKJ, 30 April 1987.

8. AJ to NKJ, 19 September 1953; KGL, 17 September 1989; NKJ to AJ, 12 August 1953 (original); quoted from NKJ to MD, undated (August 1955; draft); NKJ, 10 February 1988.

9. NKJ, 10 February 1988.

10. NKJ to GS, 18 October 1956.

11. NKJ, 26 August 1986.

12. OM to NKJ, 11 March 1956; NKJ, 12 February 1988 and 29 April 1989.

13. NKJ to GS, 28 April 1956.
14. NKJ, 29 April 1989; Jerne and Maaløe, "The effects," 1957.
15. Jerne, "The international," 1955; Christensen, *South African,* 1955.
16. Undated note (probably spring 1944). For snake symbolism, see Nussbaum, *The Therapy,* 1994, chap. 12 ("Serpents in the Soul"). For a broader discussion of the control and power motive in science, see Keller, *Reflections,* 1985, esp. chap. 6.

Chapter 17: "I'd Better Make Sure I Learn a Little about Immunology"

1. Jerne quoted in Aase Maaløe to NKJ, 29 August 1956; GS to NKJ, 19 October 1956.
2. Manuscript for speech at the Second International Meeting of Immunomicrobiological Standardization, Rome, September 1956. For a review of post–World War II international standardization work, see Cockburn, "The international," 1991, and Cockburn et al., "The international," 1992.
3. For "minimum requirements," see, e.g., Jerne, "Note," 1956.
4. NKJ to JØ, 24 April 1957 (draft); undated note (probably 1940–41); NKJ to TjJ, 12 July 1943 (draft).
5. NKJ to JØ, 24 April 1957 (draft) and undated (probably mid-February 1957; draft).
6. NKJ, 9 February 1988.
7. AJ to NKJ, 6 July 1958 and 26 October 1958.
8. HN to NKJ, 11 March 1957; Schweet and Owen, "Concepts," 1957, p. 216; Cohn, "The problem," 1957, p. 874n.
9. Jørgen Spärck, 23 May 1995.
10. Talmage, "Allergy and Immunology," 1957 (cf. "Diversity," 1957); Burnet, *Changing Patterns,* 1968, pp. 204–5; Jerne, "Burnet," 1979, p. 38. For the iconographical qualities of Ehrlich's illustrations, see Cambrosio, Jacobi, and Keating, "Ehrlich's," 1993.
11. Burnet, "A modification," 1957; Nossal, "Antibody production," 1958; Nossal and Lederberg, "Antibody production," 1958 (for Nossal's own version of the events, see "Choices," 1995, esp. pp. 5–10); Attardi et al., "On the analysis," 1959.
12. Lederberg, "Genes and antibodies," 1959. Lederberg's somewhat self-centered version of the progress of the "elective" theories was published in "Ontogeny," 1988. For the "immunobiological revolution," see Silverstein, "The dynamics," 1981.
13. Both Burnet, "The impact," 1967, p. 2, and Talmage, "Allergy and immunology," 1956, referred to Jerne as the originator of the selection theory; Holub and Jarosková, *Mechanisms,* 1960. For the importance of this and the following Prague symposiums to post–World War II immunology, see Söderqvist and Silverstein, "Participation," 1994, and "Studying leadership," 1994, and Silverstein and Söderqvist, "The structure," 1994. For an "affectionate tribute" to Šterzl, see Silverstein, "Jaroslav Sterzl," 1995.

14. Jerne, "Introduction," 1960, p. 207; NKJ to JR, 26 July 1931 (draft) and 1 January 1931 (draft); Alain Bussard, 23 June 1992.

15. NKJ to C. E. Clifton, 18 January 1960 (copy); Delavenay, *La machine,* 1959; NKJ to RP, undated (after 5 October 1960; draft).

16. Jerne, "Immunological speculations," 1960, p. 356 (see also Jerne, "Immunologic speculation," 1961).

17. NKJ, 30 April 1987; Ernest Sorkin to NKJ, 22 June 1960; NKJ, 30 April 1987.

18. NKJ, 30 April 1987; Melvin Cohn to NKJ, 20 May 1960. For a discussion of Jerne's work within the framework of a cognitive model of the immune system, see Tauber, *The Immune Self,* 1994.

19. NKJ to JØ, 24 April 1957 (draft); NKJ to RP, 29 December 1959 (copy).

20. NKJ to RP, 29 December 1959 (copy); E. Kellenberger to Irwin Bendet, 23 September 1961 (copy in Jerne's collection). The paper was later published as Kellenberger et al., "Functions," 1965.

21. NKJ to Howard Goodman, 26 August 1987 (copy); Burnet, quoted from Jerne's notes of Burnet's lecture at the Symposium on Mechanism of Antibody Formation, Liblice, 27–30 May 1959; "Introductory statement to the 2nd session of the ACMR," mimeographed report, June 1960, p. 12 (in Jerne's collection).

22. NKJ to Sir Charles Harrington, 31 January 1961 (draft). What follows about Jerne's attempts to launch WHO's immunology program in 1960–62 is reconstructed from various drafts and meeting reports in Jerne's collection and in the Archival Department, WHO, Geneva.

23. NKJ to RP, undated (after 1 December 1960; draft); Podolsky and Tauber, *The Generation,* 1997, chap. 2.

24. "Proposals for initiating a programme in general and applied immunology," undated (1961), mimeographed report (in Jerne's collection); NKJ, 30 April 1987.

25. Donald Jerne to NKJ, 18 December 1961; NKJ to GS, 27 December 1961; AJ to NKJ, 19 February 1961.

26. NKJ to GS, 9 February 1962; manuscript for presentation at the 4th session of the Advisory Committee on Medical Research, June 1962.

27. Note, 26 June 1962; NKJ to Howard Goodman, 26 August 1987 (copy); NKJ, 30 April 1987.

28. Undated note (spring 1962); note, 21 April 1962; Haurowitz quoted in RP to NKJ, 5 October 1960; lecture manuscript, "Mechanisms of immunity in infections associated with exotoxins," August 1962 (later published as Jerne, "Mechanisms," 1963; cf. Jerne, "Selektive Theorien," 1961, and "Selektive Theorien," 1962).

29. NKJ to Albert Nordin, 14 September 1962 (copy); note, 1 August 1962.

30. W. Aeg. Timmermann to NKJ, 26 February 1961.

Chapter 18: "Finally, My Precious, I Have to Be Brilliant and Make Antibodies"

1. NKJ to M. G. Candau, 15 November 1962 (copy).
2. Albert Nordin, 9 January 1992; NKJ to Ursula Kohl, undated (probably early November 1962; draft).
3. Note, 2 March 1962; Albert Nordin, 9 January 1992. For an overview of immune hemolysis, see Bibel, *Milestones,* 1988, pp. 268–70.
4. Jerne and Nordin, "Plaque formation," 1963, p. 405.
5. NKJ to Macfarlane Burnet, 28 February 1963 (copy); Burnet quoted in NKJ to GS, 14 March 1963; Edwin S. Lennox to NKJ, 17 May 1963; Hans Lautrop to NKJ, 25 May 1963; Naomi Franklin to NKJ, 12 May 1963; David Evans to NKJ, 28 May 1963; Geoffrey Edsall to NKJ, 14 May 1963; Maurice Landy to NKJ, 15 May 1963; Howard Goodman to NKJ, 9 April 1963; Emanuel Suter to NKJ, 14 May 1963; Michael Heidelberger to NKJ, 24 April 1963.
6. Ingraham, "Identification individuelle," 1963; Gustav Nossal to NKJ, 9 October 1963 (cf. Nossal, "Choices," 1995, p. 7). For multiple discovery, see Merton, "Singletons," 1973, Lamb and Easton, *Multiple Discovery,* 1984, and Cozzens, *Social Control,* 1989.
7. Jerne, Nordin, and Henry, "The agar plaque," 1963.
8. Gustav Nossal to NKJ, 9 August 1963; Garfield, "The articles," 1985; Cunningham, "A method," 1965.
9. Attardi et al., "On the analysis," 1959; NKJ to Leo Szilard, 14 June 1963 (copy).
10. NKJ to Leo Szilard, 14 June 1963 (copy).
11. Fuji and Jerne, "Morphological studies," 1965; NKJ to Morten Simonsen, 10 March 1964 (copy).
12. Henry, "Remembrance," 1981, p. 117; NKJ to GS, 19 July 1963.
13. Henry, "Remembrance," 1981, pp. 117–18; Arthur Park, 15 March 1990; Henry, "Remembrance," 1981, p. 118; NKJ to Martin Kaplan, 28 October 1963 (copy); NKJ to T. Makinodan, 1 November 1963 (copy).
14. NKJ to André Lwoff, 6 November 1963 (copy); NKJ to Aaron Novick, 31 October 1963 (copy); various lecture manuscripts, 1963–65.
15. NKJ to Macfarlane Burnet, 3 January 1964 (copy); Nossal et al., "Antigens," 1964; NKJ to GS, 27 March 1964; lecture manuscript, May 1964; Jerne et al., "The agar plaque," 1965, p. 9; Henry, "Remembrance," 1981, p. 117.
16. NKJ to GS, 7 February 1964.
17. NKJ, 8 December 1986; lecture manuscript, 18 September 1963.
18. NKJ to GS, 6 November 1963; undated note (probably 1985).
19. NKJ to GS, 11 August 1961.
20. NKJ to GS, 21 August 1961; Jerne, "Antibody formation," 1966, p. 151; NKJ to KGL, 16 April 1964 (copy); NKJ to Cynthia Lark, 29 April 1964 (copy).

21. NKJ, 7 May 1987; *Aarbog*, 1966, p. 58; NKJ to OM, 25 June 1964 (draft); NKJ to GS, 10 May 1964 and 30 September 1964.

22. IJ to NKJ, 7 December 1962; JOR, 22 March 1988.

23. RP to NKJ, 20 January 1965.

24. NKJ to Herman Kalckar, undated (probably beginning of February 1965; draft); Edgar Haber to NKJ, 6 October 1965; Jerne, "Summary," 1967.

25. Henry, "Remembrance," 1981, p. 120; NKJ to Melvin Cohn, 17 December 1964 (copy); cf. Jerne, "Studies," 1965.

26. NKJ to Göran Möller, 1 March 1965 (copy); Koros et al., "Kinetics," 1965; Fuji and Jerne, "Morphological studies," 1965; NKJ to Donald A. Rowley, 24 August 1965 (copy); Jerne et al., "The agar plaque," 1965.

27. NKJ, 25 August 1986; Bernard D. Davis to NKJ, 19 November 1965; NKJ to Albert Coons, 16 November 1965 (copy); NKJ to Bernard D. Davis, 16 November 1965 (copy); NKJ to Gustav Erhart, 24 January 1966 (copy).

28. NKJ, 7 May 1987; NKJ to GS, 10 January 1966.

29. Cairns et al., *Phage*, 1966.

30. Jerne, "The natural selection theory," 1966, p. 301. On the Kierkegaard-Jerne connection, see Schaffner, "Discovery," 1980, pp. 176–77, Golub, *Immunology*, 1987, pp. 9–10, and Piattelli-Palmarini, "The rise," 1991, p. 159. On the Kierkegaard-Bohr connection, see Jammer, *The Conceptual*, 1966, pp. 166–80, and Holton, "The roots," 1970, pp. 1040ff. For the original text, see Kierkegaard, *Philosophical Fragments*, 1985, p. 9.

31. Quoted in [Sigg], "Ich höre," 1985, p. 8; NKJ to ThS, 8 July 1993 and 5 April 1992.

32. Henry, "Remembrance," 1981, p. 118; Jerne et al., "Plaque forming cells," 1974, and Jerne et al., "Plaque techniques," 1976.

33. MB to NKJ, 13 January 1965; NKJ to GS, 10 January 1966.

Chapter 19: "Like a Log Coming Slowly to the Surface of a Lake"

1. NKJ, 7 May 1987; Ivan Lefkovits, 10 February 1988; undated note (1966). For Jerne's view of the "antibody problem," see "Das Antikörper-Problem," 1966.

2. Jerne, "Antibodies and learning," 1967. In *The Remembered Present* (1989) and other books, Edelman does not mention that Jerne had already developed a Darwinian theory of the nervous system at the Boulder meeting. For the MIT program, see Cozzens, "Knowledge," 1997.

3. NKJ to OM, 27 September 1966 (copy); NKJ, 30 April 1987; various lecture manuscripts 1966–67; NKJ to Bernard Halpern, 7 February 1967 (copy).

4. Cairns, "Foreword," 1967, p. v. For the rise of molecular immunology, see Podolsky and Tauber, *The Generation*, 1997, esp. pp. 74–80.

5. Burnet, "The impact," 1967; Cohn, "The wisdom of hindsight," 1994, p. 17; Jerne,

"Summary," 1967, p. 591; Gustav Nossal to NKJ, 24 November 1967; Gerald M. Edelman to NKJ, 13 November 1967. For a discussion of cis-immunology and trans-immunology, see Silverstein, "The dynamics," 1991.

6. Fiedler, *Waiting for the End,* 1964 (the characterization is from the dust jacket); Stent gave a series of lectures on the subject at Berkeley in 1968 (see Stent, *The Coming,* 1969); NKJ to GS, 5 February 1967 and 16 February 1969; Jerne, "The complete solution," 1969, p. 348; NKJ to GS, 16 February 1969; see, e.g., Mead, "Cybernetics," 1968.

7. Aurelia Koros to NKJ, 27 September 1967.

8. Quoted from a clipping from *The Pittsburgh Press,* 17 May 1965 (in Jerne's collection; cf. Jerne, "The regulation," 1967); Henry and Jerne, "Competition," 1968, p. 133 (cf. Fuji and Jerne, "Primary immune response," 1969); Henry, "Remembrance," 1981, p. 121; Henry and Jerne, "The depressive effect," 1967; Claudia Henry to NKJ, 2 February 1968; Henry and Jerne, "Competition," 1968.

9. NKJ to Henry G. Kunkel, 12 February 1968 (copy).

10. NKJ to GS, 20 October 1967. See further Murphy, Kiley, and Fisher-Hoch, "Filoviridae," 1990.

11. Biozzi et al., "Étude," 1966; Dutton and Mishell, "Cellular events," 1967; Göran Möller to NKJ, 22 November 1967.

12. Ivan Lefkovits, 10 February 1988; NKJ to Ernst Schneider, 19 July 1966 (copy); NKJ to Friedrich Sperl, 6 February 1966 (wrongly dated; should be 1967); NKJ to Wolfgang von Pölnitz, 6 December 1968 (copy); NKJ, 25 August 1986.

13. Information about the choice of director from Henri Isliker, 19 June, 1992 (cf. Benacerraf, *Son of the Angel,* 1990), p. 165; Lefkovits ("Conception," 1981, p. 459) suggests that the immunochemist Elvin Kabat, too, had been contacted, but there is no evidence for this in the archive, nor is it mentioned in Kabat's memoirs, "Before and after," 1988. The following discussion about the establishment of the Basel Institute for Immunology is based, beyond Jerne's collection, on Lefkovits, "Conception," 1981.

14. Rajewsky et al., "The requirement," 1969 (for the carrier effect, see Podolsky and Tauber, *The Generation,* 1997, p. 149). For the T-cell and B-cell distinction, see, e.g., Bibel, *Milestones,* 1988. See Podolsky and Tauber, *The Generation,* 1997, for a reconstruction of the contribution of molecular genetics to immunology, especially in the 1970s.

15. NKJ to J. J. van Loghem, 5 December 1967 (copy).

16. Otto Westphal to NKJ, 28 June 1968.

17. Werner Schreil to Ivan Lefkovits, 22 July 1968 (in Lefkovits's collection).

18. NKJ to Alfred Pletscher, 25 April 1968 (copy); circular letter, 21 December 1968 (draft); NKJ to GS, 16 February 1969.

19. Corner, *A History,* 1964; Lefkovits, "Conception," 1981, p. 465.

20. Lefkovits, "Conception," 1981, p. 465; Andrew Kelus to NKJ, 31 May 1969; undated note (around 1940–41); NKJ to Alfred Pletscher, 10 March 1968 (draft).

21. Lefkovits, "Conception," 1981, pp. 462, 467, 466.

22. For the antibody repertoire, see Kindt and Capra, *The Antibody Enigma*, 1984, p. 3. Podolsky and Tauber point out (*The Generation*, 1997, p. 100) that the conventional dichotomy between germ-line theories and somatic theories simplifies and obscures the recent history of immunology. I have retained it here, however, because Jerne and several other historical actors understood the contemporary situation in terms of this dichotomy. For a less historicist reconstruction, see *The Generation*, chap. 3.

23. Edelman et al., "Covalent structure," 1969; NKJ to Gerald M. Edelman, 8 February 1969 (copy). For a summary of the research situation in sequence studies up to late 1968, see Edelman and Gall, "The antibody problem," 1969.

24. Simonsen, "Graft-versus-host reactions," 1962; Simonsen, "The clonal selection hypothesis," 1967.

25. "One of my basic intentions in formulating the [somatic mutation theory of antibody diversity] was to save the clonal selection theory from the consequences of Simonsen's argument," he wrote later (Jerne, "Generation," 1970, p. 359); NKJ to GS, 8 August 1969.

26. NKJ to GS, 8 August 1969; Murdoch, *Metaphysics*, 1992, p. 400.

27. Jerne, "The generation," 1969; F. M. Burnet to NKJ, 21 August 1969; Max Delbrück to NKJ, 11 August 1969; Richard Smith to NKJ, 29 September 1969; David Talmage to NKJ, 2 September 1969 (cf. Hood and Talmage, "Mechanism," 1970). For details about Tonegawa's discovery, see Podolsky and Tauber, *The Generation*, 1997, chaps. 5 and 6.

28. MB, 4 September 1989; GS, 12 November 1988; NKJ to Alfred Pletscher, 10 March 1968 (draft).

29. For Jerne's early thymus speculations, see "The natural-selection theory," 1955, pp. 853–54; Medawar, [Discussion], 1963. For thymus research in the 1960s, see Stillwell, "Thymectomy," 1994.

30. NKJ to Morten Simonsen, 4 December 1969 (copy). For GOD, see Lennox and Cohn, "Immunoglobulins," 1967, p. 398.

31. NKJ to [name withheld], 31 May 1970 (draft); diary entry, 31 July 1945; undated diary entry (early March 1936). A year before his death, Jerne destroyed the whole collection, which comprised many hundreds of letters written between 1969 and the early 1990s.

32. Simonsen, in Jerne, "Generation," 1970, p. 363; Jerne, "The somatic generation," 1971. For an analysis of the Jerne-Simonsen-Cohn discussion, see Podolsky and Tauber, *The Generation*, 1997, pp. 143–51.

33. Michael Sela to NKJ, 31 May 1971; MD to NKJ, January 1971; Ernst Sorkin to NKJ, 26 August 1971.

Chapter 20: "I Still think That My Original Natural Selection Theory Was Better"

1. Ernst Sorkin to NKJ, 17 October 1968; John Humphrey to NKJ, 21 June 1971.
2. Anita Söderberg, 11 February 1988.
3. For Steinberg, see Wu and Lindahl, "Memories," 2001, p. 927; Tommaso Meo, 19 June 1992.
4. Jerne, "The common sense," 1977, p. 4. For the "gene lottery," see Wigzell, "The Nobel prize," 1988, p. 25. For a discussion of the "recombinant revolution," see Podolsky and Tauber, *The Generation*, 1997 (for Tonegawa's version, see "Somatic generation," 1988).
5. NKJ, 7 August 1992; Anita Söderberg, 11 February 1988; Ivan Lefkovits, 10 February 1988.
6. Jerne, "What precedes," 1972, p. 2; Wiener, *Cybernetics*, 1948; Bertalanffy, *General Systems Theory*, 1968.
7. Kunkel et al., "Individual," 1963; Oudin and Michel, "Une nouvelle forme," 1963; Oudin, "The genetic control," 1966; Jerne, "The generative grammar," 1985, p. 161. For a review of the concept of idiotypes, see Nisonoff, "Idiotypes," 1991. See also Podolsky and Tauber, *The Generation*, 1997, p. 102.
8. NKJ to Jean Lindenmann, 10 June 1971 (copy); Jerne, "What precedes," 1972, p. 9; note, 9 August 1954.
9. Jerne, "Immunological speculations," 1960, p. 341; Jerne, "The immune system," 1973, p. 59; Jerne, "Idiotypic networks," 1984, p. 19, and "Towards," 1974, p. 383. See also Tauber, *The Immune Self*, 1994, p. 292 and chap. 5, and "Historical and philosophical perspectives," 1997.
10. NKJ to Edward S. Golub, 3 April 1986 (copy); Jerne, "Towards," 1974, p. 384.
11. Jerne, "Towards," 1974, p. 387; NKJ to Antonio Coutinho, 17 May 1992.
12. E.g., Rodkey, "Studies of idiotypic antibodies," 1974 and Rajewsky and Takemori, "Genetics," 1983; Golub, "Idiotypes," 1980, p. 642 (for reviews of idiotypic research at the beginning of the 1980s, see Janeway et al., *Immunoglobulin Idiotypes*, 1981; Westen-Schnurr, *Idiotypes*, 1982; Greene and Nisonoff, *The Biology*, 1984); Moulin, *Le dernier langage*, 1991, p. 339.
13. NKJ to Richard B. Bankert, 17 September 1985 (copy); Langman and Cohn, "The 'complete,'" 1986, p. 100; Möller, "Det stora," 1988; Cohn, "Foreword," 1989, p. xxxvii.
14. NKJ to Erna and Göran Möller, 21 December 1985 (copy); NKJ to Jacques Urbain, 4 June 1985 (copy); NKJ to Antonio Coutinho, 18 August 1982 (copy).
15. Melvin Cohn to NKJ (undated; handwritten greeting on reprint of Cohn, "Conversations with Niels Kaj Jerne on immune regulation: Associative versus network recognition," *Cellular Immunology* 61 (1981): 425–36); Cohn, "Diversity," 1985, p. 25 (see also Cohn, "The concept," 1985).
16. Jerne, "Idiotypic networks," 1984, p. 20; Steffens, *Alt und Neu*, 1821, p. 102 (quoted in Cunningham and Jardine, *Romanticism*, 1990, p. 3).

17. NKJ to AJ, 10 September 1945 (draft); Jerne, "Gennemsnitskurver," 1950, p. 640.
18. Undated note (probably fall 1937); NKJ, 26 May 1989; NKJ to ThS, 8 July 1993. For metaphors we live by, see Lakoff and Johnson, *Metaphors*, 1980.
19. Quoted in [Sigg], "Ich höre," 1985, p. 2; CS, 9–10 February 1988; KGL, 17 September 1989.

Chapter 21: "Immunology Is for Me Becoming a Mostly Philosophical Subject"

1. NKJ to OM, 28 February 1983 (copy).
2. NKJ to Pauline Hogeweg and Rob de Boer, 29 March 1989 (copy); Jerne, Roland, and Cazenave, "Recurrent idiotypes," 1982; NKJ to Antonio Coutinho, 30 July 1981 (copy); NKJ to Aurelia Koros, 16 August 1982 (copy). Cf. Jerne, "The generative grammar," 1985.
3. NKJ to Jacques Urbain, 21 August 1982 (copy). For later statements about the immune sysem, see, e.g., Jerne, "The immune system," 1976, and "The immune system," 1977.
4. Steinberg and Lefkovits, *The Immune System*, 2 vols., 1981.
5. Lindmarker, "Georges Köhler . . . Jerne . . . Milstein," 1984.
6. *Les Prix Nobel 1984*, 1985 (see also http://www.nobel.se); Köhler and Milstein, "Continuous cultures," 1975; Wigzell, "The Nobel prize," 1985, p. 25.
7. Köhler, "Derivation," 1985, p. 1359; Nielsen and Nielsen, "The physiology," 2001, p. 373. For a history of monoclonals, see Cambrosio and Keating, *Exquisite Specificity*, 1995.
8. Hans Wigzell to NKJ, 15 October 1984. For Nobel Prize politics, see Nielsen and Nielsen, "The physics," 2001, and Friedman, *Politics of Excellence*, 2001.
9. Atterstam, "Tre får pris," 1984.
10. Altman, "Nobel-winning discovery," 1984; undated note (probably 1984); NKJ to AJ, undated (September 1945; draft); NKJ, 11 February 1988; NKJ to Nigel Calder, 4 June 1985 (copy).
11. Altman, "Nobel-winning discovery," 1984; NKJ to Anne Marie Moulin, 4 February 1991 (copy).
12. Noel R. Rose to NKJ, 7 November 1984; Susumu Ohno to NKJ, 22 October 1984; Jacques Miller to NKJ, 18 October 1984; Bernard Amos to NKJ, 18 October 1984; Melvin Cohn to NKJ, 30 October 1984. For an enthusiastic review of Jerne's contributions to the development of modern immunology, see Uhr, "The 1984 Nobel prize," 1984.
13. [Name withheld] to NKJ, 15 October 1984.
14. Melvin Cohn to NKJ, 30 October 1984.
15. Jerne, "The generative grammar," 1985, p. 169; NKJ to Mohan Mathen, 4 April 1986 (copy); Jerne, "The generative grammar," 1985, p. 166. Jerne referred to Chomsky, *Current Issues*, 1964. See also Podolsky and Tauber, *The Generation*, 1997, pp. 345–46.

16. Caroline Wellbery to NKJ, 13 January 1986.
17. Note, 30 April 1986.
18. NKJ to Dankward Kodlin, 28 February 1983 (copy); Varela, *Principles,* 1979; NKJ to Antonio Coutinho, 12 September 1986 (copy).
19. NKJ to GS, 28 February 1983 (copy); NKJ to Claudia Henry, 18 December 1985 (copy); NKJ to James H. Clark, 21 August 1982 (copy); NKJ to Lois [?], 28 February 1983 (copy); note, 30 April 1986.
20. NKJ to Fritz Melchers, 6 September 1983 (copy; see also NKJ to Göran Möller, 6 September 1983 (copy)); NKJ to GS, 28 February 1983 (copy); NKJ to Richard B. Bankert, 17 September 1985 (copy).
21. NKJ to OM, 16 December 1985.
22. NKJ to Erna and Göran Möller, 3 June 1985 (copy); undated note (1984 or 1985).
23. NKJ to Ejnar Tassing, 20 December 1985 (copy); NKJ to Howard Goodman, 20 December 1985 (copy); NKJ to Sandra Panem, 17 August 1987 (copy).
24. NKJ to Ejnar Tassing, 20 December 1985 (copy).
25. Levi-Montalcini, *In Praise,* 1988, p. 186.

Epilogue

1. NKJ to ThS, 17 December 1988; NKJ to Søren Ventegodt, 14 February 1989 (copy). Jerne's dismal prophecy seems to have come to nothing: see, e.g., Zachariae, *Mind and Immunity,* 1996.
2. Kaalund, *Samlede Digtninge,* 1920, pp. 278–79 (translated by Ib Ravn); IJ, 21 March 1993. Jerne may also have disliked Kaalund's poem because it was a reminder of the closeness and belongingness that he, as "a misfit," never succeeded in establishing.
3. NKJ to ThS, 12 December 1993 and 9 December 1992; NKJ, 4 July 1994.
4. Annual report from Department of Molecular Biology, University of Brussels, 1992 (in Jerne's collection).
5. NKJ, 6 August 1994; Keats, *Ode,* 1898; Crick, *What Mad Pursuit,* 1988.

UNPUBLISHED SOURCES

Almost all unpublished documents cited in this book are from Jerne's papers in the Royal Library, Copenhagen. Explicit references to them are given only in cases where one would not expect to find the cited document there; this includes correspondence between other persons, unpublished manuscripts by others, public reports, and the like.

For a full list of interviewees, dates of interviews, and the archival status of handwritten notes, tapes, or transcribed tapes, see the Danish edition of this biography (*Hvilken kamp for at undslippe*, 1998, pp. 700–702). All interview notes, tapes, and transcriptions are presently in the possession of the author.

Public Archives

Archival Department, World Health Organization, Geneva
Basel Institute for Immunology, Basel
City Archives of Assen, Rotterdam, and Twello
Department of Standardization, Danish State Serum Institute, Copenhagen
Manuscript Department, The Royal Library, Copenhagen: Niels K. Jerne's collection (Utilg. 811, 1992/84)

Medical Faculty Archive, University of Copenhagen
University Archive, Leiden

Private Collections

Perla Avegno, Rome
Ivan Lefkovits, Basel
Aase Maaløe, Copenhagen
Thomas Söderqvist, Copenhagen
Gunther Stent, Berkeley

BIBLIOGRAPHY

For a complete list of Jerne's publications, see Lefkovits's edition of the collected works, *A Portrait of the Immune System: Scientific Publications of NK Jerne* (1996), and the bibliography in Söderqvist, *Hvilken kamp for at undslippe* (1998, pp. 685–93).

Altman, Lawrence K. "Nobel-winning discovery: Honoring a 'windfall' for doctors." *International Herald Tribune,* 18 October 1984.

Andersen, Troels. *Asger Jorn: En biografi. Årene 1914–53.* Copenhagen: Borgen, 1994.

Anderson, Tom, "The activation of the bacterial virus T4 by L-tryptophan." *Journal of Bacteriology* 55 (1948): 637–49.

———. "The role of tryptophane in the adsorption of two bacterial viruses on their host, E. coli." *Journal of Cellular and Comparative Physiology* 25 (1948): 17–26.

Andrewes, C. H., and W. J. Elford. "Observations of anti-phage sera. I: 'The percentage law.'" *British Journal of Experimental Pathology* 14 (1933): 367–84.

Aarbog for Kjøbenhavns universitet, 1964–65. Copenhagen: Københavns Universitet, 1966.

Arrhenius, Svante, and Thorvald Madsen. "Physical chemistry applied to toxins and antitoxins." Pp. 3–87 in C. J. Salomonsen, ed., *Contributions from the University Laboratory for Medical Bacteriology to Celebrate the Inauguration of the State Serum Institute.* Copenhagen: n.p., 1902.

Atkins, Guy. *Jorn in Scandinavia, 1930–1953.* Copenhagen: Borgen, 1968.

Attardi, G., M. Cohn, K. Horibata, and E. Lennox. "On the analysis of antibody synthesis at the cellular level." *Bacteriological Reviews* 23 (1959): 213–23.

Atterstam, Inger. "Tre får pris för rön om immunförsvaret." *Svenska Dagbladet* (Stockholm), 16 October 1984.

Benacerraf, Baruj. *Son of the Angel.* Boston: privately published, 1990.

Benzer, Seymour. "Adventures in the rII Region." Pp. 157–65 in J. Cairns, G. S. Stent, and J. D. Watson, eds., *Phage and the Origins of Molecular Biology.* Cold Spring Harbor, N.Y.: Cold Spring Harbor Laboratory of Quantitative Biology, 1966.

Berg, Niels. "I virkeligheden er jeg et talentløst barn." *Billedbladet* (Copenhagen), 8 November 1984, 82–85.

Bergson, Henri. "Introduction à la métaphysique." *Revue de la Métaphysique et de Morale* 11 (1903): 1–36.

Bertalanffy, Ludwig von. *General Systems Theory: Foundations, Development, Applications.* New York: George Braziller, 1968.

Bibel, Debra Jan. *Milestones in Immunology: A Historical Exploration.* Madison, Wis.: Science Tech Publishers, 1988.

"Bibliography of the technical work of the Health Organization of the League of Nations, 1920–1945." *Bulletin of the Health Organization* 11 (1945): 1–235.

Biddiss, Michael D. *The Age of the Masses: Ideas and Society in Europe Since 1870.* Hassocks: Harvester Press, 1977.

"Biological standardization." Pp. 31–33 in *Official Records of the World Health Organization. Nr. 9: Report of the Interim Commission to the First World Health Assembly. Part 1: Activities.* Geneva: World Health Organization, 1948.

Biozzi, G., C. Stiffel, D. Mouton, M. Liacapoulos-Briot, C. Decreusefond, and Y. Bouthillier. "Étude du phénomène de l'immuno-cyto-adhérence au cours de l'immunisation." *Annales de l'Institut Pasteur* 110 (1966), supplement: 1–32.

Bjørneboe, Mogens. *Studier over agglutininproteinet i kaninpneumokoksera.* Copenhagen: Munksgaard, 1940.

———. "Serum proteins during immunization." *Acta Pathologica et Microbiologica Scandinavica* 20 (1943): 221–39.

Bjørneboe, Mogens, and Harald Gormsen. "Experimental studies on the role of plasma cells as antibody producers." *Acta Pathologica et Microbiologica Scandinavica* 20 (1943): 649–92.

Bloom, Harold. *The Anxiety of Influence: A Theory of Poetry.* New York: Oxford University Press, 1973.

Bowlby, John. *Charles Darwin: A New Biography.* London: Hutchinson, 1990.

Bowler, Peter J. *The Eclipse of Darwinism: Anti-Darwinian Evolution Theories in the Decades Around 1900.* Baltimore: Johns Hopkins University Press, 1983.

Boyd, William C. *Fundamentals of Immunology.* New York: Interscience, 1943.

Boyd, William C., and Sanford B. Hooker. "The influence of the molecular weight of antigen on the proportion of antibody to antigen in precipitates." *Journal of General Physiology* 17 (1933): 341–48.

———. "The influence of the molecular weight of antigen on the proportion of antibody to antigen in precipitates. Part 2." *Journal of General Physiology* 22 (1939): 281–92.

Burke, Séan. *The Death and Return of the Author: Criticism and Subjectivity in Barthes, Foucault and Derrida.* 2d ed. Edinburgh: Edinburgh University Press, 1998.

Burnet, F. Macfarlane. "A modification of Jerne's theory of antibody production using the concept of clonal selection." *Australian Journal of Science* 20 (1957): 67–68.

———. *The Clonal Selection Theory of Acquired Immunity.* Cambridge: Cambridge University Press, 1959.

———. "The impact of ideas on immunology." *Cold Spring Harbor Symposia on Quantitative Biology* 32 (1967): 1–8.

———. *Changing Patterns: An Atypical Autobiography.* Melbourne: Heineman, 1968.

Burnet, F. Macfarlane, and Frank Fenner. *The Production of Antibodies.* 2d ed. Melbourne: Macmillan, 1949.

Cairns, John. "Foreword." P. v in J. Cairns, ed., *Cold Spring Harbor Symposia Quantitative Biology* 32 (1967).

Cairns, J., G. S. Stent, and J. D. Watson, eds., *Phage and the Origins of Molecular Biology.* Cold Spring Harbor, N.Y.: Cold Spring Harbor Laboratory of Quantitative Biology, 1966.

Cambrosio, Alberto, and Peter Keating. *Exquisite Specificity: The Monoclonal Antibody Revolution.* New York: Oxford University Press, 1995.

Cambrosio, Alberto, Daniel Jacobi, and Peter Keating. "Ehrlich's 'beautiful pictures' and the controversial beginnings of immunological imagery." *Isis* 84 (1993): 662–99.

Caneva, Kenneth. *Robert Mayer and the Conservation of Energy.* Princeton: Princeton University Press, 1993.

Cassidy, David. *Uncertainty: The Life and Science of Werner Heisenberg.* New York: Freeman, 1992.

Chomsky, Noam. *Current Issues on Linguistic Theory.* The Hague: Mouton, 1964.

Christensen, Poul Agerholm. *South African Snake Venoms and Antivenoms.* Johannesburg: South African Institute for Medical Research, 1955.

Cockburn, W. C. "The international contribution to the standardization of biological substances. Part 1: Biological standards and the League of Nations, 1921–1946". *Biologicals* 19 (1991): 161–69.

Cockburn, W. C., B. Hobson, J. W. Ligthbown, J. Lyng, and D. Magrath. "The international contribution to the standardization of biological substances. Part 2: Biological standards and the World Health Organization, 1947–1990. General considerations." *Biologicals* 20 (1992): 257–64.

Cohn, Melvin. "The problem of specific inhibition of antibody synthesis in adult animals by immunization of embryos." *Annals of the New York Academy of Science* 64 (1957): 859–76.

———. "The concept of functional idiotype network for immune regulation mocks all and comforts none." *Annales de l'Institut Pasteur (Immunologie)* 137C (1985): 64–76.

————. "Diversity in the immune system: 'Preconceived ideas' or ideas preconceived?" *Biochimie* 67 (1985): 9–27.

————. "Foreword: Clippings from one immunologist's journal." Pp. xiii–xlv in Rodney E. Langman, *The Immune System*. San Diego: Academic Press, 1989.

————. "The wisdom of hindsight." *Annual Review of Immunology* 12 (1994): 1–62.

Corner, George W. *A History of the Rockefeller Institute*. New York: Rockefeller Institute Press, 1964.

Cozzens, Susan E. *Social Control and Multiple Discovery in Science: The Opiate Receptor Case*. Albany: State University of New York Press, 1989.

————. "Knowledge of the brain: The visualizing tools of contemporary historiography." Pp. 151–63 in Thomas Söderqvist, ed., *The Historiography of Contemporary Science and Technology*. Reading: Harwood Academic Publishers, 1997.

Crick, Francis. *What Mad Pursuit: A Personal View of Scientific Discovery*. London: Weidenfeld and Nicolson, 1988.

Croce, Benedetto. *Guide to Aesthetics*. Indianapolis: Hackett, 1995 [1929].

Cunningham, A. J. "A method of increased sensitivity for detecting single antibody-forming cells." *Nature* 207 (1965): 1106–7.

Cunningham, Andrew, and Nicholas Jardine, eds., *Romanticism and the Sciences*. Cambridge: Cambridge University Press, 1990.

Dal, Erik, ed. *Danish Ballads and Folk Songs*. Copenhagen: Rosenkilde og Bagger, 1967.

Daston, Lorraine. "Fear and loathing of the imagination in science." *Daedalus* 127 (1998): 73–95.

"Debat: Den eksistentielle forskerbiografi." *Personalhistorisk Tidsskrift* (1999): 247–307.

Delavenay, Émile. *La machine à traduire*. Paris: Presses universitaires de France, 1959.

Delbrück, Max. "Introduction." Pp. 39–43 in Norman H. Horowitz and Edward Hutchings, Jr., eds., *Genes, Cells, and Behavior: A View of Biology Fifty Years Later*. San Francisco: Freeman, 1980.

Desmond, Adrian, and James Moore. *Darwin*. London: Michael Joseph, 1991.

Diogenes Laertius. *Lives of Eminent Philosophers*. 2 vols. Cambridge: Harvard University Press, 1953.

Doerr, R. *Antikörper*. Wien: Springer, 1949.

Duff, Tim. *Plutarch's Lives: Exploring Virtue and Vice*. Oxford: Clarendon Press, 1999.

Dutton, R. W., and R. I. Mishell. "Cellular events in the immune response. The in vitro response of normal mouse spleen cells to erythrocyte antigens." *Cold Spring Harbor Symposia on Quantitative Biology* 32 (1967): 407–14.

Edel, Leon. *Writing Lives: Principia Biographica*. New York: Norton, 1984.

————. "Confessions of a biographer." Pp. 3–27 in G. Moraitis and G. H. Pollock, eds., *Psychoanalytic Studies of Biography*. Madison, Conn.: International Universities Press, 1987.

Edelman, Gerald M. *The Remembered Present: A Biological Theory of Consciousness*. New York: Basic, 1989.

Edelman, Gerald M., and W. Einar Gall. "The antibody problem." *Annual Review of Biochemistry* 38 (1969): 415–66.

Edelman, G. M., B. A. Cunningham, W. E. Gall, P. D. Gottlieb, U. Rutishauser, and M. J. Waxdal. "Covalent structure of an entire γ immunoglobulin molecule." *Proceedings of the National Academy of Sciences* 63 (1969): 78–85.

Ehrlich, Paul. "On immunity with special reference to cell life." *Proceedings of the Royal Society of London, Series B* 66 (1900): 424–48.

Eiduson, Bernice T. *Scientists: Their Psychological World.* New York: Basic, 1962.

Eriksson, Gunnar. "Att inte skilja på sak och person: Ett utkast till ett utkast till en biografisk metod." Pp. 103–20 in S. Åkerman, R. Ambjörnsson, and P. Ringby, eds., *Att skriva människan: Essäer om biografin som livshistoria och vetenskaplig genre.* Stockholm: Carlssons, 1997.

"Expert committee on biological standardization: Report on the first session, 9–13 June 1947." Pp. 5–7 in *Official Records of the World Health Organization. Nr. 8: Reports of Expert Committees to the Interim Commission.* Geneva: World Health Organization, 1948.

Festskrift udgivet af Københavns Universitet i Anledning af Universitets Aarsfest, 1951. Copenhagen: Københavns Universitet, 1952.

Feuer, Lewis S. "Teleological principles in science." *Inquiry* 21 (1978): 377–407.

Fiedler, Leslie A. *Waiting for the End.* New York: Stein and Day, 1964.

Fischer, Ernst Peter, and Carol Lipson. *Thinking about Science: Max Delbrück and the Origins of Molecular Biology.* New York: Norton, 1988.

Fisher, R. A. "Gene frequencies in a cline determined by selection and diffusion." *Biometrics* 6 (1950): 353–61.

———. "The analysis of variance with various binomial transformations." *Biometrics* 10 (1954): 130–39.

Fisher, R. A., and Frank Yates. *Statistical Tables for Biological, Agricultural and Medical Research.* London: Oliver and Boyd, 1938.

[Fredrik]. "Seruminstitutet under de 5 onde år." *Mikro* (State Serum Institute, Copenhagen), 8 (1952), nr. 3 (September): 29–32.

Friedman, Robert Marc, *Politics of Excellence: Behind the Nobel Prize in Science.* New York: Freeman, 2001.

Frye, Northrop. "The drunken boat: The revolutionary element in romanticism." Pp. 1–25 in N. Frye, ed., *Romanticism Reconsidered.* New York: Columbia University Press, 1963.

Fuji, H., and Niels K. Jerne. "Morphological studies of plaque-forming cells of chick spleen in primary response." *Federation Proceedings* 24 (1965): 252.

———. "Primary immune response in vitro: Reversible suppression by anti-globulin antibodies." *Annales de l'Institut Pasteur* 117 (1969): 801–5.

Garfield, Eugene. "The articles most cited in 1961–1982. Part 2: Another 100 citation classics highlight the technology of science." Pp. 218–27 in E. Garfield, *Essays of an Information Scientist: The Awards of Science and Other Essays,* vol. 7. Philadelphia: ISI Press, 1985.

Gascoyne, David. *A Short Survey of Surrealism*. London: Cobden-Sanderson, 1935.

Gaudillière, Jean-Paul. "Molecular biologists, biochemists, and messenger RNA: The birth of a scientific network." *Journal of the History of Biology* 29 (1996): 417–45.

Geison, Gerald L. *The Private Science of Louis Pasteur*. Princeton: Princeton University Press, 1995.

Geison, Gerald L., and James A. Secord. "Pasteur and the process of discovery: The case of optical isomerism." *Isis* 79 (1988): 6–36.

Giere, Ronald N. *Explaining Science: A Cognitive Approach*. Chicago: University of Chicago Press, 1988.

Glenny, A. T., and Mollie Barr. "'Dilution ratio' of diphtheria antitoxin as a measure of avidity." *Journal of Pathology and Bacteriology* 35 (1932): 91–96.

Golub, Edward S. "Idiotypes and the network hypothesis." *Cell* 22 (1980): 641–42.

———. *Immunology: A Synthesis*. Sunderland, Mass.: Sinauer, 1987.

Greene, M. I., and A. Nisonoff, eds., *The Biology of Idiotypes*. New York: Plenum Press, 1984.

Grønnegaard, Anne Marie. *Sønderhoslægter, 1630–1987*. 3 vols. Glamsbjerg: privately published, 1988.

Hadamard, Jacques S. *An Essay on the Psychology of Invention in the Mathematical Field*. Princeton: Princeton University Press, 1945.

Hald, Anders. *Statistiske Metoder: Med Eksempler paa Anvendelser indenfor Teknikken*. Copenhagen: Det private Ingeniørfond, 1958.

Hamilton, Ian. *In Search of J. D. Salinger*. New York: Random House, 1988.

Hanson, Norman R. *Patterns of Discovery*. Cambridge: Cambridge University Press, 1958.

———. "An anatomy of discovery." *Journal of Philosophy* 64 (1967): 321–52.

Haurowitz, Felix. "Biosynthese der Proteine und ihre Beeinflussung durch Antigene." *Naturwissenschaften* 46 (1959): 60–63.

Hayes, William. "Max Ludwig Henning Delbrück." *Biographical Memoirs of Fellows of the Royal Society* 28 (1982): 59–90.

Heidelberger, Michael. "Chemical aspects of the precipitin and agglutinin reactions." *Chemical Reviews* 24 (1939): 323–43.

Heilbron, John L. *The Dilemmas of an Upright Man*. Berkeley: University of California Press, 1986.

Henry, Claudia. "Remembrance of plaques past." Pp. 116–23 in Charles Steinberg and Ivan Lefkovits, eds., *The Immune System: A Festschrift in Honor of Niels Kaj Jerne*, vol. 1. Basel: Karger, 1981.

Henry, Claudia, and Niels K. Jerne. "The depressive effect of 7S antibody and the enhancing effect of 19S antibody in the regulation of the primary immune response." Pp. 421–27 in J. Killander, ed., *Nobel Symposium on Gamma Globulins*. Stockholm: Almqvist and Wiksell International, 1967.

———. "Competition of 19S and 7S antigen receptors in the regulation of the primary immune response." *Journal of Experimental Medicine* 128 (1968): 133–52.

Herf, Jeffrey. *Reactionary Modernism: Technology, Culture, and Politics in Weimar and the Third Reich.* Cambridge: Cambridge University Press, 1984.

Hershey, A. D. "Experiments with bacteriophages supporting the lattice-hypothesis." *Journal of Immunology* 47 (1943): 77–87.

Hershey, A.D., and M. Chase. "Independent functions of viral protein and nucleic acid in growth of bacteriophage." *Journal of General Physiology* 36 (1952): 39–56.

Holmes, Frederic L. "Patterns of scientific creativity." *Bulletin of the History of Medicine* 60 (1986): 19–35.

———. *Hans Krebs.* 2 vols. New York: Cambridge University Press, 1991–93.

Holton, Gerald. "The roots of complementarity." *Daedalus* 99 (1970): 1015–55.

Holub, M., and L. Jarosková, eds. *Mechanisms of Antibody Formation: Proceedings of a Symposium Held in Prague, May 27–31 1959.* Prague: Czechoslovak Academy of Sciences, 1960.

Hood, Leroy, and David W. Talmage. "Mechanism of antibody diversity: Germ line basis for variability." *Science* 168 (1970): 325–34.

Huizinga, Johan. *Homo ludens: Proeve eener bepaling van het spel-element der cultuur.* Haarlem: Tjeenk Willink, 1938.

Hunter, Michael, ed. "Psychoanalysing Robert Boyle: A special issue." *British Journal for the History of Science* 32 (1999): 257–324.

Hunter, Michael. *Robert Boyle (1627–91): Scrupulosity and Science.* Woodbridge: Boydell Press, 2000.

Ingraham, Joseph. "Identification individuelle des cellules productrices d'anticorps par une réaction hémolytique locale." *Comptes rendus des séances de l'Academie des Sciences Sér 3* 256 (1963): 5005–8.

Ipsen, Johannes. *Contribution to the Theory of Biological Standardization on the Basis of Experiments with Bacterial Toxins.* Copenhagen: Nyt Nordisk Forlag, 1941.

———. "Systematische und zufällige Fehlerquellen bei Messung kleiner Antitoximengen. II. Mitteilung. Diphtherieantitoxin." *Zeitschrift für Immunitätsforschung* 102 (1943): 369–84.

———. "A standard for antistreptolysin O of human serum, and its practical application." *Acta Pathologica et Microbiologica Scandinavica* 21 (1944): 203–13.

Ipsen, Johannes, and Niels K. Jerne. "Graphical evaluation of the distribution of small experimental series." *Acta Pathologica et Microbiologica Scandinavica* 21 (1944): 343–61.

Jacob, Francois. *The Statue Within: An Autobiography.* New York: Basic, 1988.

Jammer, Max. *The Conceptual Development of Quantum Mechanics.* New York: McGraw-Hill, 1966.

Janeway, Charles, Eli E. Sercarz, and Hans Wigzell, eds. *Immunoglobulin Idiotypes.* New York: Academic Press, 1981.

Jensen, Claus. *Die intrakutane Kaninchenmethode zur Auswertung von Diphtherie-Toxin und Antitoxin.* Copenhagen: Levin and Munksgard, 1933.

Jerne, Niels K. "Matr. nr. 11 af exercerpladsen. VI. Standardiseringsafdelingen." *Mikro* (State Serum Institute, Copenhagen) 5 (1949), nr. 6: 47–50.

————. "Gennemsnitskurver." *Ugeskrift for Laeger* (Copenhagen) 112 (1950): 639–40, 763.

————. "Matr. nr. 11 af exercerpladsen. XI. Statistisk Afdl." *Mikro* (State Serum Institute, Copenhagen) 6 (1950), nr. 2: 11–13.

————. *A Study of Avidity Based on Rabbit Skin Responses to Diphtheria Toxin-Antitoxin Mixtures.* Copenhagen: Munksgaard, 1951.

————. "Bacteriophage inactivation by antiphage serum diluted in destilled water." *Nature* 169 (1952): 117–18.

————. "Interaction T4/anti-T-serum." *Phage Information Service* 7 (1954): 5–7.

————. "The 'unit' in preference to the 'titre' as a measure of agglutinating activity." *Bulletin of the World Health Organization* 10 (1954): 937–40.

————. "The international standardization of snake antivenins: Suggestions." *WHO Expert Committee on Biological Standardization* Report nr. 333 (1955), 5 pp.

————. "The natural-selection theory of antibody formation." *Proceedings of the National Academy of Sciences* 41 (1955): 849–57.

————. "Note on basic data for a recommendation of minimum requirements for antirabies serum." *WHO Expert Committee on Rabies,* Report nr. 86 (1956), 11 pp.

————. "The presence in normal serum of specific antibody against bacteriophage T4 and its increase during the earliest stages of immunization." *Journal of Immunology* 76 (1956): 209–16.

————. "Arrhenius og immunologien." *Svensk Kemisk Tidskrift* 72 (1960), nr. 1: 17–25.

————. "Immunological speculations." *Annual Review of Microbiology* 14 (1960): 341–58.

————. "Introduction." Pp. 206–07 in M. Holub and L. Jarosková, eds., *Mechanisms of Antibody Formation.* Prague: Czechoslovak Academy of Sciences, 1960.

————. "Immunologic speculation." Pp. 74–77 in *Poliomyelitis: Papers and Discussions Presented at the Fifth International Poliomyelitis Conference, Copenhagen, Denmark, July 26–28, 1960.* Philadelphia: Lippincott, 1961.

————. "Selektive Theorien der Antikörperbildung." *Arzneimittelforschung* 11 (1961): 592.

————. "Selektive Theorien der Antikörperbildung." *Arbeiten aus dem Paul-Ehrlich-Institut* 57 (1962): 1–14.

————. "Mechanisms of immunity in infections associated with exotoxins." Pp. 410–15 in N. E. Gibbons, ed., *Recent Progress in Microbiology. Symposia Held at the VIII International Congress for Microbiology, Montreal 1962,* vol. 8. Toronto: University of Toronto Press, 1963.

————. "Studies on the primary immune response in mice." Pp. 459–61 in J. Sterzl, ed., *Molecular and Cellular Basis of Antibody Formation.* Prague: Czechoslovak Academy of Sciences, 1965.

————. "Das Antikörper-Problem." Pp. 41–46 in *Jahrbuch der Vereinigung von Freunden und Förderern der Johann Wolfgang Goethe-Universität.* Frankfurt: Klostermann, 1966.

————. "Antibody formation and immunological memory." Pp. 151–57 in J. Gaito, ed., *Macromolecules and Behavior*. Amsterdam: North-Holland, 1966.

————. "The natural selection theory of antibody formation: Ten years later." Pp. 301–12 in J. Cairns, G. S. Stent, and J. D. Watson, eds., *Phage and the Origins of Molecular Biology*. Cold Spring Harbor, N.Y.: Cold Spring Harbor Laboratory of Quantitative Biology, 1966.

————. "Antibodies and learning: Selection versus instruction." Pp. 200–205 in G. C. Quarton, T. Melnechuk, and F. O. Schmitt, eds., *The Neurosciences*. New York: Rockefeller University Press, 1967.

————. "The regulation of antibody synthesis." Pp. 17–22 in K. E. Seiffert and R. Geissendörfer, eds., *Transplantation von Organen und Geweben*. Stuttgart: Georg Thieme Verlag, 1967.

————. "Summary: Waiting for the end." *Cold Spring Harbor Symposia on Quantitative Biology* 32 (1967): 591–603.

————. "The complete solution of immunology." *Australasian Annals of Medicine* 18 (1969): 345–48.

————. "The generation of self-tolerance and of antibody diversity." *Scientific Group on Factors Regulating the Immune Response, Geneva 1–6 September, 1969*, Report nr. 69.5/Rev.1 (1969), 14 pp.

————. "Generation of antibody diversity and self-tolerance: A new theory." Pp. 345–436 in R. T. Smith and M. Landy, eds., *Immune Surveillance*. New York: Academic Press, 1970.

————. "The somatic generation of immune recognition." *European Journal of Immunology* 1 (1971): 1–9.

————. "What precedes clonal selection?" Pp. 1–15 in R. Porter and J. Knight, eds., *Ontogeny of Acquired Immunity*. Amsterdam: Associated Scientific Publishers, 1972.

————. "The immune system." *Scientific American* 229 (1973), nr. 1 (July): 52–60.

————. "Towards a network theory of the immune system." *Annales d'Immunologie* 125C (1974): 373–89.

————. "The immune system: A web of V-domains." Pp. 93–110 in *Harvey Lectures*, vol. 70. New York: Academic Press, 1976.

————. "The common sense of immunology." *Cold Spring Harbor Symposia on Quantitative Biology* 41 (1977): 1–4.

————. "The immune system: A network of lymphocyte interactions." Pp. 259–66 in F. Melchers and K. Rajewsky, eds., *The Immune System*. Berlin: Springer-Verlag, 1977.

————. "Burnet and the clonal selection theory." Pp. 34–38 in *Walter and Eliza Hall Institute of Medical Research, Annual Review, 1978–79*. Melbourne: Walter and Eliza Hall Institute of Medical Research, 1979.

————. "Idiotypic networks and other preconceived ideas." *Immunological Reviews* 79 (1984): 5–24.

————. "The generative grammar of the immune system." Pp. 157–71 in *Les Prix Nobel*

1984: Nobel Prizes, Presentations, Biographies and Lectures. Stockholm: Almqvist and Wiksell International, 1985.

Jerne, N. K., and Perla Avegno. "The development of the phage-inactivating properties of serum during the course of specific immunization of an animal: Reversible and irreversible inactivation." *Journal of Immunology* 76 (1956): 200–208.

Jerne, N. K., C. Henry, A. A. Nordin, H. Fuji, A. Koros, and I. Lefkovits. "Plaque forming cells: Methodology and theory." *Transplantation Reviews* 18 (1974): 130–91.

———. "Plaque techniques for recognizing individual antibody-forming cells." Pp. 335–70 in C. A. Williams and M. H. Chase, eds., *Methods in Immunology and Immunochemistry,* vol. 5. New York: Academic Press, 1976.

Jerne, N. K., and Ole Maaløe. "Standardization of diphtheria toxoid. Some theoretical and practical considerations." *Bulletin of the World Health Organization* 2 (1949): 49–57.

———. "The effects of ribonuclease on the bacteriophage T4, its host cell, E. coli B, and on infected coli cells." *Acta Pathologica et Microbiologica Scandinavica* 40 (1957): 362–68.

Jerne, N. K., and A. A. Nordin. "Plaque formation in agar by single antibody-producing cells." *Science* 140 (1963): 405.

Jerne, N. K., A. A. Nordin, and C. Henry. "The agar plaque technique for recognizing antibody-producing cells." Pp. 109–25 in B. Amos and H. Koprowski, eds., *Cell-Bound Antibodies.* Philadelphia: Wistar Institute Press, 1963.

Jerne, N. K., A. A. Nordin, C. Henry, H. Fuji, and A. Koros. "The agar plaque technique, the target of the antigen, and clonal selection." *Information Exchange Group No.5, Immunopathology, Scientific Memo* 46 (1965), 41 pp.

Jerne, N. K., J. Roland, and P.-A. Cazenave. 1982, "Recurrent idiotypes and internal images." *EMBO Journal* 1 (1982): 243–47.

Jerne, Niels, and Lis Skovsted. "The rate of inactivation of bacteriophage T4r in specific anti-serum. Part 1: Salt effect. Part 2: Cofactor." *Annales de l'Institut Pasteur* 84 (1953): 73–89.

Jerne, Niels, and E. C. Wood. "The validity and meaning of the results of biological assays." *Biometrics* 5 (1949): 273–99.

Johnson, Mark. *The Body in the Mind: The Bodily Basis of Meaning, Imagination, and Reason.* Chicago: University of Chicago Press, 1987.

Jong, L. de. *Het koninkrijk der Nederlanden in de tweede wereldoorlog,* vol. 1: *Voorspel.* Den Haag: Nijhoff, 1969.

Judson, Horace. *The Eighth Day of Creation: Makers of the Revolution in Biology.* London: Jonathan Cape, 1979.

Jørgensen, Jørgen. *Bertrand Russell: En praktisk idealist og hans filosofi.* Copenhagen: Ejnar Munksgaard, 1935.

———. *The Development of Logical Empiricism.* Chicago: The University of Chicago Press, 1951.

Kaalund, H. V. *Samlede Digtninge.* 2d ed. Copenhagen: Gyldendal, 1920.

Kabat, Elvin A. "Before and after." *Annual Review of Immunology* 6 (1988): 1–24.

Kalckar, Herman M. "Autobiographical notes from a nomadic biochemist." Pp. 101–76 in G. Semenza and R. Jaenicke, eds., *Selected Topics in the History of Biochemistry: Personal Recollections.* Vol. 3. Amsterdam: Elsevier, 1990.

Keating, Peter, and Abdelkérim Ousman. "The problem of natural antibodies, 1894–1905." *Journal of the History of Biology* 24 (1991): 245–63.

Keats, John. *Ode on a Grecian Urn and Other Poems.* Boston: Houghton Mifflin, 1898 [1819].

Kellenberger, E., A. Bolle, E. Boy de la Tour, R. H. Epstein, N. C. Franklin, N. K. Jerne, A. Reale-Scafati, and J. Séchaud. "Functions and properties related to the tail fibers of bacteriophage T4." *Virology* 26 (1965): 419–40.

Keller, Evelyn Fox. *Reflections on Gender and Science.* New Haven: Yale University Press, 1985.

———. "Between language and science: The question of directed mutation in molecular genetics." *Perspectives in Biology and Medicine* 35 (1992): 292–306.

Kelus, Andrew. "The ideal rabbit." Pp. 284–90 in Charles Steinberg and Ivan Lefkovits, eds., *The Immune System: A Festschrift in Honor of Niels Kaj Jerne,* vol. 1. Basel: Karger, 1981.

Kendall, F. E. "The quantitative relationship between antigen and antibody in the precipitin reaction." *Annals of the New York Academy of Sciences* 43 (1942): 85–105.

Kermode, Frank. "Strange, sublime, uncanny, anxious." *London Review of Books,* 22 December 1994, 8–9.

Kierkegaard, Søren. *Either/Or,* vol. 1. Translated by D. F. Swanson and E. M. Swanson. London: Oxford University Press, 1944 [1843].

———. *Either/Or,* vol. 2. Translated by Walter Lowrie. Garden City, N.Y.: Doubleday, 1959 [1843].

———. *Repetition.* Edited and translated by H. V. Hong and E. H. Hong. Princeton: Princeton University Press, 1983 [1843].

———. *Philosophical Fragments.* Edited and translated by H. V. Hong and E. H. Hong. Princeton: Princeton University Press, 1985 [1844].

———. *Stages On Life's Way.* Edited and translated by H. V. Hong and E. H. Hong. Princeton: Princeton University Press, 1988 [1845].

———. *Søren Kierkegaard's Journals and Papers.* Edited and translated by H. V. Hong and E. H. Hong. 7 vols. Bloomington: Indiana University Press, 1967–78.

Kindt, Thomas J., and J. Donald Capra. *The Antibody Enigma.* New York: Plenum Press, 1984.

Klein, Richard. *Cigarettes Are Sublime.* Durham: Duke University Press, 1993.

Köhler, Georges. "Derivation and diversification of monoclonal antibodies." *EMBO Journal* 4 (1985): 1359–65.

Köhler, Georges, and César Milstein. "Continuous cultures of fused cells secreting antibody of predefined specificity." *Nature* 256 (1975): 495–97.

Koros, A., C. Henry, A. A. Nordin, and Niels K. Jerne. "Kinetics of appearance of plaque-forming cells in spleens of immunized mice." *Federation Proceedings* 24 (1965): 252.

Kraus, Rudolf. "Ueber ein akut wirkendes Bakterientoxin." *Zentralblatt für Bakteriologie, Parasitenkunde und Infektionskrankheiten. 1. Abt., Originale* 34 (1903): 488–96.

Kunkel, H. G., M. Mannik, and R. C. Williams. "Individual antigenic specificity of isolated antibodies." *Science* 140 (1963): 1218–19.

Lakoff, George, and Mark Johnson. *Metaphors We Live By.* Chicago: University of Chicago Press, 1980.

Lamb, D., and S. M. Easton. *Multiple Discovery: The Pattern of Scientific Progress.* Amersham: Avebury, 1984.

Landsteiner, Karl. *Die Spezifizität der serologischen Reaktionen.* Berlin: J. Springer, 1933.

Langman, Rodney E., and Melvin Cohn. "The 'complete' idiotype network is an absurd immune system." *Immunology Today* 7 (1986): 100–101.

Lark, K. G. "Selection of somatic variation in plants." Pp. 144–49 in M. Schaechter et al., eds., *The Molecular Biology of Bacterial Growth: A Symposium Held in Honor of Ole Maaløe.* Boston: Jones and Bartlett, 1985.

Lark, K. G., and Ole Maaløe. "The induction of cellular and nuclear division in Salmonella typhimurium by means of temperature shifts." *Biochimica et Biophysica Acta* 15 (1954): 345–56.

Latour, Bruno. "Give me a laboratory and I will raise the world." Pp. 141–70 in K. Knorr-Cetina and M. Mulkay, eds., *Science Observed: Perspectives on the Social Study of Science.* Dordrecht: Reidel, 1983.

Lederberg, Joshua. "Genes and antibodies." *Science* 129 (1959): 1649–53.

———. "Ontogeny of the clonal selection theory of antibody formation: Reflections on Darwin and Ehrlich." *Annals of the New York Academy of Science* 546 (1988): 175–87.

Lefkovits, Ivan. "Conception and embryogenesis of the Basel Institute for Immunology." Pp. 459–68 in Charles Steinberg and Ivan Lefkovits, eds., *The Immune System: Festschrift in Honor of Niels Kaj Jerne,* vol. 2. Basel: Karger, 1981.

Lefkovits, Ivan, ed. *A Portrait of the Immune System: Scientific Publications of NK Jerne.* Singapore: World Scientific, 1996.

Lennox, E. S., and M. Cohn. "Immunoglobins." *Annual Review of Biochemistry* 36 (1967): 365–406.

Les Prix Nobel 1984: Nobel Prizes, Presentations, Biographies and Lectures. Stockholm: Almqvist and Wicksell International, 1985.

Levi-Montalcini, Rita. *In Praise of Imperfection: My Life and Work.* New York: Basic, 1988.

Lindmarker, Ingmar. "Georges Köhler, 38, Västtyskland: Vetenskapligt underbarn," "Niels K. Jerne, 72, Danmark: Njuter av livet och priset," and "Cesar Milstein, 57, Storbritannien: Matglad arbetsnarkoman." *Svenska Dagbladet* (Stockholm), 16 October 1984.

Lively, Penelope. *According to Mark.* London: Heineman, 1984.

Löwy, Ilana. "Variances in meaning in discovery accounts: The case of contemporary biology." *Historical Studies in the Physical and Biological Sciences* 21 (1990): 87–121.

Luria, Salvador E., and Max Delbrück. "Mutations of bacteria from virus sensitivity to virus resistance." *Genetics* 28 (1943): 491–511.

Lwoff, André. "The prophage and I." Pp. 88–99 in J. Cairns, G. S. Stent, and J. D. Watson, eds., *Phage and the Origins of Molecular Biology*. Cold Spring Harbor, N.Y.: Cold Spring Harbor Laboratory of Quantitative Biology, 1966.

Maaløe, Ole. *On the Relation Between Alexin and Opsonin*. Copenhagen: Munksgaard, 1946.

———. "Pathogenic-apathogenic formation of Salmonella typhimurium." *Acta Pathologica et Microbiologica Scandinavica* 25 (1948): 75–77.

———. "Some effects of temperature on intracellular growth of the bacterial virus T4." *Acta Pathologica et Microbiologica Scandinavica* 27 (1950): 680–94.

———. "How it all began." Pp. 1–5 in Charles Steinberg and Ivan Lefkovits, eds., *The Immune System: A Festschrift in Honor of Niels Kaj Jerne*, vol 1. Basel: Karger, 1981.

Maaløe, Ole, and Niels K. Jerne. "The standardization of immunological substances." *Annual Review of Microbiology* 6 (1952): 349–66.

MacIntyre, Alasdair. *After Virtue*. 2d ed. Notre Dame: University of Notre Dame Press, 1984 [1981].

Madsen, Thorvald. *Experimentelle Undersøgelser over Difterigiften*. Copenhagen: Det Nordiske Forlag, 1896.

———. *Statens Seruminstitut: Institutets Udvikling, 1902–1940*. Copenhagen: Bianco Lunos Bogtrykkeri, 1940.

Manuel, Frank E. *A Portrait of Isaac Newton*. Cambridge, Mass.: Harvard University Press, 1968.

Marrack, J. R. *The Chemistry of Antigens and Antibodies*. 2d ed. London: His Majesty's Stationary Office, 1938.

Mead, Margaret. "Cybernetics of cybernetics." Pp. 1–11 in Heinz von Foerster et al., eds., *Purposive Systems*. New York: Spartan, 1968.

Medawar, Peter B., [Discussion]. P. 70 in G. E. W. Wolstenholme and Julie Knight, eds., *The Immunologically Competent Cell*. London: Churchill, 1963.

Merton. Robert K. "Singletons and multiples in science." Pp. 343–70 in R. K. Merton, ed., *The Sociology of Science: Theoretical and Empirical Investigations*. Chicago: University of Chicago Press, 1973.

Miller, James. *The Passion of Michel Foucault*. New York: Simon and Schuster, 1993.

Möller, Göran. "Det stora immunologiska äventyret är över; de väsentliga upptäckterna är gjorda." *Läkartidningen* (Stockholm), 85 (1988): 3575–78.

Møller, Jens. "Nobelpristagerens liv startede som en fiasco." *Ud og Se* (Copenhagen), nr. 12 (1986): 4–7.

Monk, Ray. *Ludwig Wittgenstein: The Duty of Genius*. New York: Free Press, 1990.

———. *Bertrand Russell*, 2 vols. London: Jonathan Cape, 1996–2000.

Moraitis, George. "The psychoanalyst's role in the biographer's quest for self-awareness." Pp. 319–54 in Samuel H. Baron and Carl Pletsch, eds., *Introspection in Biography: The Biographer's Quest for Self-Awareness*. Hillsdale, N.J.: Analytic Press, 1985.

Mørch, Erna. *Serological Studies on the Pneumococci.* Copenhagen: Munksgaard, 1943.

Moulin, A. M. *Le dernier langage de la médicine: Histoire de l'immunologie de Pasteur au Sida.* Paris: Presses universitaries de France, 1991.

Multatuli [Eduard Douwes Dekker]. "Minnebrieven," in *Volledige Werken,* vol. 2. Amsterdam: Oorschot, 1951 [1861].

Murdoch, Iris. *Metaphysics as a Guide to Morals.* London: Chatto and Windus, 1992.

Murphy, Frederick A., Michael P. Kiley, and Sudan P. Fisher-Hoch. "Filoviridae: Marburg and Ebola viruses." Pp. 933–42 in B. N. Fields et al., eds., *Virology,* 2d ed. New York: Raven Press, 1990.

Nielsen, Henry, and Keld Nielsen. "The physiology or medicine prize: A survey." Pp. 373–92 in H. Nielsen and K. Nielsen, eds., *Neighbouring Nobel: The History of Thirteen Danish Nobel Prizes.* Aarhus: Aarhus University Press, 2001.

———. "The physics and chemistry prizes." Pp. 244–71 in H. Nielsen and K. Nielsen, eds., *Neighbouring Nobel: The History of Thirteen Danish Nobel Prizes.* Aarhus: Aarhus University Press, 2001.

Nietzsche, Friedrich. *Beyond Good and Evil.* New York: Prometheus, 1989 [1886].

Nisonoff, Alfred. "Idiotypes: Concepts and applications." *Journal of Immunology* 147 (1991): 2429–38.

Nossal, G. J. V. "Antibody production by single cells." *British Journal of Experimental Pathology* 39 (1958): 544–51.

———. "Genetic control of lymphopoiesis, plasma cell formation, and antibody production." *International Review of Experimental Pathology* 1 (1962): 1–72.

———. "Choices following antigen entry: Antibody formation or immunologic tolerance?" *Annual Review of Immunology* 13 (1995): 1–27.

Nossal, G. J. V., G. L. Ada, and C. M. Austin. "Antigens in immunity. Part 4: Cellular localization of ^{125}I- and ^{131}I-labelled flagella in lymph nodes." *Australian Journal of Experimental Biology and Medical Science* 42 (1964): 311–30.

Nossal, G. J. V., and J. Lederberg. "Antibody production by single cells." *Nature* 181 (1958): 1419–20.

Nussbaum, Martha. *The Therapy of Desire: Theory and Practice in Hellenistic Ethics.* Princeton: Princeton University Press, 1994.

Nye, David. *The Invented Self: An Anti-Biography from Documents of Thomas A. Edison.* Odense: Odense University Press, 1983.

Ohno, Susumu. *Evolution by Gene Duplication.* New York: Springer-Verlag, 1970.

Olby, Robert. *The Path to the Double Helix.* London: Macmillan, 1974.

Olmsted, J. M. D., and E. Harris Olmsted. *Claude Bernard and the Experimental Method in Medicine.* New York: Collier, 1952.

Oudin, Jacques. "The genetic control of immunoglobulin synthesis." *Proceedings of the Royal Society of London, Series B,* 166 (1966): 207–21.

Oudin, Jacques, and M. Michel. "Une nouvelle forme d'allotypie des globulines γ du sérum de lapin, apparemment liée à la fonction et à la spécificité anticorps." *Comptes rendus des séances de l'Académie des Sciences, Sér. 3* 257 (1963): 805–08.

Owen, Ray D. "Immunogenetic consequences of vascular anastomoses between bovine twins." *Science* 102 (1945): 400–401.

Paludan, Jacob. "Sommerdage i Løkken: Brev fra Jacob Paludan." *Nationaltidende* (Copenhagen), 12 July 1941.

Pappenheimer, A. M., ed. *The Nature and Significance of the Antibody Response.* New York: Columbia University Press, 1953.

Pappenheimer, A. M., H. P. Lundgren, and J. W. Williams. "Studies on the molecular weight of diphtheria toxin, antitoxin, and their reaction products." *Journal of Experimental Medicine* 71 (1940): 247–62.

Pauling, L. "A theory of the structure and process of formation of antibodies." *Journal of the American Chemical Society* 62 (1940): 2643–57.

Pauling, L., H. A. Itano, S. J. Singer, and I. C. Wells. "Sickle-cell anemia, a molecular disease." *Science* 110 (1949): 543–48.

Peckham, Morse. *The Birth of Romanticism, 1790–1815.* Greenwood, Fla.: Penkeville, 1986.

Pernis, B., and A. A. Augustin. [Review of Steinberg and Lefkovits, *The Immune System,* 1981.] *European Journal of Immunology* 12 (1982): 3.

Pernis, B., M. W. Cohen, and G. J. Thorbecke. "Specificity of reaction to antigenic stimulation in lymph nodes of immature rabbits." *Journal of Immunology* 91 (1963): 541–52.

Piattelli-Palmarini, M. "The rise of selective theories: A case study and some lessons from immunology." Pp. 159–72 in P.-A. Cazenave and G. P. Talwar, eds., *Immunology: Pasteur's Heritage.* New Delhi: Wiley Eastern, 1991.

Pilkington, A. E. *Bergson and His Influence: A Reassessment.* Cambridge: Cambridge University Press, 1976.

Pletsch, Carl. "On the autobiographical life of Nietzsche." Pp. 405–34 in G. Moraitis and G. H. Pollock, eds., *Psychoanalytic Studies of Biography.* Madison, Conn.: International Universities Press, 1987.

Podolsky, Scott H., and Alfred I. Tauber. *The Generation of Diversity: Clonal Selection Theory and the Rise of Molecular Immunology.* Cambridge, Mass.: Harvard University Press, 1997.

Price, Derek J. De Solla. *Little Science, Big Science.* New York: Columbia University Press, 1963.

Rajewsky, K., V. Schirrmacher, S. Nase, and Niels K. Jerne. "The requirement of more than one antigenic determinant for immunogenecity." *Journal of Experimental Medicine* 129 (1969): 1131–43.

Rajewsky, K., and T. Takemori. "Genetics, expression and function of idiotypes." *Annual Review of Immunology* 1 (1983): 569–607.

Raphael, Beverley. *The Anatomy of Bereavement.* New York: Basic, 1983.

Reichardt, Werner E. "Cybernetics of the insect optomotor response." Pp. 313–34 in J. Cairns, G. S. Stent, and J. D. Watson, eds., *Phage and the Origins of Molecular Biology.* Cold Spring Harbor, N.Y.: Cold Spring Harbor Laboratory of Quantitative Biology, 1966.

Rocke, Alan J. "Hypothesis and experiment in the early development of Kekulé's benzene theory." *Annals of Science* 42 (1985): 355–81.

Rodkey, L. S. "Studies of idiotypic antibodies: Production and characterization of auto-antiidiotypic antisera." *Journal of Experimental Medicine* 139 (1974): 712–20.

Rorty, Richard. *Philosophy and the Mirror of Nature.* Princeton: Princeton University Press, 1980.

Salk, Jonas. *Anatomy of Reality: Merging of Intuition and Reason.* New York: Columbia University Press, 1983.

Sapp, Jan. *Where the Truth Lies: Franz Moewus and the Origins of Molecular Biology.* Cambridge: Cambridge University Press, 1990.

Sato, Gordon. "Antibodies, hormones and cancer." Pp. 379–82 in Charles Steinberg and Ivan Lefkovits, eds., *The Immune System: A Festschrift in Honor of Niels Kaj Jerne,* vol. 1. Basel: Karger, 1981.

Schaechter, Moselio, Frederick C. Neidhardt, John L. Ingraham, and Niels Ole Kjeldgaard, eds., *The Molecular Biology of Bacterial Growth: A Symposium Held in Honor of Ole Maaløe.* Boston: Jones and Bartlett, 1985.

Schaffner, Kenneth F. "Discovery in the biomedical sciences: Logic or irrational intuition?" Pp. 171–205 in T. Nickles, ed., *Scientific Discovery: Case Studies.* Dordrecht: Reidel, 1980.

———. *Discovery and Explanation in Biology and Medicine.* Chicago: University of Chicago Press, 1993.

Schrödinger, Erwin. *Nature and the Greeks.* Cambridge: Cambridge University Press, 1954.

Schweet, R. S., and R. D. Owen. "Concepts of protein synthesis in relation to antibody formation." *Journal of Cellular and Comparative Physiology* 50 (1957), supplement 1: 199–228.

Segré, Emilio. *Enrico Fermi: Physicist.* Chicago: University of Chicago Press, 1970.

Sexton, Christopher. *The Seeds of Time: The Life of Sir Macfarlane Burnet.* Oxford: Oxford University Press, 1991.

Shapin, Steven. "Essay review: Personal development and intellectual biography: The case of Robert Boyle." *British Journal for the History of Science* 26 (1993): 335–45.

Shortland, Michael, ed. *Hugh Miller and the Controversies of Victorian Science.* Oxford: Clarendon Press, 1996.

Shortland, Michael, and Richard Yeo. "Introduction." Pp. 1–44 in M. Shortland and R. Yeo, eds., *Telling Lives in Science: Essays on Scientific Biography.* Cambridge: Cambridge University Press, 1996.

[Sigg, Hans]. "'Ich höre gerne zu. Jedem': Ein Gespräch mit Niels Jerne." *Roche Magazin* (Basel: Hoffman-La Roche), nr. 24 (1985): 1–17.

Silverman, S. M. "Parental loss and scientists." *Science Studies* 4 (1974): 259–64.

Silverstein, Arthur M. *A History of Immunology.* San Diego: Academic Press, 1989.

———. "The dynamics of conceptual change in twentieth century immunology." *Cellular Immunology* 132 (1991): 515–31.

————. "Jaroslav Sterzl: An affectionate tribute." *Folia Microbiologica* 40 (1995): 357–59.

————. *Paul Ehrlich's Receptor Immunology: The Magnificent Obsession.* New York: Academic Press, 2001.

Silverstein, Arthur M., and Thomas Söderqvist. "The structure and dynamics of immunology, 1951–1972: A prosopographical study of international meetings." *Cellular Immunology* 158 (1994): 1–28.

Simonsen, Morten. "Graft-versus-host reactions: Their natural history and applicability as tools of research." *Progress in Allergy* 6 (1962): 349–467.

————. "The clonal selection hypothesis evaluated by grafted cells reacting against their hosts." *Cold Spring Harbor Symposia on Quantitative Biology* 32 (1967): 517–23.

Skidelsky, Robert. "Only connect: Biography and truth." Pp. 1–16 in Eric Homberger and John Charmley, eds., *The Troubled Face of Biography.* London: Macmillan, 1988.

Smiles, Samuel. *Life of a Scotch Naturalist: Thomas Edward, Associate of the Linnean Society.* London: John Murray, 1876.

Smocovitis, Vassiliki B. "Unifying biology: The evolutionary synthesis and evolutionary biology." *Journal of the History of Biology* 25 (1992): 1–65.

————. "Living with your biographical subject: Special problems of distance, privacy and trust in the biography of G. Ledyard Stebbins Jr." *Journal of the History of Biology* 32 (1999): 421–38.

Söderqvist, Thomas. "Biography or ethnobiography or both: Embodied reflexivity and the deconstruction of knowledge-power." Pp. 143–62 in F. Steier, ed., *Research and Reflexivity.* London: Sage, 1991.

————. "How to write the recent history of immunology: Is the time really ripe for a narrative synthesis?" *Immunology Today* 14 (1993): 565–68.

————. "Darwinian overtones: Niels K. Jerne and the origin of the selection theory of antibody formation." *Journal of the History of Biology* 27 (1994): 481–529.

————. "Existential projects and existential choice in science: Science biography as an edifying genre." Pp. 45–84 in R. Yeo and M. Shortland, eds., *Telling Lives in Science: Essays on Scientific Biography.* Cambridge: Cambridge University Press, 1996.

————. "Virtue ethics and the historiography of science." *Danish Yearbook of Philosophy* 32 (1997): 45–64.

————. *Hvilken kamp for at undslippe: En biografi om immunologen og nobelpristageren Niels Kaj Jerne.* Copenhagen: Borgen, 1998.

————. "Immunology à la Plutarch: Biographies of immunologists as an ethical genre." Pp. 287–301 in Anne Marie Moulin and Alberto Cambrosio, eds., *Singular Selves: Historical Issues and Contemporary Debates in Immunology.* Paris: Elsevier, 2001.

Söderqvist, Thomas, Jan Faye, Helge Kragh, and Frank Allan Rasmussen, eds. *Videnskabernes København.* Copenhagen: Roskilde Universitetsforlag, 1998.

Söderqvist, Thomas, and Arthur Silverstein. "Participation in scientific meetings: A new prosopographical approach to the disciplinary history of science: The case of immunology, 1951–72." *Social Studies of Science* 24 (1994): 513–48.

————. "Studying leadership and subdisciplinary structure of scientific disciplines: Cluster analysis of participation in scientific meetings." *Scientometrics* 30 (1994): 243–58.

Söderqvist, Thomas, and Craig Stillwell. "Essay review: The historiography of immunology is still in its infancy." *Journal of the History of Biology* 32 (1999): 205–15.

Steinberg, Charles, and Ivan Lefkovits, eds. *The Immune System: A Festschrift in Honor of Niels Kaj Jerne,* 2 vols. Basel: Karger, 1981.

Stent, Gunther S. *The Coming of the Golden Age: A View of the End of Progress.* Garden City, N.Y.: Natural History Press, 1969.

————. "The Copenhagen spirit." Pp. 377–84 in M. Schaechter et al., eds., *The Molecular Biology of Bacterial Growth: A Symposium Held in Honor of Ole Maaløe.* Boston: Jones and Bartlett, 1985.

————. "The master and his atelier." Pp. 3–8 in I. Lefkovits, ed., *A Portrait of the Immune System: Scientific Publications of NK Jerne.* Singapore: World Scientific, 1996.

Stent, G. S., and R. Calendar. *Molecular Genetics: An Introductory Narrative.* San Francisco: Freeman, 1978.

Stent, Gunther S., and Niels K. Jerne. "The distribution of parental phosphorous atoms among bacteriophage progeny." *Proceedings of the National Academy of Sciences* 41 (1955): 704–9.

Stent, Gunther S., Gordon H. Sato, and Niels K. Jerne. "Dispersal of the parental nucleic acid of bacteriophage T4 among its progeny." *Journal of Molecular Biology* 1 (1959): 134–36.

Stillwell, Craig. "Thymectomy as an experimental system in immunology." *Journal of the History of Biology* 27 (1994): 379–401.

Streisinger, George. "Terminal redundancy, or all's well that ends well." Pp. 335–40 in J. Cairns, G. S. Stent, and J. D. Watson, eds., *Phage and the Origins on Molecular Biology.* Cold Spring Harbor, N.Y.: Cold Spring Harbor Laboratory of Quantitative Biology, 1966.

Sulloway, Frank J. *Born to Rebel: Birth Order, Family Dynamics, and Creative Lives.* New York: Pantheon, 1996.

Talmage, David. "Allergy and immunology." *Annual Review of Medicine* 8 (1957): 239–56.

————. "Diversity of antibodies." *Journal of Cellular and Comparative Physiology* 50 (1957), supplement 1: 229–46.

Tauber, Alfred I. "Historical and philosophical perspectives concerning immune cognition." *Journal of the History of Biology* 30 (1997): 419–40.

————. *The Immune Self: Theory or Metaphor?* New York: Cambridge University Press, 1994.

Tauber, Alfred I., and Leon Chernyak. *Metchnikoff and the Origins of Immunology: From Metaphor to Theory.* New York: Oxford University Press, 1991.

Teorell, T. "Quantitative aspects of antigen-antibody reactions. Part 1: A theory and its corollaries." *Journal of Hygiene* 44 (1946): 227–36.

Tonegawa, Susumu. "Somatic generation of immune diversity." Pp. 203–27 in *Les Prix Nobel 1987: Nobel Prizes, Presentations, Biographies and Lectures*. Stockholm: Almqvist and Wiksell International, 1988.

Tonkin, Elizabeth. *Narrating Our Pasts: The Social Construction of Oral History*. Cambridge: University Press, 1992.

Topley, W. W. C. *An Outline of Immunology*. Baltimore: W. Wood, 1933.

Tuchman, Barbara W. "Biography as a prism of history." Pp. 93–103 in Stephen B. Oates, ed., *Biography as High Adventure: Life-Writers Speak on Their Art*. Amherst: University of Massachusetts Press, 1986.

Uhr, Jonathan. "The heterogeneity of the immune response." *Science* 145 (1964): 457–64.

———. "The 1984 Nobel prize in medicine." *Science* 226 (1994): 1025–28.

Varela, Francisco J. *Principles of Biological Autonomy*. New York: North-Holland, 1979.

Vaughan, Roger, *Listen to the Music: The Life of Hilary Koprowski*. New York: Springer, 2000.

von Franz, Marie-Louise. *Puer Aeternus*. Santa Monica, Calif.: Sigo Press, 1981.

Walter, Maila L. *Science and Cultural Crisis: An Intellectual Biography of Percy Williams Bridgman (1882–1961)*. Stanford: Stanford University Press, 1990.

Watson, James D. "Growing up in the phage group." Pp. 239–45 in J. Cairns, G. S. Stent, and J. D. Watson, eds., *Phage and the Origins of Molecular Biology*. Cold Spring Harbor, N.Y.: Cold Spring Harbor Laboratory Press, 1966.

———. *The Double Helix: A Personal Account of the Discovery of the Structure of DNA*. New York: Atheneum, 1968.

Weevers, Theodoor. *Poetry of the Netherlands in Its European Context, 1170–1930*. London: Athlone Press, 1960.

Weindling, Paul. "Theories of the cell state in Imperial Germany." Pp. 99–155 in C. Webster, ed. *Biology, Medicine, and Society, 1840–1940*. Cambridge: Cambridge University Press, 1981.

Westen-Schnurr, I., ed. *Idiotypes: Antigens on the Inside*. Basel: Editions Roche, 1982.

Wiener, Norbert. *Cybernetics*. New York: Wiley, 1948.

Wigzell, Hans. "The Nobel prize for physiology or medicine." Pp. 24–27 in *Les Prix Nobel 1984: Nobel Prizes, Presentations, Biographies and Lectures*. Stockholm: Almqvist and Wiksell International, 1985.

———. "The Nobel prize for physiology or medicine." Pp. 25–26 in *Les Prix Nobel 1987: Nobel Prizes, Presentations, Biographies and Lectures*. Stockholm: Almqvist and Wiksell International, 1988.

Wollman, Elie, and Gunther S. Stent. "Studies on activation of T4 bacteriophage by cofactor. Part 1: The degree of activity." *Biochimica et Biophysica Acta* 6 (1950): 292–306.

Woodward, William R. "Scientific genius and loss of a parent." *Science Studies* 4 (1974): 265–77.

Woolf, Virginia. *Three Guineas*. London: Hogarth Press, 1977 [1938].

Wu, Gillian E., and Kirsten Fischer Lindahl, "Memories of a mentor: Charley Steinberg." *Genetics* 157 (2001): 927–32.

Yeats, William Butler. "The choice." P. 495 in Peter Allt and Russel K. Alspach, eds., *The Variorum Edition of the Poems of W. B. Yeats*. New York: Macmillan, 1957 [1932].

Zachariae, Robert. *Mind and Immunity: Psychological Modulation of Immunological and Inflammatory Parameters*. Copenhagen: Munksgaard/Rosinante, 1996.

Z[ibrandtsen] J[an]. "Malerinden Tjek Jerne død." *Nationaltidende* (Copenhagen), 2 November 1945.

———. "Jerne, Tjek." In Merete Bodelsen and Povl Engelstoft, eds., *Weilbachs Kunstnerleksikon*, vol. 2. Copenhagen: Aschehoug Dansk Forlag, 1949.